buy review-discussion by I. Hind in CPh   1994

Athenian Economy and Society

Athenian Economy and Society

A BANKING PERSPECTIVE

Edward E. Cohen

PRINCETON UNIVERSITY PRESS

PRINCETON, NEW JERSEY

Cohen, Edward E.
    Athenian economy and society : a banking perspective / Edward E.
Cohen.
        p.   cm.
    Includes bibliographical references and index.
    ISBN 0-691-03609-8
    1. Banks and banking—Greece—Athens—History. 2. Greece—
History—Spartan and Theban Supremacies, 404–362 B.C.   I. Title.
HG237.C65   1992
332.1′0938′5—dc20
                                                        92-5685
                                                        CIP

This book has been composed in Linotron Times Roman

Princeton University Press books are printed on acid-free paper,
and meet the guidelines for permanence and durability of the
Committee on Production Guidelines for Book Longevity of the
Council on Library Resources

Printed in the United States of America

1 3 5 7 9 10 8 6 4 2

For Betsy

אשת חיל

CONTENTS

PREFACE

I SEEK HERE to examine Athenian banking not as a disembodied theory, but as a business involving real people in actual human situations. My aim is to explain the Athenian bank in the context of the financial structure of fourth-century Athens and the lives of its inhabitants—the process of banking, not primarily its physical equipment or linguistic formulations.[1] I concentrate exclusively on this single polis during the approximately eight decades between the defeat of Athens by Sparta in the Peloponnesian War and the death of Alexander the Great in 323 B.C.[2] For this period, and this period alone, we have sufficient information—although often not accessible without effort and analysis—to understand the functioning of Athenian banking and to demonstrate its enormously important role in the economy of fourth-century Athens.

This focus on the processes of a single state for a limited period of time is not the only, or even the typical, approach to ancient economic studies. Indeed, it is sometimes assumed that any effort to analyze ancient economics should be relegated to prior development of anthropologically based universal cultural models or to the availability and acceptance of modern analyses explaining economies and economics on an overall basis, which can then be applied to particular manifestations, be they Chinese, Tolaian, or Attic.[3] In my opinion, however, far from dependence on universal models or inclusive comparative analyses, the structural differences between Athenian civilization and other

[1]This is intended as a "structuralist" study, but only in the sense of "structuralism as an 'activity' (as opposed to a subject-matter) concerned with reconstructing the mental processes through which man makes his world intelligible" (Segal 1986: 75). Cf. Barthes 1972: 213–20. On structural, synchronic, and diachronic factors in approaching ancient economic history and this study in particular, see below.

[2]Unless otherwise indicated or clear from the context, all chronological references in this volume are to be understood as "B.C." By chance, the period under study falls largely within the modern conventional denotation of "fourth century B.C.," and I too on occasion (especially as regards the transition to a market economy or the beginnings of private banking, Chapter 1) make use of this convention to avoid prolix or pedantic explanation: phenomena attributed to the "fourth century" in fact sometimes originated some years before the chronological commencement of the "fourth century," or otherwise do not exactly correspond to this later numerology.

[3]See Humphreys 1978: 3–4, 137. On the Tolaian economy, see Epstein 1969. The whole of Ste. Croix 1981 is presented as an explanation and illustration of the "value of Marx's general analysis of society in relation to the ancient Greek world" (p. 3). But despite his universalist approach, on specific issues Marx himself insisted on careful differentiation between separate periods and places in ancient history (as in his skillful exegesis of the productive position of public slaves at Athens in the fourth century: Marx 1967–70: bk. 1, vol. 2, ch. 11). In contrast, Joseph Stalin, analyzing the position of slaves in antiquity, insisted on a unitary approach (Stalin 1946: 600–601). See Gera 1975: 22.

societies mandate exclusive and continual concentration on understanding Athenian financial matters strictly in the context of Athenian institutions and values—in preference to facile analogous reference to societies distant in time, location, and circumstance.[4]

For fourth-century Athens, extensive material is available both about the functioning of its private banks and about the contemporary economy and Athens's intellectual, artistic, and material culture. Nowhere else are we provided so generously with that elusive desideratum for comparative economic studies: a technologically primitive but culturally influential financial unit, freed from modern influence by millennia, but extensively memorialized in writing and by material remains. But the sources for Athenian banking relate to a particular context, a specific world of values, cognitive processes, and historical setting. To interpret data in disregard of this world invites gross and sometimes grotesque distortion: assumptions as to "interest rates" that ignore the very different Athenian conceptualization of yield on principal; assertions as to the nature of bank activity that disregard the dominant influence of the peculiar Athenian system of taxation; concepts of ownership, derived from Roman law[5] or Anglo-Saxon experience, dictating conclusions that women could not "own" property, that ignore evidence for control of important assets by bankers' wives and women's frequent assertion of property rights.

Just as an ethnographer of the contemporary world must struggle to understand the cognitive system of his or her subject—the unique way in which a particular human culture comprehends its environment and expresses that comprehension—the historian of Athenian institutions must pay close attention to the Athenians' organization and perception of their own reality. The Athenians lived in a world of complementary opposites, embedded in the very structure of their language, influencing every aspect of their comprehension and action.[6] Where a modern banker might develop a strategic plan encompassing extended lists of possible options, the Athenian would automatically divide and contrast the possibilities: loans were either "maritime" or "landed"; assets belonged to either the "disclosed" or the "invisible" sphere of wealth; economic life separated into the public world of the community and the private arena of the household. For the Athenians, these perceptions and resultant methods of organization were key elements of reality; for this study, they are correspondingly central.

---

[4] Scholars analyzing the evolution of legal institutions have also come to recognize the need to focus on "definable historical circumstances," rather than "a sequence of developmental stages supposedly common to all societies" (Humphreys 1983b: 229). Similarly, anthropologists have acknowledged the impossibility of "a unified 'science of culture.' " (Humphreys 1983c: ix).

[5] Even for the Roman Empire itself, great care is required in extending Italian experience into the provinces. Andreau (1987: 20) significantly limits his study of Roman financiers to those functioning in the Latin-speaking part of the empire, finding no uniformity among the various eastern provinces.

[6] For extended treatment of these factors, see below, pp. 44–52, 86–90, and Chapter 6.

My focus on culture-bound processes is complemented, however, by my assumption that, as with other fundamental human drives and functions, the Athenians dealt with monetary enrichment and poverty, trade and profit in ways that reflect fundamental human responses and motivations—and these can be as clear to us as other culturally transferable human drives, emotions, and acts that we encounter in Greek literature, mythology, and art. The fundamental processes of money-lending, deposit-gathering, and currency exchange generate human reactions to materialistic advantage, to greed, corruption, and integrity. In dealing with data relating to these activities, in our case in studying "banking" in the context of an ancient society, scholarship should seek not to catalogue substance in a merely descriptive fashion but ultimately and primarily to understand the processes themselves, processes that are likely to reflect the recurrent issues and conflicting motivations that are never distant from human situations where monetary advantage is sought between creditor and debtor, and where power is derived from access to monies. If Athenian financial experiences provide, as I believe, material comprehensibly transferable to other contexts, this study—despite its avoidance of universalist or comparative methodology—may generate insights useful for universalist or comparative analysis by others.

Concomitant with my concentration on Athenian processes during the decades following the Peloponnesian War, I have sought to derive themes and conclusions solely from Athenian evidence, and from sources contemporary with the matters described or interpreted. Occasional references to other periods and places are intended essentially for clarification or for their perceived intrinsic interest, sometimes as confirmation of conclusions drawn from Athenian material, but never as independent proof by analogy of Athenian practices otherwise unknown. Material from the fourth century, however, is often preserved only in collections compiled in later antiquity (commentaries on authors, lexicographical studies, and such). Though I do not believe that we can pick and choose with reasonable accuracy those portions of this material which represent "inaccurate" traditions, I do not automatically disdain any relevant evidence so preserved; but I have endeavored to note both possible conflicts between these sources and material directly preserved from the fourth century, and suggestions made by others as to the unreliability of such later testimonia.[7] Unless the distinction is relevant to my discussion, I do not differentiate between works properly bearing the name of an ancient author and those of doubtful attribution.[8]

---

[7]On the subjectivity often shown by historians of ancient law in accepting or rejecting specific items of evidence for earlier periods preserved in the writings of later antiquity, see D. Cohen 1990a: esp. 293. Cf. Wolff 1975.

[8]Thus I cite as "Demosthenes" those speeches traditionally included in the Demosthenic corpus, and as "Aristotle" those works (even the *Problems*) similarly included in the Aristotelian corpus.

It has become fashionable to warn readers against the excessively bourgeois nature of Athenian literary sources, which were written by a privileged elite for a select audience and often dealt with unrepresentative concerns.[9] At present, however, Athenian banking is generally seen as a marginal activity affecting only marginal elements of society, and in trifling economic situations (see Chapter 1). Therefore, the mere survival of substantial literary material concerning these banks and their activities is itself important: it suggests a recognizable impact on elite financial life. Yet since many noncitizens, women, and slaves were involved in and affected by bank activity, our sources here open portals on elements of society often obscure and obscured. The clandestine orientation of the banks (see Chapter 6) further flavors the information—and offers heuristic possibilities that I have sought to exploit.

Can we properly approach even these eight decades synchronically, using in analytical tandem material from the years immediately after the Peloponnesian War and references relating to the time immediately preceding Alexander's death? Although even narrative historical writing in reality often deals not in diachronic moments but rather with periods of time,[10] social and economic historians have typically, and overtly, treated broad themes through the use of evidence from widely disparate time periods (and geographical locations). For antiquity in particular, the paucity of evidence often invites synchronicity, even the treatment of hundreds of years as a single unit,[11] with the inevitable danger that an attractive model may actually be based on the indiscriminate grouping of unrelated and diffuse items of evidence, independent of context. In the absence of diachronic differentiations, the very presentation may generate its own confirmation, through the grouping of incompatible and unrelated examples arbitrarily selected without chronological or geographical distinction, and without the guidance often provided by a structuralist detailing of related factors from the same period and society.[12] This approach, often seemingly mandated by the paucity of data, has been especially intrusive in ancient economic studies. For example, the blended amalgamations implicit in a work titled *The Ancient Economy* contrast markedly with the same author's proper refusal, in analysis of legal history, to consider together evidence from the politically distinct Greek entities of Athens and Amorgos, even where the material relates to the same era, language, and geographical area.[13]

---

[9]See, for example, Garlan 1982: 30–31; Pomeroy 1975: 10.

[10]See Dray 1971, 1978. On the necessary integration of structuralist and diachronic approaches, see Humphreys 1985a: 257–59.

[11]See Ober 1989: 36–37. An extreme example is MacMullen 1974, which considers a period of over three centuries as a single analytical entity.

[12]"Structuralism has sharply reminded us that synchronic understanding is even more necessary than diachronic history-writing" (Momigliano 1974: 68).

[13]See Finley [1951] 1985: 198 n. 17. On Finley's effort to synthesize all of "Graeco-Roman antiquity" (1985: 27–34), see the telling criticism of Andreau (1977) and Carandini (1979: 209–15). For more detailed criticisms of the "unity" of ancient Greek law, see Finley 1966: 129–42 and Triantaphyllopoulos 1968: 1–4.

Aided by a relative profusion of relevant evidence, I have been able here to focus on a fairly brief period. In some respects it may be (and has been) argued that these decades reflect a unity of values and institutions, confirmed by constitutional stability and considerable continuity in social attitudes,[14] and accordingly may be treated as a unity, as Aristotle did in his *Constitution of the Athenians* (41.2). Yet the period between the Peloponnesian War and the death of Alexander also saw rapid and complex political and military developments, and continuing, even startling, changes in social and economic processes.[15] These developments occurred within a chronological framework that must not be ignored in the inevitable tendency toward a synchronic coalescence of individual years viewed millenia later. On some issues, chronological differentiation is clearly relevant, for example the identity of Phormiōn the banker and Phormiōn "from the Piraeus," individuals active in different years but arguably the same person (see Chapter 5, pp. 176–78). But the essential continuity over some decades of the banking business, and of its practices and approaches, is not a chimera myopically conceived by modern observers. When Apollodōros seeks, after the passage of more than a decade, to collect funds borrowed from the banker Pasiōn years earlier, he undertakes detailed chronological differentiation of the facts involved, but he equates (actually using a perfective verb with present sense) the collection and loan procedures used by bankers a decade earlier and at the time of his litigation. He even denominates these practices as "customary."[16] Indeed, most of the surviving law-court speeches concerned with banking matters touch on business activities over an extended period of years, and thereby illustrate fundamental continuity in procedures.[17] Although on social and factual matters I have often focused on close chronological analysis, in the description of business practices a synchronic approach has seemed not to misrepresent economic reality.

A few words on the Athenian drachma (in this book sometimes abbreviated *dr.* for convenience).[18] The drachma, revived as the name for the modern

---

[14]See Ober 1989: 37–38, 266–68; M. H. Hansen 1982 on demographic uniformity; and Dover 1974: esp. 30–32, for attitudinal continuity.

[15]For the vast shift in social values and practices, especially after 380, see Davies 1978: 165–87. On the economic response to these societal changes, see below, pp. 3–8, 87–90.

[16]Dem. 49.4: ἀναγκαῖόν μοι δοκεῖ εἶναι ἐξ ἀρχῆς ἅπαντα διηγήσασθαι ὑμῖν, τά τε ὀφειλόμενα, καὶ εἰς ὅ τι ἕκαστον αὐτῶν κατεχρήσατο, καὶ τοὺς χρόνους ἐν οἷς τὸ συμβόλαιον ἐγένετο. θαυμάσῃ δὲ μηδεὶς ὑμῶν εἰ ἀκριβῶς ἴσμεν, οἱ γὰρ τραπεζῖται εἰώθασιν ὑπομνήματα γράφεσθαι ὧν τε διδόασιν χρημάτων καὶ εἰς ὅ τι καὶ ὧν ἄν τις τιθῆται. The debts were contracted in 373 and 372, but the presentation dates from 362. See Gernet 1954–60, 3: 7, 11.

[17]For example, the group of speeches dealing with the disputes between Pasiōn and Apollodōros (Dem. 36, 45, 46) relates to events occurring over a period of more than forty years.

[18]Inscriptional evidence attests to ancient abbreviations for various units of currency, such as "T" for "talent" or "Σ" for "stater," which could be modified to show an increase in values. The symbol for one drachma is ⱶ. Greek texts did on occasion utilize an abbreviation of δραχμαί; on inscriptions clearly financial in content, there is generally no special indication that a figure consists of drachmas (or other currency).

Greek currency, was the ancient Athenian state silver coinage. Almost all monetary values in this book are expressed as ancient Athenian drachmas.[19] Commentators have increasingly recognized the difficulty of establishing for freely traded modern monies meaningful exchange equivalencies: how can we deal with factors such as the sometimes greatly differing purchasing power, in their domestic markets, of market-established modern currency equivalents?[20] For ancient Athens, however, it is entirely nugatory (and largely irrelevant) to relate the value of its silver coinage to the unstable modern values of equivalent physical amounts of precious metals.[21] In my opinion, the best (although not entirely satisfactory) choice is to conceive of the drachma in terms of its purchasing power at Athens (approximately a day's labor by a not-unskilled individual: see Chapter 1, n. 92)—although even this conversion is subject to variation in labor costs and purchasing power in individual modern countries, changing from year to year.

Unless otherwise indicated, all translations and paraphrases of ancient sources are my own. Greek authors who are edited in Oxford Classical Text editions are generally quoted from that series; for other Greek authors, the text generally is taken from the Budé edition. The final manuscript was delivered to Princeton University Press in July 1991, and it has accordingly been impossible to consider secondary literature that has appeared thereafter.

[19] The drachma was divided into 6 obols. 100 drachmas equalled a mna; 6,000 drachmas, a talent.

[20] In theory, "absolute purchasing power parity" should prevail where exchange ratios are being set by market forces. (The formulaic expression is $P/P^* = E$, where E represents the exchange rate [domestic currency units per foreign unit], P the domestic price index, and P^* the foreign price index.) In actual practice, wide and fluctuating variations predominate, for reasons much disputed. See Krugman 1978; Roll 1979; Officer 1982.

[21] A talent of silver, equivalent to 6,000 $dr.$, weighed approximately 688 ounces (about 26 kilograms, or 57 pounds). Between 1970 and 1990, the market value of silver ranged from about $2 per ounce to a momentary high (in 1980) of $48.70 per ounce (*New York Times*, Jan. 6, 1991). Even at $48 per ounce, the composition of a single drachma would represent a metallic value of only about $5.50.

ACKNOWLEDGMENTS

I AM GLAD to acknowledge the help I have received in writing this book.

Dimitri Gofas of the University of Athens Law School read an early draft of my first musings and aided me substantially with his unparalleled knowledge of Greek commercial and legal practices. Gerhard Thür (Munich) and Claude Mossé (Paris) provided fruitful correspondence on specialized problems; Panayotis Dimakis and Sophie Adam (both of the Panteios University, Athens) offered valuable suggestions in helpful conversation, as did Lionel Casson (New York), Wesley Thompson (Davis), and Joseph Mélèze-Modrzejewski (Paris). Patricia Gibson Santangelo has been most helpful in the checking of citations, proofreading, and indexing. The two academic readers for the Princeton University Press provided insightful and helpful critiques. All who have worked with Joanna Hitchcock, executive editor for the Humanities at the Press, will understand my appreciation of her judgment and assistance.

At early stages I presented material ultimately included here to academic audiences at Princeton and Stanford Universities, the Scuola Normale Superiore di Pisa, and Bryn Mawr College, as well as to the 1987 meeting of the Association of Ancient Historians at McGill University, Hamilton, Ontario. I benefited much from lively discussions after each of these lectures, and from comments and conversation at the 1990 Symposion in Monterey, California, of the Gesellschaft für Griechische und Hellenistische Rechtsgeschichte. Early versions of parts of Chapters 2, 3, and 5 have appeared in *Classical Philology* 85 (1990): 177–90, *Classical Antiquity* 8 (1989): 207–23, and *Symposion* (1988): 57–79, respectively. The support of the American School of Classical Studies at Athens has been invaluable, especially that of its librarian, Dr. Nancy Winters, who has graciously expedited my research in Greece.

Above all, I am indebted to Michael Jameson of Stanford University, who has been, over several decades, a rare guide and mentor, a source of wisdom.

This book is dedicated to my wife, Betsy, a peerless companion.

ABBREVIATIONS

Aesch.	Aischinēs
Ail. Tact. Praef.	Ailianos, *Tactica* (Preface)
And.	Andokidēs
Arch. Delt.	Ἀρχαιολογικὸν Δελτίον
Aristoph.	Aristophanes
Ach.	*Acharnians* (425)
Ekkl.	*Ekklēsiazousai* (393 or 392)
Plout.	*Ploutos* (388)
Thes.	*Thesmophoriazousai* (411)
C.I.L.	*Corpus inscriptionum latinarum*
CIG	*Corpus inscriptionum graecarum*
Dein.	Deinarchos
Dem.	Demosthenes
DHR	R. Dareste, B. Haussoullier, and T. Reinach, eds., *Recueil des inscriptions juridiques grecques* (Paris: 1st ser., 1891–95; 2d ser., 1898–1904)
Diod. Sik.	Diodōros of Sicily
Dion. Hal.	Dionysios of Halikarnasos
Eur.	Euripides
Herod.	Herodotos
Homer, *Od.*	Homer, *Odyssey*
Hyp.	Hypereidēs
Ath.	*Against Athēnogenēs*
Dem.	*Against Demosthenes*
I.G.	*Inscriptiones graecae*
IGCH	M. Thompson, O. Mørkholm, and C. M. Kraay, *An Inventory of Greek Coin Hoards* (New York, 1973)
Isok.	Isokratēs
Just., *Cod.*	Justinian, *Codex* (second vol. of the Corpus Iuris Civilis)
Nov.	Justinian, *Novellae*
OCD	*Oxford Classical Dictionary*, ed. N.G.L. Hammond and H. H. Scullard, 2d ed. (Oxford, 1970)
Philon, *De sobr.*	Philo of Alexandria, *On Sobriety*
Plato, *Apol.*	Plato, *Apology*
Gorg.	*Gorgias*
Pol.	*The Statesman*
Rep.	*Republic*

Plut.	Plutarch
Comp.	*Comparison*
Dem.	*Demosthenes*
Mor.	*Moralia*
Polyain.	Polyainos
RE	Pauly-Wissowa, *Real-Encyclopädie der klassischen Altertumswissenschaft*, rev. G. Wissowa et al. (Stuttgart, 1894–1972)
S.E.G.	*Supplementum epigraphicum graecum* (Leyden, 1925–)
S.I.G.	*Sylloge inscriptionum graecarum I–IV*, ed. W. Dittenberger, 3d ed. (Berlin, 1915–24)
Sappho, *Suppl.*	Sappho, Papyrus fragments in E. Diehl, supplement to *Anthologia lyrica graeca*, 2d ed. (Leipzig, 1936)
SB	*Sammelbuch griechischer Urkunden aus Ägypten* (Strassburg, Berlin, and Leipzig, 1913–)
Tab. Pomp.	*Tabula Pompeiana*
Theophr., *Char.*	Theophrastos, *Charaktēres*
Thuc.	Thucydides
Xen.	Xenophon
Hell.	*Hellenika*
Mem.	*Memorabilia*
Oik.	*Oikonomikos*
Por.	*Poroi*
Symp.	*Symposion*

Athenian Economy and Society

Chapter 1

MARKET ECONOMY—BANKING REALITY

The very concept of "the economy" in the modern sense
is untranslatable in Greek, because it simply did not exist.
—M. M. Austin and P. Vidal-Naquet

The banker was little more than a money-changer
and pawnbroker.
—M. I. Finley

THIS BOOK deals with the significant role of the Athenian banks in the economy of fourth-century Athens, an impossible subject for those who deny the existence at Athens of either an "economy" or "banks." This denial presently is as fashionable as it is false, arising from the prevailing tendency to attribute a primitiveness to ancient economic activity, and a lack of sophistication to ancient businesses.[1] In fact, the fourth century at Athens witnessed two startling, and perhaps interrelated, innovations: the transition to an economy governed (in Aristotle's words) by "monetary acquisition" rather than by traditional social motivations, and the development of the world's first private businesses ("banks," *trapezai*), which accepted from various sources funds ("deposits") for which they had an absolute obligation of repayment while being free to profit from, or even lose, these monies in their own loan and investment activities.

THE ATHENIAN ECONOMY

An economy is "a system of producing, distributing and consuming wealth."[2] But anthropologists have developed models of primitive groups

[1] Hopkins terms the primitive conceptualization of the ancient economy "a new orthodoxy" (1983: xi). But "sophistication of practice" is not necessarily inconsistent with "simplicity of structure" (Starr 1987: 16) or lack of advanced technology. Even the primitivist P. Millett has now conceded that "so-called 'primitive societies' invariably have their own complexity and sophistication" (1990: 181). Cf. below, p. 62.

[2] *Webster's Unabridged Dictionary*, 2d ed., s.v. "economy." Because modern economic science has focused almost exclusively on price-making markets, anthropologists and historians have tended to equate the very term "economy" with this particular market form. See Will 1954; Lepore 1970. Such markets, however, are actually somewhat anomalous occurrences and should not be taken as definitionally determinative. See Neale 1957; Roll 1973: 371. Like "economies," "markets" in modern jargon have numerous definitions and subdivisions. The American "capital market," for example, is said to be a composite of three separate autonomous entities: the "stock market," the "bond market," and the "money market." See Stigum 1978: 7.

where production, distribution, and consumption are accomplished solely through familial or political relationships. In such societies, economic activity cannot occur without direct social significance; the economy thus is said to be "embedded" in the society itself.[3] Since no "system" for creating or dealing with wealth exists as an independent sphere, motivationally and financially distinct from other institutions, such a society can be said to lack an economy— although, more precisely, it lacks not a system of handling wealth (an "economy"), but rather the disengaged commercial activity that would permit the intellectualized concept of an economy.[4]

Fourth-century Athens was very different. The Athenians functioned through a market process in which unrelated individuals, often in the city only transiently, sometimes even operating from abroad, sought monetary profit through commercial exchange (*allagē*).[5] Not only were these transactions "disembedded from" society: they were seen by theoreticians in their writings and litigants in their court cases as threatening traditional social and familial methods of handling production and consumption.

In the *Politics* (1256a–1257b), Aristotle argues against what modern economists would call the "scarcity postulate" (a purported inability to meet overall consumer demand because of inherent absolute limitations on total potential wealth). Characteristically analyzing commercial issues in an ethical context, Aristotle poses the issue not in terms of the adequacy or expandibility of the "supply side," but as a problem of misguided desire ("demand"): true wealth, although not infinite, is sufficient to meet man's needs, properly conceived.[6] In deprecating the tendency of individuals to misconceive of wealth as monetary

---

[3]See Polanyi, Arensberg, and Pearson 1957: 68; Polanyi 1944: 63–64; Lowry 1987: 2; Humphreys 1978: 152. For similar conceptualization, cf. Parsons's "structural differentiation" (1951: chs. 4 and 5) and Mauss's "faits sociaux totaux" (1923–24).

[4]Analogously, increasing interdependence among modern economies tends to preclude the independent analysis of domestic systems through traditional monetary and fiscal tools. See Kohn 1976: 485–86.

[5]Aristot., *Pol.* 1257a31–36, b3–5: ξενικωτέρας γὰρ γενομένης τῆς βοηθείας τῷ εἰσάγεσθαι ὧν ἐνδεεῖς ⟨ἦσαν⟩ καὶ ἐκπέμπειν ὧν ἐπλεόναζον, ἐξ ἀνάγκης ἡ τοῦ νομίσματος ἐπορίσθη χρῆσις . . . πρὸς τὰς ἀλλαγὰς τοιοῦτόν τι συνέθεντο πρὸς σφᾶς αὐτοὺς διδόναι καὶ λαμβάνειν. . . . εἶτα δι' ἐμπειρίας ἤδη τεχνικώτερον, πόθεν καὶ πῶς μεταβαλλόμενον πλεῖστον ποιήσει κέρδος.

[6]Modern economists, eschewing philosophical concerns, tend incorrectly to deprecate Aristotle's approaches and analyses. See Schumpeter 1954: 57; Soudek 1952. Finley (1970) "defends" Aristotle's alleged lack of observation by insisting that, in the absence of an "economy," there was nothing to observe. Cf. Finley 1985: 21. See, however, Meikle 1979 for a critique of these "anachronistic" evaluations of Aristotle's thought (pp. 57–58). Cf. Johnson 1939: 450; J. T. Lewis 1978; Lowry 1969, 1974, 1987; Meikle 1989. In fact, Aristotle's treatment of currency-denominated exchange (in the *Politics*) and of commodity value (in the *Ethics*) won the admiration of Marx, who, like Aristotle, dealt with economic themes in a wider political and philosophical context. For Aristotle's influence on Marx, see Meikle 1985; Fenves 1986.

assets, he notes the relatively recent development[7] of a new type of economic activity that has adversely affected traditional values and methods.[8] This "monied mode of acquisition" (*chrēmatistikē ktētikē [technē]*)[9] has arisen, he says, from the new dominance of distribution by experienced businessmen motivated by profit considerations ("making money from one another").[10] The individual pursuit of profit reflects society's new functioning through the exchange of goods and services for money, not bound to societal relations, replacing the prior system of household production/consumption, which had been augmented sporadically, where necessary, by barter within defined social relationships.[11] Aristotle actually appears to be describing a system of production, distribution, and consumption actuated by a supply-demand pricing mechanism, the essence of a "market economy."[12] This commercial world of the

[7]There is general consensus that coinage was unknown prior to the seventh century, but substantial disagreement about the precise date of its introduction in the sixth century. First half of the century: Weidauer 1975: 72–109; Cahn 1977: 279–87; Kagan 1982: 343–60. Later: Cook 1946: 90–91; Robinson 1951: 156–64; Price 1976: 274–75. For the effect of the introduction of coinage on the ancient Greek economy, see Postan 1944; Kraay 1964; and Crawford 1982: 29–59.

[8]Aristotle sees the introduction of coinage as the precondition to the development of retail trade (τὸ καπηλικόν), but explicitly separates an earlier, "simple" state of this trade from the profit-seeking, complex market activity existing in his own time: πορισθέντος οὖν ἤδη νομίσματος ἐκ τῆς ἀναγκαίας ἀλλαγῆς θάτερον εἶδος τῆς χρηματιστικῆς ἐγένετο, τὸ καπηλικόν, τὸ μέν πρῶτον ἁπλῶς ἴσως γινόμενον, εἶτα δι᾽ ἐμπειρίας ἤδη τεχνικώτερον, πόθεν καὶ πῶς μεταβαλλόμενον πλεῖστον ποιήσει κέρδος (*Pol.* 1257b1–5). Modern scholars sharply differentiate the nature of economic activity at Athens in the fourth century from that prevailing earlier: see Davies 1981: 38–87; Polanyi, Arensberg, and Pearson 1957: 67 ("in Aristotle's writings we possess an eyewitness account . . . of incipient market trading at its very first appearance in the history of civilization").

[9]Χρηματιστική, an adjective, is derived from the noun χρῆμα, which carried a dual meaning of "money" and of "property" (goods, chattel, etc.). When applied to the fourth-century market, as in the Aristotelian phrase ἡ κτητικὴ χρηματιστικὴ (τέχνη) (*Pol.* 1256b40–41), the monetary notation is clearly present. Cf. Humphreys 1983c: 12 ("*chrēmatistikē*, the art of money-making"). Since Aristotle's discussion is focused entirely on the changes wrought in economic organization by the introduction of coinage, it seems unreasonable to translate χρηματιστική here by a phrase such as the "art of getting wealth" (Jowett).

[10]Aristot., *Pol.* 1258b1–4: τῆς δὲ μεταβλητικῆς ψεγομένης δικαίως (οὐ γὰρ κατὰ φύσιν ἀλλ᾽ ἀπ᾽ ἀλλήλων ἐστίν), εὐλογώτατα μισεῖται ἡ ὀβολοστατικὴ διὰ τὸ ἀπ᾽ αὐτοῦ τοῦ νομίσματος εἶναι τὴν κτῆσιν καὶ οὐκ ἐφ᾽ ὅπερ ἐπορίσθη. For Aristotle's view on the appropriate role of money, see *E.N.* 1133a18ff., 1133b16ff.

[11]Under the prior system (ἐν τῇ πρώτῃ κοινωνίᾳ [τοῦτο δ᾽ ἐστὶν οἰκία], οἱ μὲν τῶν αὐτῶν ἐκοινώνουν πάντων), barter was employed only κατὰ τὰς δεήσεις. Aristotle notes that discontinuous exchange in kind still prevailed in his time among many non-Greek nations: ποιεῖσθαι τὰς μεταδόσεις, καθάπερ ἔτι πολλὰ ποιεῖ καὶ τῶν βαρβαρικῶν ἐθνῶν, κατὰ τὴν ἀλλαγήν (*Pol.* 1257a19–25). On the entire section, see Barker's trenchant interpretation (1952).

[12]Aristotle does not examine the nature of this price mechanism, which was irrelevant to his own ethically derived concept of the "just price" (*E.N.* 1133a–b). Polanyi therefore infers that a mature pricing mechanism (in his opinion, the essence of the "market economy") arose only

market, in any event, is far removed from traditional forms of organization through the "household" (*oikos*), where production and consumption was governed not by other people's money but by societal and familial relationships and motivations. Now transactions are ephemeral and prices determined by economic considerations. Although Aristotle longs for the former system, its replacement by impersonal coined money is what he actually portrays—and rues.

This change was fundamental. In the early fifth century, the basic building-block of Athenian society, the *oikos*, had been perceived as self-sufficient, producing for its own private consumption.[13] But by the fourth century, agricultural products were increasingly being raised for cash sale;[14] consumer items were now often produced by commercial workshops;[15] aristocratic marriages for dynastic continuity had disappeared.[16] Financial stability had become dependent on the credibility (*pistis*) in the marketplace of former slaves who were able to marshal unprecedentedly large monetary resources.[17] In the sixth century, nonagricultural income and property was, for the upper classes,

---

some years later. He thus terms the fourth-century Athenian economy "market trade," the "juncture" of the "orbit of trade" and "the institution of the market" (Polanyi, Arensberg, and Pearson 1957: 83–87). For the emergence of the "market economy" in a variety of societies, see Rodinson 1973: xv–lxix; for the usefulness of Polanyi's conceptualization of the market in the study of Greek economic history, see Valensi 1974; for its inapplicability to certain aspects of the Greek world not relevant to our discussion, see Figueira 1984: 15–30.

[13]The ancient sources identify this *oikos*, rather than the individual, as the essential constituent element of Athenian society, and in recent years this judgment has come to be accepted by scholars. See below, Chapter 4, n. 113.

[14]In Attica, rents for agricultural land were by the fourth century (in contrast to the old hektemorage system) invariably paid and calculated in money, not in kind. See Xen., *Mem.* 2.7.2, 3.11.4, *Symp.* 8.25; Lysias 7.4 and §§9–10; Isaios 9.42; Theophr., *Char.* 4.5. For the significant amount of cash generated in the fourth century from the leasing of public property, including land, see R. G. Osborne 1988: 291–92. For epigraphic evidence as to the content of such leases, cf., e.g., Walbank 1983: 100–135, 177–99, 200–31; 1984: 361–68; Langdon 1987: 47–58; D. M. Lewis 1959: 239–47 (S.E.G. 18.13).

[15]The development of such shops is confirmed by the high proportion of slaves known to have been engaged in specialized craft activity in the mid-320s—in sharp contrast to the very low percentage so employed in the late fifth century. Cf. I.G. II² 1553–78 (lists reporting the manumission of 171 slaves in the 320s) (cf. Pritchett 1956: 279; Kliacko 1966: 114–27) and the Attic stelai (recording in 414 the sale of some 53 slaves; *Hesperia* 22 [1953]: 240ff., and *Hesperia* 30 [1961]: 23ff.). The earliest significant information on such commercial workshops dates from the end of the Peloponnesian War (the shield factory of Lysias and Polemarchos). Lysias 12.8, 19; Plato, *Rep.* 8; Plutarch, *Orators' Lives* 835b–c.

[16]For the period of more than forty years prior to the regime of Dēmētrios, "an exceptionally well-documented period," not a single marriage link can be discerned among political personages. Davies 1981: 120.

[17]Dem. 36.57 (of the banker, former slave Phormiōn): τοσαῦτα γάρ, ὦ ἄνδρες Ἀθηναῖοι, χρήμαθ' ὑμῖν ἀνεγνώσθη προσηυπορηκώς, ὅσ' οὔθ' οὗτος οὔτ' ἄλλος οὐδεὶς κέκτηται. πίστις μέντοι Φορμίωνι παρὰ τοῖς εἰδόσι καὶ τοσούτων καὶ πολλῷ πλειόνων χρημάτων, δι' ἧς καὶ αὐτὸς αὑτῷ καὶ ὑμῖν χρήσιμός ἐστιν. ἃ μὴ προῆσθε.

"politically negligible" (Davies 1981: 38); by the fourth century, a variety of economic bases supported the propertied citizens and "tended to obliterate differences of origin" (Mossé 1973: 49). Within his own lifetime and writings, the conservative commentator Xenophon reflects this fundamental change from embedded to market economy. Where in the earlier *Oikonomikos* he had lauded the traditional "household" as a potential solution to all of Hellas' contemporary problems, by the 350s in the later *Poroi* he actively proposes financial incentives to promote trade, to encourage immigration of economically useful aliens, and to increase the money supply.[18]

This new system naturally required new functionaries. Since hundreds of separate communities minted their own coins—and a number of dominant currencies circulated far from their own territories[19]—a prominent place in the market was taken by the money changer, who conducted business on the *trapeza* (literally, the "table" in the marketplace on which currency was exchanged).[20] Since the new price-denominated, profit-oriented market functioned through these coins, monetary exchange through the *trapeza* itself involved numerous discrete fleeting transactions, themselves further embodiment of the new economic system. Beyond the exchange of currency, however, these money changers (called *trapezitai*) provided loans, accepted deposits, and served as intermediaries in facilitating commerce, becoming what we would term "bankers" (see below). Since the provision of these functions originated not in traditional familial, social, or political relationships, but in the isolated transactions of a business environment, the *trapeza* further detached the new economy from the social fabric of traditional society.[21] Because of its commercial genesis, autonomous of traditional society, operation at Athens of a trapezitic business (a "bank") was open even to those who had no prior stake in the pre-existing fabric of relationships—to nonaristocrats, non-Athenians, even slaves.[22] These activities in turn created new personal and familial relations, further transforming both society and the economy.

[18]See Humphreys 1983c: 13. The evidence for movement to a market economy is so pervasive that Millett, in attempting "an alternative type of analysis along non-market lines" for the process of sale, is forced to concede "the appearance in the ancient literature of the external trappings of market exchange"—while turning to "modern African markets" for refutation of the Athenian evidence (Millett 1990: 168).

[19]The Cyzicene stater, for example, coinage of a state on the Sea of Marmara, was in circulation over a vast geographical area, and reached Athens itself in large numbers. See below, Chapter 5, n. 165.

[20]At Athens, these money changers occupied prominent positions in both the city marketplace and the maritime commercial emporium at the Piraeus. The Tester (*dokimastēs*), a public slave, was assigned to test monetary silver while seated "among the *trapezai*," and the law regulating the circulation of legal coinage was itself set up "among the *trapezai*." See Stroud 1974: 157, ll. 5–6, 44–46.

[21]As Humphreys (1978: 152–53) has insightfully seen.

[22]Many bankers were in fact citizens, either through birth (for example, Aristolochos, Archestratos, Antisthenēs, Antidōros) or through naturalization. See Chapter 4, n. 44.

And not only, or even primarily, the "visible" economy. Bankers actually functioned largely in a world of hidden transactions, of confidential dealings that existed in counterpoint to the "official" world of commerce. Like many basic Athenian concepts and institutions, the economy itself was dichotomously divided into "disclosed" (*phanera*) and "invisible" (*aphanēs*) markets, complementary opposites that shaped perception and activity.[23] In the disclosed market, real-estate loans were attested by boundary-stones placed openly on property, and estates were transferred with full confirmation of already-known holdings, but with virtually no mention of bank deposits, which belonged largely to the "invisible" market.[24] In the *aphanēs* market, investments and ownership were cloaked in secrecy, as protection from creditors, tax collectors, and other potential adversaries. Yet the existence of the secret sphere was much bruited, rumors of nonexistent wealth were rampant,[25] and allegations of tax avoidance or creditor evasion were frequent. For example, Demosthenes' father, who is known to have dealt extensively with Athenian banks,[26] concealed much of his property throughout his lifetime, apparently completely avoiding taxes, and possibly escaping liability for his father-in-law's debts.[27] The wealthy Stephanos was accused of acting in concert with his bankers "to conceal his wealth in order that he might obtain secret returns through the bank" (*dia tēs trapezēs*, Dem. 45.64–66). Even important foreigners came to Athens to use the *trapeza* to conceal funds from overseas rulers: an entire surviving court speech (Isokrates 17) deals with the efforts of Sopaios, a power at the Pontic court, to hide vast sums through Pasiōn's bank. (This "hidden economy," and the banks' dominant role therein, are treated in detail in Chapter 6).

THE *TRAPEZA* AS TRUE BANK

But can we legitimately consider the Athenian *trapeza* a true "bank"? For prevailing scholarly opinion, the answer is clear, and negative: only through modernizing and erroneous anachronism can these coin-changers or pawnbrokers be conceived of as "bankers."[28] Yet if "bank" is defined in its gener-

[23]For the Greek tendency to understand and organize phenomena through contrast (indeed, preferably through antithesis), see below, pp. 46–52.

[24]The "disclosed" contents of decedents' estates are thus highly misleading as to the scale of bank activity in Athens. See below, Chapter 6.

[25]Lysias 19.45: ὦ ἄνδρες δικασταί . . . οὐ νῦν μόνον ἀλλὰ καὶ ἐν τῷ ἔμπροσθεν χρόνῳ πολλῶν ἐψεύσθητε τῆς οὐσίας, οἳ ζῶντες μὲν πλουτεῖν ἐδόκουν, ἀποθανόντες δὲ πολὺ παρὰ τὴν δόξαν τὴν ὑμετέραν ἐφάνησαν. Cf. Gabrielsen 1986: 110–11, 1987: 12; Humphreys 1983c: 10.

[26]Dem. 27.11. See below, pp. 121–29.

[27]See Davies 1971: 128–29; Ste. Croix 1953: 55 n. 105; below, pp. 200–201.

[28]Austin and Vidal-Naquet 1977: 149 ("primarily money-changing establishments and pawn brokers"); Isager and Hansen 1975: 88 ("basically a money changer"); Harris 1988: 376 ("commercial banks . . . still lay far in the future").

ally accepted essence—a business having an obligation to repay funds ("deposits") received from a multitude of sources, but with the interim right to make loans and investments for its own account—the *trapeza* is undeniably a "bank." The two terms even share a common origin: Greek *trapeza* means "table," derived by metonymy from the surface on which money was handled in the marketplace; "bank" likewise means table, derived from the original Genoese "banc(h)a," denoting the money changer's work surface.[29] As a term for a financial institution, "bank" is today used in virtually every modern language—except modern Greek, which still employs *trapeza*.[30]

Between the Athenian *trapeza* and the modern bank, there are of course striking differences—in technology, legal position, and scope of operations. The *trapezai* were unincorporated businesses operated by individual proprietors or partners,[31] almost entirely free of governmental regulation; modern banks are almost always corporate institutions, invariably governed by official regulation. In contrast to the freedom enjoyed by the *trapezitai*, a bewildering variety of highly nuanced governmental differentiations govern the modern bank.[32] Yet both Demosthenes and modern banking codes fix on the same basic factors in finding the necessary essence of a bank in its generation of revenue through loans funded by outside deposits, "other people's money," which the bank must return. In the language of the United States Code, a "bank" must "(1) accept deposits" and "(2) make commercial loans."[33] For the French, a

---

[29]See Thompson 1988: 829; Bogaert 1966: 169–70.

[30]Thus the Σύγχρονον Λεξικόν τῆς ἑλληνικῆς γλώσσης (Athens, 1961) defines τράπεζα as a πιστωτικὸ ἵδρυμα, ποὺ ἐμπορεύεται τὸ χρῆμα..

[31]The Greek κοινωνός is in many respects closer to a "joint venturer" than a "partner," especially as to legal attributes. See below, Chapter 4, n. 71.

[32]Brazilian law in the 1970s, for example, provided minute, and sometimes inconsistent or unclear, differentiation between a number of institutions that appear similar: the *banco commercial*, the *banco de investimento*, the *financeira*, and the *compania de crédito imobiliário* (see Chapter 2). In France, consistent regulation proved impossible under the Banking Acts of 1941 and 1945, which applied specific and differing rules to members of the Association Française des Banques and of the Association Française des Etablissements de Crédit, and to an enormous variety of other institutions (mutual and cooperative banks, savings institutions, specialized financial organizations, etc.). Even among private "banks," inconsistent distinctions were made among *banques de dépôts*, *banques d'affaires*, and *banques de crédit à moyen et long terme*. See Colmant 1990: 51–52; Report of the Commission Bancaire (Paris, 1988).

[33]"'Bank' means any institution . . . which (1) accepts deposits that the depositor has a legal right to withdraw on demand, and (2) engages in the business of making commercial loans" (12 U.S.C.A. §1841). But U.S. courts have refused on occasion to abide literally by this proscription and have included within the definition of "bank" organizations not falling literally within the legal category: *Florida Dept. of Banking and Finance v. Board of Governors of Federal Reserve System*, C.A. 11, 1985, 760 F.2d 1135 (bank included an organization not engaged in the business of making commercial loans); *Wilshire Oil Co. of Texas v. Board of Governors of Federal Reserve System*, C.A. 3, 1981, 668 F.2d 732, *cert. den.* 102 S.Ct. 2958, 457 U.S. 1132 (institution's reservation of right to 14 days' advance notice of withdrawal from deposits did not remove the organization from the definition of "bank").

"banker" has been defined as one who accepts deposits and grants loans.[34] Ancient Roman banking likewise has been defined through the twin functions of deposit and credit, and on that basis has been isolated from other financial businesses of its period.[35] And for Demosthenes, the *trapeza* is "a business operation producing risk-laden revenues from other people's money."[36]

Most of this book is devoted to the way in which the *trapeza* accepted deposits and provided loans (thus functioning by modern definition as a "bank"), the economic significance of these activities, and their social, commercial, and legal context and implications. But the Athenian bankers performed business functions beyond the receipt of monies and the provision of credit. The *trapeza*'s involvement in currency transactions brought it a major role in the treatment of what modern economists would call "commodity money"; its handling of payment orders and provision of written payment guaranties, eliminating the need for delivery of gold or silver coin, made it, in modern terms, a creator of "bank money." Its acceptance of legal documents for safekeeping or attestation may resemble similar activities of some modern banks. But its acceptance of valuable items, such as silver bowls, is not even superficially similar to the operation of a modern "pawnshop": cash was not advanced against such items; the banker had no legal right under any circumstance to retain the goods.

Of these ancillary pursuits, none is more critical to an understanding of the Athenian economy than the bankers' involvement in the handling and creation of "money." Although modern economists generally and easily accept the differentiation of money as "commodity money" (one or more of the precious metals such as gold and silver)[37] or "bank money" (unbacked fiat money and credit in all its forms),[38] the actual place of "money" in the modern economy and the mechanics of its utilization remain a mystery. A leading "neoclassical" economic theorist, in a recent study of money and modern inflation, has noted ruefully: "The most serious challenge that the existence of money poses to the

[34]Law of 13 June 1941, defining banks and financial establishments. See Ardant 1966: 8. The 1984 Banking Act, in seeking to cover all "credit institutions" ("établissements de crédit"), describes these institutions as "legal persons carrying out banking operations as their regular business" (section 1). "Banking operations" in turn encompass the receipt of funds from the public and the provision of credit and payment mechanisms. See Colmant 1990: 53.

[35]Andreau 1987: 5. Cf. Talamanca 1955. The definition and resultant separate treatment of the *argentarii* are implicit in Kraut 1826; Guillard 1875; and Thielmann 1963.

[36]Dem. 36.11: ἡ δ' ἐργασία προσόδους ἔχουσ' ἐπικινδύνους ἀπὸ χρημάτων ἀλλοτρίων. Cf. Chapter 5, n. 1.

[37]In ancient Greece, as in many other societies, silver and gold possessed the characteristics requisite for commodity money: relative inelasticity of supply of a scarce good having inherent utilitarian value coupled with some possibility of expansion of stock through trade or production. But a variety of items (shells, for example) may possess these characteristics in differing societies and may therefore be utilized as commodity money.

[38]This division is entirely unrelated to the distinction between "inside" and "outside" money developed by Gurley and Shaw (1960). See Makinen 1977: 160.

theorist is this: the best developed model of the economy cannot find room for it" (Hahn 1982: 1). Keynesian and monetarist analyses share this perplexity: since both are based on a neoclassical synthesis, both are disturbed by the continuing and elusive search for a sound theoretical explanation of basic monetary aspects of the contemporary economy.[39]

In contrast to the diffidence of modern economists in dealing with issues relating to currency and credit, ancient historians following Finley have dogmatically asserted a simplistic, and supposedly dispositive, "truth": the money supply in Athens (and indeed in the entire ancient world at all times) was essentially inelastic because of its reliance on "coin" and the lack of "machinery for credit beyond the lending of coins." For Finley, the absence "of official banknotes or similar fiduciary money [was the] basic condition of ancient business practice and finance," and this mandated the essential "primitive" nature of all ancient economies.[40] Any deviation from this central tenet should be "rightly and briefly dismissed."[41] Reiterated forcefully over the years, this catechism has come to exert a wide influence.[42]

The dogma, however, is demonstrably untrue, for two reasons. The supposed inexorable link between primitive conditions and the absence of official paper money is theoretically insupportable. And in any event, the activities of the Athenian bankers provided the mechanism for the creation of "money" beyond the available supply of precious metals.

The Lack of Paper Currency

Finley is correct in noting the complete absence at Athens of "unbacked fiat money," paper currency whose acceptance is mandated solely by governmental designation as "legal tender." This did not, however, mandate the "primitiveness" of the Athenian economy: well into the twentieth century, paper currency functioning as unbacked fiat money was absent from both the United

---

[39]For a detailed critique of the difficulties encountered by both "real" and "monetarist" analysts in finding the mechanisms and role of money, see Rogers 1989: 73–157. Cf. Hicks 1967: ch. 1; Brunner and Meltzer 1971.

[40]Finley, "Further Thoughts," in 1985: 196–97. With increasing dogmatism, Finley insisted on this orthodoxy over several decades: cf. 1953a: 74 (with reference specifically to classical Athens), 1953b: 490–91, and the first edition (1974) of *Ancient Economy*, pp. 141–43.

[41]Finley 1985: 252 n. 83, with reference to Lo Cascio's treatment (1981: 76 n. 3) of Andreau's well-founded but limited reservations about the theory's full applicability (1977: 1143). In fact, Lo Cascio merely notes that the Roman authorities in the late Republic and early Empire took only limited action affecting the economic activity of Roman banks; accordingly, he felt it "legitimate to leave out the whole issue" of bank "creation of money" from his article concerning Roman state policy on coinage.

[42]Cf., for example, Bogaert 1968: 328, 354–55, 374–75; Rougé 1966, 3: chs. 2, 7; Humphreys 1978: 153 ("the ancient banks lacked the main function of the modern bank, that of creating credit").

Kingdom and the United States.[43] Finley erred in assuming that the absence of paper fiat notes necessitates a society's dependence on "commodity money" (and its consequent inability to increase the monetary supply because of relative inelasticity in the stock of precious metals). "Bank money," the principal source of increase in most sophisticated societies' monetary supply, has no necessary relationship to paper legal tender or other governmental fiat money. In fact, even in the absence of governmental fiat currency or state paper money, the Athenian private banks developed "paper" transfer and payment mechanisms that provided the means for expansion of the monetary supply. Elementary modern economic theory easily accommodates the feasibility of these Athenian banking mechanisms.

Unlike commodity money, whose value is equivalent to the worth of the material of which it is composed, "bank money" possesses no inherent worth. It may be composed of "representative money" ("representative" because its worth is not determined by the value of the material of which it is composed) or of "token money" (such as bank deposits, which can function as part of the money supply so long as there is confidence in their easy conversion into an acceptable means of actual payment).[44] Although representative money may be composed of coin as well as paper (and need not have a value less than its nominal worth),[45] Athens never utilized this form of money.[46] But the deposit and credit mechanisms of its *trapezai* constituted a ready source of "token money" and thus an easy means of expanding its supply of money.

Such expansion through bank deposits, without any increase in commodity (or representative) money, can be easily demonstrated.[47] If the Athenian banks

[43]Until the First World War, the Bank of England provided a physical backing of gold for its bank notes. Only in 1971 did the United States adopt unbacked fiat money (promising prior to that time to redeem all paper currency, on demand, with its equivalence in precious metals, thus providing a *de facto* gold standard for the world and a substantial subsidy to the precious-metal industries). See Melvin 1985: 138–49; Wallich 1982.

[44]See Crockett 1979: 12–13. Cf. Day 1957: chs. 1, 2; Harrod 1969: chs. 1, 2. In jurisdictions that have established representative currency as legal tender, bank deposits still cannot be recognized directly as legal tender: a bank would be entirely free of any meaningful obligation to repay depositors if it could satisfy this obligation by simply crediting another account at the same bank.

[45]For example, before decimalization, old U.K.pennies contained more than a pennyworth of copper. Until 1966, U.S. silver coins contained an amount of metal equal to the face value of the currency.

[46]To the contrary, Athens made great effort to insure the full value of its money. The 375/4 law on silver coinage provides mechanisms to test the genuineness of silver coins and penalties for transgression. See the *editio princeps* of Stroud (1974), who believes that Athens was so far committed to commodity money that it required the acceptance as "legal tender" of even counterfeit versions of Athenian coins provided that they had full silver value. In accord: Robert and Robert 1980; Engelmann 1985. Cf., however, Buttrey 1979, 1981; Wankel 1983; Cataudella 1986; Stumpf 1986.

[47]For a more complete (and complex) demonstration, adapted to contemporary realities, see Havrilesky and Boorman 1982: 10–48. Cf. Burger 1972.

had on deposit 11 talents (66,000 drachmas) of silver coinage, a combined balance sheet initially would be as follows:[48]

Assets		*Liabilities*	
Silver coinage	66,000 *dr*.	Deposits of silver coinage	66,000 *dr*.

If 3 talents (18,000 *dr*.) of loans are made by the banks, the balance sheet becomes:

Assets		*Liabilities*	
Silver coinage	48,000 *dr*.	Deposits of silver coinage	66,000 *dr*.
Loans receivable	18,000 *dr*.		

Without any increase in the banks' liabilities, there has been an increase of 18,000 *dr*. in money circulating outside the banks. If these funds are used to buy goods and services, and the recipients of the funds deposit a tenth (1,800 *dr*.) of this coinage back into the banks, the combined balance sheet now will appear as follows:

Assets		*Liabilities*	
Silver coinage	49,800 *dr*.	Deposits of silver coinage	67,800 *dr*.
Loans receivable	18,000 *dr*.		

Clearly, the total amount of bank deposits—claims that on request can immediately or eventually be turned into silver—has been increased without any corresponding increase in the amount of silver (Athenian commodity money) and in the complete absence of paper currency. The Athenian money supply would expand whenever any part of the proceeds of a bank loan was redeposited in a bank by the ultimate recipients of the funds advanced. The money supply at Athens (as in any society where banks are functioning) can thus be seen to consist of bank liabilities ("deposits") and cash in circulation.[49] The amount of increase in the bank portion of this money supply will depend on the volume and velocity of bank loans, the percentage of these loan funds immediately or ultimately redeposited in the *trapezai*, and the time period and volatility of deposits (which influence the banks' need or desire to retain currency reserves, and thus affect both the amount of additional monies available for further lending and further increase in the money supply). Monetary expansion through bank activity will be substantial if trapezitic deposits represent a signif-

---

[48]At least 11 talents, and possibly many more, were on deposit at the bank of Pasīon alone (Dem. 36.5–6 and below, pp. 129–36). This bank at the same time had at least 50 talents loaned out. On owners' capital at Athenian banks, see below, pp. 183–89. For the full and careful record-keeping of Athenian bankers, see below, pp. 124–26. On the adequacy of Athenian accounting in the Athenian (if not modern) context, see below, p. 124, n. 56.

[49]Cf. the similar definition in Fogel and Engerman 1971: 441: the money supply is "the total of bank liabilities plus currency held by the nonbank public." Purged of its jargon, this definition would have been easily comprehended by Athenians.

icant part of the total Athenian money supply, if the making of bank loans is not unduly inhibited by the volatility of deposits or other factors, and if a reasonable portion of the new purchasing power generated by these loans is immediately or ultimately redeposited in the banks. For the determination of these issues, the absence of paper currency is entirely irrelevant.

The Creation of Bank Money

The Athenian bankers did create credit and "money" beyond the available supply of precious metals. The lack of governmental scrip, in fact, lent added importance to the various banking alternatives to the physical exchange of bulky metal coins. Supplementing the banks' direct creation of money and expansion of credit through their loan and deposit processes, the *trapezai* issued guarantees of credit, expedited commerce by confirming availability of funds in bank accounts, and executed payment orders through which commercial transactions were settled and obligations met without the actual transfer of coins.

In reality, far from "the absence of credit-creating instruments and institutions remain[ing] as an unshaken foundation of the ancient economy,"[50] the Athenians utilized a profusion of credit-providing mechanisms and businesses. Although Athenian law technically required full payment of the purchase price to effectuate sale of an object,[51] thus seemingly eliminating purchases on credit and mandating laborious accumulation of hoards of metallic coins by persons saving to make a purchase (with a consequent removal of currency from circulation), in practice, credit was widely available for consumer (and other) purchases both from vendors and from banks. A seller of slaves, for example, provides financing for a 3,500 *dr.* purchase, and at a high rate of interest; a manufacturer of swords and sofas offers consumer financing on a continuing basis, apparently as a routine aspect of his business.[52] Purchasers did pay the full price, but with funds lent by sellers. As legal scholars have long recognized,[53] the procedure was simply a "legal fiction," merely a means of creating credit. No money actually changed hands: the seller did not physically transfer coins to the buyer that were then physically transferred back to the seller.[54]

---

[50]Finley 1985: 198.

[51]Pringsheim's thesis in *Law of Sale* (1950)—that the principle of cash sale prevailed throughout Greece and in Hellenistic Egypt—has long enjoyed general acceptance. See MacDowell 1978: 138; E. M. Harris 1988: 360. But Millett has recently suggested (1990: 176–78) that at Athens credit sales were freely possible, especially in light of the principle that the courts would recognize whatever arrangements private parties agreed upon (see below, Chapter 3, n. 3).

[52]Slaves: Lykourgos, *Leōkratēs* 23, with interest at almost 35% per year. Manufacturer: Dem. 27.9 (see Gernet 1954–60: 29ff., 261). Cf. Aristot., *Oik.* 2.2.8, 1347b3.

[53]See Pringsheim 1950: 245–46; Harrison 1968–71, 1: 232 n. 3.

[54]In prohibiting retail sales on credit in the *Laws*, Plato specifically sought to nullify this legal "fiction" by prohibiting the seller from waiving the physical provision of coins: ἐν τούτοις ἀλλάττεσθαι νόμισμά τε χρημάτων καὶ χρήματα νομίσματος, μὴ προϊέμενον ἄλλον ἑτέρῳ τὴν ἀλλαγήν (849e). Cf. *Laws* 915d–e.

Wide use of such "fictitious" credit permitted a marked expansion in business activity without any actual rise in coinage or bullion.

Banks were active in retail finance. A striking example: trapezitic involvement with perfume businesses, a major Athenian obsession heavily dependent on the availability of credit.[55] Banks are known to have provided funding for the ongoing operations of retail fragrance businesses (Lysias, frag. 38.1)[56] and to have been involved in the sale of perfume outlets (Hyp., *Ath.* 5–9).[57] Loans in excess of five talents (provided by suppliers and others) encumbered the latter business. The operation described in Lysias had been originally financed by the banker Sōsinomos; additional funds were advanced by others, to the point that the daily line of creditors seeking repayment is said to have resembled a funeral procession.[58] In advancing money, *trapezitai* often cooperated with other lenders: moreover, bankers routinely accepted deposits intended for specific loan areas, a type of intermediation "through the bank."[59]

Beyond consumer credit, the *trapezitai* supplied a wide variety of finance. Bankers provided loans to purchase mining concessions and processing mills (Dem. 37, 40.52), to establish a cloth-making operation (Xen., *Mem.* 2.7), to purchase land (I.G. II² 2762; *Arch. Delt.* 17 (1961–62): *Khronika* 35, no. 4), to help political leaders (Dem. 49.17, 23), to aid military operations (Dem. 49.6), to ransom friends (Dem. 53.9), to finance the import of lumber (Dem. 49.35–36), to assist business clients and their associates (Isok. 17.12, 38), to avoid creditors' execution on a ship (Dem. 33). In the dominant sphere of the Athenian economy, maritime trade, the *trapezai* held an important, perhaps a prime financing role.[60]

The bankers also expedited commerce—and concurrently enlarged the effective money supply—through credit-enhancement devices that utilized bank deposits in place of coins. As a result of legal problems arising from ship financing, a bank customer was required to post seven talents with the state: the sum was provided not in cash, but through a surety guarantee from a bank, furnished in reliance upon the customer's deposits.[61] Settlement of overseas commercial obligations by transporting monies from Athens might have significantly reduced the supply of silver circulating in Attica. By guaranteeing payment of funds at far-off locations, the banks averted this drain and allowed

[55]For the role of fragrances in Athenian life, see Webster 1969: 30, 36.

[56]The bank's loan was for *aphormē*, a funding of "what is needed to keep something going" (Millett 1983: 46). For bankers' *aphormē*, see below, pp. 183–89.

[57]Here the buyer, prior to closing on the purchase of a retail fragrance business, deposited in the *trapeza* the purchase price of 4,000 *dr.* (which had been gathered from various sources). For the bank's role in the transaction, see below, pp. 119–20.

[58]§4: τοσοῦτοι δὲ ἐπὶ τὴν οἰκίαν ἅμα τῇ ἡμέρᾳ ἀπαιτήσοντες τὰ ὀφειλόμενα ἔρχονται ὥστε οἴεσθαι τοὺς παριόντας ἐπ᾽ ἐκφορὰν αὐτοὺς ἥκειν τοῦ τεθνεῶτος.

[59]See below, pp. 121–36, 151–60.

[60]For detailed consideration of maritime lending by *trapezai*, see below, pp. 136–50.

[61]Isok. 17.44: τῶν δ᾽ ἑπτὰ ταλάντων ἐγγυητής μοι ἐγένεθ᾽ ἡγούμενος πίστιν ἔχειν ἱκανὴν τὸ χρυσίον τὸ παρ᾽ αὐτῷ κείμενον. See below, pp. 118–19.

customers to avoid the dangers and inconvenience inherent in transporting a large amount of coins or bullion. Thus when Stratoklēs needed funds available at the distant Black Sea, to which he was about to journey, he was able to leave his own money on loan in Athens and carry instead a bank guarantee of payment of principal and interest on 300 Cyzicene staters.[62] This bank commitment was issued by Pasiōn's *trapeza* in reliance on the deposits of the customer who was receiving Stratoklēs' actual currency.[63] Again, bank deposits effectively became "bank money," enhancing the supply of coinage actually in circulation in Athens.[64]

Even within the domestic economy, the *trapezai* conserved currency through bank payment orders, an alternative to coinage-consuming escrow arrangements, down payments, or the hoarding of currency to gather sufficient funds for future payment in silver. When the merchant Lykōn was leaving Athens and wanted to make payment of 1,640 *dr.* to a business colleague, he directed that funds on deposit at Pasiōn's bank be paid at a future time to Kēphisiadēs (Dem. 52.3). So routine were such transactions that standard banking procedures had been developed for effectuating them: we are told that when a private depositor ordered payment to someone, "all the bankers were accustomed" to make formulaic entries in their records setting forth the name of the person providing the funds, the sum involved, and the name of the recipient or the person who would identify the payee.[65] Since a customer's instructions were given in person, and were paid only on the recipient's personal appearance, these orders—unlike modern checks—were entirely paperless (except for the entries made in the bank's books).[66]

[62]Isok. 17.35–37: μέλλοντος Στρατοκλέους εἰσπλεῖν εἰς τὸν Πόντον . . . Πασίων' αὐτῷ συνέστησα, καὶ ὡμολόγησεν οὗτος αὐτῷ καὶ τὸ ἀρχαῖον καὶ τοὺς τόκους τοὺς γιγνομένους ἀποδώσειν. For the value of the staters, see below, Chapter 5, nn. 28, 166.

[63]§37: καίτοι εἰ μηδὲν ἔκειτο παρ' αὐτῷ τῶν ἐμῶν, οἴεσθ' ἂν αὐτὸν οὕτω ῥαδίως τοσούτων χρημάτων ἐγγυητήν μου γενέσθαι;

[64]Pasiōn's son, the bank owner Apollodōros, similarly offered to accept 3,000 *dr.* in Athens and to guarantee the condition of the ship's tackling, which Polyklēs would receive in the northern Aegean when he assumed his post as trierarch (Dem. 50.28). The guarantee was intended to permit Polyklēs not to "endanger" his money by transporting it out of Athens (κατάλιπε ἀργύριον αὐτοῦ, καὶ μὴ διακινδύνευε ἐκεῖσε ἄγων). Since Apollodōros was himself in the north, the actual surety was to be provided on his behalf (ὑπὲρ ἐμοῦ) by his close associates, Apollodōros ὁ Λευκονοεύς and Pythodōros ὁ Ἀχαρνεύς (the grandson of the Pythodōros who had acted generally as the banker Pasiōn's agent: see Chapter 4, pp. 98–99 and n. 183).

[65]Dem. 52.4: εἰώθασι δὲ πάντες οἱ τραπεζῖται, ὅταν τις ἀργύριον τιθεὶς ἰδιώτης ἀποδοῦναί τῳ προστάττῃ, πρῶτον τοῦ θέντος τοὔνομα γράφειν καὶ τὸ κεφάλαιον τοῦ ἀργυρίου, ἔπειτα παραγράφειν 'τῷ δεῖνι ἀποδοῦναι δεῖ,' καὶ ἐὰν μὲν γιγνώσκωσι τὴν ὄψιν τοῦ ἀνθρώπου ᾧ ἂν δέῃ ἀποδοῦναι, τοσοῦτο μόνον ποιεῖν, γράψαι ᾧ δεῖ ἀποδοῦναι, ἐὰν δὲ μὴ γιγνώσκωσι, καὶ τούτου τοὔνομα προσπαραγράφειν ὃς ἂν μέλλῃ συστήσειν καὶ δείξειν τὸν ἄνθρωπον, ὃν ἂν δέῃ κομίσασθαι τὸ ἀργύριον.

[66]Although "checks" (written orders negotiated by written endorsements) are today the quintessential form of payment order, a customer's instructions in the past were generally given in

Bankers routinely made written notations concerning individual accounts "so that the sums taken and the amounts received for the accounts might be clearly known."[67] Among persons commercially active, bank accounts appear to have been widely held: "all the *emporoi*" (maritime traders) had accounts—and at a single *trapeza*, that of Pasiōn.[68] Maintenance of a bank account was expected of an individual purporting to be of substance.[69] This combination of trapezitic accounts and payment orders provided a ready means for converting bank deposits into "bank money." The frequent use of these accounts for payment of debts is suggested by a litigant's scornful contempt for a creditor who resorted to collection efforts although funds to pay him were on deposit "at the bank."[70] Where payments were made not by actual transfer of coins but by entry on the books of the bank favoring the recipient's account, the need for physical coins, "commodity money," was obviously eliminated. This appears to have happened so routinely that the Athenians even had a term (*diagraphē*) for the cashless settlement of debts through bank entries.[71] To the extent that banks could anticipate handling payment orders and other calls by written memoranda (*hypomnēmata*) and not by cash, the amount of currency reserves kept by the bankers might be reduced, with a corresponding increase in the money supply through additional bank lending or bank spending.

---

person. Despite occasional scholarly references to checks in antiquity (cf. Brants 1882: 198; Guillard 1875: 9–10; Incarnati 1953: 108; Schwarze 1956: 98; Préaux 1958: 252), Andreau (1987: 561–63) has demonstrated their absence from the ancient world. Written payment orders from Graeco-Roman Egypt (in nonnegotiable form and therefore not "checks") have, however, recently been published: see *Berliner Griechischen Urkunden* 14.2401–16 (1980); cf. Bogaert 1983, 1986b: 11–13; Bagnall and Bogaert 1975. Even the highly developed banks of Hamburg and Amsterdam, as well as the Italian banks of the mediaeval period, anticipated the personal presence of payer and recipient. See Nasse 1891. At present, "checks" increasingly are being superseded by electronic transmittals, which parallel in effect, if not in technology, the Athenian payment orders, which "existed" essentially in the banks' records.

[67]Dem. 49.5: οἱ τραπεζῖται εἰώθασιν ὑπομνήματα γράφεσθαι ὧν τε διδόασιν χρημάτων καὶ εἰς ὅ τι καὶ ὧν ἄν τις τιθῆται, ἵνα ᾖ αὐτοῖς γνώριμα τά τε ληφθέντα καὶ τὰ τεθέντα πρὸς τοὺς λογισμούς.

[68]Dem. 52.3: Λύκων . . . τῇ τραπέζῃ τῇ τοῦ πατρὸς ἐχρῆτο, ὥσπερ καὶ οἱ ἄλλοι ἔμποροι. Χρῆται implied a relationship that included, but went beyond, the mere maintenance of an account: see below, pp. 65–66. For the translation "all the *emporoi*," see Mossé 1983: 60.

[69]Theophr., *Char.* 23.2: ὁ δὲ ἀλαζὼν τοιοῦτός τις οἷος . . . ἐν τῷ διαζεύγματι ἑστηκὼς διηγεῖσθαι ξένοις ὡς πολλὰ χρήματα αὐτῷ ἐστιν ἐν τῇ θαλάττῃ, καὶ περὶ τῆς ἐργασίας τῆς δανειστικῆς διεξιέναι ἡλίκη, καὶ αὐτὸς ὅσα εἴληφε καὶ ἀπολώλεκε, καὶ ἅμα ταῦτα πλεονάζων πέμπειν τὸ παιδάριον ἐπὶ τὴν τράπεζαν, οὐδὲ δραχμῆς αὐτῷ κειμένης.

[70]Dem. 47.49, 51, 57, 62, 64. The litigant does not emphasize that no payment order had been arranged!

[71]Harpokratiōn (s.v. διαγράψαντος), in citing Deinarchos's speech against Lykourgos, notes that "some people" use the word διαγράψαντος ("crossing out [a debt]," hence "paying") instead of the usual phrase διὰ τραπέζης ἀριθμήσαντος ("counting out [payment] through the bank," hence "paying through the bank"). Since Deinarchos's speech (from the fourth century) has not survived, the context of Harpokratiōn's gloss must be inferred. Cf. Hasebroek 1923b, 1920: 117–20; Bogaert 1968: 51.

Lykōn's payment order was effectuated by the bank of Pasiōn alone, without the involvement of any other *trapeza* (Dem. 52.3, 7). Indeed, the concentration of sea merchants' accounts at this single bank may have had the (intended?) effect of expediting maritime transactions by permitting noncash settlements through this *trapeza*. If businessmen commonly maintained a number of banking relationships, or if the concentration of maritime traders at Pasiōn's bank was not atypical—with practitioners in specific fields concentrating their banking activities in a single *trapeza*—then a significant volume of book-entry settlements, with a significant potential effect on the money supply, might have occurred without the involvement of a second bank.

Where numerous banks are functioning and no single *trapeza* commands a dominant position, however, cashless settlements by bank entry limited to a single *trapeza* and its clients will necessarily result in only limited expansion of the money supply. Yet where an individual pays for goods with a payment order on Bank A, Bank B may be willing to credit the seller's account with an increase in deposits even without demanding immediate transfer of silver currency from Bank A; the banker may even be willing to retain indefinitely this claim on A, which could be used to settle a debt with Banker C, D, or E at some future time. Again, the absence of "negotiable instruments" or "paper currency" would create no theoretical barrier to such interbank arrangements: the necessary entries would be carried directly on the banks' books.[72] There would have been no need of, and there is no clear evidence for, a system of interbank clearance procedures (akin to a modern "clearinghouse" or *giroverkehr*).[73]

CURRENCY EXCHANGE

Although the Athenian *trapezai* may have originated from currency-conversion counters in the central agora and at the Piraeus harbor, monetary exchange was not a bank monopoly. "Money changer" (*argyramoibos*) was a name applied to anyone engaged commercially in the testing or conversion of coins and pre-

---

[72]Although many interbank transactions in the modern world originate orally and are initially reflected only on the banks' books, they are generally confirmed by later written documentation. Increasingly, however, instead of obtaining written confirmation, banks today are recording the oral instructions in the continuing effort to reduce deliveries and retention of paper documents, so-called "truncation."

[73]A number of scholars have contended, on the basis of equivocal texts, that such a "giro" system did in fact exist at Athens. See Hasebroek 1920: 117ff. (esp. 139), and 1923b; Calhoun [1926] 1968: 93; Dopsch 1930: 74; Masi 1963: 272. Some have even written of clearing arrangements on an international basis: see Glotz 1910: 363; Toutain 1929: 98; Mondaini 1942: 29; Lévy 1964: 37. But Laum (1922) was correct in noting the total lack of any unequivocal reference to a clearinghouse system in fourth-century Athens. In accord: Bogaert 1968: 345; Kiessling, in *RE* s.v. "Giroverkehr"; Bolkestein 1958: 193; Huber 1939: 85; Westermann 1931: 39–40; Heichelheim 1964, 2:77.

cious metals.[74] There is even evidence that traders, merchants and retailers routinely engaged in the bartering of coins.[75] Although the bankers continued in the fourth century to provide exchange facilities, this was not the dominant aspect of their business: deposit and lending activities were.

The Greek world's extensive exchange activity reflected the great variety of coins in circulation, the absence of standardized values, and the danger of accepting worthless imitations of precious metals.[76] Hundreds of individual communities minted coins on many different standards.[77] Since only a few currencies commanded market acceptance outside their local areas, money changers functioned in every port and marketplace. Their task was not easy. Coins produced manually could not be standardized in weight to high precision; from wear, old coins were always slightly less heavy than those newly minted.[78] Impurities abounded.[79] Detection of counterfeit coins was challenging.[80] Information on particular pieces was inexact and often inadequate; exchange values fluctuated wildly.[81] Commissions were negotiable, often seemingly exorbitant; yet competition might be substantial.[82]

[74]Exchange: (ἀργυραμοιβοί) οἱ ἄργυρον διδόντες καὶ χρυσὸν ὠνούμενοι (scholiast to Theokritos, 12.37). Testing: Philōn, De sobr. 20 (2.219.15); De special. leg. 4.77 (5.226, 23); Loukianos 59.10.6 (ἀργυραμοιβικῶς). See Plato, Pol. 289e, quoted in note 75 below. Cf. χρυσαμοιβός (Themistoklēs, letter 6; Hesychios 4.298).

[75]Plato, Pol. 289e: νόμισμά τε πρὸς τὰ ἄλλα καὶ αὐτὸ πρὸς αὑτὸ διαμείβοντες, οὓς ἀργυραμοιβούς τε καὶ ἐμπόρους καὶ ναυκλήρους καὶ καπήλους ἐπωνομάκαμεν, μῶν τῆς πολιτικῆς ἀμφισβητήσουσί τι; For a comic allusion to money changing by merchants, see the fragment from Diphilos's Polypragmōn (Kock 2.562–63 = Edmonds 3A131–32)

[76]These complications stimulated proposals for reform: Plato suggested an international Ἑλληνικὸν νόμισμα (Laws 5.742a–b).

[77]See the list of states in Kraay 1976: 379–82. More than 1,000 are enumerated in Head 1911: 895–907. Almost 3,000 separate types are identified in Plant 1979. Fifteen different standards are known (Bogaert 1986b: 7). The profusion of issues traditionally has been attributed to the role of coins as political symbols of state sovereignty and independence (Will 1975: 102; Austin and Vidal-Naquet 1977: 56–58), but T. R. Martin (1985) has recently argued for strictly financial motivations. Cf. Giovanni 1978: 75–76.

[78]For variation in the weight of Athenian drachmas, see Bolin 1958: 41–42; Incarnati 1953: 85–86. For the minting techniques that brought about such lack of consistency, see Vermeule 1954 and 1956–57; Balog 1955; Hangard 1963: 5–27; Breglia 1964: 28–46.

[79]See Burns 1927: 158–68; Hammer 1908; Allin and Wallace 1954; Guépin 1965.

[80]For the problems confronted by "examiners" seeking to verify the genuineness of coins in fourth-century Athens, see Stroud 1974: 168–78, esp. 172 n. 54. Cf. Bogaert 1976. More generally, see Graf 1903; Schmalzriedt 1960; W. Campbell 1933. For governmental efforts to deal with the pervasive problem of counterfeit coins, see below, Chapter 5, n. 162.

[81]Even the nominal value of Greek coins was seldom indicated. See Suhle 1930; Robinson 1960. For the considerable variation in market-determined currency values, see below, Chapter 5, nn. 28, 166.

[82]Bogaert (1968: 326–29) estimates exchange fees at 5–6%, in his opinion an inappropriately high rate justified by the "shortage" of money (but this estimate is based on only a few cases that are difficult to interpret: see my discussion in Chapter 2 on the unreliability of such cliometric conclusions). More persuasive, since Athenian money changers gathered at specific locations in

We know very little about the detailed terms and procedures of specific currency transactions by bankers (or, for that matter, by anyone else). Even the identification of bankers with coin exchange depends primarily on philological, not economic or historical, evidence: the bankers' denomination as *trapezitai* (the "table-ists"), reflecting the Greek word for the surface on which money was handled.[83] But the bankers were frequently referred to by more expansive terms ("the money-men," for example), and by circumlocutions, reflecting the variety of activities they pursued.[84] Yet even into the fourth century, the *trapezitai* clearly remained active in currency exchange. A surviving fragment of the fourth-century comic playwright Menander told us that private bankers in Athens employed "evaluators" (*dokimastai*) to test the genuineness of coins,[85] and the discovery of the Nikophōn decree in 1970 confirmed the linkage of the table (*trapeza*) with currency exchange: an evaluator of the genuineness of coins was to be seated "among the *trapezai*," and the actual stele, dating from 375/4 and containing the text of the decree regulating commercial acceptance and testing of silver coinage, was to be set up "among the *trapezai*."[86] In citing the overt changing of money "at the *trapezai*" as proof that an individual had funds,[87] Demosthenes confirms the banks' continuing currency-exchange operations.

But our sources make equally clear that in the fourth century deposit-taking and money-lending became the dominant trapezitic activities—to such an extent that it has even been suggested that some bankers had entirely ceased to engage in currency exchange.[88] When we encounter the fourth-century *tra-*

---

the agora and Piraeus, is T. R. Martin's observation on the competitive prices likely to result from a "concentrated, centralized market for one commodity, which is peopled by various dealers trying to sell the same thing" (1985: 211).

[83]See above, p. 9. The letters τραπ do appear in a fragmentary inscription dated to 423/2 discovered in the Athenian agora and apparently dealing with the exchange of gold. See Meritt 1945: 119–22, no. 11 (= S.E.G. 10.87). Cf. S.E.G. 22.10.

[84]Typical periphrastic terms: οἱ γνώμῃ καὶ ἀργυρίῳ δυνάμενοι χρηματίζεσθαι (Xen. *Por.* 5.3); οἱ περὶ τὰς ἐργασίας ὄντες ταύτας (Dem. 36.29). See below, Chapter 2, n. 18.

[85]Frag. 581 Körte (Stobaios, *Eklogai* 4.22.119): ἀλλ' ἐπὶ τράπεζαν μὲν φέρειν τὴν προῖχ' ἵνα / εἰ τἀργύριον καλόν ἐστι δοκιμαστὴς ἴδῃ.

[86]See above, n. 20. Before the discovery of this inscription, it had even been conjectured that the *trapezai*, far from dealing in exchange, might be counters displaying items for sale, or even the dining rooms in South Stoa I in the agora. See Wycherley 1957: 192; Travlos 1971: 534. For the location and physical form of the *trapezai*, see below, Chapter 4, esp. n. 34.

[87]Dem. 19.114: Φιλοκράτης . . . τὸ χρυσίον καταλλαττόμενος φανερῶς ἐπὶ ταῖς τραπέζαις.

[88]Hasebroek 1920: 143. But the claim is based on no affirmative evidence, only on an unjustifiable deduction from Isokrates 17.40 (ὑμῖν μάρτυρας παρέξομαι τοὺς εἰδότας πολλά μοι χρήματ' ἐκ τοῦ Πόντου κομισθέντα, ἔπειτα δὲ τοὺς ὁρῶντάς με τῇ τούτου τραπέζῃ χρώμενον, ἔτι δὲ παρ' ὧν ἐχρυσώνησ' ὑπ' ἐκεῖνον τὸν χρόνον πλέον ἢ χιλίους στατῆρας). The likeliest witness to the speaker's possible currency transactions at Pasiōn's bank, Kittos (§12: αὐτὸν ἐπὶ τῇ τραπέζῃ καθήμενον), was unavailable to testify (the reason for his absence is a major subject of dispute between the parties to the litigation; see §§11–14). His testimony might

pezitai (and our detailed sources relate only to this period), they are never personally engaged in money-changing. Kallippos, the representative of the Hērakleōtes in Athens, seeks out the banker Pasiōn: he finds him not "at the table," but "in the city" (Dem. 52.8). To obtain the deposit information requested by Kallippos, Pasiōn suggests that they go to the bank proper at the Piraeus harbor. In fact, when Kallippos had been "at the bank" some time earlier, he found there not the banker himself, but his chief functionary, Phormiōn (52.5–6). Already early in the fourth century, it is the banking assistant (and alleged slave), Kittos, who is "seated at the table" handling large sums of currency (Isok. 17.12). The bank owner is pictured in Isokrates' presentation as personally and intimately involved in trapezitic business, but on a level sharply removed from currency exchange: providing sureties, negotiating claims, offering guarantees and personal advice to important customers. Similarly, when the politician and military leader Timotheos needed funds, he found Pasiōn not at the bankers' tables, but at the harbor itself (Dem. 49.6). Indeed, surviving sources deal in detail with a great variety of banking activities—lending directly and through intermediation, protecting collateral, accepting deposits, negotiating damages for failure to protect deposits, investing in real estate, making provisions for continuity of banking businesses, executing purchase orders, safeguarding documents, and so on. We see the bankers in a variety of settings—at home, at the assembly,[89] at the harbor, in the temples, in transit between the civic center (*agora*) and the harbor. But we never see the bank owners or operators themselves personally engaged in the changing of money. More importantly, in the entire corpus of surviving banking disputes and litigation, not one case involves issues arising from money-changing activities.

From this it should not be inferred that currency-changing and money-dealing occurred only on a petty scale and only involved small sums.[90] The bank clerk

---

in any event have been controlled by the speaker's adversary, the banker Pasiōn. The other witnesses to his dealings with Pasiōn (τοὺς ὁρῶντάς με τῇ τούτου τραπέζῃ χρώμενον) might well have confirmed currency dealings. (On the congeries of business activities, presumably including coin exchange, encompassed in the term χρῆσθαι, see below, pp. 65–66.) The fact of his currency transactions with unnamed persons (quite possibly other banks) does not prove anything about the level of bankers' exchange activities in the early fourth century. In providing witnesses, the speaker is seeking not to offer information about exchange facilities, but to confirm his claims that he disposed of a considerable amount of cash at an earlier time.

[89]Dem. 21.215. In a famous incident, the banker Blepaios approached Demosthenes in the *ekklēsia*, supposedly to offer him a bribe for dropping the prosecution of Meidias. Since only adult male citizens had the right to attend the *ekklēsia* (Hansen 1987: 7, 124), Blepaios is clearly an Athenian citizen. For the (false) claim that virtually no bankers held Athenian citizenship, see Chapter 4, n. 44. This Blepaios made the commercial mining loan reported at Dem. 40.52. A "Blepaios son of Sōklēs," contractor for work on the temple at Eleusis in the 330s (I.G. II² 1657.32), is almost certainly the same man: Sōklēs is one of the bankers mentioned at Dem. 36.29. There is also a reference in Alexis 227 (Kock) to Blepaios as wealthy.

[90]As Bogaert claims: "Les changeurs ne disposaient pas de grosses sommes de monnaies étrangères et souvent ils ne pouvaient satisfaire à la demande de leurs clients" (1968: 328).

Kittos in the early fourth century handled currency in such daunting amounts that he could be accused of improperly paying out to two customers 36,000 *dr.* in silver.[91] (This was about six months' pay for a warship's complement of 200, a year's earnings for about 120 skilled artisans).[92] In a relatively short period, a single individual was able to exchange in a series of transactions 1,000 staters, equivalent to perhaps 25,000 *dr.*, with no suggestion that the dealings were at all exceptional.[93] Precisely because currency dealings were a bank activity—and the bankers controlled large amounts of other people's money [94]—such massive exchanges of cash or bullion could be accomplished at Athens. Once *trapezitai* as true bankers came to hold monetary deposits, their stock of "other people's money" gave them a natural competitive advantage over other dealers in currency, especially where a substantial amount of currency was required. In turn, their exchange operations were highly compatible with the vagaries of overseas lending, especially maritime finance.[95] The Athenian banker could be an effective commercial money-changer only because he was not "little more than a money-changer and pawnbroker" (Finley 1981: 74).

FALSE ANACHRONISM: THE MODERN INVENTION OF THE ATHENIAN PAWNSHOP

In moving from their money-changing origins to acceptance of deposits and extension of credit, the Athenian *trapezitai* created the world's first private banks.[96] Bankers undertook various fiduciary activities: witnessing transac-

---

[91]Isok. 17.12: ἐγὼ καὶ Μενέξενος διαφθείραντες καὶ πείσαντες αὐτὸν ἐπὶ τῇ τραπέζῃ καθήμενον ἓξ τάλαντ' ἀργυρίου λάβοιμεν παρ' αὐτοῦ. Cf. §21.

[92]Craftsmen in the period 409–6 received a single drachma per day, in exceptional cases 1½ *dr.* Erechtheion accounts: I.G. I² 373–74 = I.G. I³ 475–76. See Randall 1953: 208. The architect himself received a single drachma, but his assistant only 5 obols. See Paton 1927: 330. The later Eleusinian accounts (I.G. II–III² 1672–73: 329/8 and 327/6) report pay of 1½ *dr.* for unskilled laborers, 2 or 2½ *dr.* for skilled workmen. Cf. A.H.M. Jones [1957] 1977a: 135 n. 1; Stockton 1990: 9–10. Humphreys (1978: 174) values at "18,000 days' pay at contemporary rates" an Athenian mercenary's two-talent estate (the subject of Isaios 4). For similar estimates, see Davies 1971: xxii n. 6, 1981: 9. For the cost of living at Athens and its effect at various times on wages, see Gallo 1987: esp. 57–63.

[93]Isok. 17.40 (for the Greek text, see above, n. 88).

[94]Cf. Isok. 17.2: χρήματα πολλὰ διαχειρίζουσι; Dem. 45.72: bank functionary as χρημάτων κύριον πολλῶν; Dem. 36.57 (regarding the banker Phormiōn): τοσαῦτα χρήμαθ' ὑμῖν ἀνεγνώσθη προσηυπορηκώς, ὅσ' οὔθ' οὗτος οὔτ' ἄλλος οὐδεὶς κέκτηται.

[95]See below, pp. 149–50.

[96]There is no evidence for individual banking activity preceding that of the Athenians: Bogaert (1966: 132–33) has convincingly demonstrated the error in modern references (by Cavaignac [1951: 18] and others) to private bankers at Ephesos in the seventh and sixth centuries. Evidence for other loan or deposit activity is equivocal. Greek religious complexes, such as that at Samos, may have performed some banking functions in the archaic period (see Heichelheim 1964: 73–74; Bogaert 1964a: 107–20). Despite cavalier references in modern literature to Mesopotamian

tions, safeguarding documents, accepting valuables for safekeeping.[97] Yet, despite frequent scholarly assertions that they were essentially "pawn-brokers,"[98] the bankers never pursued activities at all akin to modern pawn-broking: they never accepted for deposit personal property against which they lent small sums on the understanding that, as their sole remedy, they would keep the property if the funds advanced were not repaid within a specified period. To the contrary, persons delivering physical goods to a *trapeza* did so solely for safekeeping and had an absolute and unconditional right to the return of these items.[99] Individual borrowers were always personally liable for repayment of a loan: although no law or regulation prohibited "nonrecourse" financing, not a single example is known of such lending at Athens. And there is no basis at all for the modern juridical underpinning for the "pawnshop" concept of Greek credit, the theory of "substitutive" collateral (namely, the assertion that in the event of a default on a loan, a creditor who had accepted property as security for the debt was entitled only to take ["substitute"] the asset in full satisfaction of the debt, rather than to sell the collateral and pursue the borrower for any shortfall).[100]

Bank loans were not limited to inconsequential sums, nor were borrowers marginal creatures who could obtain credit nowhere else. In fact, the smallest bank loan known (Dem. 49.22) is in the amount of 100 *dr.*, a sum equivalent to perhaps 150 days' earnings or the better part of a year's compensation at then-prevailing rates (see n. 92 above). Yet these 100 drachmas were merely a small part of the bank's advances to this borrower: he had previously received, and still had outstanding, more than 2,350 *dr.*[101] And shortly thereafter, the same debtor obtained a credit extension of an additional 1,750 *dr.*, bringing his total obligation to the bank to more than 4,200 *dr.* (in excess of two-thirds of a

---

"bankers" (see, for example, Imbert 1965: 27; Rostovtzeff 1930: 8,661), earlier evidence is even more difficult to evaluate. See Bogaert 1966: 43–66 and the bibliography there cited. Cf. Lehmann 1980: passim. The financial dealings of large estates in Mesopotamia, attested perhaps as early as the seventh century, did not involve outside clients but were intimately connected with estate administration (Heichelheim, *OCD* s.v. "banks").

[97]Witnessing transactions: Dem. 35.10 (on this banking function, see below, pp. 178–79). Safeguarding papers: Dem. 34.6, 56.15; I.G. II² 2741 (Finley no. 39) ll. 4–6. Accepting valuables: Dem. 49.31–32.

[98]Salin 1921: 503–4; Pöhlmann 1925, 2: 531; Bolkestein 1958: 127–28

[99]The only case known to us in detail establishes this clearly: when leaving Athens on business, Timosthenēs, an Athenian citizen engaged in overseas trade, deposited some money with the banker Pasiōn. At the same time he also delivered to him two valuable bowls. This delivery is not an example of "pawning" goods in return for an advance of money: Timosthenēs simultaneously was depositing cash with the banker. During the trader's absence, the bowls were "inadvertently" (ἀπὸ τύχης) given to another client. The banker remained obligated for the return of the containers: Pasiōn and Timosthenēs ultimately negotiated a price of 237 *dr.* as compensation for the items (Dem. 49.31–32).

[100]See below, p. 212, n. 132.

[101]Dem. 49.6: 1,351 *dr.* 2 *ob.*; 49.17: 1,000 *dr.*

talent). When analyzed in terms of its purchasing power, this sum—an amount sufficient to buy thousands of days of skilled labor—would be a meaningful credit extension for even the largest modern financial institutions. The borrower was also notable: Timotheos, scion of a distinguished Athenian family, aristocratic by birth and policy, for decades an important political leader and naval commander, and an intimate of the Athenian banker Pasiōn.[102] Credit in an amount so substantial, to a recipient so prominent, does not reflect the marginal dealings of a marginal source of financing.

The remaining corpus of Athenian bank loans confirms the significance of bank credit. Analysis of a much-quoted summary by Bogaert, purporting to cover all known Athenian bank loans,[103] reveals that *every* credit on this list involves substantial funding. The loan of 300 *dr.*, itself a sizeable sum, reported at Isokrates 17.38 is actually only one—and the *smallest*—of at least five separate credit extensions described in that litigation. The others range as high as 7 talents. A sixth loan can be added if the two credits, each of 6 talents, described at sections 12 and 50 are actually separate transactions.[104] The ship financing at Demosthenes 33.7 involves 3,000 *dr.* of bank money—only part of a total loan of 4,000 *dr.*[105] The 2,000 *dr.* described at Demosthenes 40.52 financed the purchase of mining concessions. At Demosthenes 45.28, two loans, each of 6,000 *dr.*, are enumerated. Although the exact amount of the financing at Lysias, frag. 38.1, is not known, the credit was sufficient to fund the ongoing operations of a perfume business (see above, n. 56). Bogaert disregards as extraordinary a financing of 15,600 *dr.* (Dem. 36.38). He does include a loan of 1,000 *dr.* (Dem. 53.9) secured by personal property (drinking cups and a golden crown), but there is no suggestion in the text that the borrower was not personally liable for repayment of the loan. Some of these loans are entirely unsecured.[106] Where collateral was obtained, the *trapezai* advanced funds against a great variety of assets: real estate, imported lumber, cash on deposit at the bank, ships, or maritime cargo.[107]

Far from relegation to unsavory marginality, as a group bankers enjoyed high esteem and credibility. An individual litigating against a *trapezitēs* complains to the jurors of his disadvantage in having a banker as an adversary: the

[102]For the dealings between Pasiōn and Timotheos, see, for example, Dem. 49.6, 27 (ὧν αὐτῷ δεηθέντι ὑπηρέτηκεν [sc. ὁ Πασίων], τούτων, ἄν ποτε δύνηται, χάριν ἀποδώσειν). On Timotheos, see below, Chapter 2, n. 24.

[103]Bogaert 1968: 370 n. 391. For the inadequacy of this catalogue, which omits a number of definite bank loans and numerous probable credit extensions, see below, pp. 32–33, 170–71. Cf. Thompson 1979: 230–33.

[104]On these loans, see below, pp. 38–40.

[105]See below, pp. 154–57.

[106]Dem. 49.2, 23. See below, pp. 201–7.

[107]Real property: Dem. 36.6; I.G. II² 2762; *Arch. Delt.* 17 (1961–62): *Khronika* 35, no. 4. Lumber: Dem. 49.35–36. Cash: Isok. 17, passim. Maritime collateral: Dem. 33.7, various loans enumerated below, pp. 170–83.

trapezitai had wide networks of relationships, disposed of considerable monies, and were accorded unquestioned credibility.[108] Even foreign-born bankers found their place among the Athenian elite and themselves established grand households in the tradition of the Hellenic aristocracies.[109] The loans described above uniformly involve Athenians of significance, and foreigners of wealth and power: Menexenos, the scion of one of the "wealthiest and most distinguished" Athenian houses;[110] Apollodōros, the son of an Athenian banker, most politically influential of the new citizens of the fourth century, a name redolent with conspicuous wealth and civic service;[111] the son of Sopaios, closely related by politics and marriage to the ruler of Bosporos (himself a prime "benefactor" of Athens);[112] and the well-known and influential Athenian citizen Pythodōros.[113] This reality of borrowers, often of high political and social stature, routinely seeking and obtaining substantial loans, sometimes even without pledging assets, refutes with finality any suggestion that the *trapeza* was in economic essence not a bank, but a pawnshop.

[108]Isok. 17.2: φίλους πολλοὺς κέκτηνται καὶ χρήματα πολλὰ διαχειρίζουσι καὶ πιστοὶ διὰ τὴν τέχνην δοκοῦσιν εἶναι. For these attributes, cf. Chapter 4.

[109]For bankers' *oikoi*, see below, pp. 82–90.

[110]Davies 1971: 145. Cf. Mathieu and Brémond [1929–42] 1963, 1: 74 n. 1. The family's wealth consisted primarily of real property (Isaios 5.43). For Menexenos's bank borrowings, see Isok. 17.12 and below, pp. 39–40.

[111]On Apollodōros's extravagant expenditures on clothes, women, and servants: Dem. 36.8, 45. His extravagant outlay on liturgies: Dem. 50.7. Cf. Dem. 36.39, 45.78, 50.26. For Apollodōros's career in the courts and in public life, see Schäfer 1885–87, 3.2: 130–99; Pearson 1966. On Apollodōros as "a member of the aristocracy of Athens," see Austin and Vidal-Naquet 1977: 150. Cf. Davies 1971: 437–42.

[112]See Isok. 17.57; I.G. II² 212, esp. ll. 20–24. Cf. Dem. 20.29ff., 36ff. For the importance of grain supplied by the Bosporan rulers, see below Chapter 6, n. 83.

[113]Isok. 17.33; Dem. 54.7.

Chapter 2

A METHODOLOGICAL ALTERNATIVE TO THE MISUSE
OF STATISTICS

Nothing is intelligible until it has been put into statistics
—Fernand Braudel (disapprovingly)

ALTHOUGH IT DEALS with money and finance, this book does not rely on statistics. Instead it focuses on a close reading of texts in an effort to understand economic and social interrelationships. Whereas such eschewing of numerical calculation might be inconceivable in studies of contemporary societies, in the Athenian context it is virtually mandated by the source material: the absence of sources that would facilitate a mathematical approach, and the fortuitous survival of forensic material offering extensive insights into the subjects here considered.

Although it has become fashionable to deprecate as "impressionistic" studies based on interpretation of source material rather than on compilation of data,[1] the same allegation of "subjectivity" is no less applicable to mathematically oriented efforts to interpret Athenian banking and finance. Yet the attraction of cliometric generalization has inhibited the use of an often preferable "forensic" methodology that is available for the study of Athenian finance. We possess extensive evidence for Athenian business and banking in the form of litigants' presentations in the law courts. Since such speeches were delivered to juries numbering in the hundreds, and since persuasion was a speaker's only goal, it seems reasonable to posit—even in the absence of statistical data—that the presence of a general practice is confirmed by a litigant's claim that presupposes such a practice, even if we cannot establish the truth of the particular assertion (provided, of course, that the generalized phenomenon would have been known to Athenian jurors). For example, from Apollodōros's claim that he borrowed money from a banker to ransom a friend (Dem. 53.6–13), "we can be confident" (Thompson 1979: 224) that Athenian bankers did make loans to ransom friends, even if we cannot establish that Apollodōros borrowed money

---

[1]Starr 1987: 66. The presupposition underlying the whole of Xenophon's *Oikonomikos* is the substantial role played by wives in the economic activity of the household. The entire work would be meaningless if this were not true, even though such involvement by women cannot be established statistically. Nonetheless, even Foxhall, who generally makes incisive use of otherwise ignored material, feels compelled to characterize Xenophon's material as "anecdotal" (1989: 36).

for this purpose in this particular case. Historians of Athenian law have long
employed this methodology,[2] which we might term "forensic attestation." The
merits of forensic attestation, on which the present study heavily relies, can be
illustrated as follows, through an examination of the extent to which Athenian
bankers provided credit for commercial loans. Whereas the prevailing view,
that bankers play no appreciable role in such finance, is based on flawed
"mathematical" studies, forensic attestation reveals the routine and substantial
involvement of the bankers in financing Athenian business.

THE PERILS OF CLIOMETRICS

Historians of the ancient economy, apparently influenced by contemporary
economists' reliance on mathematically based models, have often resorted to
statistics to provide for their findings a patina of mathematical precision or
scientific objectivity.[3] The "ignominious truth," however, is that "there are no
ancient statistics."[4] Our sources do, of course, report numbers, perhaps as
many as a million for all aspects of classical antiquity and for a period exceed-
ing 1,000 years,[5] but these are not statistics: to have produced statistics, ancient
authors would have had to assemble, classify, and tabulate numerical data in a
systematic fashion so as to present significant information about a specific
ancient subject. Such material does not appear in antiquity. Modern historians'
efforts to overcome this difficulty have often been frustrated,[6] especially by the

---

[2]See Humphreys 1978: 11. This method is to be differentiated from the superficially similar
common-law "judicial notice" utilized by judges, especially on the appellate level, to accept
without proof matters so generally known as to compel court recognition even without their
assertion by the litigants. For "judicial notice" in the context of evidentiary procedures in
Athenian courts, see Todd 1990a: 20.

[3]See Finley 1986: 27–29. Cf. D'Arms 1981: vii; Goldsmith 1987: xi.

[4]A.H.M. Jones, Introduction to his inaugural lecture (1948). Cf. the similar observation by
Momigliano in his own inaugural lecture (1952).

[5]Finley 1986: 27–28. The total (1,000,000 items of numerical data) gains perspective when
contrasted with material available to chroniclers of the modern economy: in the single year 1986,
payment orders ("checks") initiated by customers of American banks alone numbered 45 billion
(*American Banker*, March 16, 1987, p. 22) and is anticipated to increase to 57.4 billion by 1992
("Nilson Report," *American Banker*, February 22, 1989, p. 2).

[6]But on occasion they have succeeded brilliantly. Cf., for example, D. M. Lewis's comments
on Andreyev's analysis of the Athenian "Rationes Centesimarum" (1973: 188–91). More recently, see M. H. Hansen 1986: ch. 1 (the cover of Hansen's *Demography* is fittingly graced by
an "Age Pyramid . . . Model West, Mortality Level 4, Growth Rate 5.00"). This age pyramid
is "based on the reasonable assumption that the demographic structure of Greece in the fourth
century B.C. was basically the same as the demographic structure of the early Roman empire" (p.
11). Although Hansen's work is largely and persuasively dedicated to refutation of Jones's
demographic analyses, Jones actually utilized as early as 1955 graphs likewise based on the
assumption that Athenian age distribution was similar to that "in Carthage and Africa under the
Principate" (A.H.M. Jones [1957] 1977b: 82–83).

deficiencies of the data base: the notorious unreliability of numbers transmitted over thousands of years by confused and sometimes contradictory manuscripts;[7] the patent impossibility of assuming that material that has survived largely by chance constitutes a scientifically appropriate sampling; and the total absence for many issues of any data at all.

We do have significant data concerning the utilization of credit by Athenian borrowers, primarily from dozens of speeches relating to court cases and preserved through manuscripts. In the corpus of thirty-three "private speeches" by Demosthenes, at least 130 separate extensions of credit can be identified. Approximately two dozen references to maritime loans alone are contained in five speeches attributed to Demosthenes that focus on maritime finance, all dating from the fourth century (Demosthenes 32, 33, 34, 35, 56). Much more information is available from a variety of additional sources—literary, epigraphic, numismatic, papyrological. Perhaps 1,000 separate loans can be identified from classical Greek antiquity,[8] with a disproportionately high percentage from Athens in the period here under study.

Unfortunately, analysis of the provision of credit at Athens, a prime function of Athenian banks, illustrates the limitations of quantitative studies. Here the lure of a statistical approach has been irresistible: some data is available, and by its nature this information is numerical, for the credit function in its very essence is arithmetical, requiring the calculation of amounts expended and repaid, the determination of sums due, the valuation of underlying collateral and means of repayment. Surviving evidence, however, does not lend itself to mathematically precise use. The fragmentary nature of the material has exacerbated the subjectivity inherent in scholarly selection of sources deemed relevant. Efforts to marshal this evidence in a scientific manner have often resulted only in an objective wrapping, seemingly authoritative to the nonspecialist, for what often remains an entirely subjective analysis, yielding (at best) inconclusive results.

Thus statistical analysis of Athenian trade and finance takes two forms: (1) the "comparative percentage" methodology, which is applied to two or more groupings of data, and (2) the "conclusory generalization," which either determines (from the presence of a few examples) that a phenomenon was generally

[7]Difficulties are encountered even where the manuscript tradition is consistent and clear. For example, all codices of the book text of Thucydides report that the highest amount of coined silver ever maintained on the Akropolis amounted to 10,000 talents (Thuc. 2.13.3). Meritt, however, finds this number "impossible not only because no sum even approaching 10,000 talents can ever have been accumulated on the Acropolis," but also because of the evidence provided by the so-called second of the two "Kallias decrees." See Meritt 1982: 114. An alternative to the text of the codices is provided by a scholion to Aristophanes' *Ploutos* (line 1193); this alternative reading, which omits the number "10,000," has been defended by D. M. Lewis 1952.

[8]Cf. Millett (1983: 43), who mentions having catalogued almost 900 transactions, "drawn from the whole of classical Greece."

present, or concludes (from the absence of many examples) that a phenomenon was generally absent. Both approaches have been applied, with thoroughly unsatisfactory results, to the study of Athenian credit and banking.

Subjectivity of Data Selection

In contrast to the sort of "traditional" scholarship that explicitly conveys the subjective judgment of its author—and that often gains acceptance because of a particular scholar's perceived wisdom—cliometric analyses tend to be presented and perceived as "objective." Two relatively recent compilations, however, are good examples of the subjectivity that has in fact characterized arithmetical studies of Athenian credit.[9] Both studies attempted "a statistical test of Hasebroek's theories on the organization of trade" (Millett 1983: 37). One analysis found that in maritime finance the majority (more than 59 percent) of identifiable lenders at Athens were citizens; the other study found just the opposite: most of the identifiable lenders (over 63 percent) were noncitizens. The first established that virtually no lenders were active as traders; the other, that the majority of lenders (57 percent) were so engaged. Finally, the two studies found that noncitizens either clearly dominated, or "certainly did not dominate," the conduct of Athenian foreign trade.

The explanation for these contradictions is simple. Each analysis was intended to prove a thesis: the authors set out either to uphold or to refute Hasebroek's model of Athenian trade, wherein Athenian citizens form a class of *rentiers* who provide funds for commerce, but only passively, with no personal involvement in trade itself (the actual merchants, on this view, are predominantly impoverished noncitizens who borrow because of need). Despite their divergent conclusions, both studies illustrate a problem inherent in the mathematical sampling of ancient sources: the selection and categorization of examples ultimately represents the subjective judgment of the selector. The source material does not lend itself even to random selection: the speeches of the Attic orators are skillful contrivances that describe personal characteristics, not so that we can determine an individual's status but for rhetorical purposes of their own.[10]

Furthermore, the universe from which the data are selected is determined by the selectors' knowledge, and the information marshalled may be far from exhaustive. Thus, in defining the characteristics of the Athenian maritime lenders, a scholar familiar with Athenian comedy uses a sampling in which comic sources are appropriately represented; another scholar, without such

[9]Erxleben 1974: 462–82; Isager and Hansen 1975: 70–74. The methodological difficulties of such numerical analyses are further suggested through yet another study, and variant interpretation, of the underlying data: M. V. Hansen 1984: 71–92.

[10]Wolff 1969: 1–13; Millett 1983: 38.

specialization, "takes no cognizance of New Comedy."[11] The same ancient individual, described in a single ancient source and in a single context, is for one cliometrician a well-capitalized businessman (*emporos* or *nauklēros*); for another, not a "businessman" at all but a mere passive creditor. Obviously, the divergent judgments will cause the percentile relationships to differ in lists of investors and traders.[12] Such information can be tabulated, but doing so does not negate (though it might obfuscate) the fact that these "statistics" present the same subjective views as would a conventional narrative.

Most significantly, however, these "comparative percentage analyses" invariably start from the view that only private lenders are relevant, since banks supposedly provided little credit for nonconsumptive purposes.[13] If, however, bank monies from numerous depositors provided a substantial source of funding for Athenian trade, then studies that ignore the role of the banks and the characteristics of bank customers are necessarily inadequate. In fact, there is no sound basis for the prevailing "quantitatively" grounded view that Athenian banking had little or no role in business finance.

Generalization from Inadequate Evidence

It is easy, but often invalid and sometimes even irrational, to conclude that a practice at Athens was unimportant because it is attested in only a few isolated pieces of evidence. The evaluation of the banks' role in business finance especially has suffered from this habit of negative generalization, which has been used improperly to establish that Athenian banking must have been unimportant because we know of few functioning bankers, and that "productive credit" must have been an insignificant aspect of bank lending because so few "productive loans" are attested.

Although ample by comparison with some other periods and places in antiquity, our evidence for fourth-century Athenians by name and occupation is, taken absolutely, very limited. We are unable to identify, even by name, so much as one percent of the Athenians chosen to perform festival liturgies,[14] even though liturgical honors were reserved for those Athenians having the largest and most conspicuous property holdings; and we are able to name even this small number only after decades of intensive analysis of both long-known sources and newly discovered inscriptions. It would therefore seem ill-advised

---

[11]Casson (1976: 45 n. 40), who includes in his analysis relevant material from comedy.

[12]Cf. the treatment of Andokidēs (Lysias 6.19, 49); Androklēs (Dem. 35.10, 49); Diodotos (Lysias 32.4, 24); Leōkratēs (Lykourgos 1.55); Nikippos (Dem. 50.17); and Nikoboulos (Dem. 37.6, 46, 54). Erxleben 1974: 473–77; M. V. Hansen 1984: 72–75.

[13]Bogaert 1965a: 140–56, 1968: 356–57, 411–12; Isager and Hansen 1975: 88, 97; Erxleben 1974: 490–91.

[14]Davies 1971: xxviii–xxx.

to judge the importance of a particular profession from the mere number of persons who are known to us as practitioners in the field.

Yet such judgments are freely made. The conclusion that "there was no real-estate market, properly speaking, in Athens at all" is alleged to be proven in part by the further assertion that "not one Athenian is known to us who earned his livelihood by dealing in real estate" (Finley 1981: 71). The apparent absoluteness of the statement— "not one Athenian is known to us"—obscures the subjectivity inherent in determining the actual source of income for any ancient Athenian.[15] The same author uses the same method in his derisive dismissal of Athenian banking—and here it is still more clearly illegitimate. Given the relatively small population of fourth-century Athens, the highly fragmentary nature of the evidence, and the correspondingly reasonable expectation that even a popular profession might be poorly attested, I find it remarkable that more than thirty bankers at Athens from the fourth century alone are known by name and profession. It does not, however, seem remarkable to Finley: for him, partial proof of the "rudimentary" nature of Athenian banking is supplied by the assertion that "not thirty Athenians are known from the whole of the fourth century who are specifically identified as bankers, a reflection of the rarity of the occupation."[16]

But was Greek literature also rudimentary and rare? For all of the Greek world, for all of the centuries until the Byzantine period, we know fewer than 3,000 authors;[17] and this includes not only every genre of writing, both poetry and prose, from the mere compilation of lists through lyric poetry to pornography, but also even anonymous writers whose work (or allusion thereto) has chanced to survive without specific identification of the author, although Greek authors did not generally seek to hide their identities—in contrast to the inherently confidential (or rather, clandestine) functioning of Athenian banking (see below, Chapter 6). In many cases, moreover, even where there is a reference to an individual clearly involved in making loans, holding funds or documents, or performing other banking activities, our sources would have no reason explicitly to identify that person as a banker (*trapezitēs*). Indeed, because Athens did not license banks or otherwise legally define "bankers," in actual usage

---

[15]More than one Athenian seems to me likely to have "earned his livelihood by dealing in real estate." Aristolochos appears even to have speculated in real-estate acquisition (Dem. 36.50). Aristaichmos and his co-guardian had no apparent difficulty in converting significant liquid funds into investments in land and multiple-dwelling buildings (Dem. 38.7). Xenophon describes entire classes of individuals engaged in ongoing construction of houses for profit who "sell the houses as soon as they are completed and then build others" (*Oik.* 20.29), as well as persons systematically engaged in the purchase of farms for speculation and the business techniques they employed (ibid., 20.22–28). The Athenians even had a term for speculators in rental real-estate (σταθμοῦχοι). See Boeckh [1842] 1976: 141. For speculation in land in the fourth century, see Mossé [1962] 1979: 35–67; French 1991: 38.

[16]Finley 1981: 73.

[17]See Berkowitz and Squitier 1986: xi.

"bankers" are frequently denominated by circumlocution—"the money-men" or "the lenders"—thus reducing still further the validity of conclusions drawn from an arithmetical counting of persons explicitly named as "bankers."[18]

Yet the bankers are ubiquitous. From Finley's own specialization, the *horoi*-stones, there is a striking example: among the more than 200 inscriptions recording creditors' interests, only two professions are represented by practitioners who are identified by name and occupation: medicine and banking.[19] "The banker Euklēs" in fact appears, not as a creditor or a debtor, but in his professional capacity as the recipient of the written agreement underlying the debt. No one would argue that the single reference to a doctor among these inscriptions proves "the rarity of the occupation" (whose prominence in classical Greece is of course well attested by literary and epigraphical materials). Relatively frequent and (under the circumstances) often unexpected references to Athenian bankers cannot—even by aberrant statistical method—establish that bankers were absent from, or insignificant in, Athenian life.[20]

Numerical analysis is also said to demonstrate that Athenian bank loans were made predominantly for purposes of "consumption." For Bogaert, author of the standard source survey on Greek banking, cliometric analysis establishes that bank loans for consumption were "five times more numerous" at Athens than "productive" loans.[21] This finding has itself become the basis for extended argumentation and sweeping conclusions by others.[22] But the fragility of the underlying data base is instructive.

Bogaert's analysis is actually based on only eleven bank loans.[23] Here again

---

[18]Thus Xenophon (*Por.* 5.3) refers to bankers as οἱ γνώμῃ καὶ ἀργυρίῳ δυνάμενοι χρηματίζεσθαι. Cf., for example, Dem. 36.29: οἱ περὶ τὰς ἐργασίας ὄντες ταύτας. Bogaert ignores this in suggesting (1968: 80 n. 118) that Xenophon's phrase was intended to have broader application. (Cf. Thiel 1922: 34; Knorringa [1926] 1961: 44; and Ziebarth 1929: 73, all of whom relate the phrase solely to "bankers.")

[19]Banker: Finley [1951] 1985: 39 (= I.G. II² 2741). Physician: Finley [1951] 1985: 135 (= I.G. II² 2660).

[20]Fourteenth-century Florence and seventeenth-century Osaka provide useful standards for comparison. Through the chronicle of Giovanni Villani (A.D. 1338), significant demographic and commercial data have been preserved about Florence. This economic colossus, which at the time ranked among the five largest cities in Europe, employed 30,000 workers in the woolen clothing industry alone, and monopolized banking and trade in Italy and internationally. At that time the city had a total of some eighty banking and money-changing businesses. See Brucker 1983: 51–56, and, generally, Goldthwaite 1980. In Osaka, the commercial and financial center of seventeenth-century Japan, ten large banking houses (with about 150 affiliated bankers) served a centralized economy with a population of about 25 million, larger than any European country at the time. See Crawcour 1961; Hirschmeier and Yui 1975: ch. 1.

[21]Bogaert 1968: 356–57, 411–12; 1986a: 26.

[22]See, e.g., Finley 1985: 141, 208. Cf. Millett 1983: 42–47.

[23]Bogaert 1968: 370 n. 391. Cf. Bogaert 1986a: 24–26. Andreau correctly objects that if knowledge of bank loans were truly limited to eleven examples, it would be invalid to derive from such data Finley's sweeping characterizations of Greek financial practices (Andreau 1977: 1144–48.

the data selected reflect only the selector's own sense of appropriateness and relevance. Since Bogaert believes (erroneously in my opinion; see below, Chapter 5) that Athenian banks did not make maritime loans, he ignores the relatively large number of "productive" loans that would necessarily be included in any analysis that recognized the Athenian banks' ongoing role in sea finance. Furthermore, his choice of nonmaritime examples is far from exhaustive, and it is highly subjective even in the loans that it does recognize. For example, Bogaert includes only one citation from the speech preserved as Isokrates 17, whereas close reading of the oration reveals numerous other examples (see below). Again, of the eleven loans in Bogaert's canon, four involve a single "consumer," Timotheos, and are the subject of a single litigation (argued at Demosthenes 49). But Timotheos is a highly atypical Athenian consumer: for an extended period in the fourth century, he was also a prominent political leader and naval commander.[24] Extension of credit to him could not be totally free of political or military considerations.

Even beyond the nature of the sampling, the subjectivity of Bogaert's analysis belies the numerical dogma. To prove that loans were made almost exclusively for personal consumption, Bogaert merely asserts that only two of his eleven loans were for "productive" purposes. He does not, however, attempt to establish that the other nine loans were in fact made for "consumption." Not surprisingly, a later investigator concluded that the purpose of three of the loans could not be known and that one additional loan should actually be considered "productive" (Thompson 1979: 230). On this interpretation, statistical analysis could be said to "prove" that only a minority of all bank loans were for consumption. Since four of the five remaining "consumer" loans involve the distinguished leader Timotheos, and certainly cannot be considered "consumer" loans in any meaningful sense, Thompson has argued that only one of Bogaert's examples, a loan to a bank owner (Apollodōros) providing funds "to ransom a friend" (Nikostratos) can properly be considered a loan for consumption (ibid. 231). If we wished to generalize from inadequate evidence, this finding could justify a claim that Athenian bank loans were "overwhelmingly" directed away from consumption, since Bogaert was able to produce "only a single example" of a loan for personal use.

Furthermore, even this single example is suspect, since it is not without business coloration. By characterizing Nikostratos as a social intimate[25] who failed to repay a loan, the bank owner Apollodōros perhaps better justified his own extreme efforts to collect the alleged debt; his court presentation nevertheless reveals the business relationship that complemented their social dealings. Apollodōros employed Nikostratos "for administration and management" of

---

[24]See K. Klee, in *RE* 6 A (1937) 1324ff., s.v. "Timotheos" (3); Kallet 1983; Tuplin 1984; Cawkwell 1962: 45–49. Still useful is Rehdantz 1845.

[25]§4: γνωρίμως μέν μοι εἶχεν καὶ πάλαι, . . . καὶ μᾶλλον ἀλλήλοις ἤδη ἐχρώμεθα διὰ τὸ γείτονές τε εἶναι καὶ ἡλικιῶται.

his farm (Dem. 53.4): indeed, during Apollodōros's lengthy absences, Nikostratos had been left in charge of every aspect of the property (ibid.). And even if the defendant had been "only" a friend, the loan still would not necessarily be characterized properly as a loan made for "consumption": since cultivation and retention of friends was explicitly recognized as an important business asset for Athenian bankers (Isok. 17.2), it was commercially vital for a bank owner to preserve such social relationships.[26] If this financing is not to be characterized as a loan made for "consumption," there is—*mirabile dictu!*— not a single Athenian bank loan positively known to have been intended for consumption.

The orthodox view of the purpose of bank loans is supposedly confirmed by yet other statistical studies; but the confirmation is derived from the same flawed use of the same flawed method. Millett asserts that from "[his] own catalogue of almost nine hundred loan transactions of all types, drawn from the whole of classical Greece, there are perhaps five—excluding maritime loans— which might conceivably be classed as productive" (1983: 43). In fact, however, it is not the hundreds of items, but the five, from which the sweeping generalization is drawn: "The case could hardly be clearer, and the five exceptions do serve to prove the rule that Greek credit was overwhelmingly unproductive" (ibid.). The methodological excess also could hardly be clearer. Maritime loans themselves, of course, constitute the overwhelming majority of credit transactions about which we know enough to evaluate the purpose; and even Millett is forced to admit that these loans were "apparently productive": as evidence for "productive borrowing in a society supposedly dominated by a profoundly unproductive mentality, they are an embarrassment" (ibid.: 42, 44).

But even if we ignore the "embarrassment" caused by these dozens of nonconforming examples, one massive group of loans remains: the *horoi*, which number well over 200 separate inscriptions attesting to creditors' property interests in Athenian real-estate. These secured transactions have received enormous scholarly attention, not least from Finley and his student Millett, who perhaps are the two scholars most insistent on the primacy of consumption credit at Athens. These loan transactions, which represent about one-quarter of all known financings from the classical Greek world, are overwhelmingly from Attica and fall chronologically (where this can be determined) between the beginning of the fourth century and the first part of the third. They constitute a corpus larger in number, if not in economic significance, than even the group of maritime loans, which both Finley and Millett, with varying explanations, have been forced to classify as "productive."[27]

---

[26]Herman (1987: 94) assumes an incompatibility between "friendship" and profit-oriented commercial practice. In fact, at Athens itself there are numerous examples of loans at interest to relatives and friends, including several of which Herman is aware (ibid., 94 n. 69).

[27]Finley: "productive" because used "to purchase or improve income-producing property" ([1951] 1985: 87). Millett: "apparently productive" because "they seem to have been contracted in order to increase the existing wealth of the borrower" (1983: 42).

How many of these *horoi*-loans can be shown to have been made for consumption? Not a single one. As Finley recognizes, "the *horoi* maintain almost complete silence about the reasons for the indebtedness they publicised."[28] But the silence is not total, although again the limited information available is "embarrassing." Millett is able to identify the purpose of at least one of the stones (Finley no. 3), and this single example he finds "productive."[29] Even new discoveries dog the old orthodoxy. A decade after the original publication of Finley's monograph on the *horoi*, another embarrassing stone was reported: in language paralleling that of "Finley no. 3," it too confirmed a "productive" purpose.[30]

But the classification of a loan's purpose finally and necessarily remains a subjective process. The fungibility of money means that the ultimate use of funds can never certainly be determined from their immediate application: a loan secured by personal assets or used directly for social purposes may free other money for business use or may actually be related to a borrower's commercial activity; the tendency for private financial transactions to remain confidential will limit the information available even to contemporary observers. What is required, then, is a flexibility that will seek to understand the Athenian process of credit extension in terms appropriate to the fourth century. If examples are to be categorized, the categories should correspond to ancient, not modern, terms and concepts. Modern scholars, however, actually warn against "the invention of categories to match up with the types of loans found in the sources" and insist on analyzing Athenian loans through modern (or actually protomodern) terminology.[31]

Even for present-day bankers, to whom data are generally available in smothering overabundance, determining the purpose of a loan presents substantial theoretical and practical conundra. For example, banking regulations often limit the percentages of loans of different types that may legally be provided by certain kinds of institutions. Thus "thrift institutions" in the United States have been required to invest the bulk of their funds in "real-estate loans," with a strict limitation on the percentage of their assets that may be committed to "consumer loans."[32] But the differentiation of a "real-estate loan" from a "consumer" or "commercial loan" is often quite arbitrary and

---

[28]Finley 1981: 70. Similarly Finley [1951] 1985: 81, 83–84.

[29]Millett 1983: 43. *Horos* no. 3 in Finley [1951] 1985 (= I.G. II² 2762); Dittenberger 1915–24: 1194.

[30]*Arch. Delt.* 17 (1961–62): *Khronika* 35, no. 4 (now 12A in the expanded 1985 reprint of Finley 1951). Millett (1983: 188 n. 15) concedes it to be a "possible" analogue to Finley no. 3.

[31]Millett 1983: 43. For an effort to relate categorization to the "types of loans found in the sources," see Pleket's useful comments (1971: 433–37).

[32]Under laws and regulations presently in force, federally chartered savings institutions cannot provide "consumer loans" in excess of 30% of the institution's total assets. Yet certain loans likely to be for consumer purposes are not included in the category of "consumer loans," for example "home equity loans," which are secured by the equity in the borrower's residence but are not necessarily used for the purpose of home improvement.

ultimately dependent on subjective criteria. There is, for example, a dilemma in classifying a bank's loan to a commercial business when the financing is secured by a mortgage on real property and periodic rental receipts are expected to provide the funds for servicing the loan. Is this a commercial or a real-estate credit?

Modern banking organizations have been unable to resolve the problems inherent in determining the purpose of a loan. In the late 1960s in the United States, the Federal Reserve Board strongly discouraged banks from extending credit for the purpose of financing corporate acquisitions (so-called "acquisition loans"). The fungibility of money meant, however, that the expansion of "normal" credit-lines might make available for acquisition purposes corporate funds that were otherwise available (but perhaps unneeded) for ongoing business operations. Serious disputes, never resolved, arose over the purpose of credit extension.[33] In Brazil, at about the same time, similar questions, also never fully resolved, arose as to the types of loans permitted to various financial institutions: the *banco commercial*, the *banco de investimento*, the *financeira*, and the *compania de crédito imobiliário* all could accept deposits and provide specified but never fully clarified types of loans.

In the case of ancient Athens, the reconstruction of economic process (together with the "antiquarian" goal of determining the underlying "facts") necessarily precedes meaningful analysis of economic and social issues.[34] Even cliometric studies will ultimately benefit from the overtly analytical (and factually oriented) tools offered by "forensic attestation."

"FORENSIC ATTESTATION": AN ALTERNATIVE APPROACH

Forensic analysis reveals a credit structure at Athens manifestly in conflict with the cliometric conclusions examined above. Litigants' claims presuppose the ongoing provision of commercial loans by banks in their normal business activity. For example, the son of Sopaios demands the return of funds allegedly on deposit with the bank of Pasiōn, who replies by insisting (*inter alia*) that bank funds, far from constituting deposits, actually have been used to make or secure commercial loans (Isok. 17): whatever his obligation to repay the alleged deposits, the banker would certainly not claim, without elaboration, that monies were used for business credit if the explanation would contradict the jurors' general knowledge or expectation of a bank's activities. Similarly, when the Athenian general Timotheos denies that he is personally liable for the

---

[33]These definitional difficulties presumably were among the reasons that, after resolution of the "credit crunch" of the late 1960s, the U.S. Federal Reserve Board has sought to avoid channeling of financial resources into specifically categorized areas.

[34]On the integration of philosophical history (emphasizing the interpretation of events) and antiquarian history (focusing on the collection of facts), see Momigliano 1950: 285–86. Cf. Veyne 1971: ch. 1.

repayment of a bank loan, since the financing was in fact a business advance to a trader that Timotheos did not guarantee or otherwise legally obligate himself for (Dem. 49), the extent of the officer's actual involvement may be beyond our knowledge, but his contention compels the inference that Athenian banks did not avoid making commercial loans.

Although interpreting litigators' assumptions (like selecting and compiling numerical data) involves some subjectivity, the validity of the conclusions drawn from forensic attestation can be tested directly and independently: one need only read the texts cited. Generalizations based on cliometric analysis can be challenged only if the reader has the time and expertise to compile all the data anew (which of course rarely happens), or if (as here) the statistical conclusions directly contradict the premises clearly underlying arguments being made by Athenian litigants. The following cases show the conflict between sweeping conclusions made by econometric studies as to the absence of commercial financing by banks, and the courtroom arguments presupposing such loans.

Demosthenes 49

Pasiōn the banker advanced 1,750 drachmas to Philōndas. These funds were used to pay transportation charges for the shipment of lumber by sea from northern Greece to Athens. The creditor, seeking to hold Timotheos personally responsible, asserted that the funds were advanced to Philōndas at Timotheos's prior arrangement; that the loan was understood really to be to Timotheos; and that in any case the lumber was taken to the general's house in the Piraeus. But in denying responsibility for repayment of the loan, Timotheos insisted that the advance was made to Philōndas alone, strictly "for the sake of trade."[35]

We cannot say who was telling the truth. The text, however, necessarily presupposes an Athenian audience's willingness to believe that a banker would provide business financing. In his efforts to establish Timotheos's personal use of the loan, the creditor appealed to the jurors' personal knowledge and sought to construct a proof from reasonable assumption and argumentation (ek tek-mēriōn, §34), directing such argumentation specifically to this loan. But at no point did he deprecate as inherently incredible Timotheos's contention that the loan was made merely "for the sake of trade."

If Athenian banks were known to specialize in consumer loans and to engage only rarely, if ever, in business-related loans, then the creditor, in an argument explicitly relying on "probabilities," would necessarily have suggested that "the pattern of Greek moneylending for non-productive purposes is indubitable" (Finley 1985: 141). Instead, the creditor confirms the opposite. Apol-

---

[35]ἐμπορίας ἕνεκα: Dem. 49.35, 36, trans. A. T. Murray (1936–39). Timotheos apparently characterized Philōndas as "a businessman who imported the timber in order to sell it" (Thompson 1979: 231).

Iodōros actually explains how a loan "for the sake of trade" would normally have been handled by the bank (§35): "If the lumber had been brought in for the sake of trade . . . do you think that my father [the banker Pasiōn] . . . would have permitted Philōndas to convey the lumber out of the harbor—when it was pledged to him as security for the freight charges? Would he not have guarded it, stationing there somebody from his staff (*tina tōn oiketōn*), and taken the revenue from the lumber as it was sold, until he had recovered his advances?"

Isokrates 17

The case reported at Isokrates 17 focuses entirely on the relationship between a banker, Pasiōn, and a client (known to us only as the "son of Sopaios") deeply involved in maritime commerce. Indeed, the transactions described—regardless of the protagonists' differing claims and interpretations—presuppose extensive commercial activity by the bank. No fewer than five credit extensions, ranging from 300 drachmas to 7 talents, are alleged, and a sixth can be added if the two loans of 6 talents each described at sections 12 and 50 are in fact separate transactions.

The gravamen of the case is the client's claim to repayment of substantial sums allegedly deposited with the banker Pasiōn. The banker, for his part, insists that the client is indebted to the bank for various financings, primarily related to maritime finance, and in amounts "frighteningly" large.[36] As usual in such cases, the speech is filled with arguments from probability and with "proofs" (*tekmēria*) based on plausibility.[37] But though the client disputes his liability for these alleged borrowings, he nowhere argues that it was inconceivable or unlikely or even rare for an Athenian banker to extend credit to facilitate maritime trade.

Indeed, the entire relationship is set in the context of business activity and commercial finance. The bank's client, an important person in the Bosporan kingdom, is clearly and significantly involved in maritime trade. He reports coming to Athens for trade (*kat' emporian*) with two ships filled with grain and with considerable money (§4; cf. §1). His involvement in maritime commerce is chronicled: we find him lending large sums on a Delian cargo ship (§42); with the aid of the bank, he uses funds that were otherwise being conveyed to the Pontos (§§35–37); and when he demands return of his own deposits it is to facilitate a trip to Byzantion (§8). He claims to have played a major role in supplying Athens with food in times of scarcity when the Bosporans sent away empty the ships of the "other merchants" (*emporoi*, §57). When the Bosporan king allegedly wishes to be helpful, he summons persons active in maritime operations (*nauklēroi*) and asks them (§52) to aid the client and not to "stand

---

[36]Cf. 17.43: the potential lender Philippos κληθεὶς καὶ ὑπακούσας, δείσας τὸ μέγεθος τοῦ κινδύνου ἀπιὼν ᾤχετο. The banker provided the credit.

[37]For example, see §§31, 36, 53 (τεκμήρια); §§46, 54 (εἰκός).

aside while [he is] being treated unjustly." The appeal is comprehensible only if the bank's client had been engaged in maritime commerce, a participant in the so-called "world of the *emporion*."[38]

Not surprisingly, then, the client reports a virtual loan portfolio of banking credits, acknowledged and disputed, involving a spectrum of maritime commerce. First, as a result of the client's substantial financing of a cargo vessel allegedly owned by a Delian, he required surety for seven talents—a very large sum, but one that Pasiōn was able to provide through Archestratos "from the bank" (*ton apo tēs trapezēs*, §43): from an economic aspect, provision of a guarantee represents no less an extension of credit than does a direct loan. Another example of indirect bank financing for maritime trade is related at §§35–37, where the client reports that he borrowed 300 staters from Stratoklēs, but only after the bank, at Stratoklēs' request, guaranteed both principal and interest. For the bank, this guarantee was of course the functional equivalent of any other form of loan: if repayment were not made as agreed, bank funds would be expended to honor the guarantee,[39] and the banker would have to collect this loan from the beneficiary of the guarantee. Again, nothing in the speech suggests that the transaction was regarded as unusual in any way, even though it would have been to the client's advantage to brand the transaction implausible if he could have done so.

Even when the client does dispute the actual receipt of a loan—300 drachmas that he had previously acknowledged (§38)—he attempts to explain away his prior admissions, instead of arguing that an Athenian bank would probably not have extended credit to a foreign businessman. Although we do not know the alleged purpose of this loan, the fungibility of money and the client's financial involvement in trade suggest that any funds loaned to him would have been available for business purposes, either directly or by freeing some of his other resources for commerce.

Other extensions of credit are mentioned. Although the client admits that he "permitted" his associate Hippolaidēs to borrow at the bank (§38), he denies Pasiōn's claim that he himself (with his associate Menexenos) had borrowed a further six talents from the bank (§12).[40] But again the actual nature of the

[38]Reference to "the *emporion*" has become scholarly shorthand for the physical, financial, and ideological sphere encompassing businessmen involved in maritime trade and finance. See Vélissaropoulos (1977: 61–85), who expands on Gernet's earlier use of the phrase (1955b: 185 n. 5); see also below, Chapter 3, n. 35.

[39]Financing, as here, through suretyships and guarantees of repayment, rather than through actual handling of bulky coins or bullion, enormously increased the credit-providing capacity of the Athenian bankers. See above, pp. 14–18.

[40]The funds had been disbursed by Kittos, who had been at the exchange counter and was allegedly "persuaded" and "bribed" to let them take six talents of silver. The banker would have insisted that the transaction was an actual loan (Thompson 1979: 232–33), not a theft (κλοπή), as the client characterizes the banker's position. This comports with the tendency of Athenian litigants to present contractual dispute as the rhetorical equivalent of "theft" (cf. D. Cohen 1983: 23).

advance is of no importance: the failure of the client to treat the disputed loan as "improbable" is critical. Funding of such magnitude could not have been intended for "consumption," especially in view of the involvement of Menexenos, the scion of one of the "wealthiest and most distinguished" Athenian houses.[41]

Demosthenes 33

Hērakleidēs' bank extended a loan of 3,000 drachmas to Apatourios, a ship owner (*nauklēros*) from Byzantion, so that he could repay commercial-maritime creditors seeking to execute on his vessel (§7). Although this financing would appear to be a prime example of maritime lending by a bank, it has actually been counted in one statistical analysis as an example of nonproductive credit since it was used merely for "the repayment of a loan" (Bogaert 1986: 28). Such number-counting ignores the reality set forth clearly, in context, in the courtroom presentation.

The financing was arranged in the *emporion*, the commercial portion of the Piraeus (above, note 38), by an individual engaged full-time in maritime finance after years as a seagoing merchant (§4); he was particularly active in trade between Byzantion and Athens (§5). This bank transaction was not an isolated case: the merchant-financier had an established relationship with the banker (§7), and the bank's ongoing involvement in maritime finance is further confirmed by its skill in fashioning the loan[42] and by its subsequent success in effectuating repayment through the sale of the security (§12).

All this evidence is ignored by the cliometric approach. The speech not only presupposes, but indeed explicitly and implicitly describes, lending activity in the *emporion* for which the banks are an ongoing and natural source. For the arithmetician, however, the financing is merely another "nonproductive loan" to be statistically catalogued.

[41]Davies 1971: 145.

[42]Note the personal guarantee by a third party, the participation with another lender, the written loan agreement, and the taking of the ship as security. There is no basis for Bogaert's assertion (1986a: 28) that the financing was made against the personal guarantee alone: indeed, the bank loan was repaid with funds generated by the sale of the vessel; the speaker's "purchase" of the ship is specifically referred to as an "amendment" of the terms of the transaction, presumably in contrast to the form of security-interest held by the original lenders, who on default had not been able promptly to obtain possession of the vessel (note the imperfect [ἐνεβάτευον, §6]). For a fuller discussion of this loan, see below, pp. 154–57.

Chapter 3

FINANCIAL CONTEXT AND CONCEPTS

ENTIRELY UNREGULATED by government, the *trapeza* functioned in cultural and economic contexts alien to present-day business activity. Yet recurring scholarly disputes as to the banks' operations almost invariably have been framed in specialized modern terms and concepts: efforts to differentiate "interest on time deposits" from "interest on demand deposits" (Thompson 1979: 225ff.; Bogaert 1986a: 19ff.), discussions of "clearing systems" between banks and "giro transactions" between accounts at the same *trapeza* (Hasebroek 1920: 113ff.; Pöhlmann 1925: 2:530 n. 3), analogies to "commercial account(s) in a modern bank" (Calhoun [1926] 1968: 101), and so forth. In contrast, we propose Athenian context and Athenian concepts as the necessary bases for explication of Athenian banking phenomena. At Athens, banking "powers" and business arrangements were determined without state interference—by economic, not legal, constraints. Governmental "charters" permitting specified activities, or limiting competition, were nonexistent. But in exercising their freedom, or in abstaining from opportunities, the bankers operated in a cultural and commercial universe molded by societal concepts and business realities, an Attic *weltanschauung* continually being fabricated by the actuality of fourth-century, eastern Mediterranean, Hellenic living. This life, far more than the business concepts and experiences of other civilizations,[1] is critical to comprehending the operations of the *trapeza*.

---

[1]Ancient societies are frequently referred to as "precapitalistic" (see, for example, Garlan 1982: 202) since they were dependent on "the forms of slavery, serfdom etc." that preceded the utilization of nominally free wage labor (Marx 1967–70, 3: 8.19). "Precapitalistic" is then equated with "primitive," often without overt recognition, and used to justify analysis of Athenian economic processes primarily through anthropological reference to "primitive" modern societies rather than through ancient evidence. (For a conspicuous example, see the treatment of exchange in Millett 1990). But definitions of capitalism, and hence of "precapitalism," are notoriously impressionistic. If capitalism is understood in Weberian terms as "an actual adaptation of economic action to a comparison of money income with money expenses," then "the capitalistic enterprise and the capitalistic entrepreneur, not only as occasional but as regular entrepreneurs, are very old and were very widespread . . . as in Babylon, Hellas, India, China, Rome" (Weber 1976: 19–20). Cf. Weber 1961; Salvioli 1907; Gernet 1907: 203–4. Athenian banking, in fact, was an "operation" focused on money income and expense (cf. Dem. 36.11): bankers, in particular, were οἱ γνώμῃ καὶ ἀργυρίῳ δυνάμενοι χρηματίζεσθαι (Xen., *Por.* 5.3).

Freedom from Regulation and Oligopoly

In sharp contrast to virtually all modern systems, and to some ancient arrangements,[2] loans from the *trapezai* were explicitly independent of parochial legal governance. Indeed, concerning contractual provisions, Athenian law seems to have mandated the primacy of "whatever arrangements either party willingly agreed upon with the other."[3] The maritime-loan document preserved at Demosthenes 35.10–13,[4] the sole surviving text of an actual Athenian sea-finance agreement, provides explicitly that regarding the matters encompassed therein, "nothing else [shall] have greater validity than [this] contract,"[5] a clause specifically characterized in the text as giving the contract priority over laws and decrees (§39).[6] The same provision of overriding effect was found in the written agreement that is the subject of litigation in Demosthenes 56.[7]

The primacy of private arrangements partly explains why at Athens, shortly before the beginning of the fourth century, the world's first "private banks" arose.[8] These *trapezai* operated entirely independently of governmental regulation or constraint, an autonomy highly compatible with the prevailing minimal state involvement with trade and finance. Harbor authorities, presumably from fiscal motivations, did record the cargo content of ships,[9] and did perform limited police and administrative functions.[10] Athenian law encouraged the

---

[2]The financial operations of religious complexes (so-called Greek "temple banks") utilized funds belonging to a particular deity to offer loans intended to finance cult expenses. The public authorities who controlled the shrines were intimately involved with these operations. Indeed, the best-attested of these banks, that at Delos, was controlled by Athens both before 314 and after 166. See Thompson 1988: 832. In Hellenistic times, there appeared "public banks" (δημόσιαι τράπεζαι), primarily committed to receiving and spending tax monies: for Athens, see I.G. II² 1013, ll. 4, 27.

[3]In contractual contexts there is frequent reference to Athenian law mandating absolute governmental noninvolvement in the conditions and terms of nongovernmental dealings (τοῖς νόμοις τοῖς ὑμετέροις [sc. Ἀθηναίοις] οἳ κελεύουσι, ὅσα ἂν τις ἑκὼν ἕτερος ἑτέρῳ ὁμολογήσῃ κύρια εἶναι: Dem. 56.2). Cf. Dem. 42.12, 47.77; Hyp., *Ath.* 13; Dein. 3.4; Plato, *Symp.* 196c.

[4]Despite earlier attacks by Schucht (1892; 1919: 1120ff.), this document is now generally accepted as genuine. See Harrison 1968–71, 2: 111; Drerup 1898: 315ff.; Gernet 1955b: 197; Purpura 1987: 203ff. On the authenticity of other documents in Demosthenes, see Schläpfer 1939.

[5]κυριώτερον δὲ περὶ τούτων ἄλλο μηδὲν εἶναι τῆς συγγραφῆς. Cf. I.G. XII 7.67, 27 and 76.

[6]ἡ μὲν γὰρ συγγραφὴ οὐδὲν κυριώτερον ἐᾷ εἶναι τῶν ἐγγεγραμμένων, οὐδὲ προσφέρειν οὔτε νόμον οὔτε ψήφισμα οὔτ' ἄλλ' οὐδ' ὁτιοῦν πρὸς τὴν συγγραφήν.

[7]Although the written agreement has not been preserved, §26 confirms the provision.

[8]"Private bank" here refers to a banking operation conducted by an individual or individuals for their own account (ἴδιος). The corresponding Greek phrase (ἰδιωτικὴ τράπεζα), however, is not attested before Hellenistic times (see Preisigke 1910: 32; 1915: 172; 1925–66, 3: 172). For the absence of earlier private banks, see above, Chapter 1, n. 96.

[9]See, for example, Dem. 20.32, 32.18, 34.7, 35.29.

[10]Government officials included ἀγορανόμοι ("controllers of the market") concerned with maintaining order in the public markets and preventing the sale of adulterated or impaired goods

import of grain to Athens: persons resident in Attica were not to ship cereals to other *emporia*; maritime lenders at Athens might provide funds for trade in grain only if the cereals were to be transported to Athens.[11] But the government did not even set standards or otherwise regulate the seaworthiness of vessels, their safe equipage or operation, today universal manifestations of governmental oversight.[12] Financial arrangements were subject to no control other than that of market conditions: "commerce in Athens was never an affair of the state."[13]

Nor was the market controlled by oligopolies able through economic dominance to force conformity to a cartel's business practices and decisions on seemingly independent operators.[14] Even maritime commerce—despite its operation on the vast scale necessary to provide food and other goods for many thousands of Attic residents[15]—was characterized by extreme market fragmen-

---

(Aristot., *Ath. pol.* 51.1; Dem. 20.9; Hyp., *Ath.* 14); μετρονόμοι ("controllers of measures") responsible for the weights and measures used by merchants (*Ath. pol.* 51.2); and, for retail and wholesale trade in grain respectively, σιτοφύλακες ("guardians of grain") and ἐπιμεληταὶ τοῦ ἐμπορίου ("supervisors of the *emporion*") (*Ath. pol.* 51.3, 4). On the ἀγορανόμοι and μετρονόμοι, see Stanley 1979. For regulatory interaction between the σιτοφύλακες and the ἐπιμεληταὶ τοῦ ἐμπορίου, see Figueira 1986: 150–51; Alesia 1949: 20; Kohns 1964: 147, 158–59. An inscription found in 1970 in the Athenian agora provides for supervision of the Piraeus's silver tester (δοκιμαστής) by the ἐπιμεληταὶ τοῦ ἐμπορίου (Stroud 1974: 183).

[11]On the prohibition of grain shipment to other ports, see Dem. 34.37, 35.50; Lykourgos, *Leōkratēs* 27. For limitations on lenders, see Dem. 35.50–51, 56.6, 11; Lykourgos, *Leōkratēs* 27. Cf. Dem. 24.136 with schol.; Dem. 58: Hypothesis, 5, 12.

[12]See Adam 1989: 283–84.

[13]Mossé 1983: 53. Cf. Adam 1989: 291; Garland 1987: 88; Hasebroek 1978: 43; Gernet 1955b: 186.

[14]For the practical considerations limiting concentration in the Athenian grain market and precluding, "for example, 4 or 5 firms controlling 60 or 70% of sales," see Figueira 1986: 158–59. For a general analysis of dynamic factors curtailing operation of cartels, see Machlup 1952. Not surprisingly, the best-attested effort to dominate a market during the fourth century originated outside Athens, the "cornering" of the grain market by Kleomenēs, who had been given significant political power and complete financial control of Egypt by Alexander in 332 (although Tarn [1948, 2: 303 n. 1] doubts whether he was actually appointed "satrap," as reported by various ancient authors). On his efforts to control the market, see Dem. 56.7–10 and Aristot., *Oik.* 1352a16–b25 (2.2.33). Cf. Riezler 1907: 33–34; Andreades 1929: 1ff.

[15]Even the most conservative estimates of Athenian food requirements in the fourth century make clear the enormous burden carried by maritime trade: Garnsey (1985: 62–75) has recently suggested that in any particular year, Attic needs for grain alone might not have exceeded 400,000 medimnoi ("enough to feed around 90,000 people," p. 74), a shortfall considerably less than that suggested in earlier studies (cf., e.g., Jardé 1925; Gomme 1933: 28–33), but still requiring an enormous mobilization of resources relative to the limited population of Attica, the size of ships, and the absence of governmental finance (see below, Chapter 5, n. 126). Importation of food by sea was an inherent feature of Attic life: it clearly predated the Peloponnesian War (see Gauthier 1981: 5ff.), although claims of reliance on foreign grain as early as the seventh century (Grundy 1948: 67–69) appear unfounded (cf. Noonan 1973 and Bloedow 1975). The volume of imports needed did, of course, vary with the vagaries of local production (see Jameson 1983: 6–16).

tation: there existed at Athens no single owner of a multiship fleet,[16] no dominant trading companies, no enterprise controlling the harbor. In every maritime
financing known to us in any detail, there is always more than a single lender (a
bank, of course, represents by definition a combination of resources). A single
ship itself would carry many "traders" (*emporoi*), and each of these *emporoi* or
groups of *emporoi* would have separate cargo securing individual loans from
groups of lenders. The ship itself might be secured by a separate loan from yet
other lenders, and the ship owner might be carrying cargo for his own account
subject to a loan or loans from yet other lenders.[17]

Unregulated by oligopolistic or governmental controls, Athenian bankers
were free to vary the conduct of their operations, free to commingle "bank"
and individual funds, free to engage in speculative investment.[18] No rule
required all bankers to pay "interest" on customers' deposits, or to treat all
clients and situations uniformly. No activity was governmentally proscribed; no
activity was governmentally mandated.

But bankers were not free of all proscriptions and mandates: they were still
subject to those inherent in the conceptions and organizing principles of their
society—which did not rely, as ours does, on financial concepts of "interest,"
or on such derivative notions as "interest-free demand deposits." Theirs was a
system largely based upon complementary opposites, a system whose dominant influence on financial activities was exercised in a manner that has gone
largely unnoticed in modern analysis of the Athenian economy.

In Lieu of Interest: "Maritime" and "Landed" Yields

At Athens, unlike the modern world, bank "deposits" could be made not only
in coin, but in valuable drinking cups (Dem. 49.31); in addition to money,
clients on occasion borrowed mattresses, cloaks, and tableware from their
bankers (Dem. 49.22). The term "deposit" (*parakatathēkē*, *enthema*) was
applied without differentiation to both bank and nonbank placements (Korver
1934: 28–39), and even to "deposits" of contracts (Dem. 34.6). Nor did
"interest" correspond to the modern concept: to the contrary, Athenians dealt

---

[16]Phormiōn is frequently said to have been the only person in Athens known to have owned
more than a single merchant ship (Dem. 45.64). Cf. Ste. Croix 1974: 50 n. 31, 1981: 558 n. 3.
But this is true only if we assume that the wealthy son of Sopaios was not the owner of the two
ships that he brought to Athens filled with grain (Isok. 17.4). The statement also assumes that
Phormiōn the banker was the owner (as Bogaert insists: 1986b: 27), and not (through his bank?)
the financier of the ships (as suggested by Erxleben 1974: 491–92). Cf. Isager and Hansen 1975:
73; Chapter 5, n. 123 below. We have no specific knowledge of the shadowy Lampis, who
"fitted out the city and *emporion*" for the Aiginetans (Dem. 23.211): his characterization as "the
largest shipowner in Hellas" (Vince 1935) is probably too free a translation of Demosthenes'
μέγιστα ναυκλήρια κέκτηται τῶν Ἑλλήνων (literally, "has acquired the greatest maritime
[interests] in Hellas").

[17]For the fragmentation of maritime finance, see below, pp. 136–50.

[18]See below, pp. 62–66.

with "yield" (*tokos*) conceptualized in a binary pattern of "maritime yield" (*tokos nautikos*) and "landed yield" (*tokos eggeios*) utterly removed from twentieth-century categorization. Although this distinction has sometimes been recognized in passing,[19] its significance, critical to understanding Athenian finance and banking activity, has not been pursued.

On the assumption that "maritime yield" represents the equivalent of what in modern usage we term "interest," reference is frequently made to the "very high interest rate, known as 'maritime interest' " (Isager and Hansen 1975: 74), charged by maritime lenders.[20] "Interest," however, like its cognates in other modern languages, is generally defined as the rate of payment for the use of money "expressed as a percentage per unit of time."[21] "Interest" thus is a return on funds related strictly to the passage of time.[22] In contrast, the Greek word *tokos* essentially conveys the meaning of a "bringing forth" or "birth," and only metaphorically is extended in usage to cover "the produce or usance of money lent out."[23] Since *tokos* is not inherently time-related, it is best translated in English as "yield," rather than "interest."

Athenian "maritime yield" bore no relationship to time-denominated "interest." In turn, for the Athenians, with their tendency to antithetical but imprecise financial conceptualization, "landed yield" derived meaning essentially through contrast to "maritime yield." Extensions of credit were conceived and grouped antithetically ("maritime loans," *daneismata nautika*, and "landed loans," *daneismata eggeia*), and each group was characterized by a different method of calculating financial return: a "maritime yield," normally used in sea finance, determined by entrepreneurial factors; and a "landed yield," calculated on the basis of the passage of time. The term "landed yield" is strictly a counterpoint to "maritime yield": the Athenian tendency to antithetical conceptualization resulted in characterization of loans and yields as "landed," in contexts where the alternative financing was "maritime," even where the "landed" loan lacked any special real-property context. Significantly (contrary to both the prevailing assumption[24] and modern expectation), "land-

---

[19]Lipsius [1909–15] 1966: 721; Harrison 1968–71, 1: 228 n. 3; Korver 1934: 125ff.

[20]Cf., for example, Austin and Vidal-Naquet 1977: 150; Biscardi 1982: 39; Bleicken 1985: 74; Davies 1981: 64; Gauthier 1976: 95; Ste. Croix 1974: 41, 43; Vélissaropoulos 1980: 302.

[21]*Webster's Unabridged Dictionary*, 2d ed.

[22]A return on funds related to profitability, rather than time passage, is described in modern commercial usage by the phrase "participation." By "participating" in the net revenues of a borrower, "Islamic" banks are able to obtain a return on funds advanced, without violating Koranic prohibitions against charging interest.

[23]Liddell-Scott Lexicon, sv. τόκος. Aristotle explains this extended usage: ὁ δὲ τόκος αὐτὸ [sc. τὸ νόμισμα] ποιεῖ πλέον (ὅθεν καὶ τοὔνομα τοῦτ' εἴληφεν· ὅμοια γὰρ τὰ τικτόμενα τοῖς γεννῶσιν αὐτά ἐστιν, ὁ δὲ τόκος γίνεται νόμισμα ἐκ νομίσματος): *Pol.* 1.1258b5. Cf. Plato, *Rep.* 8.555c; 6.507a.

[24]At least since Büchsenschütz (1869: 490), scholars have interpreted "landed yield" as applicable solely to loans relating to "land," rather than as a measure of calculating return on

ed yield" was not applied solely to loans secured by land or buildings. Nor was there anything "abnormal" about the calculation of maritime returns; contrary to oft-repeated shibboleth,[25] there is no basis for assertions that rates in Hellenic antiquity were "normally" calculated through multiples determined by the passage of time.

In short, the Athenians' financial categorization was unique to their civilization. Recognition of their unique conceptualization clarifies elements of their economy and banking operations that have defied modern comprehension.

Polarization in Financial Terminology

A dominant characteristic of classical Greek culture is its tendency to understand and to organize phenomena through contrast, preferably through antithesis.[26] The Greek language itself was molded on polarity: the most obvious example is the characteristic *men . . . de* construction, particles indicating the balance or opposition of two elements, sometimes words but often longer phrases or even sentences. Aristotle even provided philosophical justification for structured polarization (antithesis provides pleasure and aids understanding: *Rhetoric* 1410a20ff.).[27] Indeed, "binary division" was so central to Hellenic culture that it has been said to have "dominated Greek thought."[28]

---

principal. Cf. Billeter 1898: 31; Korver 1934: 127–28. For example, editors have consistently misinterpreted Lysias 32.15 where reference is made to funds "lent at landed interest" (ἐγγείῳ ἐπὶ τόκῳ δεδανεισμένας). The passage is treated as though the text referred explicitly to a borrowing secured by real property. See, e.g., Adams 1905; Morgan 1895. Cf. Davies 1981: 63. Similarly, a borrowing at Dem. 34.23 is explicitly described as made at "landed yield" (ἐγγείων τόκων), but the passage is generally translated as if it spoke of a "borrowing at interest upon real security" (Doherty 1927: 765). Cf. Murray 1936–39; Carey and Reid 1985: 196; but note Gernet's accurate "à intérêt terrestre" (1954–60). Thompson (1980: 144 n. 57) correctly denies that the term means a loan secured by land and compares the phrase to two other passages involving land/sea antithesis, but he does not explicitly interpret ἔγγειοι τόκοι as relating to yield. Paoli did see sixty years ago that "landed loans" are characterized not through the security of real property but by their "simple antithesis" ("semplice contrapposto") to "maritime loans" ([1930] 1974: 60 n. 5, 93 n. 1).

[25]For example, Finley notes that "interest rates in antiquity were normally in multiples or fractions of twelve, i.e. at so much per month" (1985: 187 n. 50). Cf. Boeckh [1842] 1976: 141. On calculation of rates generally in the classical period, see Billeter 1898; Heichelheim 1963, s.v. "Geld- und Münzgeschichte"; Michell 1957: 342ff., 347ff.; Wille 1984; Tilli 1984.

[26]This characteristic has been much studied in recent years in a proliferation of "structuralist" studies: see especially Lévi-Strauss 1967; Vernant and Vidal-Naquet 1969; C. Segal 1986: 43–45. Such cognitive opposition has been identified as characteristic of Mediterranean cultures in general: see Bourdieu 1977: 87–95; Hertzfeld 1985: 53ff., 90–91, and 1986: 215ff.

[27]The author of the *Rhetorica ad Alexandrum* (1435b27) is explicit in granting higher approval to that antithesis which is simultaneously opposed in meaning *and* terminology, as against the solitary contrast of meaning *or* terminology.

[28]See Garner (1987: 76), who lists numerous examples of the phenomenon (pp. 75–83). For the critical role in Greek thought of theories based on opposites, see Lloyd [1965] 1987: 15–85.

Dramatized contrast was a basic element in most literature and art.[29] Indeed, the state gathered the entire population for the presentation in festival of institutionalized antinomies. Here extreme polarization was inherent in the art form itself (for example, the *strophē-antistrophē* choregic pattern, whose precise metrical mirroring produced contrast without explicit statement, merely through placement of a word or image in one or the other dramatic component). Conflicted popular reaction to artists such as the divine, the reviled Euripides[30] was consonant with a culture where "throughout Greek tragedy systems of linked polarity—mortal and divine, male and female, man and beast, city and wild—operated . . . to include not just the emotional, interior world of the individual character or spectator but the whole of society" (C. Segal 1986: 57).

In a world perceived in opposites, no structural polarity was more basic than the fundamental contrast between land and sea, between the nonmaritime and maritime spheres. Thus the Athenian historian Thucydides perceived the Peloponnesian War as, in essence, a land/sea conflict—"a land-power seeking to overcome a sea-power."[31] As a result, the otherwise unremarkable Lakedaimonian attack by sea against the Athenians based at Pylos becomes for Thucydides a reversal of the natural order of maritime and nonmaritime roles between Athens and Sparta, an amazing upheaval of fortune (*tychē*; Thuc. 4.12.3), not a minor strategic inversion occasioned by the Athenian fleet's efforts to reach Sicily expeditiously. Indeed, this sea/land counterpoint was so basic to Greek thinking that generations of Greek professors have explained to their students the appropriateness of the exclamatory joy expressed by Xenophon's Ten Thousand—"The Sea! The Sea!"—after battling their way through the land mass of Asia Minor (*Anabasis* 4.7.24). Illustrative of this characteristic alternation of the maritime and nonmaritime, it is this same Xenophon who instinctively characterizes an interest rate higher than 1 percent per month not as "usurious," as modern writers might, but as "maritime,"[32] and then emphasizes the nonmaritime nature[33] of his own proposed yields on capital.

---

[29]See Kennedy 1963: 34. Even the seemingly straightforward Herodotos handled eyewitness reports in an adversarial manner (Collingwood 1946: 25). Cf. Kleber 1890: 1, and Norden 1923: 27. J. H. Finley, Jr. (1938: 64–67) has shown that dramatic conflict was so inherent in the intellectual structure of Athenian civilization that it is nugatory to search for mutual influence in the "antithetical styles" of Euripides and Thucydides; rather, both manifest the centrality of contrast in Athenian society.

[30]Extreme contrasts of feeling about specific individuals illustrate this inherent tendency toward polarization. Thus Jaeger (1939: 380) finds that his contemporaries "adored Euripides like a god." But in his entire lifetime he won first prize in the dramatic competitions only four times. See E. Segal 1983: 252.

[31]Gomme, Andrewes, and Dover 1956–81, 2: 449. Gomme considers this sea/land contrast, for Thucydides, "the chief strategic interest of the war."

[32]Xen., *Por.* 3.9: ὥσπερ ναυτικόν.

[33]καὶ ταῦτα ἐν πόλει: 3.10. Gauthier (1976: 95) notes "la valeur locative de ἐν." The contrast, however, is present in the text without regard to the correctness of Gauthier's suggestion

Xenophon is not alone in promulgating his revenue proposals within these two categories, for the contrast of land and sea was implicit, and often explicit, in Athenian conceptualization and characterization of commercial—and banking—activity. Physically and culturally, in the very construction and placement of their communities, the Greeks often manifested a basic binary business dichotomy: the nonmaritime city proper (*to astu*) with its "landed" financial center (*agora*), and the separate maritime commercial center (*emporion*), generally on the coast and away from the "landed" center.[34] The ultimate embodiment of this separation, of course, is Athens, with its elaborate agora city-center miles from the sea, and its incomparable Piraeus harbor and maritime center directly on the water and constituting the *emporion par excellence*.[35]

This physical separation was paralleled in financial matters by a corresponding, pervasive conceptualization of all loans as either "landed" (*eggeia*) or "maritime" (*nautika*).[36] This dichotomy reflected both Greek conceptualization and economic reality. The Hellenic tendency to antithesis essentially focused on *complementary* opposites. Complementary characteristics—male and female, wet and dry, hot and cold—exclude other possibilities; their antithesis precludes continuity on a spectrum. An item must be either one or the other.[37] This bifurcation limited financial possibilities to "landed" or "mar-

---

(pp. 97ff., with which I agree) that Xenophon was proposing a "contribution obligatoire, conforme à . . . l'eisphora athenienne" (p. 98), not a scheme for voluntary investment (as seen by Bolkestein 1939: 265–66) nor a public loan (Thiel 1922: 48–50; von der Lieck 1933: 41; Giglioni 1970: 84).

[34]Greek *emporia* were often subsidiary to a *polis* but seldom at any distance from the sea coast (Vélissaropoulos 1977: 61). Because of the threat from pirates, Greek cities had originally been situated away from the sea coast, and in classical times the traditional cities (such as Athens, Argos, and Knossos) retained their inland locations (Thuc. 1.7).

[35]The *emporion* was the physical, financial, and ideological sphere at Athens encompassing businessmen involved in maritime trade and finance. Physically the area encompassed the western portion of the Piraeus harbor and centered on the *deigma* (δεῖγμα). (See Dem. 35.29, 50.24; Xen., *Hell.* 5.1.21; Pollux 9.34; Suidas, s.v. δεῖγμα. Cf. Amit 1965: 79–80; Panagos 1968: 208–14; Gofas 1970: 28ff.) The dichotomous business life of Athens is confirmed by the parallel but separate provisions for the *emporion* at the Piraeus and the agora in the city set forth in the silver-testing law found in the Athenian agora in 1970. Special provision is made even for the placement of the inscribed text of the decree separately at the two centers. See Stroud 1974: esp. ll. 37ff. Similarly Xenophon, in his proposals for increasing revenues at Athens, makes parallel provision for capital expenditures καὶ ἐν Πειραιεῖ καὶ ἐν τῷ ἄστει (*Por.* 3.13). Regarding the juridical implications of this urban dualism, cf. Paoli 1976: 197–99.

[36]Hellenistic Egypt provides striking confirmation that the division between "landed" and "maritime" goods was perceived as an all-encompassing categorical partition. There the stereotypical phrase ἔγγαια καὶ ναυτικά in the contractual clause was replaced by a new verbal formula permitting "plus brièvement la saisie de 'tous les biens' de la partie coupable, sans comporter de précision sur la nature de ces biens" (Gauthier 1980: 205).

[37]See Foxhall 1989: 23: "They cannot be permanently or inextricably linked into a continuous chain of meaning: they simply do not coalesce tidily into a structuralist framework." For scholarly failure to recognize a similar antithesis between "invisible" (ἀφανής) and "visible" (φανερά) assets, see below, pp. 191–94.

itime," and forced into one of these categories items that we might consider belonging to neither, or sharing characteristics of both or of others. Here Athenian perception corresponded to Hellenic reality. In the modern world, the maritime sphere may still constitute an important part of total economic activity, but technological developments and multifaceted mechanisms of communication have reduced marine trade to one factor among many, in some countries no longer even a significant factor. In the Hellenic world, however, there was no alternative to physical transportation by sea or land. Indeed, because of the pervasive pattern of Greek settlement along the coasts of the Mediterranean and Black Seas (rather than inland), and because of the primitive nature of the mechanisms available for transportation and communication over the harsh terrain, the dominant area of a commercial world limited to land and sea was probably the maritime.[38] And, of course, maritime business was especially important to Athens.[39]

Not surprisingly, then, in commercial usage, "landed" or "maritime" characterizations are usually set as the sole alternatives. Lexicographers juxtapose the terms in explaining loan phrases.[40] A contract can be "landed" (*eggeion*) or "maritime" (*nautikon*): when the speaker in Demosthenes 33 is justifying his use of a jurisdictional objection (the *paragraphē*), he insists that there is no agreement (*symbolaion*)—"neither maritime nor landed"—between himself and his adversary.[41] Assets are grouped as maritime or nonmaritime: in the loan agreement preserved at Demosthenes 35, execution is permitted against property "both landed and maritime."[42] In Xenophon's *Symposion*, "maritime"

[38]See, for example, Biscardi 1982: 28: "Le vrai commerce a toujours été, dans l'Antiquité grecque et romaine . . . le commerce en gros par voie de mer." The primitive nature and high cost of overland transportation meant that most long-distance trade was by sea. See Ste. Croix 1974: 42; Bleicken 1985: 73; Garland 1987: 85.

[39]Most Athenians were economically dependent on sea-related activity. See Xen., *Hell.* 7.1.4, where an envoy asserts explicitly to the Assembly, "μὴν τάς γε τέχνας τὰς περὶ ταῦτα πάσας οἰκείας ἔχετε. καὶ μὴν ἐμπειρίᾳ γε πολὺ προέχετε τῶν ἄλλων περὶ τὰ ναυτικά· ὁ γὰρ βίος τοῖς πλείστοις ὑμῶν ἀπὸ τῆς θαλάττης· ὥστε τῶν ἰδίων ἐπιμελόμενοι ἅμα καὶ τῶν κατὰ θάλατταν ἀγώνων ἔμπειροι γίγνεσθε." Cf. Starr 1989: 47; Andreades [1933] 1979: 243 ("the foreign policy of the Athenians was largely a grain policy").

[40]Pollux 3.84: ἔγγεια δανείσματα, ναυτικά. (An alternative reading is ἔγγυα δανείσματα. The spelling probably reflects manuscript confusion resulting from the post-classical Greek confusion, and ultimate assimilation, of the vowel sounds "ει" and "υ." On instability in Attic vowel usage as early as the fifth century B.C., see Browning 1969: 32–33.) To be sure, in explaining the difference between "invisible" (ἀφανής) and "visible" (φανερά) property, Harpokratiōn characterizes "visible" as "landed" (ἔγγειος) property. Although Harpokratiōn proceeds to characterize "invisible" property as "personalty" (ἡ ἐν χρήμασι καὶ σώμασι καὶ σκεύεσι—a "gloss . . . hardly credible" [Gabrielsen 1986: 101]; but see below, pp. 193–94), actual usage tended to merge the ἔγγειος/ναυτικός and the ἀφανής/φανερά contrasts. Thus in Isokrates 17 the sums deposited with the bank and redeployed to facilitate maritime finance are characterized by the Bosporan depositor as ἀφανής (Isok. 17.7–10).

[41]οὔτε ναυτικοῦ οὔτ' ἐγγείου (Dem. 33.3).

[42]καὶ ἐγγείων καὶ ναυτικῶν (35.12).

and "landed" possessions are in antithesis.[43] Indeed, for Athenian finance, the "maritime"/"landed" opposition is so prevalent that in a case dealing with maritime finance,[44] the speaker can counter an opponent's argument partly by pointing out the inherent implausibility of a maritime trader's borrowing at "landed interest"[45] in order to repay a maritime financing.

At Lysias 32, a speech dealing with an estate dispute showing "close similarity of family circumstances to those of the orator Demosthenes" (Davies 1971: 151), the assets—largely cash and loans—are carefully separated between landed and maritime loans, just as in Demosthenes' own treatment of his father's assets at Demosthenes 27.11 (see below, pp. 52–53). The juxtaposition in Lysias is explicit: aside from cash, the bulk of the estate of Diodotos is comprised of receivables on two types of loans, separately characterized as "maritime" and "at landed interest."[46] Earlier in the speech (§6), reference is made to Diodotos having personally delivered to his brother at least a portion of his property—and there, too, the assets are separated out as cash, maritime loans, and nonmaritime financing (2,000 *dr.* in the Chersonese,[47] apparently a loan relating to land[48]). At §6, some of the assets later claimed to be part of the estate are not mentioned (an omission that may merely reflect Diodotos's delivery at that time of only some of his property), but editors generally have conjectured a lacuna (see the text set forth in note 47). So pervasively juxtaposed in Athenian usage are the terms "maritime loan" and "landed loan," however, that as early as 1841, Sauppe insisted on filling the supposed lacuna with the specific phrase "landed loans" (*eggeious*)—thereby making explicit the landed/ maritime contrast,[49] which in any event is implicit in the text as transmitted.

---

[43]*Symp.* 4.31: νῦν δ' ἐπειδὴ τῶν ὑπερορίων στέρομαι καὶ τὰ ἔγγεια οὐ καρποῦμαι καὶ τὰ ἐκ τῆς οἰκίας πέπραται, ἡδέως μὲν καθεύδω. Similar wording is found in the loan contract between the city of Arkesinē and the Naxian Praxiklēs: ἔγγαια καὶ ὑπερπόντια (line 14, Dittenberger 1915–24: no. 955, 4th–3rd century B.C.). Vélissaropoulos is correct (1980: 308 n. 177) in rejecting Dittenberger's suggestion that ὑπερπόντιος here signifies *transmarinus*. Cf. Gauthier 1980: 197ff.

[44]τὰ χρήματα ἐπὶ τῆς νεώς: Dem. 34.2.

[45]ἔγγειος τόκος (Dem. 34.23).

[46]ναυτικά: Lysias 32.14; μνᾶς ἐγγείῳ ἐπὶ τόκῳ δεδανεισμένας: §15.

[47]δίδωσι καὶ πέντε τάλαντα ἀργυρίου παρακαταθήκην· ναυτικὰ δὲ ἀπέδειξεν ἐκδεδομένα ἑπτὰ τάλαντα καὶ τετταράκοντα μνᾶς [lacunam indicaverunt editores], δισχιλίας δὲ ὀφειλομένας ἐν Χερρονήσῳ.

[48]Lysias later makes reference to corn "coming in every year from the Chersonese" (φοιτᾶν σῖτον ἐκ Χερρονήσου καθ' ἕκαστον ἐνιαυτόν: Lysias 32.15). Editors long have theorized that "this grain was sent annually as payment of the interest" on the 2,000 *dr.* loan (Adams 1905). Return paid not in money but in crops would be appropriate only to a loan relating to land. The recurring yearly payment suggests a calculation of yield related strictly to the passage of time (i.e., "interest"). (Payment of overseas obligations in kind is not without parallel, as demonstrated afresh by the discovery in 1986 in the Athenian agora of an Athenian law of 374/3 providing for tax payment in grain by Lemnos, Imbros, and Skyros. See Shear 1987.)

[49]After μνᾶς: ἐγγείους δὲ δισχιλίας δραχμὰς δεδανεισμένας. Other scholars have made similar suggestions (e.g., Fuhr: ἑκατὸν δ' ἐγγείῳ ἐπὶ τόκῳ δεδανεισμένας).

The same maritime/landed investment categorization is continued for the guardian's actual investments in Lysias 32. Diogeitōn is accused of having actually invested the children's property in maritime finance (§25); he should instead have invested in real estate (§23). Even more explicitly in another case, when a guardian makes financial arrangements allegedly inappropriate for orphans' accounts, Lysias rebukes him for placing the funds on a "maritime," not a "landed," basis.[50] And when Hypereidēs accuses Demosthenes of investing in maritime finance, he immediately couples the charge with criticism of Demosthenes' real-estate investment activity.[51]

Even in Hellenic communities outside Greece proper, and in contexts only peripherally commercial, the landed/maritime contrast persists. In a marriage contract dating from the fourth century B.C.,[52] found at Elephantine Island in Egypt, more than a thousand kilometers from the Mediterranean, the groom agrees to possible execution against his property, which here, too, is dichotomously categorized within the landed/maritime differentiation. Strikingly, the actual words are identical to those of the maritime contract at Demosthenes 35.[53]

This binary commercial categorization was so basic to Hellenic thinking that its perseverance in the Greek Mediterranean for centuries should not be surprising.[54] This continuity is confirmed by a unique papyrus first published in 1957 that preserves a notice of payment from a banker.[55] Although not an actual loan agreement, the text describes in some detail a maritime financing of the second

---

[50]Lysias, frag. 91 (Thalheim): τοῦ νόμου κελεύοντος τοὺς ἐπιτρόπους τοῖς ὀρφανοῖς ἔγγειον τὴν οὐσίαν καθιστάναι, οὗτος δὲ ναυτικοὺς ἡμᾶς ἀποφαίνει.

[51]Hyp., Dem., col. 17: [καὶ νῦν δὲ ναυ]τικοῖς ἐργάζῃ [τι]σὶν καὶ ἐκδόσεις δί[δως], καὶ πριάμενος ο[ἰκί]αν.

[52]P. Eleph. I = Mitteis and Wilcken [1912] 1963: 283 = Meyer 1920: 18. Cf. Hunt and Edgar 1952: no. 1.

[53]ἐγγαίων καὶ ναυτικῶν: line 13. Mitteis recognized the expression as "eine spezifisch griechische Wendung" (Mitteis and Wilcken [1912] 1963: pt. 2, p. 318). Modrzejewski (1970: 141 n. 35) has suggested that the similarities between the *syngraphē* at Dem. 35.12 and the Elephantine papyrus illustrate the great extent to which notarial practice introduced the substance of Greek legal principles to Egypt. Wolff, however, believes that the papyrus confirms the extent to which, already in 311, the Greeks in Egypt had abandoned certain fundamental principles relating to marriage (Wolff 1952: 167). *Contra*: Vatin 1970: 165–67.

[54]Gofas (1970: 5 n. 1), for example, relates the term σάλβα ἤντερα (sic) in an arbitrators' decision of A.D. 1709 to ἡ ἀντίθεσις "ἐγγείων καὶ ναυτικῶν" at Dem. 35.12. Cf. the contrast found in the Rhodian Sea Law (a much later legal code possibly incorporating Hellenistic elements—see Rougé 1981: 165): τὰ μὲν χρήματα ἔγγαια, οἱ δὲ τόκοι ναυτικοί (3.ιη).

[55]P. Vindob. G 19792 = S.B. VI 9571 (ed. prin.: Casson 1957). Improved readings are offered in Youtie 1960: 262 n. 87. A definitive text, verified against the original and with legal commentary, is found in Biscardi 1974: 211–14. That text is reproduced with additional commentary in Casson 1986. On the characteristics of bank notices preserved in Egypt, see Wolff 1978: 96–97. Full bibliographical reference to work on maritime loans in the Roman period is contained in Kupiszewski 1972: 378 nn. 24–27.

century A.D.[56] With the sole exception of the maritime contract at Demosthenes 35, which itself explicitly presents the landed/maritime categorization (§12), this is the only document we have at present that deals with maritime finance in the ancient Mediterranean.[57] In the papyrus, contiguous reference is made to a "maritime" loan, a "maritime" contract, and a "landed" contract.[58]

Differentiating "Maritime" from "Landed" Yield

A remarkable passage from Demosthenes illustrates both the fundamental Athenian categorization of property into maritime and nonmaritime assets, and the differing methods employed in calculating return on loans pertaining to each sphere.

At 27.9–11, Demosthenes sets forth the individual assets comprising his father's estate. He first groups all the estate's domestic assets (*tauta oikoi panta*) and remarkably includes therein not only items such as furniture, jewelry, and cash kept at home, but also a talent of silver lent at the fixed interest rate "of a drachma [per mna],"[59] a typical nonmaritime arrangement representing a cost of 1 percent per month.[60] Indeed, Demosthenes explicitly calculates on a time basis the return on these nonmaritime loans: an "annual rate" (*tokos tou eniautou hekastou*) of "more than 700 *dr.*" (actually 720 *dr.*). The maritime loans are described immediately after, but in a category clearly separate from the "domestic" loans.[61] Because maritime financing carried no annual or other time-related rate, Demosthenes is unable to indicate the yield on these substantial assets,[62] an omission damaging to his efforts to establish the

[56]For the view, properly rejected by Casson and Biscardi, that the text deals with an *actio exercitoria*, see Seidl 1957: 360. Cf. Purpura 1987: 268 n. 230.

[57]A fragmentary maritime loan contract from the first half of the second century B.C. provides for the financing of a voyage to Somalia. (P. Berol. 5883 and 5853 = SB III 7169 [see Wilcken 1925].)

[58]Lines 7–8: εἰς ἔκτεισιν δάνιον ναυτικὸ(ν) κατὰ ναυτικὴν συγγραφὴν ἧς ἡ ἔγγειος παρ' ἐμοὶ τῷ τραπ(εζίτῃ).

[59]Dem. 27.9: ἀργυρίου δ' εἰς τάλαντον ἐπὶ δραχμῇ δεδανεισμένου.

[60]Cf. Ste. Croix 1974: 46 n. 20: "The Greeks and Romans usually calculated their interest by the month ('1 per cent interest' in an ordinary Greek or Roman transaction would mean 1 per cent per month unless the contrary was stated)."

[61]In an estate otherwise extremely varied, the nonmaritime assets are grouped (μὲν); then the maritime loans (δ'). Dem. 27.11: καὶ ταῦτα μὲν οἴκοι κατέλιπεν πάντα, ναυτικὰ δ' ἐβδομήκοντα μνᾶς, κ.τ.λ. Maritime loans directly or indirectly constituted all of the estate's nondomestic assets. See Paoli [1930] 1974: 20 n. 2.

[62]Polemical confusion has resulted from commentators' failure to perceive this differentiation between maritime and nonmaritime assets. Because Demosthenes characterizes as ἐνεργά the three assets first enumerated (the two workshops and the talent of domestic loans: καὶ ταῦτα μὲν ἐνεργὰ κατέλιπεν, in contrast (μέν) to other assets, it has been assumed that all of the estate's other assets were ἀργά. See Davies 1971: 127; Thompson 1979: 227. Since maritime loans clearly were yield-producing but were not included in the initial list of items specifically termed ἐνεργά, prolonged but unsuccessful efforts have been made to reconcile the apparent conflict.

magnitude of the cash flow available to his guardians at the time of his father's death: the absence of a time-related interest calculation for maritime finance and the variability of the entrepreneurially established yield on sea loans apparently made it impossible for him to determine the return on investments made when he was not more than seven years old (Dem. 27.4).[63]

Similarly, nonmaritime funds advanced in the Chersonese, contrasted at Lysias 32.6 with the same principal's maritime loans, yield a return to an Athenian creditor denominated strictly by time.[64] An agora-based lender is characterized by Theophrastos as lending at a yield calculated "by the day."[65] Xenophon's proposed capital financing for Athens is presented within the landed/maritime antithesis. Return on capital will range from more than 100 percent to not less than 18 percent— "just as maritime finance."[66] But this high yield will not involve the risks of the sea; it will be "in the city," generated with the highest degree of safety.[67] Despite the explicit reference to the high level of return on maritime finance, Xenophon is equally explicit in holding to the characteristic time-oriented yield calculation of nonmaritime lending. For Xenophon's "landed" capital-providers, the return would, of course, be on a per-diem basis ("three obols per day").[68] In contrast, "maritime yield" was determined by contractual agreements focusing on commercial considerations, especially degree of risk and anticipated profitability.[69] Since the degree of

---

See Korver 1942: 8ff.; Bogaert 1986a: 21. But once the further distinction between "domestic" and "maritime" assets at §11 is noted (ταῦτα μὲν οἴκοι κατέλιπεν πάντα, ναυτικὰ δ'), the explanation is clear: among the domestic items, the first three (workshops and interest-bearing loans) were ἐνεργά, precisely as the orator says, but the other domestic assets were nonearning (ἀργά)—inventories of ivory, iron, wood, dye, and bronze; the family home; furniture, jewelry, and clothing; money held in cash. All of these assets, ἐνεργά and ἀργά together, constitute the nonmaritime property, contrasted with the marine assets, which are listed separately, pursuant to Athenian categorization.

[63]Cf. Jaeger [1938] 1963: 24–25.

[64]Lysias 32.15: καθ' ἕκαστον ἐνιαυτόν.

[65]Char. 6.2 (τῷ ἤθει ἀγοραῖός τις), 6.9 (πολλῶν ἀγοραίων στρατηγεῖν, καὶ εὐθὺς τούτοις δανείζειν καὶ τῆς δραχμῆς τόκον τρία ἡμιωβόλια τῆς ἡμέρας πράττεσθαι). Cf. Char. 10.2: οἷος ἐν τῷ μηνὶ ἡμιωβόλιον ἀπαιτεῖν ἐλθὼν ἐπὶ τὴν οἰκίαν.

[66]Xen., Por. 3.9: ὥσπερ ναυτικόν.

[67]Ibid., 3.10: ἀσφαλέστατόν τε καὶ πολυχρονιώτατον.

[68]τριώβολον τῆς ἡμέρας. Gauthier (1976: 95) observes that Xenophon's comparison relates only to rate and to relative risks of land and sea ventures, not to the nature or characteristics of the proposed financing.

[69]Recognition of the "yield" on maritime loans as representing a return different from time-related "interest" may partially explain why maritime finance appears to have been excepted from the frequent efforts by the Roman authorities to place limits on maximum returns on loans. See Paulus, Sententiae 2.14.3. Evidence for Roman maritime lending practices is equivocal: however, prior to Justinian's legislation in the sixth century A.D. (see de Martino 1982: 211, and Cassimatis 1931: 53–55), great flexibility appears to have prevailed in the actual terms of such loans (τρόπους εἶναι ποικίλους τῶν τοιούτων δανεισμάτων; modos esse varios talium mutuorum: Just., Nov. 106). Such independence concerning contractual term, although compati-

risk, the expectation of gain, and the relative bargaining power of the parties might vary enormously, it is not surprising that reported yields also show enormous variation,[70] in contrast to landed rates, which seem to have been relatively stable.[71]

Insight into these business factors is provided by the only actual sea-finance contract surviving from fourth-century Athens, the agreement set forth in full in Demosthenes 35[72] and there frequently characterized as "maritime" (§§1, 17, 27, 43, 54, 56). Merchants sailing from Athens are to purchase in Mendē or Skiōnē (both located on a peninsula in the northern Aegean) 3,000 containers of Mendaian wine, intended as collateral security for a loan of 3,000 *dr.* From there the wine is to be shipped to the Bosporan kingdom for sale—or, at their option, the borrowers are authorized to proceed as far north on the western coast of the Black Sea as Borysthenēs (on the Dnieper River, today part of the Ukraine).[73] The borrowers also had the option to avoid the Black Sea altogether. Provided that the trip back from the Pontic area commenced before the rise of Arktouros (mid-September)—but otherwise without regard to the course chosen or time required—the lenders were to receive a fixed yield of 675 *dr.* to be paid, in addition to principal, within 20 days of the ship's return to Athens.[74]

---

ble with Athenian practice, was in sharp contrast to the inflexibility of other Roman business arrangements (see Paoli [1930] 1974: 61ff.). Justinian's legislation in A.D. 528 limiting return on maritime loans (*traiecticii contractus*) to an interest rate calculated on a time basis (Just., *Cod.* 4.32.26[2]), itself revoked by *Nov.* 106, clearly was intended to alter prior practice.

[70]Reported yields vary between 12½% (Dem. 50.17) and over 100% (if the reference in Lysias 32.25 is actually to a maritime loan). Failure to differentiate maritime from landed yields results in such errors as Finley's lumping of "interest rates on maritime loans" with "interest rates in the Greek and Roman worlds," all of which he assumes to have been "stable locally over long periods" (1985: 23).

[71]Interest rates on landed loans tended to such uniformity that some scholars have even conjectured that there were "normal interest rates" that would be "presumed by the law" in the absence of a specific arrangement by the parties (Paoli 1976: 60–61; see also Paoli [1930] 1974: 61).

[72]For its authenticity, now generally accepted, see above, n. 4.

[73]Ἀθήνηθεν εἰς Μένδην ἢ Σκιώνην, καὶ ἐντεῦθεν εἰς Βόσπορον, ἐὰν δὲ βούλωνται, τῆς ἐπ' ἀριστερὰ μέχρι Βορυσθένους, καὶ πάλιν Ἀθήναζε. It is generally assumed (e.g., Ste. Croix 1974: 45; Murray 1936–39) that the reference in the text to "Bosporos" is not to the Black Sea but to the kingdom located in Crimea, and that the borrowers have complete freedom to select either of these totally different itineraries. An alternative interpretation would reduce somewhat the borrowers' choice of itinerary: under the contract the borrowers were authorized to enter the Black Sea (Βόσπορον) after purchasing wine at the Chalcidic peninsula, and could follow the west coast of that sea (τῆς ἐπ' ἀριστερὰ) no further than the Dnieper River. On this interpretation of the *syngraphē*, the ship's travel to the Crimea would have violated the contract's provisions—but the borrowers are accused of violating virtually every other relevant contractual clause!

[74]§13: Ἐὰν δὲ μὴ εἰσβάλωσι, μείναντες ἐπὶ κυνὶ ἡμέρας δέκα ἐν Ἑλλησπόντῳ . . . καὶ ἐντεῦθεν καταπλεύσαντες Ἀθήναζε τοὺς τόκους ἀποδόντων τοὺς πέρυσι γραφέντας εἰς

The western coast of the Black Sea was much closer to Athens than the Crimea. Ancient sailing vessels would have encountered wind conditions of extreme variability, particularly in the Black Sea.[75] The arrangements of this contract clearly anticipated, and explicitly permitted, extreme variability both in possible itinerary and in the consequent period of time during which lenders' funds would be outstanding. Yet the venture, whether extended or expedited, brought the lenders the same basic return of 3,675 *dr.* on an investment of 3,000 *dr.*

In every case where information about the amount of return on maritime creditors' funds is preserved, yield is calculated on the same fixed basis. At Demosthenes 50.17, a fixed yield of "one-eighth" is payable on a maritime loan for a relatively short one-way journey between Sēstos and Athens.[76] In Demosthenes 34, relating to maritime trade between Athens and Bosporos, the yield for the financing is set at 600 *dr.* on a principal sum of 2,000 *dr.* (§§23, 25). In the negotiation of a maritime loan secured by a ship (Dem. 56.5), yields governed by destination, Athens or Rhodes, are proposed, rather than interest calculated by passage of time.[77] And at Demosthenes 33.6, Apatourios owes 4,000 *dr.* on a maritime loan covering the sea journey that has just been completed—but there is no indication that interest is continuing to run on a daily or monthly basis, as in the case of a nonmaritime loan.

Variations in length of voyage would arise not only from sailing conditions or from the borrowers' exercise of contractual options, but also from commercial circumstances. For example, as was common in fourth-century sea trade, the ship in Demosthenes 35 carried numerous merchants and agents pursuing their own separate transactions.[78] Reconciliation of their needs might result in delay. The chaotic buyers' market in the Pontic area for the goods offered by Phormiōn (described at Dem. 34.8–9) resulted in conflict between the captain's sailing schedule and the merchant's business needs. In the event, Phormiōn utilized other (later) means of transport (Dem. 34.9), but the lenders' return did not increase.

τὴν συγγραφήν. Murray (1936–39) correctly explains the reference to "last year's yield" (although he does so in terms of "interest rate"): "If the return voyage is delayed until the legal year has expired (at the summer solstice) the rate of interest is to remain unchanged."

[75]Casson 1971: 291 n. 93.

[76]For the Greek text, see n. 94 below. The "plain meaning" of the passage, indicating a single and not a periodic payment on principal, is confirmed by ancient definition. Harpokratiōn cites this specific passage (Dindorf ed., p. 132) to define the fourth-century Athenian use of the word ἐπόγδοον: "one-eighth" refers to a loan where return to a lender would be exactly that fraction of the principal sum advanced (εἴη δ' ἂν ἐπόγδοον τὸ οὕτω δεδανεισμένον ὥστε τοῦ κεφαλαίου τὸ ὄγδοον μέρος δοθῆναι τῷ δανειστῇ, οἷον τριώβολον τοῦ τετραδράχμου).

[77]ἔλεγον ὅτι βούλονται δανείσασθαι ἐπὶ τῇ νηί, ἐφ' ᾧ τε πλεῦσαι εἰς Αἴγυπτον καὶ ἐξ Αἰγύπτου εἰς Ῥόδον ἢ εἰς Ἀθήνας, διομολογησάμενοι τοὺς τόκους ‹τοὺς› εἰς ἑκάτερον τῶν ἐμπορίων τούτων. Indeed, throughout Dem. 56, yields are referred to as determined not by time, but by destination (cf. §§12, 28 [τοὺς εἰς Ῥόδον τόκους], 29).

[78]For the various arrangements, see below, pp. 146–47.

In fact, under the contract at Demosthenes 35, certain variations in yield were provided, but were solely conditional on marine contingencies, unrelated to mere passage of time. Thus, if jettison of cargo were required, repayment was reduced relative to the proportion of cargo surviving (§11). Return of principal and yield was also to be proportionately lower if payments were extracted by pirates (§11). If the entire cargo were lost as a result of any of these contingencies, no repayment on the loan would be required.[79]

Maritime risk explains even the provision for an increase in yield from 225 *dr.* per thousand to 300 *dr.* if the trip back from the Pontic area did not commence until after the rise of Arktouros (mid-September): travel after this date would involve, in Greek judgment, sharply increased maritime risk for the lender—and the possibility of substantially increased profits for the debtor. As emphasized by Apollodōros at Demosthenes 50.21, dangers at sea from the weather and from piracy rose sharply after Arktouros.[80] But these perils might be offset by opportunity for enhanced profit following the star's rise: traders might take advantage of the post-Arktouros grain shipments from the Pontos.[81] None of this relates to the mere passage of time, as in the case of "landed yield"—indeed, in the context of the optional itineraries permitted by the contract of Demosthenes 35, a journey to the Crimea that concluded entirely before Arktouros might actually have taken longer than an alternate voyage, occurring after Arktouros, to the less distant western coast.

In the fourth century, utilization of time-based yields would have been incompatible with prevailing mercantile conditions. Maritime profits, like maritime risks, were extremely high, on occasion offering a return of at least double the funds invested[82] for sea voyages that seldom required more than a few weeks.[83] But the period of commercial activity, generally restricted to the summer sailing season, was relatively brief.[84] If funds could be redeployed several times during a single season, vast monetary reward might be obtained; if repayment were delayed even a few weeks during the period of good weather, additional opportunities for high return might be lost. In this commercial context, it would have been nugatory to relate return on funds to passage of time: if

[79]§11: σωθέντων δὲ τῶν χρημάτων Ἀθήναζε, ἀποδώσουσιν οἱ δανεισάμενοι τοῖς δανείσασι τὸ γιγνόμενον ἀργύριον κατὰ τὴν συγγραφήν.

[80]Indeed, Apollodōros attributes his men's subsequent severe disheartenment to the ensuing dangerous weather conditions: "rain and thunder and wind because of the time of the year" (Dem. 50.23).

[81]Cf. Dem. 50.19: ἀνηγόμην ἐπὶ τὴν παραπομπὴν τοῦ σίτου . . . ἕως ὁ ἔκπλους τῶν πλοίων τῶν μετ' ἀρκτοῦρον ἐκ τοῦ Πόντου ἐγένετο.

[82]Cf. Lysias 32.25. But, in Thompson's view (1978: 417), "maritime lending was so chancy that no calculation of normal profits is possible."

[83]A voyage from the Crimea to Rhodes might take as little as ten days (Diod. 3.34.7). (Because of prevailing wind conditions, the northerly journey, of course, would take much longer.) Cf. Casson 1971: 281–91.

[84]Rougé 1975: 15–16; Biscardi 1982: 30–31.

repayment were delayed for half a month, additional "interest" at the standard "landed" rate of 1 percent per month would have meant only an additional 15 *dr.* on a loan of 3,000 *dr.* But the delay might eliminate opportunities for maritime reinvestment that might yield, as in Demosthenes 35, an additional 675 *dr.* or more in a relatively short period.

Although return on maritime funds did not increase if a voyage consumed more time than anticipated (or decrease if fewer days were used), profit considerations and contractual provisions together sharply limited maritime borrowers' possible exploitation of the absence of daily interest accruals. Required payment of principal and yield was precipitated not by passage of time, but by a ship's arrival at an agreed-upon port (e.g., Dem. 33.6, 34.26, 35.11, 50.17). Permitted itineraries were specifically agreed upon (as detailed in Demosthenes 35 and 56, the two fullest surviving descriptions of maritime-loan arrangements). Since a considerable portion, often half, of the capital required for a maritime venture was contributed not by the creditors, but by the debtors,[85] borrowers shared with lenders a strong motivation to complete the journey expeditiously and to redeploy the funds on additional ventures.[86] In many cases, a maritime borrower was merely one of many merchants on a particular ship,[87] and thus was not in a position to control the ship's itinerary, the timing of its arrival at a particular port, and the subsequent maturation of the obligation of repayment. Ship operators (*nauklēroi*), borrowing against the security of their vessels, would be constrained not only by agreements with their own creditors, but also by their transport agreements with shippers of goods being carried by the vessel.

To be sure, once the ship reached the designated port, the debtors did have a specified period of time within which to pay the sum due, twenty days under the contract at Demosthenes 35. To secure prompt repayment, creditors were entitled to take possession of the cargo securing their loan (Dem. 32.17, 34.8, 35.11), or even of the ship itself, if pledged as security (Dem. 33.6), but under the fixed-yield provisions of sea finance, no interest was payable for the period following the ship's arrival in port and preceding the repayment date. If the loan were not repaid within the permitted period, again, time-related interest did not begin to accrue; instead, a specified "penalty" sum (*ta epitimia*), sometimes twice the amount advanced by the creditors, might become immediately payable.[88]

---

[85]Dem. 34.6, 35.18. See Ste. Croix 1974: 50; Thompson 1978: 413 n. 48.

[86]Even on routes where sailing (and consequently maritime trade) was possible throughout the year, such as Rhodes to Alexandria, efforts were made to maximize the number of trips by utilizing the same funding for two or three journeys. Cf. Dem. 56.30: ἐκεῖσε μέν γε ἀεὶ ὡραῖος ὁ πλοῦς, καὶ δὶς ἢ τρὶς ὑπῆρχεν αὐτοῖς ἐργάσασθαι τῷ αὐτῷ ἀργυρίῳ.

[87]See below, Chapter 5, nn. 149, 150.

[88]The contract in Dem. 35 does not contain such a penalty provision, but cf. Dem. 34.26, 33; 56.20, 27, 38, 45. On "penalty clauses" in Athenian maritime contracts, see Paoli [1930] 1974: 136–37; and on their "reception" into Roman law, see Biscardi 1978.

A singular controversy confirms the complexity of "maritime yield" and its difference from easily calculable, time-related "landed yield." Lykōn had advanced 4,000 *dr.* as a maritime loan in connection with an anticipated voyage to Akē, on the Phoenician coast (Dem. 52.20). When it was decided not to undertake the journey, the maritime lender brought suit, charging that he had been "hoodwinked . . . about the yield."[89] Precisely because the journey was aborted before it began, a dispute about "yield" would have been most unlikely if maritime return, like that on other loans, were calculated on a time basis. The amount of interest owed would have been easily determinable by applying the predetermined percentage of principal to the period between disbursement and proffered repayment. And if yield were calculated on a time basis, the anticipated venture's early cancellation would have involved a relatively insignificant amount of interest, and little likelihood of litigation "about the yield": for each full month, at a rate, for example, of a drachma per mna, only 40 *dr.* would have been owed. But apply the same calculation to "maritime yield," and there is much to dispute "about the yield": a relatively high amount, perhaps 1,000 *dr.*, would have been in question, and its payment would have been governed by complex provisions, exculpatory or punitive, contained in a detailed maritime agreement that was likely to refer to numerous contingencies.

Meaning of "Landed" Yield

"Landed yield" has been generally defined as interest payable on loans secured by grounds or buildings,[90] a definition derived from the assumption that "landed loans" (*daneismata eggeia*) were financings secured by real property. But there is no evidence to support these definitions: in the few cases in which the phrases are employed in contexts allowing evaluation of the interpretations proffered, the ancient sources conflict with the modern explanation.

Thus "landed loans" are attested where there is no possibility of collateralization by real property. The speaker at Demosthenes 33.3, for example, explicitly denies having either a "landed" or a "maritime" loan arrangement with Apatourios.[91] If a landed loan required real-estate collateral, no denial would have been necessary, for Apatourios, the alleged borrower, was clearly a Byzantine having no right to own real estate (*egktēsis*) at Athens; he therefore could not be a party to a contract at Athens requiring his pledge of Attic

---

[89]περὶ τῶν τόκων ὡς ἐξηπατημένος. This evidence is especially valuable since the dispute is mentioned, in passing, in Dem. 52, an entirely independent case involving different litigants and issues unrelated to the gravamen of Lykōn's prior suit. Cf. Thompson 1987: 600–601; see the discussion below, p. 120.

[90]See n. 24 above. Korver is explicit in connecting the two terms: "῎Εγγειος se dit . . . d'un prêt, qui se fait sur un gage immobilier: on peut même dire τόκος ἔγγειος de l'intérêt qui est exigé dans un cas pareil" (1934: 150).

[91]ἄλλου δὲ συμβολαίου οὐκ ὄντος ἐμοὶ πρὸς τοῦτον, οὔτε ναυτικοῦ οὔτ' ἐγγείου.

property as security. (Real property elsewhere would not be subject to Athenian jurisdiction, and hence would be irrelevant.) Accordingly, the adjective "landed" here cannot reflect an object of security.

Similarly, Phormiōn effectuates a loan at "landed interest,"[92] but he does so at Bosporos while in the midst of a round-trip journey from Athens. The loan is described in some detail[93]—the interest rate, the currency utilized (Cyzicene), even the prevailing exchange ratio for conversion into Athenian drachmas, but there is no indication in the text that the loan was secured by real estate. Indeed, the borrower, an individual residing at Athens but temporarily in need of funds at the far reaches of the Black Sea, cannot be assumed to have had, at Bosporos, land or buildings to pledge as security.

Demosthenes 50.17 nicely illustrates the difference between maritime loans and landed loans—and also shows how editors, unaware of the nature of this distinction, have introduced into manuscripts inappropriate emendations. In this passage two loans are described, one of which is explicitly denominated "maritime."[94] Apollodōros, while serving as trierarch of an Athenian warship in the northern Aegean, claims to have borrowed 1,500 dr. from a certain Archedēmos, and an additional 800 dr. through a "maritime" loan[95] from Nikippos the nauklēros, "who happened to be at Sēstos." The maritime financing was at a "yield" of "one-eighth" (12½ percent), with the principal and interest to be repaid if and when the ship returned to Athens. The return on the

---

[92]Dem. 34.23: δανεισάμενος ἐγγείων τόκων.

[93]§24: δεῖ δὴ μαθεῖν ὑμᾶς ὅσα φησὶν χρήματα ἀποδεδωκέναι. τῶν μὲν γὰρ ἑκατὸν εἴκοσι στατήρων γίγνονται τρισχίλιαι τριακόσιαι ἑξήκοντα, ὁ δὲ τόκος ὁ ἔγγειος ὁ ἔφεκτος [τῶν τριάκοντα μνῶν καὶ τριῶν καὶ ἑξήκοντα] πεντακόσιαι δραχμαὶ καὶ ἑξήκοντα· τὸ δὲ σύμπαν κεφάλαιον γίγνεται τόσον καὶ τόσον. Although the speaker insinuates that his adversary actually paid a full year's interest on the money borrowed at landed yield, the absence of a fixed return on "landed" loans prevents his actual calculation of the sum allegedly repaid, hence the evasive τόσον καὶ τόσον.

[94]δανεισάμενος ἐγὼ ἀργύριον παρ᾽ Ἀρχεδήμου μὲν τοῦ Ἀναφλυστίου πεντεκαίδεκα μνᾶς ἐπίτοκον, ὀκτακοσίας δὲ δραχμὰς παρὰ Νικίππου τοῦ ναυκλήρου ναυτικὸν ἀνειλόμην, ὃς ἔτυχεν ὢν ἐν Σηστῷ, ἐπόγδοον, σωθέντος δὲ τοῦ πλοίου Ἀθήναζε ἀποδοῦναι αὐτὸ καὶ τοὺς τόκους.

[95]There is no basis for Erxleben's insistence (1974: 471, 477) that such a maritime financing was "impossible" ("unmöglich"). The lender may well have been advancing funds available to him in Sēstos (resulting from transit fees or other income generated on the outgoing passage from Athens) but needed to repay loans maturing only when his ship successfully returned to Athens. In fact, several other examples are known of financing provided by a nauklēros in the course of a sea journey. In Dem. 34, Phormiōn suggests that he had borrowed funds in the Crimea from Lampis the nauklēros (see Thompson 1980: 144ff.). At Kalaureia, Philip the nauklēros provided funds to Timotheos, who was about to sail to Athens (Dem. 49.14). And at Dem. 56.17, Parmeniskos, apparently a nauklēros, is accused of obtaining "maritime yields" (ναυτικοὺς τόκους) from others, even as he himself worked the Rhodes-Egypt route and was obligated for repayment of a sea loan contracted at Athens. Similarly, while in the Pontos, Lakritos's brother, an emporos, lends to a nauklēros the proceeds of a maritime loan originally made to himself at Athens (Dem. 35.36).

sea loan, of course, is not related to the amount of time that the funds will be outstanding. Whether the journey takes a few days or many, the yield will still be "one-eighth" (plus return of principal, of course: *auto kai tous tokous*). The other loan is reported merely to have been "at a yield" (*epitokon*).

Since the earliest critical editions, the speaker's silence about the nature of and the amount of return on the first loan has been seen as inconsistent with his specificity about the maritime loan. Already in the eighteenth century, Reiske (1770–71) had suggested reading "at 'landed yield' "[96] instead of merely "at a yield." In his interpolation of an explicit counterpoint between landed and maritime loans, Reiske was early supported by Salmasius.[97]

At Demosthenes 50.17, Boeckh's reasoning ([1842] 1976: 135 n. 654) ultimately prevailed: "*epi tokon* is added" to communicate that the loan was "for interest" even though obtained "from his friend and countryman."[98] But Boeckh's explanation, although in support of a paleographically sound conclusion, ignores the textual counterpoint. The contrast of the loan "at a yield" (*men*) and the "maritime" loan (*de*) obviously indicated something more than statements that both loans were "for interest": these were compatible, not counterpointed, assertions. In the light of our analysis, it seems clear that these statements would have communicated to an Athenian audience, as they did to Reiske in the eighteenth century, a contrast between maritime and landed loans. But the text as transmitted poses no difficulty, since for an Athenian audience, the nonmaritime loan would have needed no further explanation. Interest on "landed loans" appears to have adhered to a standard or "market" rate; to jurors attuned to the maritime/landed contrast, the statement "at a yield" would have been intelligible as meaning "at the prevailing rate for landed loans at that time in such area." Similarly, the formulaic "with interest and costs added" used by American courts conveys to the court's audience the (unstated) added meaning "at the statutory interest rate and legally established charges." The text as transmitted also makes rhetorical sense: since Apollodōros is emphasizing the extraordinary expenses to which he has been subjected, he has reason to specify the high fixed charge (one-eighth) of a maritime loan, not the relatively low, time-related interest on a landed loan, which, if repaid in a relatively short time, would have been even more inexpensive.

---

[96]ἐγγείων τόκων vel ἐγγείου τόκου.

[97]Salmasius suggested ἐγγύῳ. These textual suggestions mirror the similar effort by Sauppe and Fuhr, among others, to insert an explicit "landed" (ἐγγείους) reference into the text at Lysias 32.6 (see above, p. 50).

[98]The reading ἐπίτοκον itself reflects an emendation by Schäfer and not the actual manuscript reading (ἐπὶ τόκον), which editors uniformly reject.

Chapter 4

WIVES, SLAVES, AND THE ATHENIAN BANKER

FUNCTIONING WITHIN a legal system that did not recognize businesses as autonomous persons for juridical purposes, the Athenian bank was not an "institution," but an intensely personalized "operation" (*ergasia*) conducted by individuals having considerable skill in finance.[1] Because Athenian banking was closely involved with the "invisible" (*aphanês*) economy, which avoided taxes and creditors, the bankers also needed discretion. But aside from the important and challenging matters of financial significance, banking as an ongoing business necessarily involved a multitude of mundane functions. The bankers could not employ free Athenians to handle these tasks. Although individual citizens might undertake specific, limited assignments—representation in a particular commercial dispute, expedition of a financing through provision of a guarantee, and the like—societal values inhibited citizens from working on a continuing basis under another person's control; public maintenance allocations provided the financial means to permit even the most impoverished Athenian to avoid "servile" (*doulika*) employment.

But slaves and dependent family members could not muster philosophical and moral objections to avoid participation in banking operations. As a result, even in a patriarchal and repressive "slave society," bankers' slaves had unusual opportunities for personal wealth and social acceptance, and bankers' wives could have detailed knowledge of, and influence in, the functioning of the banks. On the death of its proprietor, control of a banking business—with corresponding power and property—was routinely left not to a male descendant, but to a male slave and the proprietor's widow—who were then joined in marriage. Although the pattern was somewhat surprising even to Athenian citizens (and has been largely ignored by modern scholarship), this combination of spouse and slave was a natural response to legal, social, and economic factors inherent in the structure of Athenian life. Athens was a society antithetically divided between the public sphere of politics and state, where the male citizen held exclusive suzerainty, and the private domain of the "household" (*oikos*), where the leading role of the male citizen was sharply circumscribed by economic reality and social custom. The *trapeza*—often operated by noncitizens, always functioning through household members, and often utilizing as

---

[1]Thus Xenophon (*Por.* 5.3) refers to bankers as οἱ γνώμῃ καὶ ἀργυρίῳ δυνάμενοι χρηματίζεσθαι.

the "banking house" the banker's own residence, but still dealing of necessity in the public arena of law and business—belonged fully to neither domain. Banking's bifurcated orientation, yet critical economic role, mandated adaptations in Athenian practices that offer important social and legal insights into Athenian life.

A "STRICTLY PERSONAL" BUSINESS

The Athenian bank was not an institution in the sense of an "establishment" perceived as having an existence independent of the personalities of the persons involved with it.[2] At Athens the banker, like the doctor or the sculptor—and in sharp contrast to the typical modern financial business—was perceived not as a participant in a corporate organization, but as an individual practicing a *technē*, a craft or trade requiring personal commitment, knowledge, and skill.[3] For modern economic historians, this Athenian characterization has resulted in dual confusion: the assumption that since the form of organization was simple, the business conducted must have been insignificant or simplistic; and the equally enticing but incorrect conclusion that because of the complexity of the business undertaken, Athenian banks must have required an operational organization similar to that of modern enterprises.[4] In reality, the Athenian *trapeza* was a relatively simple organization (as discussed in this chapter) with a complex business function (as set forth more fully in Chapters 5 and 6).

---

[2]The English word "institution," along with its cognates in other modern languages, is derived from the Latin "institutio," which itself has an essential meaning of "establishment." Cf. *Oxford Latin Dictionary*, s.v. "institutio"; *Webster's Unabridged Dictionary*, 2d ed., s.v. "institution."

[3]See Xen., *Oik.* 1.1: ἆρά γε ἡ οἰκονομία ἐπιστήμης τινὸς ὄνομα ἐστιν, ὥσπερ ἡ ἰατρικὴ καὶ ἡ χαλκευτικὴ καὶ ἡ τεκτονική; . . .Ἡ καὶ ὥσπερ τούτων τῶν τεχνῶν κ.τ.λ. Cf. Pollux 4.7, 22. The *technē* of banking was to be "taught," just as any other *technē*: (Dem. 45.71) τοῦτον [sc. Φορμίωνα], ἡνίκ᾽ ὤνιος ἦν, εἰ συνέβη μάγειρον ἢ τινος ἄλλης τέχνης δημιουργὸν πρίασθαι, τὴν τοῦ δεσπότου τέχνην ἂν μαθὼν πόρρω τῶν νῦν παρόντων ἦν ἀγαθῶν. ἐπειδὴ δ᾽ ὁ πατὴρ ὁ ἡμέτερος τραπεζίτης ὢν ἐκτήσατ᾽ αὐτὸν καὶ γράμματ᾽ ἐπαίδευσεν καὶ τὴν τέχνην ἐδίδαξεν . . .

[4]Thus, for example, Calhoun correctly sees the complexity and large scale of banking operations ([1926] 1968: 99–106): he is, however, quickly found referring to "maturely developed banking institutions" (p. 94), finding "close analogy to the growth of a modern bank's capital stock and surplus" (p. 108), and even fantasizing about a "hint" of "state supervision or control comparable to the attempts of modern governments to safeguard the interests of depositors" (p. 111). In contrast, Austin and Vidal-Naquet correctly deny the institutional nature of Athenian banks but immediately conclude that "they were primarily money-changing establishments and pawn-brokers" (1977: 149). Humphreys is alone in utilizing a more sophisticated (and more appropriate) approach: although she characterizes the banks as "only one-man businesses" that "depended on the ability of a single owner," she sees that "the Athenian banks, like modern banks, served to reconcile discrepancies between lenders' and borrowers' needs" (1978: 152–53).

Since Athenian law did not accord independent legal standing to the *trapeza*,[5] Athenians generally did not differentiate between the banker himself and his banking entity. This absence of separate legal standing for a bank apart from its owner(s) conformed to general Athenian treatment of businesses: for legal purposes they were assimilated into the persona of their owners. In contrast to modern systems, which freely recognize the corporation as an "artificial person," Athens did not accord juridical status to commercial entities.[6] Yet in popular parlance, and even in legal documents,[7] the banking business as a functioning operation was referred to and recognized under the term *trapeza*, just as other Athenian businesses were recognized as operating entities, although they did not possess legal identification apart from the person of their owners (for example, Demosthenes' father's bed-producing workshop [*klinopēgion*] and the banker Pasiōn's shield factory [*aspidopēgion*]). For the Athenians, these were not "unincorporated enterprises" but *technai*.[8] As with modern proprietorships, which lack independent juridical status, this popular recognition, without legal effect, meant that clients and others did not in their

[5]See Finley [1951] 1985: 262 n. 3; Welles 1970: 805–6. On Greek "associations," see Ziebarth 1896; Endenburg 1937; Pantazopoulos 1946. For the business and legal implications of these relationships, see below, n. 71.

[6]Absence of juridical recognition for business proprietorships or partnerships is a phenomenon entirely independent of the law's treatment of social or demipolitical associations. There is little ancient evidence to support the view, universally held in recent times, that Athenian law never recognized the existence of, or accorded legal standing to, such groupings. Although there is no inherent necessity for a legal system to accord these associations independent standing (see E. M. Harris 1989: 339 n. 1], assertions that Athens failed to do so rest essentially on a single tenuous argument: Attic documents do not differentiate consistently between the members of an association and the entity itself (Harrison 1968–71, 1: 242 n. 1). Property, for example, is said to be characterized indiscriminately as hypothecated either to a deme (as an associated entity) or to the demesmen themselves. See Finley [1951] 1985: 260 n. 14; Kränzlein 1963: 136. Thus, in I.G. II² 2670, property is hypothecated to the Kekropidai, the Lykomidai, and the Phlyans (members, respectively, of a tribe, genos, and deme); in I.G. II² 2699, land is sold ἐπὶ λύσει to *eranistai* τοῖς μετὰ Ἀριστοφῶντος Εἰρεσίδου. But in I.G. II² 2631, land is said to belong to the *koinon* of the Eikadeis. Cf. *Hesperia* 5 (1936): 397, ll. 175ff., where a tribe itself is described as a creditor (ἐνοφείλεσθαι τῆι Αἰαντίδι φυλῆι). But such interchangeability actually is entirely consistent with Greek usage: routinely, independent political jurisdictions are indiscriminately mentioned by reference either to the citizens of the polis (for example, οἱ Ἀθηναῖοι) or to the polis itself (αἱ Ἀθῆναι). Despite this "inconsistent" usage, the Greeks obviously did develop autonomous political units. Allowance must also be made for the Athenian tendency to utilize legal terminology without rigorous definition (see Chapter 5, nn. 215, 219) and for the Greek proclivity to differentiate only antithetical relationships (see Chapter 3).

[7]Cf. the lease of Pasiōn's bank: "ΜΙΣΘΩΣΙΣ· κατὰ τάδε ἐμίσθωσε Πασίων τὴν τράπεζαν Φορμίωνι" (Dem. 45.31). Although the authenticity of the "lease" has been challenged (see below, Chapter 5, n. 322), its contents are in every detail directly deducible from Dem. 45 (and 36).

[8]Thus Pollux includes all three (the τράπεζα, the ἀσπιδοπήγιον, and the κλινοπήγιον) in his listing of τέχναι (7.170, 7.155, and 7.159). Cf. Dem. 27.9, characterizing his father's workshops as τέχνης οὐ μικρᾶς ἑκάτερον.

dealings consistently or necessarily differentiate between the owner and the business, either linguistically or professionally.

In fact, surviving evidence establishes clearly the pervasive Athenian practice of equating the banker and his bank, of referring to them interchangeably. The *trapeza* is, on occasion, referred to as a business having a perceptible independent identity, as at Demosthenes 36.5,[9] where Pasiōn is reported to have owed money "to the bank" (*eis tēn trapezan*), in this case his own *trapeza*. But just as routinely, the Athenian bank is assimilated to the identity of its proprietor. A striking example of this interchangeability occurs in Demosthenes 45, where in an astounding juxtaposition the speaker reports the claim that Pasiōn personally owes money *to* the bank, and in the very next sentence describes this alleged obligation of the bank's owner as a debt *of* the bank itself.[10]

Similarly, the Athenians tended to refer to money on deposit at the bank as money placed not in the bank, but "with the banker." Throughout Isokratēs 17, for example, funds allegedly on deposit in the bank of Pasiōn are denominated as funds "with Pasiōn" (§§7, 8, 35–37, 39, 44).[11] But the same monies are also alluded to as on deposit "at the bank."[12] In the discussion of Demosthenes' father's estate, the bankers Xouthos and Dēmomelēs and their banks are treated as interchangeable.[13] Likewise, funds owed to a bank are described as owed to its individual proprietor.[14]

Since third-party deposits with the bank were perceived as funds entrusted to the banker personally, the bankers tended, not surprisingly, to commingle these deposits with their own personal funds. Deposits totaling eleven talents are employed among fifty talents of "private" loans made by Pasiōn.[15] An advo-

---

[9]Other examples: Hyp., *Ath.* 5; Dem. 36.11, 23, 37, 51; 45.29, 30, 41, 47.

[10]After the text of the lease at Dem. 45.31 (ὀφείλει δὲ Πασίων ἐπὶ τὴν τράπεζαν ἔνδεκα τάλαντα εἰς τὰς παρακαταθήκας), the speaker repeats (§32): προσγέγραπται δὲ τελευταῖον 'ὀφείλει δὲ <u>Πασίων</u> ἔνδεκα τάλαντα εἰς τὰς παρακαταθήκας.' But immediately thereafter he argues: ἔστι δ᾽ ὅστις ἄν, δι᾽ ὃν ὠφειλήκει τοσαῦτα χρήμαθ᾽ ἡ <u>τράπεζα</u>, τούτῳ τὰ λοίπ᾽ ἐπέτρεψεν; (emphasis added).

[11]In every one of these examples, the situs of the bank deposit is described by παρὰ ("with") followed by the appropriate personal reference. Indeed, at §§35–37 Pasiōn personally (οὗτος) agrees to guarantee repayment of a loan from Stratoklēs, although the security for the commitment is money on deposit at the bank, which, of course, itself is personalized as having been placed with the individual banker (εἰ μηδὲν ἔκειτο παρ᾽ αὐτῷ τῶν ἐμῶν, οἴεσθ᾽ κ.τ.λ.).

[12]Isok. 17.44: πολλὰ χρήματ᾽ . . . ἐπὶ τῇ τούτου τραπέζῃ κεῖταί μου, explicitly characterized at §45 as τὴν παρακαταθήκην.

[13]Cf. Dem. 27.11: παρὰ Ξούθῳ for "with Xouthos" = "at the bank of Xouthos"; παρὰ Δημομέλει for "with Dēmomelēs" = "at the bank of Dēmomelēs." On Xouthos and Dēmomelēs, see below, pp. 121–29.

[14]Isok. 17.39: ὁμολογῶ καὶ τούτῳ προσομολογῆσαι τριακοσίας δραχμὰς. Isok. 17.7: ὀφείλοντά με καὶ τούτῳ καὶ ἑτέροις ἐπὶ τόκῳ. Bogaert (1968: 65) correctly terms this a debt "to the bank" ("envers la banque"), despite the Greek text's clear attribution of the asset to the individual banker.

[15]Dem. 36.5: ἀργύριον δὲ πρὸς ταύτῃ δεδανεισμένον ἴδιον πλέον ἢ πεντήκοντα τάλαν-

cate warns that confirmation of claims against a banker might result in the destruction of not only the banker's own assets, but also the assets of other persons—even where the litigation involves charges only against the banker in his personal capacity, not against his bank in its ongoing business operations.[16] In the same context, it is reported that all of the personal assets of Sōsinomos, Timodēmos, and other bankers had been lost when they were unable to repay bank deposits.[17] And in personally collecting large sums owed to his father, Apollodōros uses the bank's records as evidence, confirming again the routine interconnection of personal funds and bank loans.[18] The commingling of personal and banking assets may even have extended to real-estate purchases: Aristolochos the banker is reported to have acquired land "while obligated to numerous persons"—after which these persons came to own the property.[19] There is no suggestion of impropriety on Aristolochos's part: the Athenian fusion of bank and banker into a single judicial and popular identification mandated the almost inevitable loss of some bank deposits as a result of investments that modern systems would term "personal."

The banker's personal network of friends and his prestige as a professional were as significant as even the possession of vast monetary resources.[20] Indeed, banking was so intensely personalized at Athens that business and social relations tended to coalesce. Clients are said to "use" (*khrēsthai*)[21] bankers—the mariner in Demosthenes 33 employs the word to describe his close relationship with the bank of Hērakleidēs. But "use" implied not only a business relationship but also a social intimacy. The son of Sopaios "used" the bank of Pasiōn (Isok. 17.4): when a personal crisis arose (§6) he immediately consulted with Pasiōn, for their relationship was such that he "trusted" the banker "exceedingly, not only about money, but about all other matters as well."[22] In fact,

---

τα. ἐν οὖν τοῖς πεντήκοντα ταλάντοις τούτοις ἀπὸ τῶν παρακαταθηκῶν τῶν τῆς τραπέζης ἔνδεκα τάλαντ' ἐνεργὰ ἦν. See below, pp. 129–36.

[16]Dem. 36.49. For other evidence of Phormiōn's continued activity as a banker after termination of this lease, see Chapter 5, n. 268.

[17]Dem. 36.50: καὶ τὸν Σωσίνομον καὶ τὸν Τιμόδημον καὶ τοὺς ἄλλους τραπεζίτας, οἵ, ἐπειδὴ διαλύειν ἐδέησεν οἷς ὤφειλον, ἐξέστησαν ἁπάντων τῶν ὄντων. Διαλύειν in this context carries the technical meaning "to repay depositors." For analogous transitive meanings of διαλύειν, see Kussmaul 1985: 39.

[18]Dem. 36.20: πολλὰ χρήματ' εἰσέπρακται, γράφων εἰς τὰ ἐγκλήματα "ἔβλαψέ με ὁ δεῖνα οὐκ ἀποδιδοὺς ἐμοὶ τὸ ἀργύριον, ὃ κατέλιπεν ὁ πατὴρ ὀφείλοντα αὐτὸν ἐν τοῖς γράμμασιν."

[19]Dem. 36.50: ποτ' εἶχεν ἀγρόν, εἶτά γε νῦν πολλοί· πολλοῖς γὰρ ἐκεῖνος ὀφείλων αὐτὸν ἐκτήσατο.

[20]Cf. Isok. 17.2: φίλους πολλοὺς κέκτηνται καὶ χρήματα πολλὰ διαχειρίζουσι καὶ πιστοὶ διὰ τὴν τέχνην δοκοῦσιν εἶναι.

[21]Applied to relationships with clients, the basic meaning of the verb is to "use" a person for an end or purpose. See *Liddell-Scott Lexicon*, s.v. "χράομαι." The Greek term does not carry the negative connotation sometimes present in colloquial English "use" of someone.

[22]Isok. 17.4, 6: ἐχρώμην τῇ τούτου τραπέζῃ . . . οὕτω γὰρ οἰκείως πρὸς αὐτὸν δι-

Pasiōn's bank is reported to have been "used" generally by merchants (*emporoi*) at Athens (Dem. 52.3).

Financial "use" of an individual implied close involvement with him in other aspects of life.[23] A passage in Demosthenes 52 (§§20–22) describes, in a commercial context, the business-cum-social relationships implied in "using" (*khrōmenos*) someone. In a dispute over funds on deposit with a banker, Apollodōros asks the jurors to recognize that Lykōn could not have "used" Kallippos since he never involved him in his "matters" (*pragmata*) and was never called upon by Kallippos for assistance in the latter's personal affairs. Throughout an extended commercial dispute, Lykōn never turned to Kallippos, but instead called upon other "friends," including Archebiadēs, who reconciled the disputants. The banker's dealings with Timosthenēs and Timotheos in Demosthenes 49 further illustrate the link between business and social relationships. Timosthenēs, an Athenian citizen engaged in overseas trade, was not only a customer of Pasiōn's bank, but a business partner and intimate of the banker's slave, Phormiōn (§31). On leaving Athens, he had deposited not only money but also two bowls "of Lycian work."[24] When the prominent general Timotheos sought one evening to "borrow" various items, including cloaks, bedding, bowls and cash, needed to entertain visiting dignitaries, he sent his servant to the banker Pasiōn, who lived nearby (§§22–24). Unfortunately, Timosthenēs' two valuable containers were "inadvertently" (*apo tychēs*) lent to Timotheos (who did not return the cash or the bowls), resulting in a comic vignette when Timosthenēs came to claim them, and necessitating some complex financial maneuvering by Pasiōn (§32). This mixture of social and commercial anticipations from "use" of a banker further personalized the *trapeza*. The banker's utilization of household members in bank operations, then, would not only reflect the difficulty of obtaining hired "employees"; it would also conform to the expectations of clients for whom business with the bank meant close involvement with the banker and his associates.

ASSETS, HUMAN AND OTHER

The Athenian bank's business value rested almost entirely upon its "human assets," essentially the proprietor himself and his dependents. Any physical items pertaining to the bank were entirely ancillary, and were immaterial in

---

εκείμην ὥστε μὴ μόνον περὶ χρημάτων ἀλλὰ καὶ περὶ τῶν ἄλλων τούτῳ μάλιστα πιστεύειν.

[23]This dimension is entirely overlooked by Bogaert when he states (1968: 355 n. 293) that the phrase "χρᾶσθαι τῇ τραπέζῃ signifie 'y avoir un compte.'" In fact, a basic meaning of χρᾶσθαι is "to be intimate with" someone, especially with reference to sexual intimacy. See Herod. 1.99; Xen., *Mem.* 1.2.29, 2.1.30; Isaios 3.10; Dem. 59.67. For the Greek-language tendency to extend a multitude of basic verbal concepts into sexual context corresponding to basic meanings, see the list of verbs in Pollux 5.92 and Bain 1991.

[24]On the legal implications of such noncash deposits, see Weiss 1923: 364 n. 31.

comparison to the profit-producing potential of the banker's money-raising and money-management skills,[25] network of relationships, and high credibility,[26] the essence of the banking "operation" (*ergasia*).[27] The banker's own money was not essential: the banking business, in Demosthenes' words, produced revenues "from other people's money."[28] Bion, a student of the fourth-century Athenian philosopher Theophrastos, even commented on Athenian bankers' seemingly total dependence on funds not their own.[29] While some *trapezitai* may have lacked the means to provide even their own operating monies, and thus were unduly vulnerable to financial reversals (see below), a *trapeza*'s value was not dependent on equity provided by a rich owner: the bank of Pasiōn, an incredibly wealthy man,[30] was leased for a substantial rental at a time when Pasiōn, far from having contributed significant private funds, is said to have personally owed eleven talents to the bank.[31]

The possible value of a *trapeza* is shown by the considerable annual rental at which Pasiōn's bank was leased, first to Phormiōn for eight years, then to others for at least ten years (Dem. 36.37). But the tangible assets of an Athenian bank would not have justified any substantial payment. An adversary of Phormiōn makes this clear by rhetorically asking: "Is there anyone who for the counter and the premises and the records would undertake to pay such a rental obligation?"[32] In fact, we now know from the Nikophōn decree (discovered in 1970 in the Athenian agora) that the physical premises of the banks were quite compatible with the etymological origins of the word *trapeza* ("table"): the

---

[25]Dem. 36.57 refers to the enormous sums that could be raised by bankers from third parties: τοσαῦτα γάρ, ὦ ἄνδρες Ἀθηναῖοι, χρήμαθ᾽ ὑμῖν ἀνεγνώσθη προσηυπορηκώς, ὅσ᾽ οὔτ᾽ ἄλλος οὐδεὶς κέκτηται. πίστις μέντοι Φορμίωνι παρὰ τοῖς εἰδόσι καὶ τοσούτων καὶ πολλῷ πλειόνων χρημάτων, δι᾽ ἧς καὶ αὐτὸς αὐτῷ καὶ ὑμῖν χρήσιμός ἐστιν.

[26]A clear summary of these intangible assets is set forth at Isok. 17.2 by a litigant who felt himself disadvantaged by these banking characteristics: Ἔστι δ᾽ . . . πάντων χαλεπώτατον τοιούτων ἀντιδίκων τυχεῖν. Τὰ μὲν γὰρ σομβόλαια τὰ πρὸς τοὺς ἐπὶ ταῖς τραπέζαις ἄνευ μαρτύρων γίγνεται, τοῖς ἀδικουμένοις δὲ πρὸς τοιούτους ἀνάγκη κινδυνεύειν οἳ καὶ φίλους πολλοὺς κέκτηνται καὶ χρήματα πολλὰ διαχειρίζουσι καὶ πιστοὶ διὰ τὴν τέχνην δοκοῦσιν εἶναι. The proper interpretation of συμβόλαια continues to be in dispute: see Kussmaul 1985: esp. 35–39. The term here could refer to either "agreements" (Van Hook's "contracts" [1945] is too limited) or "obligations" ("engagements"; Mathieu and Brémond [1929–42] 1963).

[27]The term ἐργασία was so thoroughly inclusive of the entire banking operation that τραπεζῖται could be described simply as οἱ περὶ τὰς ἐργασίας ὄντες ταύτας (Dem. 36.29). Cf. below, Chapter 5, n. 1.

[28]Dem. 36.11: ἡ δ᾽ ἐργασία προσόδους ἔχουσ᾽ ἐπικινδύνους ἀπὸ χρημάτων ἀλλοτρίων.

[29]Telēs 36.7–8 (ed. Hense²): πῶς δὲ οἱ τραπεζῖται, φησὶν ὁ Βίων, χρημάτων [sc. σπανίζουσιν], ἔχοντες αὐτά; οὐ γὰρ αὐτῶν ὄντα ἔχουσιν.

[30]The amount of Pasiōn's personal fortune has been variously estimated: between 40 and 70 talents in antiquity (see Erxleben 1973: 117); between 35 and 74 talents by modern scholars (Bogaert 1986a: 42).

[31]Dem. 36.4–6. On this passage, see below, pp. 129–36.

[32]Dem. 45.33: ἔστιν οὖν ὅστις ἂν τοῦ ξύλου καὶ τοῦ χωρίου καὶ τῶν γραμματείων τοσαύτην ὑπέμεινε φέρειν μίσθωσιν;

"tables" themselves were so insubstantial that the Tester (*dokimastēs*), a public slave, could be assigned to test monetary silver while seated "among the *trapezai*," and the actual stele, containing the text of the decree, could also be set up "among the *trapezai*."[33] Although the Nikophōn decree itself was uncovered in the northwestern section of the agora,[34] no evidence has been found, despite decades of excavations in the agora, of banking edifices supplementary to the "tables."[35] The disappearance of all traces of the "tables" themselves likely reflects their construction from insubstantial materials.

In most cases, the permanent physical premises of an Athenian bank were probably coextensive with the personal residence of the *trapeza*'s proprietor: we specifically know this to be true in the case of Pasiōn's bank (see Dem. 49.22, 52.8, 52.14). Many professions and crafts (*technai*) are known to have been conducted at home.[36] Since residences even of persons having no connection with the banking business might include substantial security features,[37] there is no reason to believe that valuables and documents would be any less

[33]καθήμενος μεταξὺ τῶν τραπεζῶν (Stroud 1974: 157, ll. 5–6); μεταξὺ τῶν τραπεζῶν (ibid., ll. 44–46). For other tasks of "public slaves" (δημόσιοι, sc. δοῦλοι), see Garlan 1982: 80–81. Cf. Jacob 1926 and [1928] 1979.

[34]Since the stone containing the decree was re-used in the Great Drain, its place of discovery (built into the West Wall of the Great Drain in front of the Royal Stoa) is of little significance in establishing the initial location of the stele and derivatively of the *trapezai*. The decree itself locates the "tables" only "in the city" (ἐν [ἄσ]τει, line 45). Plato, however, situates the "tables" in the agora (*Hippias minor* 368b; *Apol.* 17c), and Stroud (1974: 167) argues for placing the banking tables possibly in the northwest corner of the agora. This appears a reasonable inference, since there is some evidence that stoas were utilized for banking tables (see Bogaert 1968: 186, 231, 253, 375), and a number of stoas appear to have been located in the northwest corner of the agora (Thompson and Wycherley 1972: 171). Threpsiades and Vanderpool (1963: 108–9) place the Stoa of the Herms here (for the possible interconnection of the Herms and the tables, see Theodoretos, *Therapeutika* 12.175.17). Another possible location for the "tables" is the so-called South Stoa I, along the south side of the agora square. See Camp 1986: 122–23.

[35]Much commercial activity, however, appears to have taken place in shops and workrooms located in buildings immediately adjacent to the agora. We know, for example, of establishments belonging to persons involved in finance that were located behind the Stoa Poikilē (Loukianos, *Hetairikoi logoi* 8.2; *Ploion* 13) and at the Diomeian Gate (Alkiphron, *Epistulai* 3.3). This commercial quarter "in a very real sense belonged to and indeed *was* the agora" (Wycherley 1978: 91), and much of it has been explored as part of the ongoing agora excavation.

[36]Jameson 1990b: 185. Aischines (1.124) conjectures that a single house might be used as a business-place and a home in turn by a doctor, a smith, a fuller, and a carpenter, and could even be used as a brothel.

[37]The most characteristic feature of the country house is its tower, intended for domestic security. See Young 1956: 122–46; cf. Osborne 1985: 31–34, 63–67; Pečirka 1973: 123–28. At Dem. 47.56, for a dramatic example, female slaves lock themselves into the tower when the house is attacked by a creditor of the residence's owner. Cf. Pesando 1987: 51, 56. Again, at Thorikos, in the mining area of Attica, homes were built with special attention to security, apparently to protect the silver present at times in the washing-rooms (Jones 1975: 121–22). Similar protective efforts, albeit without the tower, could well be anticipated in town homes. Jameson, analyzing Greek utilization of domestic space, specifically notes that in general "the

secure in such private residences than in separate business edifices: in fact, additional protection would be provided by the continual presence of persons related to the banker.

The equipment utilized in the banking business had little value. There was, of course, the table itself (Isok. 17.12; Dem. 45.33). Transactions might require a scale (Dem. 49.52) or a touchstone (Theophrastos, *On Stones* 45; Theokritos 12. 36–37). An abacus might be used (Lysias, frag. 134; *Anth. Pal.* 9.435).[38] Papyrus rolls (or wax tables) were presumably required for the all-important records of account (Dem. 49.5, 52.4–5); although this material was not inexpensive,[39] even in bulk it did not constitute a monetarily significant capital asset. Not surprisingly, then, the substantial value attributed in Demosthenes 36 to the physical assets of Pasiōn's shield workshop (*aspidopēgion*) is contrasted with the lack of worth applicable to the equipment and location of the bank. The workshop's value was increased by its physical facilities (*ktēma*); the bank's was not. In contrast to the value of the shield facility as a tangible asset, the bank is deprecated as an "operation" dependent on third-party deposits (Dem. 36.11).[40]

But the value of this operation, the capacity to generate revenues from third-party deposits, justifying the payment of substantial rentals,[41] should not be characterized, as it sometimes is,[42] by the term "goodwill." Even in the analysis of modern enterprises, the rubric "goodwill" has little usefulness since it is variable with the nature and content of individual businesses.[43] Unless the underlying asset value of specific concerns has been determined,

---

country house is remarkably similar to the town house . . ." (1990a: 103). There is, then, no basis for Hasebroek's assumption that keeping money in a bank offered greater "external security than keeping it in a private house . . ." (1978: 86 n. 4). Cf. Hasebroek 1920: 116ff.

[38]On the abacus, cf. Lang 1957 and 1964.

[39]In 323/2, a small "tablet," sufficient to record a complex maritime contract, had a value of about 1/24 *dr.* (Dem. 56.1), about 2% of a craftsman's daily wages. (The Eleusinian accounts, from 329/8 and 327/6, record payments to skilled workers of 2 or 2½ *dr.* per day: I.G. II–III² 1672ff.; cf. Chapter 1, n. 92.) For the general cost and use of papyrus in antiquity, see Turner 1968: 5, 181 n. 22; N. Lewis 1934: 154–55.

[40]Dem. 36.11: τὸ μὲν γὰρ κτῆμ' ἀκίνδυνόν ἐστιν, ἡ δ' ἐργασία προσόδους ἔχουσ' ἐπικινδύνους ἀπὸ χρημάτων ἀλλοτρίων.

[41]Not all Athenian *trapezai* possessed such value. The speaker at Dem. 36.51 notes that Phormiōn was able to continue lease payments even when other bankers, μίσθωσιν οὐ φέροντες, ἀλλ' αὐτοὶ ἑαυτοῖς ἐργαζόμενοι, failed.

[42]See Calhoun [1926] 1968: 107; Welles 1970: 806; Hopper 1979: 122. Cf. Davies (1971: 429), who terms Pasiōn's assumption of the bank of Archestratos and Antisthenēs, supposedly without payment, as "an outright gift of goodwill."

[43]The U.S. Accounting Principles Board emphasizes how little an attribute's essence is explained by its characterization as "goodwill": "The excess of the cost of an acquired company over the sum of identifiable net assets, usually called goodwill, is the most common unidentifiable intangible asset" (Opinion no. 17, "Intangible Assets"). Kieso and Weygarndt (1980: 563) note that "goodwill type intangibles may create some right or privilege, but it [sic] is not specifically identifiable, has an indeterminable life, and its cost is inherent in a continuing business."

"goodwill" is relatively meaningless; once such values have been defined, resort to "goodwill" is unnecessary, and perhaps even obfuscating. Moreover, "goodwill" is most likely to be found, and most easily valued, in an "institutional" setting, where successive owners and operators can pay for the reputation and other intangible properties of a business enterprise having an identification and legal existence separate from that of its shareholders and employees. In the highly personalized Athenian bank, real value lay in living, tangible assets—not in persons merely hired for a business function, but in the individuals legally owned and physically controlled by the bank's proprietor.

UNAVAILABLE AND UNDESIRABLE: FREE CITIZENS AS BANK EMPLOYEES

At Athens, citizens were simply not available for "employment" in banks.[44] Although many free Athenians were self-employed in craft or trade—unable or unwilling to attain the philosophically expressed ideal of leisurely dedication to cultural and social activities[45]—they avoided service under others.[46] Employment by a master for brief periods, a day or two, might have been

[44]Some bank proprietors were Athenian citizens, however, sometimes by birth. For example, the banker Aristolochos is known to have been born an Athenian citizen (Davies identifies him with Aristolochos Χαριδήμου (I) Ἐριχιεύς [1971: 60–61]. Cf. Gluskina 1970: 19.) A number of bankers received Athenian citizenship through naturalization (Osborne 1981–83, 4: 196; see below, pp. 88–89). Although for most *trapezitai* we have no direct information as to their place of birth or citizenship, circumstantial factors are sometimes informative. Thus Archestratos provided surety for a non-Athenian (Isok. 17.43). Since such guarantees were accepted only from citizens, Archestratos must have been an Athenian. His associate Antisthenēs also appears to have been an Athenian (Kirchner 1901–3: 1187 and 2405). Antidōros of Phaleron, clearly an Athenian citizen (see I.G. II² 1612, ll. 352ff.; 1622, ll. 128ff.; 1609, l. 70) appears to have been engaged in the banking business with Aristolochos (cf. Davies 1971: 35–36). The banker Blepaios is known to have attended the Assembly, which was restricted to adult male citizens (Dem. 21.215; see above, Chapter 1, n. 89).

[45]But working persons were not entirely absent from cultural pursuits: at his workshop, the shoemaker Simōn, for example, is reported to have discussed philosophical questions with Socrates, a stonemason. See Diogenes Laertios (2.122–23), who claims that Simōn preceded Plato in using the dialogue form to preserve reminiscences of Socrates. (Through a graffito, Simōn's workshop has now been located immediately adjacent to the agora: D. B. Thompson 1960: 234–40; Hock 1976: 41–53.) For the "positive self-assessment of free workers in Athens," see E. C. Welskopf 1980: 23ff.

[46]See Hopper 1979: 140; Finley 1981: 99; Ehrenberg 1962: 162. Rejection of working under a master should not be confused with antipathy about labor itself. For the distinction, and an analysis of its historical basis, see Wood 1988: 126–45, esp. 139. While "metic-status was autonomous, ambiguous, and did not 'naturally' gravitate either down toward slaves or up toward citizens" (Whitehead 1977: 115), metics of free Greek origin would likely have harbored the same attitudes as Athenian citizens toward "servile" employment, and metics of servile origin (if not already independently involved in banking) would have attained their freedom through other skills or for other purposes.

acceptable to a few citizens,[47] but extended service was intolerable: in Aristotle's words, "the nature of the free man prevents his living under the control of another."[48] Even for those unable to support themselves from their own property or from independent craft or business,[49] the availability of public maintenance funds for citizens provided a practical means to avoid employment arrangements considered demeaning: the Athenian state offered paid service in the armed forces, and compensation for frequent jury duty and assembly meetings; for "incapacitated" citizens of limited means, there were outright public grants.[50]

Since ongoing banking operations required regular and repetitive service over an extended period of time, bank employment was inherently incompatible with the "work ethic" of free Athenians. Although in many fields at Athens the same functions might be performed either by slaves or by free persons hired for a specific task or for a limited period of time,[51] in the provision of banking services slave involvement was presumed.[52] When free persons are utilized on bank-related matters, their service is never extended, nor is it exclusive to a single employer: rather, we encounter businessmen working on their own (as in the case of the maritime entrepreneur who introduces a client to the bank of Hērakleidēs [Dem. 33.7]) or agents used for specific purposes (for example,

[47]Although most of those standing daily for hire at Kolonos Agoraios in Athens were slaves, some might have been free men (Pherekratēs, frag. 134 [Edmonds 256]). Cf. Fuks 1951: 171–73.

[48]Aristot., *Rhet.* 1367a33: ἐλευθέρου γὰρ τὸ μὴ πρὸς ἄλλον ζῆν. Cf. Isaios 5.39: τοὺς δὲ περιεώρα εἰς τοὺς μισθωτοὺς ἰόντας δι' ἔνδειαν τῶν ἐπιτηδείων. Cf. also Isok. 14.48; Dem. 57.45; Xen., *Mem.* 2.8.1–5. See also Humphreys 1983c: 10.

[49]For the many Athenian citizens who followed entrepreneurial pursuits, see Thompson 1983. For the place of such activities in the ancient world, see Goody 1986: 177–84.

[50]For welfare payments see Aristot., *Ath. pol.* 49.4 (cf. Lysias 24); for compensation for attendance at the *ekklēsia* and *dikastēria*, see *Ath. pol.* 62.2. In the fourth century, at least 6,000 Athenians (perhaps 20% of the citizen body) attended the Assembly, which lasted only part of the day, with compensation as high as 1½ *dr.*, a sum comparable to earnings otherwise available. Hansen 1987: 14–19, 46–48; Markle 1985: 266; Gallo 1987: 51–52; below, Chapter 1, n. 92. Cf. Jones [1957] 1977: 109 (normal attendance well over 5,000) and (less persuasively) Staveley 1972: 78 (attendance generally only 2,000–3,000). Six thousand jurors received ½ dr. for each day actually served. From the mid-fourth century on, there were forty assemblies annually (Hansen 1987: 23; Ober 1989: 7–8); the courts were probably in session between 150 and 200 days each year (Sinclair 1988: 225). Jameson (1977–78: 124) warns against considering jury service and Assembly attendance "full-time employment." This public funding, however, certainly supplemented resources available to citizens from other sources. In any event, regular presence at Assembly and court would have interfered with employment at a job that demanded daily attendance.

[51]See Ehrenberg 1962: 183, 185. For parallel functioning by slave and free labor in the construction trades, see Randall 1953.

[52]Thus, in questioning whether collateral security had actually been delivered to a bank, a creditor demands to know, "Who brought the copper . . . hired men or slaves?" (εἶτα τίνες ἦσαν οἱ ἐνέγκαντες τὸν χαλκὸν . . . ; μισθωτοὶ ἢ οἰκέται;). But regarding receipt at the bank, the question is limited to slaves: "Which of our slaves was the one receiving [it]?" (τίς ὁ παραλαβὼν τῶν οἰκετῶν τῶν ἡμετέρων;) (Dem. 49.51).

Archestratos's provision of the bond for Pasiōn [Isok. 17.43] or Stephanos's relationship to the banker Aristolochos at Dem. 45.64). In any event, use of Athenian citizens as permanent bank employees would have ill served the banker's business interests; the proprietor's use of his own slaves as staff better reflected the intense identification of the *trapeza* with its proprietor. The handling of customers' affairs by employees who, as part of the proprietor's household (*oikos*), might be accepted as human extensions of the banker himself accords with a client's "use" of an individual *trapezitēs* in a relationship that transcended routine banking transactions (see above). By utilizing his own slaves, too, the *trapezitēs* would be better able to restrict within the banking "house," often his own residence (see above), the private matters and documents entrusted to him, thus better maintaining confidentiality.

Although it was not necessarily less expensive than the use of free employees,[53] using a staff of slaves did minimize the risk of employees' usurpation of client relationships. Because bank transactions, alone among routine commercial activities at Athens,[54] depended on written documentation,[55] staff members involved even in routine transactional matters could not be left illiterate: indeed, bank employees necessarily enjoyed opportunities to develop substantial skills (Dem. 45.71). Since banking personnel other than the proprietor often dealt directly with customers on important and complex matters (see below, pp.74–75), employees might, and did, develop their own relationships with clients.[56] With such skills and connections, free employees would have been able to establish competing banking businesses, a realistic possibility in a state that did not license or otherwise restrict the establishment of *trapezai*. The possibility of purloined customers and independent business relationships is

---

[53]By analogy to more recent conditions in the Western Hemisphere, it has been generally assumed that the primary reason for utilizing slave labor in antiquity was economic, to provide cheap labor (see Wiedemann 1987: 30). Unfree labor, however, appears to have had no inherent cost advantage, especially if appropriate allowance is made for capital investment. See Hopkins 1983: xviii. Analysis here of the nonfinancial advantages of banking slaves confirms other recent studies suggesting that, in classical Greece, utilization of free or slave labor (or a combination) was generally determined by factors far more complex than mere minimization of labor costs. See Garlan 1982: 84–85; Nenci 1978: 1287–1300.

[54]Hasebroek 1923a: 393ff.; Pringsheim 1955: 287–97. Cf. below, pp. 178–79.

[55]Bankers' book entries (τὰ γράμματα) were basic to trapezitic transactions (cf. Dem. 36.20, 21, 36; Dem. 49.43, 44, 59; Dem. 52.5, 19), and bankers' books were proverbially detailed: cf. Hyp., *Dem.*, frag. 2: Καὶ συκοφαντεῖς τὴν βουλήν . . . ἐρωτῶν . . . πόθεν ἔλαβες τὸ χρυσίον καὶ τίς ἦν σοι ὁ δούς, καὶ ποῦ· τελευτῶν δ' ἴσως ἐρωτήσεις καὶ ὅ τι ἐχρήσω λαβὼν τῷ χρυσίῳ, ὥσπερ τραπεζιτικὸν λόγον παρὰ τῆς βουλῆς ἀπαιτῶν. Gluskina even notes that to the extent that written agreements lacked "notarial validity as proof," the proprietor's "personal and professional" dependence on his slaves would increase (1970: 43). For the special evidentiary significance accorded in litigation to bankers' business records, see below, Chapter 5, n. 57.

[56]Thus Menexenos and the son of Sopaios were allegedly able to "persuade" Kittos, a bank employee, to advance six talents to them, apparently without authorization by the bank proprietor (Isok. 17.12). See below.

confirmed by Pasiōn's insistence on a "noncompetition" covenant even in leasing his bank to Phormiōn, his own former slave and trusted assistant.[57] And on his deathbed, Pasiōn felt even this legal protection insufficient: he determined that "the only salvation" for the bank, and for his family's economic position, lay in returning Phormiōn legally to the family, as guardian of his minor child and husband of his widow.[58]

Phormiōn's situation was not unique. The practical impossibility and commercial undesirability of utilizing free labor in the Athenian bank made the slave-owning *trapezitēs* dependent on his enslaved banking staff, a reliance that would have increased as age limited the proprietor's own capacity to conduct business (cf. Dem. 46.13, 49.30). Opportunities for the bankers' slaves to advance often resulted, as "strictly personal" businesses, for strictly selfish reasons,[59] became "family" operations, uniting bankers' slaves and wives.

SLAVES AND WIVES

[At Athens] men and women purchased as slaves are no
less free than their purchasers. And in the relationships of
women to men and of men to women, how much equality
through law, and liberty is developing!
—Plato, criticizing fourth-century Athens[60]

It has now become dogma that at Athens virtually every citizen was a slave owner,[61] functioning in a "patriarchal" society that has been seen as more brutal and exploitative than modern repressive cultures,[62] a tyranny of male

[57]The lease document, although exceedingly brief, specifically forebade Phormiōn to pursue banking activity on his own account. Dem. 45.31: μὴ ἐξεῖναι δὲ τραπεζιτεῦσαι χωρὶς Φορμίωνι, ἐὰν μὴ πείσῃ τοὺς παῖδας τοὺς Πασίωνος. Cf. §34.

[58]Dem. 36.30: Πασίων . . . μόνην ὁρῶν σωτηρίαν τοῖς ἑαυτοῦ πράγμασιν, εἰ τοῦτον [sc. Φορμίωνα] ἀνάγκη ποιήσειεν οἰκεῖον ὑμῖν.

[59]Similarly, it has been conjectured that Roman slaves engaged in commercial pursuits often received their freedom primarily for the slave-owners' business advantage. See F. W. Wilson 1935: 66; Meiggs 1973: 224; Hopkins 1978: 123, 129–32.

[60]*Republic* 8.563b (written sometime in the first half of the fourth century): οἱ ἐωνημένοι καὶ αἱ ἐωνημέναι μηδὲν ἧττον ἐλεύθεροι ὦσι τῶν πριαμένων. ἐν γυναιξὶ δὲ πρὸς ἄνδρας καὶ ἀνδράσι πρὸς γυναῖκας ὅση ἡ ἰσονομία καὶ ἐλευθερία γίγνεται.

[61]"Dependent labour systems were bound to be prevalent in the ancient world, given the low level of productivity. . . . In classical Athens, where the price of a slave was equivalent only to the cost of maintaining him for one to two years, all but the very poor could afford to own at least one slave" (Garnsey 1980: 1). Starr (1958) dissents from the dogma, finding slavery less prevalent and less significant than posited by the prevailing orthodoxy (but see Degler 1959 and Oliva 1960). Cf. Wood 1988. (In recent years, interest in ancient slavery has been extremely high: the *Bibliographie zur Antiken Sklaverei* [1983], although incomplete, still lists 5,162 separate items. The best bibliographical survey remains Brockmeyer's *Antike Sklaverei* [1979].)

[62]It is generally agreed that Athenian society was "an extremely patriarchal one in theory, not only legal theory but the generally accepted social understanding of the people" (Schaps 1979:

citizens in which women and slaves (*douloi*)[63] were equally without rights and similarly victimized.[64] Athenian banking did involve both bankers' wives and enslaved banking employees, and not surprisingly attributed to them identical legal status: the banker was "master" (*kyrios*) of both his slaves and his wife.[65] But though the roles of wife and slave were indeed important and in fact interrelated, their actual situations were far more complex than the stereotype of exploitation that might be anticipated.

The banker's slaves routinely performed critical functions, independently handling substantial sums of money (Dem. 45.72). Slaves would receive and evaluate security for loans (Dem. 49.52). Deposits, in cash and in valuables, and in sizeable amounts, might be received by *douloi* alone, who could freely dispose of such items without supervision (Dem. 49.31). Indeed, a slave functionary at Pasiōn's bank was "persuaded" by clients to disburse the substantial sum of 36,000 *dr*. (Isok. 17.12). Despite the legal focus in subsequent litigation

---

96; cf. Pomeroy 1975: 58). Athenian patriarchy in practice was yet more "severe and crass" than that of modern "patriarchal industrial societies" (Keuls 1985: 12), although societal male-dominance in actual practice might have been substantially modified by power yielded indirectly by women through personal and economic relationships (as Schaps argues [1979: 92–96]; Gallo [1984] similarly seeks to clarify possible differences between legal theory and social reality). For an overview of women's role in democratic Athens, see Lacey 1968: 151–76, with bibliographical reference at p. 300 n. 1 to earlier contributions.

[63]Although Roman law defines all persons as either free or slave—there is no other category (Just., *Inst.* 1.3.)—in ancient Greece the great variety of personal statuses in the various political entities (cf. Pollux 3.73–83) has generated inconsistency in modern terminology. For example, the phrase "serf" is used to describe the unfree Spartan "helot" group. Since the word "slave" is derived from the mediaeval term for war captives of Slavic or Eastern European origin and bears more recent, racially oriented connotations, Lauffer (1961) has suggested that historians not employ the word "slave" for unfree persons in ancient Greece. Although Finley has warned that another term, even a Greek word, would soon engender its own connotations (see Finley 1975: 63–64), such associations would at least derive from the ancient Greek rather than the modern world. To denote unfree persons in Athens, therefore, I here freely interchange "slave" and *doulos* (δοῦλος; plural *douloi*), the basic Greek word for "slave." I use the English as a reminder that we are describing actual "unfree persons" and not merely a specialized juridical status, the Greek as a reminder that the "unfree persons" appear in a specific historical context.

[64]See (already in 1923) Wright [1923] 1969: 1. Cf. Vidal-Naquet 1986: 206–7; Cantarella 1987: 38; Schuller 1985: passim. Ancient literature in general stereotypically attributes to women and slaves similar negative attributes (see Just 1985). Keuls argues that "the two categories" (slave and wife) are explicitly connected at Athens through "a considerable number of references and symbols": for example, "the legal term for wife was *damar*, a word derived from a root meaning 'to subdue' or 'to tame.' " (1985: 6). Aristotle treated women and slaves together: the woman's inferiority possibly was to be contrasted with the slave's utter worthlessness (*Poetics* 1454a21–2: καίτοι γε ἴσως τούτων τὸ μὲν χεῖρον, τὸ δὲ ὅλως φαῦλόν ἐστιν).

[65]"Master," rather than "guardian," is generally accepted as the closest modern equivalent to κύριος. See the comments by Wolff (whose mother tongue was German) 1944: 46–47 n. 22. Since the Athenian *kyrios* can only be understood in the context of the *oikos* (where the wife had considerable responsibility for management and supervision; see below), the word probably is best left transliterated, rather than translated into modern languages that have no approximate equivalents.

on whether the customers had obtained a legitimate advance or had "stolen" the monies,[66] from an economic perspective the striking aspect of this vignette is that a *doulos* independently, without his banker-owner's involvement, had the power to effectuate so large a monetary transaction. Indeed, much of the discussion in Isokrates 17 relates to legal complications arising from the conduct of important trapezitic business by slaves.[67] Pasiōn himself, while still a slave, had gained the confidence of his masters by handling banking matters requiring integrity and discretion.[68]

Similarly, the slave-manager of Pasiōn's bank (Dem. 45.33) routinely acted on his own, even in complex, sometimes disputed matters. Thus, pursuant to a loan request from an Athenian general (Dem. 49.6), Phormiōn delivered loan proceeds to one of the commander's financial assistants (Dem. 49.7)—a disbursement for which the general later denied personal responsibility and refused repayment (Dem. 49.4, 44). The same slave deals directly with the official representative at Athens of a foreign city (Dem. 52.5) and has control of the bank's all-important books of record (*ta grammata*) (Dem. 52.6, 29). On his own he pays out to a third party the 1,640-odd drachmas that had been the object of interest for a foreign *proxenos* (Dem. 52.7). Slaves are even reported to have been dispatched to deal with foreign potentates concerning significant bank deposits at Athens by their nationals.[69] On other occasions, items involving the utmost discretion are handled by slave-bankers acting in conjunction with the bank's proprietor (e.g., Dem. 49.17, 29).

Pursuant to formalized contractual arrangements, slaves actually operated

---

[66]Under Athenian law, the "bribery" of Kittos (διαφθείραντες αὐτόν), resulting in bank assets being taken against the will of the bank's owner, would have constituted "theft" (κλοπή), a criminal offense; "persuasion" (πείσαντες αὐτόν) would have permitted only a noncriminal claim for return of the funds. See Dem. 21.44–45 for this Athenian differentiation between private contractual disputes (where by mutual consent a party obtains money and then fails to repay it) and offenses involving the state (i.e., "criminal" acts), characterized for Demosthenes by a taking of funds contrary to the will of the owner (βίᾳ δὲ τοῦτ' ἀφέληται). Definitional problems are inherent in a legal system's attempts to distinguish between the criminal act and the commercial contractual dispute; for the Athenian treatment of this issue (with consideration of how it is handled in other systems), see D. Cohen 1983: 10–33. Isokrates 17 itself provides good examples of the Athenian court speakers' tendency to present contractual dispute as the rhetorical equivalent of "theft" (cf. ibid., p. 23).

[67]Because of the pivotal role of Kittos (τὸν παῖδα ὅς συνῄδει περὶ τῶν χρημάτων . . . αὐτὸν ἐπὶ τῇ τραπέζῃ καθήμενον, Isok. 17.11–12) and his alleged status as a slave, evidentiary procedures available only for use with unfree persons, including interrogation by torture, were sought by the banker's adversary (Isok. 17.13).

[68]Dem. 36.43: παρὰ τοῖς αὑτοῦ κυρίοις Ἀντισθένει καὶ Ἀρχεστράτῳ τραπεζιτεύουσι πεῖραν δοὺς ὅτι χρηστός ἐστι καὶ δίκαιος, ἐπιστεύθη.

[69]Isok. 17.51. Although Kittos is said to have claimed that he had obtained his freedom by the time he undertook a mission to the Bosporan kingdom, the speaker insists that he remained a slave: only if *douloi* normally undertook such missions could the speaker credibly insist both that Kittos was a slave (a fact important to the speaker's case) and that Kittos had undertaken this important representation.

entire banking businesses. Pasiōn's bank, perhaps the largest Athenian trapezitic operation,[70] was operated initially by Pasiōn as successor to his own
masters, and later by his own former slave, Phormiōn. In noting explicitly (at
Dem. 36.4) that Phormiōn had already obtained his freedom when he entered
into operating leases giving him complete control of the bank and of a shield
workshop, the speaker clearly implies that slave status would not have barred
him from entering into these substantial obligations; otherwise, the mere fact of
his being lessee of the businesses would have established his status as free. And
we know that even as a slave having significant banking authority and responsibility, Phormiōn conducted maritime trading activities as a principal.[71] Even
more strikingly, Phormiōn was succeeded at the bank by four individuals—
Xenōn, Euphraios, Euphrōn, and Kallistratos—who entered into a lease with
their own masters, the bank's owners, and for ten years paid rent of a full talent
per year conducting this major banking business (Dem. 36.13, 37)—while still
slaves.[72]

But commercial contractual arrangements were not the only path to bank
proprietorship for *douloi*: often a banker would, on his death, entrust both his
bank and his wife to a slave-successor (see below). Although such an arranged
marriage might have been intended solely as a property transfer (with the
widow's personal attributes of no importance), the operation of the Athenian
bank through the banker's household, especially when it was physically situated in the residence itself, would have encouraged the development of personal
relationships between slave and nonslave members of the banker's retinue.
Indeed, Phormiōn's involvement with Pasiōn's family, even before Pasiōn's
death, was so close that he was accused of having fathered a child, Pasiklēs,
born during the banker's lifetime to Pasiōn's wife, Archippē (Dem. 45.84).[73]
"Friendship" between males and females dependent on their master conforms

---

[70]Even Thompson, who sees banks as "insignificant" in the Athenian economy, recognizes
the significance of "the lendable deposits (and) private resources of a tycoon like Pasion"
(Thompson 1979: 240).

[71]See Dem. 49.31, where Timosthenēs, active in overseas commerce (ἀφικνεῖται κατ᾽ ἐμπορίαν ἰδίαν ἀποδημῶν), is characterized as Phormiōn's κοινωνός at a time when Phormiōn
was still a *doulos*. Κοινωνός is difficult to translate: although it often approximates the word
"partner" as popularly used in English, the legal attributes of partnership under Anglo-American
law (especially automatic joint liability) are entirely absent from Athenian life and law. See E. M.
Harris 1989: 339, esp. nn. 1 and 2. At other times, the word takes on a connotation closer to
"participant" (one of a group of individuals engaged in a commercial or other enterprise). Such
collective undertakings (*koinōniai*) were common at Athens. See Endenburg 1937; Ziebarth
1896; Pantazopoulos 1946. Davies (1971: 432) sees "Phormiōn's later activity as a shipowner"
as having its "roots" in this earlier business involvement in maritime trade.

[72]Only later did their owners ἐλευθέρους ἀφεῖσαν ("enfranchised them," Dem. 36.14; see
Harrison, 1968–71, 1: 175 n. 2) . See below for an analysis of the legal bases supporting slaves'
capacity to enter into business contracts juridically cognizable at Athens.

[73]Archippē's background has defied meaningful elucidation. Even her nationality and ultimate
receipt of Athenian citizenship present conundra unresolved in studies as early as Paley and
Sandys [1896] 1979 (in which it is suggested [xxxviii and 144n.] that she was non-Athenian, a

to modern models for nonhierarchical relationships:[74] in striking confirmation of the perceived equivalence between slaves and wives, newly purchased *douloi* and newly wed brides were welcomed into the Athenian household with the same ceremony (*katachysmata*).[75]

In any event, Archippē was thoroughly conversant with trapezitic business: she had access to the bank's records, and detailed knowledge of its complex operations. The extent to which Pasiōn's personal monies were utilized to fund loans, the use by the bank of proprietor's "capital" (*aphormē*), the legal arrangements under which the bank was leased during Pasiōn's lifetime, the terms of rental to successor lessees after his death—"all this" Archippē was knowledgeable about, "with specificity."[76] Indeed, after her husband's death, Archippē had such control over the bank's records that she was even accused of having destroyed them, allegedly to prevent the development of legal claims against Pasiōn's successor, her second husband Phormiōn.[77] Again, even in the absence of quantifiable evidence for the number of bankers' wives who had access to such information or control of such records, the mere presentation of this charge in an Athenian court presupposes the jurors' anticipated acceptance of the scenario as reasonably likely in actual practice.

It appears to have been commonplace for women to have knowledge of their male relatives' business and lending practices. The wife of Diodotos, for example, was familiar with his financial resources and dealings (Lysias 32.5), and after his death was able to produce documentary proof (*grammata*) of her husband's investment of seven talents and forty mnai in maritime loans, despite her own father's efforts to purloin these records (ibid., §§7, 14). At the time of her husband's death, she personally possessed at least 2,000 *dr.* and 30 staters (ibid., §15), and she exhibited detailed knowledge of Diodotos's financial affairs while persuasively refuting allegations concerning his estate (§§15–18).[78] Similarly, in a complex case involving substantial financial assets, largely hidden,[79] the defendants insist that it is, *inter alia*, the death of the plaintiffs' mother, "who was knowledgeable of all these matters," that permit-

---

suggestion that is not supported by Dem. 46.23) and as recent as Carey 1991. See below, pp. 103–6.

[74]Foucaultian descriptive and feminist ideological models both anticipate such association: see Foucault's comments (1984: 381–82) and Dreyfus and Rabinow 1983: 233. Cf. Ackelsberg 1983, and Diamond and Quinby 1988: passim. In comedy, slaves, free women, and children are portrayed as allies in contesting free adult male authority. See Humphreys 1983c: 76 n. 6.

[75]On the introduction of slaves, see below, n. 121. For brides, see Licht [1932] 1953: 42–56; Ehrenberg 1962: 194 n. 1.

[76]Dem. 36.14: ἡ πάντ' ἀκριβῶς ταῦτ' εἰδυῖα.

[77]Dem. 36.18: τὰ γράμμαθ' ἡ μήτηρ ἠφάνικε πεισθεῖσ' ὑπὸ τούτου, καὶ τούτων ἀπολωλότων οὐκ ἔχει τίνα χρὴ τρόπον ταῦτ' ἐξελέγχειν ἀκριβῶς.

[78]The verbally persuasive skills of Athens's female "companions" (*hetairai*) have long been recognized. Dimakis even envisions these women as contributing to the redaction of speeches by leading orators and *logographoi* (1988: 43).

[79]Dem. 38.7: τὴν οὐσίαν Ξενοπείθης καὶ Ναυσικράτης ἅπασαν χρέα κατέλιπον, καὶ φανερὰν ἐκέκτηντο μικράν τινα.

ted the plaintiffs to proceed with their improper claims (Dem. 38.6). And when creditors went to a debtor's farm in an attempt to seize his property when he was absent, his wife was able to disclose to them that their efforts were unnecessary since the funds owed were on deposit "at the bank" (Dem. 47.57).

Although gender-derived differentiations created serious barriers to a woman's direct vindication of legal rights (see below), and hence indirect obstacles to full business involvement, no social or legal prohibitions absolutely precluded a wife's direct participation in banking activities outside the home. Husbands and wives are known to have worked together in retailing activities.[80] Many goods were sold by women, especially in the agora where the bankers' "tables" were set.[81] Consumer trade in certain commodities, perfumes for example, was actually dominated by female retailers.[82] Even the Eleusinian treasurers dealt with at least two women (I.G. II²1672, ll. 64, 71), purchasing from one of them, a certain Artemis of Piraeus, reeds for building materials having a value of at least 70 *dr.*[83] This commercial freedom necessarily reflected, as Aristotle recognized, the practical impossibility of keeping poor women from earning money in the public sphere of commerce.[84] But in the prosperous, established households, it was deemed important to restrict severely women's public activity.[85] To the extent that bankers and their customers shared or acquired these elite values, the wives of the *trapezitai* would have found it increasingly difficult to engage directly and openly in the banking business.

Accordingly, although we know of hundreds of loans extended by men (see above, p. 28), very few women are known to have functioned as principals in extending credit. Aristophanes, in the *Thesmophoriazusai* (839–45), describes Hyperbolos's mother as engaged in lending money at interest; although this reference is contained in a comic sally, similar lending by a woman is mentioned in a sober court presentation (Dem. 41.7–9, 21). There, the wife of Polyeuktos is reported to have lent Spoudias 1,800 *dr.* at interest: on her death,

[80]S.I.G.³ 1177 = I.G. III¹, app. 69 (Artemis the gilder working in a shop with Dionysios the helmet-maker); I.G. II² 1561, ll. 22–30 (two sesame-sellers: see Schaps 1979: 61).

[81]See Herfst (1922: 40–48), who enumerates, with source reference, the variegated types of goods retailed by women. Cf. Balabanoff 1905, and Lewy 1885: passim. Females were so active in the agora that they "seem to have had, if not a monopoly, at least a privileged position in the market-place" (Lacey 1968: 171). There is, however, no basis for Becker's belief (1877–88, 2: 199–202) that a particular section of the agora, the *gynaikeia agora*, was reserved for female merchants, rather than for goods intended for women.

[82]Pherekratēs, frag. 64 Kock. But there were male perfume-sellers. See Athenaios 13.612a–e (= Lysias, frag. 1 Thalheim), 15.687a.

[83]But these same records (I.G. II² 1672–73) reveal scores of transactions with men.

[84]Aristot., *Pol.* 4.15, 1300a6–7: πῶς γὰρ οἶόν τε κωλύειν ἐξιέναι τὰς τῶν ἀπόρων; 6.8, 1323a: τοῖς γὰρ ἀπόροις ἀνάγκη χρῆσθαι καὶ γυναιξὶ καὶ παισὶν ὥσπερ ἀκολούθοις διὰ τὴν ἀδουλίαν.

[85]See, for example, Aristoph. *Thes.* 425, 519, 783ff.; Aristot., *Oik.* 1343b7–1344a22 (1.3–4); Xen., *Oik.* 7.33; Lysias 3.6; Theophr., *Char.* 28.

her own records (*grammata*) survived as evidence of the transaction. (This does not appear to have been an isolated transaction: the speaker in Demosthenes 41 implies that he himself had borrowed money from the woman.) A woman is even reported on a fragmentary *horos*-inscription as one of the lenders in a real-estate financing.[86] Women participated in bank-related matters independent of a familial role. In one of the few instances in which information has survived regarding the circumstances that generated a specific bank deposit, it is a woman, Antigona, who induces a would-be business purchaser to marshal the substantial funds, forty mnai, deposited in a *trapeza* as an apparent "good-faith deposit." Even her adversary recognizes her leading role in this complex financial transaction.[87] Although such examples are rare, it is not their frequency but their possibility that is important.

Women could operate as principals in loan transactions because by the fourth century, in actual practice (if not initially in legal theory), they were often recognized as the true owners of property. A vignette preserved in our sources confirms this: a woman confronts creditors seizing her husband's assets and forbids them to touch various items of property, because they are hers (*hautēs*), not her husband's.[88] Modern scholars may argue that these assets, part of her dowry, actually were "owned" by her husband, as her "master" (*kyrios*), or by another male relative, as protector of her interest;[89] but confronted by her husband's creditors, she asserted not her male relatives' ownership, but her own.

Because of the highly confidential nature of Athenian banking, related to the widespread utilization of the banks to "hide" property and funds,[90] knowledge of bank transactions itself attested to the holder's critical position in the bank operation. Possession of such information by slaves and wives—and more importantly, the power to act on the information—joined them to the bank's proprietor in a pivotal economic function. In an environment of personal, not institutionalized, banking businesses dependent on the skills of the owners' slaves, in a city whose legal and social structure permitted independent business activity by *douloi*, where bankers' spouses had detailed knowledge of bank activities and were potentially able to resolve business-related personal conflicts,[91] a *trapezitēs* could seek to preserve his business by installing a

[86]Fine 1951: no. 28. Cf. Finley [1951] 1985: 188.

[87]Hyp., *Ath.* §§4–5. On the form of the bank placement, see below, pp. 119–20.

[88]Dem. 47.57: τὰ δ' ἐκ τῆς ἄλλης οἰκίας ἐξέφερον σκεύη, ἀπαγορευούσης τῆς γυναικὸς μὴ ἅπτεσθαι αὐτοῖς, καὶ λεγούσης ὅτι αὑτῆς εἴη ἐν τῇ προικὶ τετιμημένα.

[89]See Schaps 1979: 4–16; Harrison 1968–71, 1: 236; Sealey 1990: 38–39; Ste. Croix 1970: 276–77. I discuss below the considerations through which women's right to own property came to be accepted, and the social reality underlying these adaptations.

[90]Bogaert notes this prevailing practice matter-of-factly: ". . . im 4. Jahrhundert benutzte man die Banken, um einen Teil seiner Einkünfte vor dem Fiskus zu verbergen, auf griechisch ἀφανίζειν" (1986b: 16). See below, pp. 202–7.

[91]A striking example: although Apollodōros and Phormiōn avoided legal disputes during Ar-

highly regarded slave as his successor—and might even, upon the principal's death, unite his wife in marriage with his slave-successor. This means of succession is clear and well attested. The speaker at Dem. 36.29 calls upon the jurors' personal knowledge: "anyone could cite many examples" of slaves who had been freed by their owners, entrusted with the master's bank, and married at the owner's direction to his widow.[92] Indeed, the speaker insists that many of the jurors were personally aware that, just as in the case of Phormiōn's bank, Sōkratēs, "that well-known banker," had provided for the marriage of his wife to his former slave, Satyros—in fact, Sōkratēs himself had been freed by his masters and (the speaker implies) established as the head of their bank. Another example: the Athenian banker Sōklēs similarly had given his wife to Timodēmos, formerly Sōklēs' *doulos*.

This trapezitic practice was not limited to Athens.[93] In Aigina, for example, Strymodōros had married his wife to Hermaios, "his own slave"; after she died, the banker again provided for the marriage of his own daughter to the former slave.[94] Although editors have not embraced the obvious implication that the Aiginetan banker had transferred his wife along with his bank during his own lifetime,[95] the "plain meaning" of the text clearly illustrates the speaker's insistence on the need for bankers, in protecting banking assets, to behave in a manner appropriate for bank proprietors, even if unacceptable by conventional social values.[96] This information is provided in a defense of Phormiōn's behavior, and more particularly in defense of the authenticity of legal documents (Pasiōn's purported will and the alleged text of the bank's lease to Phormiōn)

---

chippē's lifetime, immediately upon her death—allegedly because of the removal of her detailed knowledge of the bank's arrangements—litigation commenced. See Dem. 36.14.

[92]οὐδ' αὐτὸν λέληθεν, οὐδ' ὑμῶν πολλούς, ὅτι Σωκράτης ὁ τραπεζίτης ἐκεῖνος, παρὰ τῶν κυρίων ἀπαλλαγεὶς ὥσπερ ὁ τούτου πατήρ, ἔδωκε Σατύρῳ τὴν ἑαυτοῦ γυναῖκα, ἑαυτοῦ ποτὲ γενομένῳ. ἕτερος Σωκλῆς. . . . καὶ οὐ μόνον ἐνθάδε ταῦτα ποιοῦσιν οἱ περὶ τὰς ἐργασίας ὄντες ταύτας . . . ἀλλ' ἐν Αἰγίνῃ. . . . καὶ πολλοὺς ἄν ἔχοι τις εἰπεῖν τοιούτους (Dem. 36.28–29).

[93]Another famous slave-banker is Hermias, who succeeded his master, Euboulos, in the banking business and apparently also as "tyrant" of Assos and Atarneus, towns on the Aiolic coast of Asia Minor, near the island of Lesbos. See Strabo 13.1.57, 67; S.I.G. 229 = Tod 1948: no. 165. Since Hermias is said to have been a eunuch (see Wormell 1935: 55ff., and Bidez 1943: 133ff.), not surprisingly there is no tradition saying that he also received Euboulos's widow in marriage. However, Hermias did arrange the marriage of his niece and adopted daughter, Pythias, to Aristotle, under whom he had studied in Athens and who later resided at Assos between 348/7 and 345/4. Cf. Diogenes Laertios 5.3.

[94]καὶ τελευτησάσης ἐκείνης ἔδωκε πάλιν τὴν θυγατέρα τὴν ἑαυτοῦ. The text clearly states that Strymodōros gave both his wife and his daughter in marriage to Hermaios.

[95]It has even been suggested that the first arrangement was only planned, not effectuated, and was in fact preempted when Strymodōros's wife predeceased him, or that the "original will contained the proviso 'and if my wife shall die' " (Pearson 1972: 226).

[96]Dem. 36.30: τοῖς γένει πολίταις, οὐδὲ ἕν' πλῆθος χρημάτων ἀντὶ τοῦ γένους καλόν ἐστιν ἑλέσθαι· τοῖς δὲ . . . τῇ τύχῃ δ' ἐξ ἀρχῆς ἀπὸ τοῦ χρηματίσασθαι καὶ ἑτέρων πλείω κτήσασθαι καὶ αὐτῶν τούτων ἀξιωθεῖσιν, ταῦτ' ἐστὶν φυλακτέα.

that together provided for Pasiōn's former slave to exercise substantial control over Pasiōn's banking assets during his lifetime and, at his death, to become his widow's second husband and guardian of his minor child. Although the jurors might be aware that such arrangements were not unusual for bankers, the speaker still felt it necessary to explain their appropriateness in social and business context: citizens by birth ought not to choose "piles of cash" (*plēthos khrēmatōn*) over pedigree; bankers fortunate enough to have obtained wealth through their trapezitic activities, and citizenship as a "gift," were obligated to protect their assets (Dem. 36.30).

These normative values are confirmed throughout the history of the best-attested Athenian banking business, the *trapeza* operated by Pasiōn from the 390s until the late 370s. Prior to 394,[97] this bank had belonged to Antisthenēs and Archestratos: Pasiōn, their successor, had been their slave (Dem. 36.43, 46, 48). Although we know that Antisthenēs had at least one son, Antimachos, apparently an individual of reasonably good reputation,[98] Pasiōn's "diligence" (*philergia*) and "integrity" (*khrēsotēs*) were said to have won him the bank (Dem. 36.43–44).[99] In turn, Pasiōn during his lifetime entered into a lease of his banking business to his own slave, Phormiōn[100]—although at the time of the transaction Pasiōn's eldest son, Apollodōros, was already an adult and possibly was about the same age as Phormiōn.[101] After Pasiōn's death, and after Phormiōn had operated the bank under lease for eight years, the bank

[97]Pasiōn was already fully established as a τραπεζίτης before August 394, when Konōn prevailed in the naval battle at Knidos. See Isok. 17.43. Cf. Mathieu and Brémond [1929–42] 1963, 1: 83 n. 2.

[98]Antimachos was still alive in 351/50 (the date of Dem. 36: see Isager and Hansen 1975: 177), but was not prospering "as he deserved" (Dem. 36.45: πράττων οὐ κατ᾽ ἀξίαν).

[99]Reputation was critical to banking success, since transactions were effectuated without witnesses (Isok. 17.2). See above, n. 55, and below, pp. 178–79.

[100]Dem. 36.4, 11, 37; 45.31–32. The lease was entered into with Phormiōn ἤδη καθ᾽ ἑαυτὸν ὄντι.

[101]Apollodōros was born in 395/4 (cf. Dem. 36.22, 46.13). Although we do not know Phormiōn's date of birth, he was accused by Apollodōros of having fathered Pasiklēs (born not earlier than 380: Schäfer 1885–87, 3: 132), and by 373 he was handling significant matters for the bank (Dem. 45.33, 49.17). From these indicia, Phormiōn's birthdate has been inferred as about 410 (Gaspars 1943: 47, cited in Bogaert 1968: 74 n. 73) or "by 400 at the latest" (Davies 1971: 431). But this evidence is equally compatible with a somewhat later birth date. We know of "teenagers" undertaking important economic and legal matters at Athens; for example, Demosthenes handled substantial claims against his guardians while not more than 18 years old and successfully conducted major litigation against them shortly thereafter. Women at Athens were expected to commence sexual activity at an early age, extremely so by modern Western standards: women were normally married by fourteen or fifteen. (See Garland 1990: 21; Keuls 1985: 103; cf. Lacey 1968: 107 ["not later than about sixteen"]; Pollux 8.107 [s.v. φράτορες"]. For even earlier marriage in the Roman world, see Plut., *Lykurgos and Numa* 4.1–3; Rousselle 1983: 32–33.) In a society where slaves and wives were assimilated in other contexts, there should be nothing surprising about a charge (even an unfounded one: see Davies 1971: 429) of sexual misconduct between a banker's wife and a teenage *doulos*.

was leased again to slave-assistants, one of whom, Euphraios, actually had been employed at the bank even prior to its lease to Phormiōn (see above, p. 76).[102]

These slave-bankers acquired great wealth, power, and social prestige, as a virtually inevitable result of the unique nature of the Athenian *trapeza* and its special place in the economy. The bankers then used these accoutrements to establish their own quasitraditional households.

THE BANKING HOUSEHOLD: A TRADITIONAL FORM TRANSFORMED

By the middle of the fourth century, the banker Phormiōn was among the most powerful benefactors of the Athenian state, a titan of wealth and prestige. When Demosthenes, already a prominent political leader, and scion of a prominent Athenian family, prepared his important speech *Against Meidias*, he sought to equate his own financial contributions to the city with those of the "wealthiest" Athenians, naming Phormiōn, the former slave, first among a trinity of "leading" citizens (*hēgemones*).[103]

The other two named by Demosthenes, Lysitheidēs and Kallaischros, were Athenians of the highest standing. Lysitheidēs is explicitly characterized as *kalos k' agathos* (Dem. 52.30), an epithet appropriate to aristocratic delineation. Already before 353, he had received the high honor of a crown from the state for his public benefactions (Isok. 15.94). In the mid-fourth century, he appears to have been a substantial landowner in the mining regions of Attica:[104] this real estate may have been the basis of his fortune. Although Kallaischros also has been identified as having significant mining interests, his wealth and prestige likely derived principally from his family, to which Solon the Athenian lawgiver and Plato the philosopher themselves belonged, an *oikos* enriched by prosperous marriage arrangements.[105]

---

[102]Along with Phormiōn, Euphraios had disbursed loan funds to Timotheos in 373 at Pasiōn's direction (Dem. 49.44). See Bongenaar 1933: 207.

[103]Dem. 21.157: ἡγεμὼν συμμορίας ὑμῖν ἐγενόμην ἐγὼ ἔτη δέκα, ἴσον Φορμίωνι καὶ Λυσιθείδῃ καὶ Καλλαίσχρῳ καὶ τοῖς πλουσιωτάτοις. For identification of this Phormiōn with his homonyme, the banker, see Kirchner 1901–3, 2: 392; Davies 1971: 436; MacDowell 1990: 376. Cf. below, pp. 176–78.

[104]See *Hesperia* 19 (1950): 210, no. 5, line 55; p. 219, no. 6, line 110; p. 236, no. 14, lines 5–6. Cf. Crosby's restoration (1950: 277, no. 29, lines 4 and 7–8) of Lysitheidēs' children as owners of land at Thorikos. Again, near the middle of the fourth century, Lysitheidēs' son Lysikratēs is named as the owner of real estate at Laureion (ibid., p. 210, no. 5, line 49).

[105]Kallaischros, while a relatively rare name, is not so uncommon as to permit family attribution only on an onomastic basis. Davies (1971: 591) suggests identification of the ἡγεμών in Dem. 21.157 with the head of a family with silver-mining interests. This Kallaischros had served as a trierarch some years earlier (I.G. II² 1609, line 27). His name can probably be restored on two fragmentary mining texts dating from near the middle of the fourth century: as a registrant for a mine (*Hesperia* 19 [1950]: 210, no. 5, line 2), and as a land owner in the mining district (*Hesperia* 26 [1957]: 2, no. S2, line 8). His name may also be recognizable in another fragmen-

Phormiōn's origins were far different. Demosthenes had litigated with errant guardians over their waste of his father's substantial estate (Dem. 27–31); Lysitheidēs had been among the earliest pupils of Isokratēs (Isok. 15.93), the preeminent Athenian educator who prepared his students for the elitist ideal of the citizen's life; Kallaischros of Phegous would have been born around the time his kinsman Plato began his famed Academy. But Phormiōn had come to Athens an ignorant non-Greek slave:[106] his sole education was "learning the lettered accounts" at the bank where he slaved (Dem. 45.72). Years later, after Phormiōn had performed enormous public and private benefactions for the Athenians (Dem. 36.55–57) and had attained almost unparalleled prosperity (Dem. 45.54 and 72), both as an independent banker[107] and as a maritime businessman (Dem. 45.64), Apollodōros tells him in open court that all his success and accomplishment were entirely dependent on a single vagary of chance: his purchase by a banker, in whose employ a slave might rise to blessed heights at Athens, but

> you [jurors] all know that if a caterer, or an artisan of some other skilled calling (*technē*), had purchased Phormiōn, then—having learned the *technē* of this master—he would have been far from his present benefits.[108] But since . . . a banker acquired him and taught him lettered accounts and instructed him in this *technē* and made him responsible for large sums of money, he has become prosperous, taking as the foundation of all of his present prosperity the good fortune that brought him [to a banking family].[109]

tary mining document (*Hesperia* 19 [1950]: 240, no. 15, lines 4 and 10). But Kallaischros the trierarch was an *isotelēs*, and therefore is unlikely to have been registered as an Athenian land owner (unless he had previously attained *egktēsis*). A better candidate would seem to be one of the members of the family of Kritias, whose affiliates include Solon and Plato, and whose wealth may have partly derived from marriage links with the prosperous families of Andokidēs and Pyrilampēs. A chronologically appropriate possibility would seem to be Kallaischros of Phegous, who served as διαιτητής in 325/4 (I.G. II² 1926, line 22) and would therefore have been born in 384/3.

106Phormiōn spoke Greek so poorly that he was apparently unable to participate meaningfully in a court proceeding in Greek (Dem. 36.1; cf. Apollodōros's mockery of Phormiōn's Greek at Dem. 45.30).

107Phormiōn was still engaged in banking many years after the end of the lease pursuant to which he had operated the bank of Pasiōn (Dem. 45.64, 66). Cf. Paley and Sandys [1896–98] 1979, 2: xxiii; Beloch 1912–27, 3: 334; below, Chapter 5, n. 268.

108Of course, an Athenian citizen working as an artisan in a field other than banking was equally unlikely to achieve the financial success possible as a *trapezitēs*. But, theoretically at least, a citizen would have been able to change his profession; the slave, theoretically at least, had no such choice.

109Dem. 45.71–72: οἶμαι γὰρ ἅπαντας ὑμᾶς εἰδέναι, ὅτι τοῦτον, ἡνίκ᾽ ὤνιος ἦν, εἰ συνέβη μάγειρον ἢ τινος ἄλλης τέχνης δημιουργὸν πρίασθαι, τὴν τοῦ δεσπότου τέχνην ἂν μαθὼν πόρρω τῶν νῦν παρόντων ἦν ἀγαθῶν. ἐπειδὴ δ᾽ ὁ πατὴρ ὁ ἡμέτερος τραπεζίτης ὢν ἐκτήσατ᾽ αὐτὸν καὶ γράμματ᾽ ἐπαίδευσεν καὶ τὴν τέχνην ἐδίδαξεν καὶ χρημάτων ἐποίησε κύριον πολλῶν, εὐδαίμων γέγονεν, τὴν τύχην, ἣ πρὸς ἡμᾶς ἀφίκετο, ἀρχὴν λαβὼν πάσης τῆς νῦν παρούσης εὐδαιμονίας.

A variety of factors—the personalized nature of the *trapeza*; legal procedures and social mores facilitating business enterprise by slaves; the importance of natural abilities and dependability in the potentially lucrative but "dangerous" *technē* of banking (Dem. 36.11); the rise of a new "mixed aristocracy" joining the traditional Athenian-citizen elite with influential resident foreigners and even wealthy former slaves—combined in fourth-century Athens to make possible enormous upward mobility for bankers' slaves. In this environment, a Phormiōn could be linked to the descendants of Solon and to the mercantile-citizen *oikos* of Demosthenes. But possibility was transmuted into reality only through the economic self-interest of the bankers themselves, and through Athenian society's basis on households, not individuals.

Although the citizenry appears to have had some reservations about insuring bank continuity by marrying a banker's widow to a slave who was assuming the proprietor's responsibilities,[110] bankers were merely adapting the fundamental, free Athenian social organization of the *oikos*, making it a mechanism for perpetuating a business producing wealth for persons of largely servile and non-Athenian background.[111] The ancient sources identify the *òikos*, rather than the individual, as the basic element of Athenian society,[112] and in recent years this judgment has come to be accepted by scholars.[113] All individuals of every status were members of a household; adult men appear even to have been registered in *demes*, a critical unit of political life, as members of an *oikos*, not independently.[114] Not surprisingly, then, the *oikos* is fundamental to the interaction of a banker, his wife, and his slaves in operating and perpetuating the *trapeza*.

Translated most easily by the word "household," *oikos* actually encompassed the physical attributes of the group's "house," the complement of members living in that house ("persons"), and the "property" belonging to

[110]Dem. 36.30: ὑμῖν μὲν γάρ, ὦ ἄνδρες Ἀθηναῖοι, τοῖς γένει πολίταις, οὐδὲ ἐν πλῆθος χρημάτων ἀντὶ τοῦ γένους καλόν ἐστιν ἑλέσθαι· τοῖς δὲ . . . ἀπὸ τοῦ χρηματίσασθαι καὶ ἑτέρων πλείω κτήσασθαι καὶ αὐτῶν τούτων ἀξιωθεῖσιν, ταῦτ' ἐστὶν φυλακτέα.

[111]Jameson has noted that archaeological evidence shows "no obvious distinction" between citizen and metic houses, and that in fact "the classical house on a small scale" replicates "the essential features of the archaic aristocratic establishment" (1990b: 195 and n. 42).

[112]See Aristot., *Pol.* 1252a–b; Xen., *Oik.* Not surprisingly, tragedy, with its concern for the essence of Greek life, accords the *oikos* a central position; as a corollary, every extant play (except Sophocles' *Philoktētēs*) has female characters. See Humphreys 1983c: 18. Euripides' *Alkestis* even focuses on the heroine's self-sacrifice to preserve the *oikos*. See Burnett 1971: 34–35.

[113]See, for example, Foxhall 1989: 22; Fisher 1976: 2, 5ff.; Hallett 1984: 72–76; Hunter 1981: 153; Jameson 1990b: 179. In a constitutional sense, "the πόλις was an aggregation of οἶκοι" (Wolff 1944: 93).

[114]Lacey 1968: 129, 293–94 n. 21. For the role of the household in modern Greece, see du Boulay 1974: ch. 1; for its importance in other societies, see Netting, Wilk, and Arnould 1984: xxii.

those members.[115] The term is often encountered in Greek literature, from its early denotation of the physical "house" (especially clear in the works of Homer) to the tripartite sense (found frequently in the Athenian orators) combining residence, people, and assets. Although "the different senses of the word" can be studied separately[116]—and a particular aspect may be emphasized in context[117]—the unique signification of the word lies in its denotation, at least in the fourth century, of an *entity* encompassing physical place, persons associated with that place, and assets of value belonging to those persons. For each of the separate notations, Greek offered a plenitude of alternative terms, most particularly *oikia* for the physical house, *klēros* for the assets, and *agchisteia* for a circle of related persons. But Greek had no term for "family," in the modern sense of a nuclear or extended grouping of people living together.[118] Greece knew only the *oikos*. Its members included all the persons living in a particular house—in Aristotle's words, a "natural association for everyday purposes."[119] Slaves are explicitly included by Aristotle as members of the *oikos*, along with husband, wife, and children (*Pol.* 1253b4–7).[120] Indeed, in a ceremony analogous to that which greeted the entry of a bride, a newly purchased slave was welcomed into the *oikos* with an outpouring of figs, dates, and other delicacies intended to portend a "sweet and pleasant" future.[121]

Although its dominance as a societal element appears to have been greater in Attica than in other Greek areas,[122] the "household" was not a uniquely Athenian social form. The *oikos* was clearly known in concept and by name

[115]For the fullest discussion of the word in its various attributes, see MacDowell 1989b: 10–21. Cf. Karabēlias 1984: 441–54.

[116]As MacDowell does: 1989b: 11–17.

[117]For example, the physical premises are specifically meant in Antiphon's reference to the man asleep ἐν οἴκῳ (Ant. 2d.8).

[118]In explaining the importance of the *oikos*, Aristotle points out the lack of a descriptive term in Greek for the nuclear family (husband and wife): ἀνώνυμον γὰρ ἡ γυναικὸς καὶ ἀνδρὸς σύζευξις (*Pol.* 1253b9–10). Finley notes: "The necessity never made itself felt to provide a specific name for the restricted concept evoked by our word 'family'" (1985: 18–19). Cf. Humphreys 1983c: 67.

[119]*Pol.* 1252b.12–14: ἡ μὲν οὖν εἰς πᾶσαν ἡμέραν συνεστηκυῖα κοινωνία κατὰ φύσιν οἶκός ἐστιν. Cf. 1253b.4: οἰκία δὲ τέλειος ἐκ δούλων καὶ ἐλευθέρων.

[120]In fact, the slave, as a member of the *oikos*, was frequently referred to as an *oiketēs*.

[121]Lex. Seguer. (Bekker) 269.9: καταχύσματα ἰσχάδες καὶ φοίνικες καὶ κάρυα ἄλλα τοιαῦτα ἐδώδιμα κατέχεον αἱ κύριαι τῶν οἴκων κατά τι ἔθος ἐπὶ τὰς κεφαλὰς τῶν ἄρτι ἐωνημένων δούλων παραδηλοῦσαι, ὅτι ἐπὶ γλυκέα καὶ ἡδέα πράγματα εἰσεληλύθασιν. Cf. Aristoph., *Plout.* 768 and schol.; Dem. 45.74; Pollux 3.77; Harpokratiōn and Suidas, s.v. "καταχύσματα." See Licht [1932] 1953:42–56; Ehrenberg 1962: 194 n. 1.

[122]See Schaps 1979, which offers numerous examples of greater individual rights of ownership in other Greek societies supporting his conclusion: "Elsewhere in Greece, the *oikos* did not occupy the same position of importance" (p. 4).

throughout Greece, attested by the "national bard," Homer,[123] and through the legendary "houses" that were the subjects of the tragedies presented at the great festivals. Aristotle in the *Politics* places the *oikos* in the broadest possible context. In the *Republic*, Plato utilizes it as a fundamental standard of reference; ultimately in the *Laws*, he offers it as the basis for all social organization.[124] Even the palace, family succession, and material possessions of the Great King of Persia constituted in Greek perception an *oikos*.[125] Organization of their personal and business lives through the "household" was natural, therefore, even for those bankers who were not Athenian or even Greek, but who now sought to assimilate to an Athens where they had already attained financial success. But these new *oikoi* were not being formed in an egalitarian society. The great Athenian "houses," with their traditions and pretensions, had for generations pursued (and largely attained) social and political preeminence. Their interrelation with the emerging economically powerful *oikoi* of the bankers tells much about the Athens that evolved after the Peloponnesian War.

A new *oikos*, however, did not find in the established dynasties its sole point of reference. Like the complementary financial opposites of the landed and maritime spheres and the cultural predisposition to antithesis reflected in the division of the economy into "invisible" and "visible" sectors,[126] the household, as a focus of Athenian private living, took its form from its contrast with the public world of the community. Gender, the complementary contrast of male and female, was for the Athenians a basic cognitive and social opposition, again expressed through separation of physical areas: the private world of the household, with women and slaves as significant members, cut off from the public world of the community, a contrasting political domain excluding all but the individual adult male citizen.[127]

Banking, however, necessarily partook of both worlds. A business that functioned through the *oikos* with its membership of women and slaves, the *trapeza* was nonetheless legally and socially assimilated to the persona of its male operator. Since it dealt in monetary assets and their intangible legal resultants of debts and receivables (that is, rights relating to "property," an essential aspect of the very definition of the *oikos*), the bank could not separate itself from the household. Yet these same rights to property necessarily brought

---

[123]For the importance of the οἶκος in Homeric times, see, for example, Knox 1989: 43.

[124]*Laws* 4.720e–721e. For the large extent to which Plato's precepts for the Cretan city of the *Laws* actually reflect contemporary Athenian practice, see Morrow 1960: passim.

[125]Themistoklēs thus was able to remind King Artaxerxes of the damage he had done to the royal *oikos*: ἥκω παρὰ σέ, ὃς κακὰ μὲν πλεῖστα Ἑλλήνων εἴργασμαι τὸν ὑμέτερον οἶκον (Thuc. 1.137.4).

[126]For the landed/maritime dichotomy, see above, Chapter 3; for the visible/invisible economic antithesis, see above, Chapter 1, and below, Chapter 6.

[127]For the fullest treatment of these factors, see Humphreys 1983c: 1–21 and 58–78. Cf. Foxhall 1989: 22–25; D. Cohen 1990b: 153–54.

the *trapeza* into contact with the laws and the courts, the officials and the rules located in the public sphere, which were traditionally controlled exclusively by male citizens. In the household, the wife might have substantial responsibility for management and supervision.[128] In the business world, the male slave as an independent functionary was "at home" (see below), but the woman was essentially out of place.

Because of the conflicting demands of the two spheres, and because of the complementary contributions offered by spouse and slave to the operation and perpetuation of the *trapeza*, a banker's joining of wife and slave to continue the business and protect the family property and wealth,[129] far from an anomaly impossible to explain, was probably in many cases the only economically viable solution to the divergent demands of public community and private household. A banker could not leave his business to his wife alone: the public domain's social and legal strictures prevented this.[130] He could not leave the bank to his slave alone: his property was necessarily intertwined with his family through the institution of the *oikos*.

By the fourth century, however, the traditional *oikos* had been significantly transmuted, permitting its continued viability during a period of massive societal change. The *oikos* of the early fifth century had been perceived as self-sufficient, producing for its own private consumption, pursuing in its marital couplings dynastic arrangements of aristocratic purity intended to perpetuate the *oikos* and thereby preserve control of the polis for its "best" citizens (*aristoi*).[131] By the fourth century, a "market economy" had arisen: money and goods, including agricultural products, were exchanged in fleeting transactions; commercial workshops produced consumer items.[132] Yet the *oikos* continued, in altered and idealized form, but still enticing to the parvenu, still appealing to the aristocrat. Indeed, volumes were written by upper-class ideologues lauding the *oikos* as the very basis of civilization (as in Xenophon's *Oikonomikos*, which saw in the traditional "household" the solution to virtually all of Hellas's contemporary problems).

But in economic matters, the *oikos* was form, the market economy was reality. Organization of quasi-*oikoi* by persons of servile background confirmed the economic form, but perpetuated a new social reality. The appearance of

[128]Xenophon's guide to household management makes this clear: *Oik.* 3.10–15; 7.32, 36–42; 9.15, 19. Because of the domestic separation of sexes (doors between the male and female parts of the house might actually be locked: Lysias 3.6–7, Dem. 47.56; but see Lysias 12.16), the wife's direct supervision over male slaves would be limited. This was especially true in agricultural families, where almost all male *douloi* worked outdoors. See Jameson 1977–78.

[129]This is precisely the justification offered by Demosthenes (36.30–31).

[130]On the social and legal adaptations that permitted the solution adopted by the bankers, see below, pp. 101–10.

[131]See Connor 1971: 3–84; Humphreys 1983c: 10ff.

[132]For the transition from the "household" (οἰκονομική) economy to the market economy (which Aristotle terms χρηματιστική), see Chapter 1.

banking *oikoi* of slave origin signaled the rise of a new "mixed" Athenian establishment,[133] which was infusing the traditional Athenian upper classes with wealthy resident foreigners, former slaves, naturalized citizens.[134]

For any participation in the public life of the city, key to the function of the traditional *oikos*, Athenian citizenship was necessary. This could be obtained through naturalization, albeit with difficulty, since it required actual legislation, a special resolution of the Assembly. Such grants were not routinely given: in principle they were reserved for persons who had been extraordinary benefactors of the state.[135] Still, evidence survives even today for scores of persons who so obtained citizenship.[136] And among such honorees, bankers had a startlingly high representation.[137] Indeed, "it is on the whole fair to say that banking was not so much a way by which citizens became rich as a way by which slaves and metics were able to buy themselves citizenship" (Davies 1981: 65–66). When bankers did become enfranchised, through such contributions as providing choruses, equipping ships, and paying special levies, they continued to meet civic expenses disproportionate to their numbers.[138] In the Athens of the fourth century, where influence and prosperity, after the crushing defeat in the Peloponnesian War, were derived not so much from military as from economic factors,[139] these *trapezitai* found considerable opportunity for integration with the traditional Athenian upper class. Even political power was affected by wealth: maintenance of influence through dynastic marriages, necessarily open only to aristocratic citizens, seems to have ended completely;[140] but wealth, distributed far beyond the traditional (citizen) upper class, never

[133]A "striking transformation" (Davies 1981: 38) in sources of wealth occurred between the sixth and the fourth centuries. Davies surveys this transformation at length (1981: 38–87). Cf. Mossé 1973: 49.

[134]The acceptance of metics as social equals is perhaps best illustrated by the portrayal of Kephalos's family in Plato's *Republic*. Pečirka succinctly describes "a new social structure based on 'economic' wealth not bound to status and indifferent to the status monopolies of the citizens of Athens, a structure which cut across the status groups of the community of the citizens" (1976: 28). For the fullest analysis of societal relationships in the fourth century ("l'évolution des rapports sociaux en Attique au IVᵉ siècle"), see Mossé [1962] 1979: 133–215. Mossé explicitly connects fourth-century developments in commercial banking with "l'apparition d'une mentalité nouvelle en contradiction avec l'éthique de la cité" (1972: 143).

[135]See, for example, Dem. 23.199ff.; 20 passim; 45.78; 59.13, 88ff. Cf. Dem. 23.194ff.

[136]Osborne 1981–83, 4: 204–6.

[137]Ibid., 4: 196. Financial contributions were prominent among the desiderata for naturalization (ἀνδραγαθίαν εἰς τὸν δῆμον τὸν Ἀθηναίων: Dem. 59.89). Hence the not-surprising overrepresentation of bankers among those attaining citizenship. Cf. Whitehead 1983: 70.

[138]Of the seven bankers known to have been enfranchised, at least three, and possibly four, themselves are recorded as having undertaken liturgical contributions, and their offspring and relatives increase this number. In contrast, for the entire fourth century, only about 700 Athenians have been identified as undertaking liturgies. See Davies 1971: xxvii–xxx.

[139]See, for example, Dem. 50.7, 11–19, 35. Cf. Humphreys 1978: 174; Jordan 1975: 213–15.

[140]See above, Chapter 1, n. 16.

ceased to be an important political factor.[141] A number of naturalized citizens even immersed themselves in the maelstrom of Athenian political life,[142] although none is known to have pursued politics more extensively than the bank-owning Apollodōros, son of Pasiōn.

Banking offers compelling examples of this amalgamation of wealth and influence. Even relatively early in the fourth century, in a suit against a *trapezitēs* who had only recently obtained his own freedom, a foreign litigant closely related by politics and marriage to the ruler of Bosporos (himself a considerable "benefactor" of Athens) complains of the networks of "friends" and the high credibility attained by the Athenian bankers (Isok. 17.2)—indeed, the speaker himself had enjoyed the closest personal relationship with the banker/former *doulos* (Isok. 17.6). Furthermore, Menexenos, scion of an establishment family with a fortune derived from Attic land,[143] was also joined closely in bank dealings with both the foreigner and the ex-slave, a financial "use" combining social and commercial aspects (see above, pp. 65–66). Indeed, Menexenos's relationship with the formerly(?)[144] enslaved bank clerk Kittos was so close that, together with the foreigner, he had allegedly obtained by "persuasion" an advance of six talents from the bank (Isok. 17.12). The foreigner Pythodōros (from Phoenicia) "introduces" potential clients to Pasiōn (Isok. 17.4), with whom his namesake, the well-known citizen Pythodōros, is extensively involved (Isok. 17.33; Dem. 54.7). In short, already early in the

[141]The racing victories of Dēmadēs and Dēmētrios, and the continuing private financing of public works are suggestive of this connection as late as the 320s. Pečirka (1967: 24) has seen a "patent contradiction" between the important social and economic position of wealthy noncitizens and their lack of direct political rights. But noncitizens of wealth and influence were precisely the individuals most likely to be able to obtain enfranchisement: there are frequent complaints that money, especially that of bankers, was a dominant factor in motivating important political leaders to effectuate the legislation required for naturalization. (Cf. Dein. 1.43; Aischinēs 3.85; Hyp., *Dem.* col. 25). As Pečirka himself has shown, even the right to own land in Attica, available to non-Athenians through grants of *egktēsis*, was given to wealthy noncitizens already actively involved, in the most significant ways, in Athenian public affairs (as attested by the few cases where the exact status and reasons for the grants are known). Pečirka 1966: 68–70, 80–81. Cf. I.G. II² 351 and 624.11–20; I.G. II² 505.7–41.

[142]For example, Menōn of Pharsalos, Apollodōros of Kyzikos, Phanosthenēs of Andros, Hērakleidēs of Klazomenai, and Charidēmos of Oreos.

[143]For the attribution, see Davies 1971: 145ff.; Mathieu and Brémond [1929–42] 1963, 1: 74 n. 1. The family's wealth consisted primarily of substantial real property (Isaios 5.43)—but in the new Athens, not surprisingly, much of it was subject to creditors (ibid., §21).

[144]One of the issues raised by Isok. 17 involves the status of Kittos, whether freed or still enslaved. An individual named Kittos appears many years later as a banker in a position of high trust (Dem. 34.6). Mathieu and Brémond ([1929–42] 1963) identify the homonymes as the same individual; if correct, this is another indication of the economic and social mobility available through banking to slaves in Athens. But in view of the many years' interval between the two litigations, the "Kittos" at Dem. 34.6 "peut être son descendant" (Gernet 1954–60, 1: 155 n. 1).

fourth century, Isokrates 17 presents, as general characteristics of the profession, bankers of humble origin networking with wealthy foreigners and well-placed citizens.

The subsequent co-options into the new mixed "aristocracy" of both Pasiōn's son, Apollodōros, and Pasiōn's successor, the former slave Phormiōn, were thus not anomalies, but elements of a pattern whereby the disadvantages of inferior origin could be overcome through relationships based on acquired prestige and financial capability.[145] But just as the bankers sought to utilize traditional Athenian forms to provide stability and continuity for their business enterprises, existing Athenian social and legal practices proved adaptable to emerging commercial requirements. Because of banking's integral connection to the household, these adaptations of necessity focused on finding accommodation in the community for banking slaves and bankers' wives.

Adaptation to Slave Enterprise

Social and economic realities at Athens facilitated independent operation of banks by men who were not free. A contemporary commentator even noted the difficulty at Athens of distinguishing at a glance free men from slaves.[146] In daily life, this might lead to embarrassing, and legally explosive, contretemps. During a raid on a citizen's farm by persons seeking to enforce a judgment, the debtor's son was carried off—he was assumed to be a slave (Dem. 47.61). A young citizen was sent into a neighbor's garden to pluck flowers in the hope that, mistaking the intruder for a slave, the neighbor might strike or bind him and thus become subject to legal action (Dem. 53.16). The maltreatment of a free woman at Dem. 47.58–59 suggests that female slaves were also difficult to differentiate.

This physical similarity helps explain Demosthenes' insistence (45.71–72) that the Athenian banks offered unique opportunities to a *doulos*. "Slave opportunity" is, of course, oxymoronic in the context of the racially based servitude of more recent North American history, which insisted on the permanent ex-

---

[145]Demosthenes teaches the citizens of the necessity of cultivating such prestige and funding powers: τοσαῦτα γάρ, ὦ ἄνδρες ᾿Αθηναῖοι, χρήμαθ᾿ ὑμῖν ἀνεγνώσθη προσηυπορηκώς, ὅσ᾿ οὔθ᾿ οὗτος οὔτ᾿ ἄλλος οὐδεὶς κέκτηται. πίστις μέντοι Φορμίωνι παρὰ τοῖς εἰδόσι καὶ τοσούτων καὶ πολλῷ πλειόνων χρημάτων, δι᾿ ἧς καὶ αὐτὸς αὑτῷ καὶ ὑμῖν χρήσιμός ἐστιν. ἃ μὴ προῆσθε (36.57).

[146]Xen., *Ath. pol.* 1.10: εἰ νόμος ἦν τὸν δοῦλον ὑπὸ τοῦ ἐλευθέρου τύπτεσθαι . . . πολλάκις ἂν οἰηθεὶς εἶναι τὸν ᾿Αθηναῖον δοῦλον ἐπάταξεν ἄν· ἐσθῆτά τε γὰρ οὐδὲν βελτίων ὁ δῆμος αὐτόθι ἢ οἱ δοῦλοι καὶ οἱ μέτοικοι, καὶ τὰ εἴδη οὐδὲν βελτίους εἰσίν. Winkler (1990: 180) suggests that this absence of physical differentiation might have resulted in increased intimidation of slaves by citizens seeking "invisible markers" of status. In fact, Athenian law (in contrast to that of certain other Greek jurisdictions) prohibited persons other than a slave's owner from striking him—although an exception was allowed in the case of a slave caught stealing produce from a farmer. See MacDowell 1978: 81.

ploitation of the slave as a member of an inferior group;[147] which actively sought to prevent social relationships, especially marriage, that might blunt the perpetual easy differentiation of slave and free groups;[148] and which enacted legislation[149] and made other efforts to deny professional skills, and even literacy, to the black.[150] At Athens, the situation was much different. Far from being racially based and inherently perpetual, servitude was a misfortune that could happen to anyone,[151] sometimes under conditions that, if set forth in a work of fiction, would have been highly comic. Witness the experience of

[147]In America, for example, in a landmark case, the U.S. Supreme Court held that freed blacks could not ever be United States citizens and that even after obtaining their freedom blacks "had no rights which the white man was bound to respect" (*Dred Scott v. Sanford*, 60 U.S. 393, 407 [1857]). In contrast, in Islamic society, military command and high political positions were often held by slaves (who until the nineteenth century were frequently white). See B. Lewis 1990: 12, 15. For the legal structure of Islamic slavery, see Santillana 1926: 111–26. (Gordon's recent work [*Slavery in the Arab World* (1989)] deals mainly with the modern period.)

[148]The Supreme Court of the northern U.S. state of Pennsylvania in 1837 denied free blacks the right to vote under the Pennsylvania constitution and laws, but held out the hope that this ruling might be reversed if black "blood . . . may become so diluted in successive descents as to lose its distinctive character" (*Hobbs v. Fogg*, 6 Watts 553, 560 [1837]). But even the northern state of Massachusetts prohibited interracial marriage in its statutes of 1705 and 1786, and in its revised code of 1836 actually increased the penalties for transgressions.

[149]Even in racially based slave cultures where commercial activity may be contrary to the literal tenets of the written law, slaves' independent practice of trades may nonetheless persist for economic reasons. In the American South, despite restrictive legislation in some jurisdictions intended to prevent their education, many slaves lived and worked in cities on their own account, paying their masters monetary compensation from fees and wages earned as craftsmen, generally receiving from employers and customers compensation equivalent to that paid to free black or white practitioners. See Goldin 1976.

[150]Many U.S. states attached criminal sanctions to the prohibition on teaching a slave to read or write. See, for example, the *Va. Code* (1848), pp. 747–48. Slaves were severely restricted by the laws of many states from engaging in the professions or in business transactions. See generally Higginbotham 1978. At Athens, in contrast, special efforts were made to provide young slaves with a skill (see Forbes 1955: 321–40 and, for Egypt in the Hellenistic period, Biezunska-Malowist 1966b: 65–72).

[151]As Watson has said of Roman slavery, "The moral and economic nature of slavery is fundamentally affected by whether or not slavery is racist in character. If it is not, then the existence of slavery is not a statement of a world view of ethnic hierarchy. To be a slave is a misfortune for the individual, assuredly a grave one, but it is not inevitable, natural or necessarily permanent" (1987: 3). At Athens, no legal barrier existed to the enslavement of a citizen of another Greek state (Harrison 1968–71, 1: 165), although Plato objects theoretically to the enslavement of other Greeks (*Rep.* 469b), and the Spartan commander Kallikratidas refused, in actual practice, to sell as slaves Greeks captured in the siege of Methymna during the Peloponnesian War (except for Athenians). (Xen., *Hell.* 1.6.14: οὐκ ἔφη ἑαυτοῦ γε ἄρχοντος οὐδέν' ἂν Ἑλλήνων εἰς τὸ ἐκείνου δυνατὸν ἀνδραποδισθῆναι.) But at Athens, "Greekness" was a cultural, not a racial concept (Isok. 4.50: ἡ πόλις ἡμῶν . . . τὸ τῶν Ἑλλήνων ὄνομα πεποίηκεν μηκέτι τοῦ γένους, ἀλλὰ τῆς διανοίας δοκεῖν εἶναι, καὶ μᾶλλον Ἕλληνας καλεῖσθαι τοὺς τῆς παιδεύσεως τῆς ἡμετέρας ἢ τοὺς τῆς κοινῆς φύσεως μετέχοντας; cf. Herodotos 8.144.2). In fact, many slaves, although apparently not the majority, clearly were of Greek origin. See Finley 1981: 104.

Nikostratos, erstwhile friend of the bank owner Apollodōros. After the death of his father Pasiōn (who himself had entered banking as a slave), Apollodōros moved his residence to the country. There he was Nikostratos's neighbor, and the two, who were quite close in age, became quite friendly. Shortly after 370, however, while Apollodōros was away transporting Athenian emissaries to Sicily in the warship that he, as a prominent Athenian, had equipped and was commanding, three *douloi*—two given by Apollodōros to Nikostratos, and a third belonging to the latter—ran away. Nikostratos went after them. But during the pursuit he was himself captured by a hostile warship and taken to the island of Aigina, off the Attic coast. There he was sold into slavery. Apollodōros returned to learn of the "misfortune" (*symphora*; Dem. 53.4–6). (The story has a bittersweet denouement: Greek slavery always being potentially transitory, Nikostratos's freedom was protected through a loan effectuated by the banker's son; lending being always dangerous [*epikindynos*, Dem. 36.11], Apollodōros subsequently encountered great animosity from Nikostratos.)

Such potential reversal of position between master and slave may partly underlie Plato's advice that masters should treat their slaves well, not so much for the slaves' advantage, but for the masters' (*Laws* 6.777d). For the great philosopher himself, however, a transition between freedom and slavery was not merely theoretical: an aristocratic Athenian by birth (a member of the family of Kritias, with descent from Solon), he is reported to have personally experienced enslavement in a situation like that of Nikostratos (and similarly purchased into freedom through his friends' efforts).[152] Indeed, so pervasive was the need to free Athenian citizens fallen into the control of others that in seeking favorable consideration from jurors Lysias lists, among a litany of routine civic undertakings (paying regular and special taxes, not causing difficulties, obeying the law, creating no enmity), his family's "ransoming of many Athenians from the enemy" (Lysias 12.20).

This potential for both slavery and freedom and the essential interchangeability of servant and master necessarily influenced economic function. The slave-owning banker was driven by his own economic interest to offer advantage to those slaves playing key roles in the banking "operation." Ongoing banking transactions demanded skillful handling by *trapeza* employees, sometimes operating in close conjunction with the proprietor, but often, as we have seen, functioning alone. Thus it should not be entirely surprising that Phormiōn's successors, still enslaved, were able to lease the bank of Pasiōn from their own masters, the bank's owners, or that Phormiōn himself, while still a slave, also seems independently to have entered into such arrangements.[153]

Male slaves, like male citizens, could work in the public world of community and commerce without affronting social values; unlike wealthy female citizens,

---

[152]See Diogenes Laertios 3.18–21, among others, for the full, possibly apocryphal tale.
[153]See Dem. 36.4, 13, and 37, and above, pp. 80–82.

they were not restricted to the private sphere of the *oikos*. Slaves involved in businesses not focused (as banking was) on the household could even live and work away from the family residence. At Athens, slave craftsmen employed in the construction trades are known to have received wages in money; when not actually living in the master's quarters, these unfree laborers paid a portion of their compensation to their masters.[154] A group of "nine or ten" slave leatherworkers are reported (Aischinēs 1.97) to have operated a workshop: the slave in charge (*hēgemōn tou ergastēriou*) paid their master a fixed sum of three obols per day, and the other slaves paid two obols. Milyas, who was reponsible (*diōikēsen*) for the manufacturing businesses left by Demosthenes' father, is said to have been entitled to keep the profits from the operation of the businesses, while paying the heirs only a fixed fee.[155] Slaves skilled in the production of pottery functioned on similar terms.[156] *Douloi* are known to have operated retail businesses without supervision: Meidas and his two sons ran a perfumery; their master received an accounting only monthly (Hyp., *Ath.* 9, 19). For service *technai*, such as medicine and teaching, similar practices have been posited, although the paucity of evidence and the absence of specialized studies have prevented the emergence of "a clear picture" as to "what the different juridical, social, and economic relationships might be . . ." (Wiedemann 1987: 33). But the detailed evidence for slaves' involvement in banking may clarify the position of slaves in other *technai* requiring skill and trust.

In banking, economic considerations provided the slave with a stature compatible with his business obligations. The bank's position might be endangered if slave functionaries were intimidated by free customers. A slave-banker had occasion to question the demands of highly connected citizens (such as the esteemed *proxenos* of the Herakleōtes, whom Phormiōn challenged at Dem. 52.5–6), and he necessarily had access to large sums of money (as with Kittos, who was in a position to advance 36,000 *dr.* to customers: Isok. 17.4). If slaves working at a *trapeza* had felt compelled to defer to free customers, their employer's monetary interests would have suffered. At least one contemporary observer saw this clearly. Noting (and lamenting) the elevated economic and social position of Athenian slaves, including their failure to show acquiescence to free persons,[157] the author of the Xenophonic *Constitution of the Athenians*

[154]See Randall 1953; Burford 1963. Cf. the charcoal-burner in Menander's *Epitrepontes*, a slave who lives outside the city with his wife and merely pays to his owner a portion (ἀποφορά) of his earnings (see l. 380). Cf. Bienzunska-Malowist 1966b: 65–72.

[155]See Francotte 1900: 12; Bolkestein 1958: 63. Demosthenes, many years later, refers to Milyas as "our freedman" (ὁ ἀπελεύθερος ὁ ἡμέτερος; Dem. 27.19), but there is no indication that Milyas was not still a slave when he was operating the workshops.

[156]See Webster 1973. For Roman practices considered analogous (Wiedemann 1987: 33), see Prachner 1980; Harris 1980; Tapio 1975.

[157]§10: οὔτε ὑπεκστήσεταί σοι ὁ δοῦλος.

(1.10–11) lays the blame on money (*apo khrēmatōn*): for persons receiving a share of the earnings of their slaves (*apophoras*), "it is not profitable" to have their slaves "fear" the free persons whom they encounter. Indeed, "if your slave fears me, there will be a danger that he will give over the money in his possession so as not himself to be at risk."[158]

The social and economic circumstances fostering slave enterprise, so offensive to the author of the *Constitution of the Athenians*, were critical to the operation of an Athenian bank. Perhaps predictably, the legal system also provided multifaceted accommodation to business needs, including recognition of slaves' responsibility for their own business debts, court acceptance of slaves and free noncitizens as parties and witnesses in banking and certain other commercial litigation (in contravention of the general rules allowing access to polis courts only to citizens of the polis), and acceptance of mercantile "agency" as a mechanism to overcome remaining legal disabilities.

Limitation on a Master's Liability for a Slave's Business Debts

In the nineteenth century, the sands of Egypt yielded the text of an Athenian courtroom presentation dealing with responsibility for business debts: a slave engaged in a retail perfume business with his two sons was purchased by a buyer who undertook in the purchase agreement responsibility for the shop's debts. These amounted, unexpectedly (he says), to five talents: the purchase price for the three slaves was only two-thirds of a talent. The buyer claims to have assumed these debts only because of the seller's fraudulent misrepresentation of the amount of the business's liabilities (Hyp., *Ath.*, delivered between 330 and 324).[159] Although the legal dispute here focuses only on the obligation of a buyer who assumes business debts incurred by slaves, the text actually provides remarkable evidence that the *douloi*, and in particular the father, Midas, were at least primarily liable for these commercial obligations: on several separate occasions Midas is explicitly characterized as personally obligated for the debts.[160]

Evidence of this obligation, business-related and personal, merely confirms a legal precondition logically necessary for slaves' involvement in Athenian banking. The participation of *douloi* in banking—as lessees, managers, proprietors, or even functionaries—was dependent upon the law's recognition of a *doulos*'s capacity to enter into commercial contractual arrangements. In turn, a slave's capacity to enter into business contracts is the prerequisite to a slave's responsibility for business debts.

[158] ἐὰν δὲ δεδίῃ ὁ σὸς δοῦλος ἐμέ, κινδυνεύσει καὶ τὰ χρήματα διδόναι τὰ ἑαυτοῦ ὥστε μὴ κινδυνεύειν περὶ ἑαυτοῦ.

[159] For the date, see §31: Alexander's decree of 324, restoring Greek exiles to their native cities, had not yet been issued; the Troizēnian cooperation with Athens in 480 is referred to as having occurred more than 150 years earlier.

[160] §6: ὅσον μέντοι ὀφείλουσιν ἀργύριον. §10: καὶ εἴ τῳ ἄλλῳ ὀφείλει τι Μίδας (purportedly the actual language of the purchase agreement). §20: ὀφείλοντα Μ[ίδαν].

Under statute attributed to Solon, the legendary Athenian lawmaker,[161] the slave's master was clearly liable for noncontractual wrongs ("torts") committed by a *doulos*. To resolve responsibility where the slave was acquired by a new owner only after occurrence of the delict, the law (cited in Hyp., *Ath.*) appears even to have specifically placed liability on the person owning the slave at the time that a tortious wrong was committed.[162] But, as with other surviving evidence relating to an owner's responsibility for a slave's wrongdoing,[163] this law is entirely silent about a master's liability for contractual obligations incurred by slaves. Since the debts at issue in the Athēnogenēs case arose entirely from business commitments, Gernet has argued (1955a: 161–62) that an owner's liability for such debts was not addressed by any specific statutory law: otherwise the litigant would have appealed to such legislation, instead of utilizing the early law dealing with slaves' wrongful "actions," at most applicable only by analogy to "contractual obligations."[164]

The law's ambiguity is not surprising: the independent operation of businesses by *douloi* represented a commercial reality of the fourth century that undoubtedly was not foreseen by the sixth-century "lawgiver." In many instances, however, on a number of obvious theoretical bases (characterization of the *doulos* as agent for his owner, joint liability for joint undertakings, etc.), a master could have been held liable for contractual obligations incurred by his slaves, even in the absence of an owner's general liability for the contractual commitments of a *doulos*. Master's liability would easily and clearly have arisen from conventional banking operations by a proprietor and his staff of slaves. Indeed, we know of several cases where a slave was in fact sued directly, as a named defendant, but where the master insisted, at least partly for tactical reasons, that the suit should instead have been brought directly against the slave's owner (Dem. 37.52, 55.31–32).

This evolving law of a master's possible responsibility for or freedom from liability for a slave's contractual commitments may explain bankers' use of leases to "preserve" their banks.[165] Lease of a *trapeza* provided a fixed rental to the owner in return for the lessee's retention of income resulting from bank operation, including the collection of loans and the repayment of depos-

---

[161]See Gagarin 1986: 71–72; Ruschenbusch 1966.

[162]*Ath.* §22: [Σόλων] εἰδὼς ὅτι πολλαὶ ὠναὶ [γίγνον]ται ἐν τῇ πόλει ἔθηκε νόμον δί-καιον . . . τὰς ζημίας ἃς ἂν ἐργάσωνται οἱ οἰκέται καὶ τὰ ἀ[——]ατα διαλύειν τὸν δεσπότην παρ' ᾧ [ἂν ἐργασ]ωνται οἱ οἰκέται. For ζημίαν ἐργάζεσθαι as descriptive of a slave's noncontractual wrongdoing, see Wyse [1904] 1967: 506.

[163]Only tortious wrongs are referred to in Dem. 37.21–22 (specific tort described), 37.51, 53.20 (ὁπότε κακόν τι ἐργάσαιτο), and 55.31–32 (master's insistence that his slave οὐδὲν ἀδικεῖ).

[164]Cf. Pringsheim 1950: 454ff.; Harrison 1968–71, 1: 173–74; Meyer-Laurin 1979: 267; MacDowell 1978: 81.

[165]Thus Pasiōn's arrangements for his bank, including its lease to Phormiōn, are described as μόνην σωτηρίαν τοῖς ἑαυτοῦ πράγμασιν (Dem. 36.30). For the financial and economic aspects of the μίσθωσις of Athenian banks, see below, Chapter 5.

its.[166] Further, although all assets under the slave's control, including all of the *trapeza*'s assets, would remain exposed to creditors, the bank owner's other assets would be protected from bank obligations incurred after commencement of the lease. Of course, the owner would still have been liable for repayment of deposits left with him prior to effectiveness of the lease: Athenian law's non-recognition of businesses as juridical persons insured that liability. But a formal lease would have eliminated any inference that a slave was acting as agent for his master in entering into a banking commitment, or that they were coventurers, possible bases for finding a master legally responsible for a slave's contractual debts, even in the absence of general legislation mandating this obligation.

In contrast, such a rental arrangement between a bank owner and slave would have lacked economic justification if the master had remained potentially liable for bank obligations incurred after the lease had become effective: the owner would then have limited his right to receive income while retaining unlimited liability for losses. But the slaves of Apollodōros and Pasiklēs paid their masters exactly the same rent as the free person who had previously leased the *trapeza* (Dem. 36.12), not an increased sum, as might be expected if their status as slaves had in fact increased their masters' liability for contractual obligations incurred by the bank during the period of their lease.

Acceptance of Slaves and Noncitizens as Parties and Witnesses in Banking Litigation

Contractual arrangements with slaves had meaning (because legally enforceable) only if slaves could be parties to commercial litigation. In fact, there is significant evidence that the Athenian courts—in a marked departure from traditional and widespread Hellenic insistence on citizenship as a prerequisite to enforcement of legal rights—substantially disregarded personal status in mercantile matters.[167] In essence, the same Athenian courts that did not recognize the bank as an independent juridical entity were willing, in certain commercial areas, entirely to disregard personal status as a prerequisite to utilization of, and participation in, the judicial system.

Slaves appear to have had full court access, as parties and as witnesses, in cases involving commercial matters. This acceptance is best attested in the important "commercial maritime" cases and courts (*dikai emporikai*), where "standing" was accorded without regard to the personal status of litigants.[168]

---

[166]Dem. 36.13: τὰς παρακαταθήκας καὶ τὴν ἀπὸ τούτων ἐργασίαν αὐτὴν ἐμισθώσαντο. Cf. Dem. 36.6: μισθούμενος . . . τὴν ἐργασίαν αὐτὴν τῆς τραπέζης καὶ τὰς παρακαταθήκας λαμβάνων. See Thompson 1981: 92 n. 18 for retention of λαμβάνων, eliminated without paleographical justification by editors following Blass. Cf. below, Chapter 5, n. 324.

[167]Cohen 1973: 69–74, 121; Gernet 1955a: 159–64; McKechnie 1989: 185. For the general exclusion of noncitizens, cf. n. 219 below.

In the case of slaves, this represented a unique accommodation, for (with the exception of testimony in cases of murder, perhaps only against the alleged murderer of their master[169]) slaves were otherwise absolutely deprived of the right even to be witnesses in legal proceedings.[170] "Commercial maritime" disputes, however, were not the only cases encompassed in the special procedural category of "monthly cases" (dikai emmēnoi). "Banking cases" (dikai trapezitikai) are also denominated by Aristotle as among these "monthly cases" (Ath. pol. 52.2). Although little is known with certainty as to the nature of "banking cases,"[171] there is no reason to assume criteria of standing or evidence substantially different from those of the "allied sphere" (Harrison 1968–71, 1: 176) of commercial maritime cases. Likely similarity of procedure is further suggested by the substantial involvement of slaves and foreigners in both Athenian sea trade and banking.[172] Strikingly, the clearest example of a slave having the right to testify and participate in an Athenian court, that of Lampis the nauklēros in Demosthenes 34, involves a doulos who provided credit to a borrower who was the recipient of a number of other loans—some of which may have been provided by bankers.[173] And Pankleōn, engaged in commercial pursuits in a fuller's shop, seeks to avoid a court action (Lysias 23) on the grounds that he is a Plataian, only to be met by the plaintiff's introduction of evidence that he is in fact a slave. Of course, the plaintiff's presentation of proofs of servitude would justify pendency of the case only if slaves actually could be parties to business-oriented lawsuits.[174]

There is independent evidence that certain slaves, the so-called douloi "living on their own" (khōris oikountes) or "self-supporting" (misthophoroun-

[168]Garlan (1982: 55), who asserts regarding the legal capacity of douloi, "Surtout à partir du IVe siècle, il fallut enfin adapter empiriquement ses capacités juridiques aux fonctions économiques qui lui étaient confiées." Cf. Paoli [1930] 1974: 106–9.

[169]See Gernet 1955a: 151–55. Cf. Grace 1974: 34–56.

[170]For slaves' general inability to bring lawsuits, see Plato, Gorg. 483b; Dem. 53.20. Their testimony could be utilized only to the extent that it was extracted under formalized torture, a form of proof that indeed emphasized the normal evidentiary incapacity of the doulos. See Thür 1977; Soubie 1973–74: 127; Humphreys 1985b: 356 n. 7. Isokrates 17, with its convoluted references to possible testimony under torture by the banking slave Kittos, is no guide to procedure in the δίκαι ἔμμηνοι: the speech relates events from the 390s; the δίκαι ἔμμηνοι arose only sometime after 355. See Harrison 1968–71, 1: 21; Gernet [1938] 1955: 175–79; Cohen 1973: 189–90.

[171]On the δίκαι τραπεζιτικαί, see Gernet [1938] 1955: 176–77.

[172]For noncitizen involvement in maritime commerce, see above, pp. 29–30.

[173]For Lampis's advance of 1,000 dr., see Dem. 34.6 and Thompson 1980: 144–45. Cf. the discussion below, pp. 179–80. At Dem. 34.5 Lampis is termed the οἰκέτης of Diōn, at 34.10 the παῖς of Diōn. For his clear testimonial capacity, see §31. Seager (1966: 181 n. 82) notes that although a slave, Lampis is rhetorically treated in Dem. 34 as though he were an "independent agent."

[174]The speech is a late work of Lysias, probably delivered about 387 B.C. (Lamb 1930). The procedural confusion implicit in the argument may reflect the novelty of the recognition at Athens of slaves' procedural capacity.

tes),[175] were able, at least for some matters, to participate as parties to litigation in the Athenian courts. Since slaves living outside the master's house appear to constitute essentially *douloi* engaged in commercial pursuits on their own,[176] evidence of their right to litigate further confirms court standing for *douloi* in commercial matters.[177] Although Harrison notes, somewhat expansively, that "Ps.-Xen. *Ath. Pol.* 1.11 implies that [these] slaves could sue in the courts,"[178] the comment by "Xenophon" is strictly in the context of the commercial activity and business value of Athenian slaves.[179] Menander portrays a "self-supporting" slave as competent to protect his own rights through bringing suit—but the example again is limited to property rights.[180] Recognition of the rights of the slaves by Theophrastos (*Char.* 30, §§9, 15) again is limited to their property, especially their earnings.[181]

Agency as Legal Mechanism

In banking matters, the legal acceptability of acting through agents facilitated the operation of *trapezai* by non-Athenians, both free and unfree. During his early years of banking activity, before obtaining citizenship, perhaps while still a slave,[182] Pasiōn utilized the citizen Pythodōros "to do and say all things" for

---

[175]Anec. Bekk. ([*Lex. rhēt.*] 316 s.v. "χωρὶς οἰκοῦντες") includes δοῦλοι χωρὶς οἰκοῦντες τῶν δεσποτῶν in the definition of χωρὶς οἰκοῦντες, and some scholars have equated the χωρὶς οἰκῶν with the δοῦλος μισθοφορῶν. See Partsch 1909: 136; Clerc 1893: 281. But Suda and Harpokratiōn seem to limit inclusion among τοὺς χωρὶς οἰκοῦντας to freedmen. For various, ultimately unsuccessful efforts to resolve the issue, see Whitehead 1977: 25 n. 87. For a general consideration of the two categories, see Perotti 1972 and 1976.

[176]See above, pp. 92–94.

[177]Ste. Croix has suggested that Lampis was a slave χωρὶς οἰκῶν (Seager 1966: 181 n. 82).

[178]Harrison 1968–71, 1: 167 n. 6. Sparseness of evidence precludes even hypotheses as to the precise date of the Athenian courts' initial recognition of slaves' standing in commercial matters. But since the Xenophonic *Ath. pol.* seems clearly to date from relatively late in the fifth century (see Moore 1986: 20; Gomme 1940; Forrest 1970), tendencies toward recognizing slaves' litigational capacity in business disputes must have been present in the Athenian system even before the flowering of banking activity in the fourth century.

[179]ὅπου γὰρ ναυτικὴ δύναμίς ἐστιν, ἀπὸ χρημάτων ἀνάγκη τοῖς ἀνδραπόδοις δουλεύειν, ἵνα λαμβάνωμεν ὧν πράττῃ τὰς ἀποφοράς, καὶ ἐλευθέρους ἀφιέναι. ὅπου δ' εἰσὶ πλούσιοι δοῦλοι κ.τ.λ. On ἀποφορά as the earnings of slaves involved in business pursuits for their own account, see above, n. 154 and text thereto.

[180]*Arbitr.* 203fK (δοῦλος μισθοφορῶν). Although Gernet suggests that δικάζεσθαι in this context is entirely humorous (1955a: 175 n. 3), even for a joke some factual context must be posited.

[181]In a recent study, Todd has argued persuasively that the objection to slaves' testimony was not that the *doulos* "cannot be trusted to tell the truth" but that the *doulos* lacked the financial "capacity to be sued" for perjury (1990a: 28). The slave-businessman alone could sustain this burden, and so alone appears to have been permitted to testify.

[182]Pasiōn played an important role in the banking business of his masters (Dem. 36.43, 48): J. W. Jones (1956: 186) has even suggested that Pasiōn, while still a slave, was entirely responsible for the operation of the bank. Although it is always assumed that he was manumitted prior to the events described in Isok. 17 (cf. Davies 1971: 429–30), in fact we do not know when he obtained his freedom.

him.[183] When Pasiōn employed bank funds to provide a bond of seven talents for a client (Isok. 17.42–43), neither the bank (not a cognizable "person" for legal purposes) nor he himself (since not a citizen) could effectuate the bail directly.[184] But the problem was surmountable by agency: the banker utilized the citizen Archestratos to accomplish the pledge, and the court accepted this agency.[185] Pasiōn also used the citizen Agyrrhios (of Kollytos) as a confidential representative in litigational matters (Isok. 17.31ff.). Even citizen-bankers appear to have acted through or with other persons. Thus Aristolochos was so closely involved with Antidōros of Phaleron, also a citizen (see above, n. 44), that the two seem to have functioned much as joint venturers in the banking business: Antidōros's apparent avoidance of Aristolochos's bankruptcy suggests that he was probably not liable for the *trapeza*'s debts and therefore was not an actual partner in Aristolochos's bank.[186]

Agents were employed sometimes merely for the principal's convenience.[187] Stephanos was dispatched to represent a banker's interests at Byzantion (Dem. 45.64), and the money-lending Dēmōn sent Aristophōn to Kephallēnia to resolve a commercial maritime dispute (Dem. 32.10–12). But on other occasions, the law's acceptance of agents permitted noncitizen or slave-bankers to overcome barriers to their business activities. Despite the Athenian courts' preference for direct oral presentation by the parties to an action, Phormiōn, whose Greek was poor, utilized Demosthenes to speak for him in an important bank-related litigation.[188] Agency might also resolve the otherwise disabling incapacity of a slave-banker (or any other non-Athenian) to foreclose on security for a loan provided in the form of Attic land, which could be owned only by citizens or by those given special permission by individual act of the Assembly (the so-called right of *egktēsis*).[189] When the noncitizen Phormiōn, on undertaking operation of a bank pursuant to a lease, wanted to be able to execute on those loans which the bank had extended "on land and multiple dwellings" (*epi gēi kai synoikiais*), he arranged for the bank owner, his former master, to retain nominal ownership of these receivables, in form as a debtor of

---

[183]Isok. 17.33: ὑπὲρ Πασίωνος ἅπαντα καὶ λέγει καὶ πράττει. This Pythodōros (ὁ σκηνίτης), whose shops situated near the Leōkorion were well known to Athenians (cf. Dem. 54.7), is not to be confused with Pythodōros (ὁ Φοίνιξ) who was also utilized by Pasiōn for the introduction of potential clients (cf. Isok. 17.4). But he appears to have been the grandfather of Pythodōros "ὁ Ἀχαρνεύς," who acts for Pasiōn's son Apollodōros at Dem. 50.28. See Mathieu and Brémond [1929–42] 1963, 1: 81 n. 1; Davies 1971: 481.

[184]See Whitehead 1977: 93; Gauthier 1972: 138–41, 145.

[185]Isok. 17.43: Πασίων δ' Ἀρχέστρατόν μοι τὸν ἀπὸ τῆς τραπέζης ἑπτὰ ταλάντων ἐγγυητὴν παρέσχεν. For Archestratos's status, see above, n. 44.

[186]Antidōros is known to have performed at least two trierarchies independently of Aristolochos: *Eudia* (I.G. II² 1622, ll. 128ff.), and *Epipedōsa* (I.G. II² 1622, ll. 137ff.).

[187]A number of individuals carried out tasks with which their principals did not wish to be openly connected. See Lofberg 1917: 48–59.

[188]The orator opened his presentation by noting Phormiōn's ἀπειρίαν τοῦ λέγειν, καὶ ὡς ἀδυνάτως ἔχει Φορμίων (Dem. 36.1).

[189]On this grant, see generally Pečirka 1966; Steltzer 1971.

the bank, so that "he might be able to execute" against such real property.[190] This utilization of Athenian citizens as agents, through the mechanism of a formalistic intermediate loan, effectively permitted noncitizens operating banks to engage freely in real-estate lending.[191]

True to the highly personal nature of Athenian banking, these agents invariably were closely involved with the bank proprietors.[192] Archestratos, for example, was one of Pasiōn's former masters, with whom Pasiōn, while still a slave, had developed a relationship of the highest trust.[193] Phormiōn, before obtaining his freedom, utilized the citizen Timosthenēs as his business partner in maritime operations, but the relationship, as usual, was both mercantile and personal.[194] Antidōros collaborated as syntrierarch with Aristolochos on no less than six liturgies, a cooperation without known parallel.[195]

This free use of representatives, permitting businessmen to accomplish through third parties undertakings that were otherwise prohibited, constituted a remarkable legal innovation. Other systems of law have had significant difficulty even in developing a mechanism through which actions otherwise permitted can be effectuated through third parties. Only with bewildering intricacy did the Roman law develop distinctions circumventing the absolute preclusion of agents for any purpose;[196] modern legal systems have been resistant in varying degrees to the binding of a third party by arrangements made through others.[197] But Athenian law, precisely because it had not developed rigorous systems of juridical requirements for the creation of obligations,[198] was able easily to give legal effect through representatives, even to commitments that might not be undertaken directly by principals—provided that the representatives themselves had capacity to effectuate those undertakings. Without some concept of agency, banking as an ongoing business is impossible. Through its acceptance of slave bankers' representation by citizens where necessary, Athenian law satisfied both traditional form and contemporary legal requirement, while facil-

---

[190]Dem. 36.6: οἷός τ' ἔσοιτ' εἰσπράττειν ὅσα Πασίων ἐπὶ γῇ καὶ συνοικίαις δεδανεικὼς ἦν.

[191]See below, pp. 133–36.

[192]This agency relationship should not be confused, or even compared, with the very different "patronus/libertus" equation of Roman civilization (for which see Schiller 1971: 24–31; Treggiari 1969: 68–81; Juglar 1902: 60–69). See Millett 1989. The Athenian prostatēs seems to have had no function beyond certifying initially that a noncitizen was a person suitable for registration as a metic, the status assumed by "immigrants" and by slaves on obtaining freedom. See MacDowell 1978: 78 (but cf. Whitehead 1977: 90–91).

[193]Dem. 36.44: παρὰ τοῖς αὑτου κυρίοις 'Αντισθένει καὶ 'Αρχεστράτῳ τραπεζιτεύουσι πεῖραν δοὺς ὅτι χρηστός ἐστι καὶ δίκαιος, ἐπιστεύθη.

[194]Dem. 49.31: ἐπιτήδειος δὲ ὢν Φορμίωνι καὶ κοινωνὸς ὁ Τιμοσθένης. See above, n. 71.

[195]See Davies 1971: 35.

[196]See Wenger 1906: 125; Nicholas 1962: 201–4.

[197]For the inherent opposition to agency, and its partial resolution in modern Britain and the United States, see Buckland and McNair 1952: 214–15.

[198]See Wolff 1968; J. W. Jones 1956: 224–25

itating the operation of the banking household, and the concomitant realization of a market economy.

WOMEN, LAW, AND PROPERTY

In accommodating slaves' business activity, the law was not in conflict with Athenian social customs or structures: male *douloi* were traditionally involved in economic activity outside the home. Here the law's adaptation to changing business circumstance created no inherent tension. Financial rights for women presented entirely different, and far more difficult, considerations.

At Athens, a woman's direct economic prerogatives were, under prevailing law, substantially inferior to the property rights of females in other, similarly male-dominated Greek communities, and any effort to alter this inequity directly challenged social values and perceptions mandating a woman's exclusion from the public world of the community. Overt exercise of legal rights would have brought women into the very sphere from which they were excluded: the public community, with its courts and other law-connected entities restricted to men alone, where legal rights were created and vindicated. At Athens, social sanctions restricted women to the world of the household.[199] Yet the household itself involved dominion over assets, items of wealth, things of value. "Property" was an integral part of the very definition of the *oikos* (see above): indeed, for the Athenians, "ownership" of property was not even conceivable outside the context of the household.[200]

The banking *oikos*, however, offers unique insight into the accommodation of the demands of the two spheres. Although banking was an activity integrally tied to the household and thus accessible to women, the *trapeza* also functioned, necessarily and prominently, in the public community. This conjunction of bank and household, bank and community, brought the *trapeza* to straddle the boundary between the two worlds. The bank's needs, the wife's rights, the social structure of Athens, the alien origins of many bankers all influenced the law. And here too we will find the law adapting to economic reality by accommodating the personal and property needs of bankers' wives. This acceptance took the form of a silent tolerance:[201] the law refrained from applying statutory

---

[199]It is, of course, an exaggeration to conceive of women as literally locked into their homes: separation and seclusion are not identical. But the ideal of separation, and its partial physical realization (see D. Cohen 1989, 1990b: 156–63), presented an inherent barrier to the law's acceptance of women's direct exercise of economic rights.

[200]Xenophon presents the most striking example: the property of the *oikos* is not restricted to the house itself; even goods owned in another city belong to the household. Οἶκος δὲ δὴ τί δοκεῖ ἡμῖν εἶναι; ἆρα ὅπερ οἰκία, ἢ καὶ ὅσα τις ἔξω τῆς οἰκίας κέκτηται, πάντα τοῦ οἴκου ταῦτά ἐστιν; Ἐμοὶ γοῦν, ἔφη ὁ Κριτόβουλος, δοκεῖ, καὶ εἰ μηδ᾽ ἐν τῇ αὐτῇ πόλει εἴη τῷ κεκτημένῳ, πάντα τοῦ οἴκου εἶναι ὅσα τις κέκτηται (*Oik.* 1.5).

[201]Legal systems often utilize such tacit mechanisms when social and economic realities are at variance with prevailing ideology. See Humphreys 1985a: 256–57. For example, Brazilian law in the nineteenth century was unable to resolve explicitly the conflict between the legal system's

provisions that would otherwise bar a banker's arrangements regarding family and property. This juridical response simultaneously achieved two ends: it accommodated economic needs, yet it kept the banking wife and her banking *oikos* from direct contact with the male sphere of courts and community.

A Wife's Personal Legal Status

Before the law could deal with a wife's property rights, it had to bring within its cognizance the woman herself. Here the institution of marriage provided a necessary point of intersection for the public and private spheres. Marriage, at the heart of the *oikos*, was also a critical concern for the Athenian state, which rigorously limited citizenship, the sole source of all political rights,[202] to individuals born within specified marital arrangements.[203] Yet aside from birth, there was another—albeit highly restricted—path to citizenship: naturalization. At Athens, this was no routine procedure: naturalization required on an individual basis a specific resolution of the male citizen body in Assembly.[204] But bankers were unusually successful in winning citizenship (see above, pp. 88–89). In thus bringing into the political system disproportionate numbers of *trapezitai*, the Athenians not only facilitated the creation of new great households, and their integration into prevailing society; they also dealt with (or, rather, failed to deal with) wives' personal status in a way that has been baffling to modern scholars (see n. 73 above), but that in fact reflects juridical adaptation to the needs of banking households.

The prominent banker Pasiōn had been naturalized as an Athenian citizen not long before his death in 370/69.[205] By then, grants of citizenship were in

---

liberal ideology and the country's regressive social reality. The result: recognition in practice of unequal agreements between freedmen and their ex-owners, but silence in the codified law, which could not explicitly countenance the reality of rural relations of dependence. See da Cunha 1985. Cf. Whitcombe 1985 (written law's silence on traditional relations between Indian zamindars and their dependents).

[202]See Wolff 1944; Patterson 1981. Cf. Paoli 1976: 197–99.

[203]Citizenship was given only to persons born from marital unions in which both parents were Athenian citizens. For the triumph of this requirement of double endogamy over alternative criteria, see Davies 1977–78.

[204]Mass grants are known to have occurred only in two exceptional wartime circumstances: to Athens's Plataian allies in 427, and in order to provide desperately needed sailors for the Arginousai campaign in 406.

[205]Dem. 46.13. He was not a citizen at the time that Isok. 17 was argued (late 390s): see §33 (use of Pythodōros the citizen as his agent) and §41 (his inclusion among the ξένοι εἰσφέροντες). Davies (1971: 430) reasonably infers that Pasiōn's receipt of citizenship resulted from his military and naval benefactions to the city (Dem. 45.85, 59.2). There would have been little opportunity for such benefactions during the tranquil period stretching from 386 to 377, when Athens was carefully avoiding actions that might endanger the Peace of 387/6. Cf., for example, the terms of renewal of Athens's alliance with Chios in 384/3 (I.G. II² 34, ll. 6–16) intended to avoid disturbance of the Peace.

general explicitly extended to descendants of the honorands,[206] and Pasiōn's children and grandchildren, male and female, are known to have been recognized as Athenian citizens.[207] Yet the status of his wife-widow Archippē is unknown: in contrast to their explicit grant of citizenship to the descendants of male honorands, Athenian naturalization decrees ignore wives.[208] And unlike certain other Greek states of the fourth century,[209] Athens did not enfranchise women in their own right. As a result, despite preservation of a number of court cases in which Archippē's family situation, role in the banking household, and disposition of property are discussed in detail, Archippē's own citizenship is never explicitly mentioned. This ellipsis in itself presented no ideological inconsistency or practical difficulty: the essence of an Athenian woman's citizenship lay in the capacity to give birth to Athenian citizens.[210] In providing for the offspring of male honorands, therefore, the Assembly was fully meeting conventional family needs through legislation compatible with community social values. But for bankers, this omission raised the likelihood that their typical testamentary directions would result in gross violation of Athenian law. Archippē's situation is graphic: whether she is considered a citizen or a foreigner, Pasiōn's arrangements are *prima facie* patently unlawful.

On his death in 370/69 (Dem. 46.13), Pasiōn in his will "gave" his wife Archippē to Phormiōn, to whom he had previously leased his bank.[211] Although Phormiōn did not obtain Athenian citizenship until 361/60,[212] he was married to Archippē in 368.[213] If Archippē were a citizen, this marriage blatantly violated the statutory prohibition of a noncitizen's cohabitation in marriage with an Athenian citizen: male noncitizens in such relationships were to be sold into slavery, and their goods confiscated.[214] But if Archippē were not

---

[206]Sometime after 388 (but prior to 369/8), offspring began to be routinely included in grants of citizenship. Osborne 1981–83, 4: 151–52.

[207]His son Apollodōros, born in 395/4 (24 years old at the time of his father's death in 370/69: Dem. 36.22, 46.13), refers to himself as a naturalized citizen, κατὰ ψήφισμα πολίτης (Dem. 53.18), ποιητὸς πολίτης (Dem. 45.78). Pasiōn's granddaughter, married to the citizen Theomnēstos, clearly held Athenian citizenship. See Dem. 59.1–15.

[208]Osborne 1972: 147 n. 75; 1981–83, 4: 150.

[209]See, for example, S.E.G. 15.384, 18.264, 19.425, 23.470. Roman citizenship grants explicitly mentioned wives: see, for example, C.I.L. 16.1.10–13.

[210]See Sealey 1990: 19; Just 1989: 24. The right to motherhood was recognized as a moral claim of women: see Isaios 2.7–8, 8.36. For the peripheral aspects of female citizenship, see Patterson 1986; for the concept of "passive" citizens, see Mossé 1979a; Lotze 1981.

[211]Dem. 45.28: δίδωμι τὴν ἐμαυτοῦ γυναῖκα 'Αρχίππην Φορμίωνι, καὶ προῖκα ἐπιδίδωμι 'Αρχίππῃ, τάλαντον μὲν τὸ ἐκ Πεπαρήθου, τάλαντον δὲ τὸ αὐτόθεν, σονοικίαν ἑκατὸν μνῶν, θεραπαίνας καὶ τὰ χρυσία, καὶ τἆλλα ὅσα ἐστὶν αὐτῇ ἔνδον, ἅπαντα ταῦτα 'Αρχίππῃ δίδωμι. Cf. Dem. 36.8.

[212]Dem. 46.13. Cf. Dem. 36.6 and 47.

[213]Dem. 45.3; Dem. 46.20–21.

[214]The text of the law is quoted at Dem. 59.16: ΝΟΜΟΣ: 'Εὰν δὲ ξένος ἀστῇ συνοικῇ τέχνῃ ἢ μηχανῇ ἡτινιοῦν, γραφέσθω πρὸς τοὺς θεσμοθέτας 'Αθηναίων ὁ

an Athenian citizen, Phormiōn's parallel directions providing her with
ownership of substantial real estate (a multiple-dwelling apartment house, or
synoikia) would have been clearly illegal: noncitizens were precluded from
owning real estate in Attica.[215] Archippē's situation was not unique or insignificant: Demosthenes makes clear that for bankers such arrangements were
actually the norm, at Athens and elsewhere, as evidenced by such archetypical
exemplars as the Athenian bankers Sōkratēs, Satyros, Sōklēs, and Timodēmos
(Dem. 36.29; see above, pp. 79–80). Metic and slave bankers who obtained
citizenship at Athens, and thereafter left their banks and their wives to their
slaves, would have confronted the same dilemma: the wife, if a citizen, could
not lawfully marry the banker's noncitizen successor; if not a citizen, she could
not own the house that was an integral part of the *oikos* that the banker was
seeking to perpetuate.

Analyzed on general juridical principals, Archippē's personal situation presents a conundrum resistant to solution.[216] Athens could not easily avail itself
of the modern response of including a spouse automatically in citizenship
decrees or extending to a woman a separate right of naturalization (a step known
to have been adopted by at least some other ancient Greek communities; see
above, n. 209). At Athens, institutions situated in the male world of the community sought to avoid all contact with, and even mention of, living women.
This effort reflected an ethical norm so deeply held that in Athenian litigation,
speakers consistently employed complex circumlocution even to avoid mentioning their own female relatives by name: with alacrity, litigants freely referred by name to their opponents' female connections, tacitly excoriating

βουλόμενος . . . ἐὰν δὲ ἁλῷ, πεπράσθω καὶ αὐτὸς καὶ ἡ οὐσία αὐτοῦ, . . . ἔστω δὲ καὶ
ἐὰν ἡ ξένη τῷ ἀστῷ συνοικῇ κατὰ ταὐτά. Under the earlier law prevailing from the mid-fifth
century, offspring of citizen/noncitizen marriages would have been denied Athenian citizenship,
but it is uncertain whether the relationship itself would have been invalid: cf., for example,
Hignett 1952: 343, and MacDowell 1978: 67, 87 (invalid) with Harrison 1968–71, 1: 26, and
Patterson 1981: 29 n. 3, 95 n. 57, 99 (permitted but discouraged). By the time of Archippē's
marriage to Phormiōn, the law quoted at Dem. 59.16 appears already to have been in effect (cf.
Whitehead 1986b: 111). By 350/49, the approximate date of the first definitive confirmation of
the law's effectiveness (cf. Biscardi and Cantarella 1974: 104; Gernet 1954–60: 4, 67 n. 3), the
speaker of Dem. 36 is explaining to his audience the ubiquity of the bankers' practice of arranging
for the marriage of their wives to their slave-assistants (§§28–29).

[215]Although the provisions of Pasiōn's will might be read as purporting to convey the property
to Archippē only as her dowry, her husband Phormiōn (at this time a noncitizen) could not
lawfully have held ownership of the real estate as her *kyrios*. Since an alien was absolutely
precluded from owning real estate at Athens, even for a brief period, the dilemma is not resolved
by assuming that the property was to be sold immediately upon receipt by Archippē: if she could
not take legal title, she could not effectively convey the property. For the possibility of noncitizen
bankers securing loans by real estate and executing thereon, see below, pp. 133–36.

[216]For the recurring inability of scholars to reconcile the various apparent contradictions, see
Whitehead 1986b. Carey (1991) is no more successful: in arguing that Archippē always remained
an alien, he is forced to suggest that she ceased to be Pasiōn's wife after he attained citizenship—
although Pasiōn himself in his will terms her "my wife" (τὴν ἐμαυτοῦ γυναῖκα, Dem. 45.28).

adversaries' impropriety in intermixing, to their women's disgrace, the antithethical worlds of court and *oikos*.[217] To be sure, the names of women no longer alive might properly be mentioned in court, just as in naturalization decrees citizenship could be bestowed, without sexual differentiation, on the descendants of the naturalized male: female children were thus included without the necessity of specific mention and consequent violation of their personae.[218] For modern legal systems, failure to resolve the wife's civil status would create an unacceptable void. For the Athenian system, however, it generally presented no difficulty, since citizenship rights (other than the privilege of procreating new citizens) could be exercised exclusively within the judicial and political systems, institutions entirely outside the sphere of the *oikos* where wives functioned. A banker's wife was an exception, since she was involved with a family business that necessarily functioned in both the public and the private areas.

The adaptation espoused by the law, not surprisingly, was consistent with its basic avoidance of women (and of foreigners):[219] it permitted an inherently equivocal citizenship status to the wives of naturalized bankers. This ambiguity allowed alien bankers to make arrangements for their wives and property compatible with the banks' needs, while still obtaining for themselves the citizenship necessary to their integration into Athenian life.

Under Athenian law, Archippē was neither exclusively an Athenian citizen nor exclusively an alien. As Whitehead has suggested, the law granted her both legal statuses as circumstance required, a position of "Janus-like duality" (1986b: 114). This equivocality is explicitly recognized by Apollodōros when he suggests that even if Pasiōn's will had "given" Archippē in marriage to Phormiōn, the latter should not have acted on his own in effectuating that testamentary direction. Instead, Apollodōros insists, "if Phormiōn wished to act properly," he should have sought through the formal legal system confirmation of the will's provision, bringing a declaratory action "before the archon if he claimed her as a citizen, and before the polemarch, if as a foreigner."[220]

---

[217]Highly contorted periphrasis occurred when women were central to the issues in litigation or where presentation of the facts required reference to many females. For a demonstration of the consistency with which litigants adhered to these patterns, see Schaps 1971. Cf. Gould 1980: 45; Bremmer 1981.

[218]American newspapers still generally follow a long-established practice of not reporting the names of female victims of rape, an anonymity limited, however, to women still alive at the time of reporting.

[219]In the absence of special arrangements (such as those arising from interstate treaty or connected with residence rights obtained by foreigners), the Greek cities allowed access to their courts only to their own citizens. See Cohen 1973: 59–62; Gernet [1938] 1955: 181–82; Gauthier 1972: 149–56. Even the right to reside at Athens may have been granted initially through a procedure in which the foreigner did not directly participate: Levy 1987: 60.

[220]Dem. 46.23: Οὐκοῦν αὐτόν, εἴπερ ἐβούλετο ὀρθῶς διαπράττεσθαι, λαχεῖν ἔδει τῆς ἐπικλήρου, εἴτε κατὰ δόσιν αὐτῷ προσῆκεν εἴτε κατὰ γένος, εἰ μὲν ὡς ὑπὲρ ἀστῆς, πρὸς τὸν ἄρχοντα, εἰ δὲ ὡς ὑπὲρ ξένης, πρὸς τὸν πολέμαρχον.

In actual practice, just as in Archippē's case, the issue of the wife's status would normally never be raised, and her citizenship never resolved. Although an outsider might seek a determination in the courts about an adversary's relationship with a woman, as in the famous case of Neaira (Dem. 59), both law and societal values tended to preclude such litigation by family members. It was, of course, the law's silence that had left Archippē's status ambiguous when her husband was explicitly raised from alien to citizen through naturalization. Far from bringing female family members into the "outside" court system,[221] male family members would normally struggle to protect their female relatives from the dishonor of being publicly discussed. Accordingly, despite his averred outrage, during his mother's lifetime Apollodōros avoided court hearings that would have raised any of these issues.[222] Only after her death did he proceed against Phormiōn. And even then, he made only the most veiled suggestion that his mother's status might have invalidated the marriage,[223] a muted implication without effect, offered many years after her death in an independent action against the unrelated Stephanos.

Women's Property Rights

The intense personalization of the Athenian *trapeza*, legally inseparable from the persona of its proprietor, meant that proprietors' assets were intermingled with bank receivables (see above, pp. 62–66) and that *trapezitai* were personally liable for repayment of deposits. For bankers, this interrelationship of business and household called for some workable arrangement permitting the successful continuation of both *oikos* and *trapeza*. As we have seen, testamentary provision of marriage between wives and slaves was a common solution.

Here, too, however, the situation of Archippē presents difficulty. The basic nature of property ownership at Athens has baffled modern scholars, who have asserted that in fact the Athenians never developed a true concept of

[221] "Inside" (pertaining to the household) and "outside" (pertaining to the public sphere) are themselves terms basic to the Athenian universe of complementary opposites. For the "inside" as the wife's area of management, see Xen., *Oik.* 7.3; Aristot., *Oik.* 1343b7–1344a22 (1.3–4). Pasiōn appropriately bequeaths to Archippē all the items "inside" (ὅσα ἐστὶν αὐτῇ ἔνδον, ἅπαντα ταῦτα Ἀρχίππῃ δίδωμι: Dem. 45.28).

[222] Although the γραφὴ ξενίας presumably was available, he never brought an action to clarify her marital situation and thereby his own claims. Nor did he bring a private suit (δίκη ἰδία); he withdrew before trial the γραφὴ ὕβρεως that he did present (Dem. 45.3–4).

[223] In accord with Athenian values, Apollodōros in litigation never speaks with specificity about the circumstances surrounding his mother's marriage, asserting rather the inappropriateness of a son's speaking in detail in court about a mother, even one long deceased: οὐκ ἴσως καλὸν υἱεῖ περὶ μητρὸς ἀκριβῶς εἰπεῖν, Dem. 45.3.

"ownership," or even a term for it.[224] Nonetheless, it has been uniformly agreed that in Athens women were unable to own property directly in their own name and their own right.[225] This legal incapacity may have been vitiated in daily life by their exercise of practical control over certain goods, in particular their own clothing and jewelry, and perhaps a little money,[226] and it has even been suggested that in some ways property should be conceived of as held not as his own by the male head of the household, but in a representative capacity on behalf of the *oikos* as an entity.[227] But either approach dismisses direct female ownership: if property is understood as owned through households, the male head of the family controlled it through his position as *kyrios* ("master") of the members of the family; if property is understood as owned individually, women were unable to function as owners because of their dependence on masters who alone were legally capable of controlling assets.[228]

This analysis still cannot explain Archippē's position with respect to property attributed to her. She seems clearly to have had monetary assets fully recognized, in legal context, as her own: Apollodōros is accused in court of seeking 3,000 *dr.* from her estate "in addition to the 2,000 *dr.* that she had given to Phormiōn's children."[229] Pasiōn states in his will that he "gives to Archippē as dowry one talent from Peparēthos, another talent here at Athens, a *synoikia*

---

[224]Wolff 1944: 63; Harrison 1968–71, 1: 201. MacDowell terms the Athenian property laws "primitive" (1978: 133). Scholars have tended to cite Aristot., *Rhet.* 1361a (1.5.7) as the sole known Greek definition of ownership (see, e.g., Jones 1956: 198; but note Kränzlein's reservations, 1963: 33, 51–52). In *Rhetoric*, Aristotle focuses on the power to alienate (ἀπαλλοτριῶσαι) as the essence of "proprietorship" (τοῦ οἰκεῖα εἶναι). Athenian law specifically prohibited women from engaging in any contractual dealings involving more than one medimnos of barley (ουμβάλλειν μηδὲ γυναικὶ πέρα μεδίμνου κριθῶν [Isaios 10.10; cf. Aischinēs 1.18]). On the practical significance of the limitation, see Kuenen-Janssens 1941: 212.

[225]Even Foxhall, who demonstrates the economic importance of focusing on the right to use property rather than on the capacity to alienate, can argue only "that it is inappropriate to consider property solely as a function of individual ownership," while noting the *opinio communis* that "women in ancient Athens could not and did not own property" (1989: 22, 23).

[226]Sealey (1990: 45–49) equates this right of control to a "negative account of ownership," in which women's fundamental rights are not entirely eliminated by her *kyrios*'s "authority to administer her property for the specific purpose of her upkeep and the protection of her interests" (p. 48).

[227]This view has ancient support from Sōsitheos, who, in the struggle for the estate of Hagnias (Dem. 43), maintains that the concept of ownership by household is fundamental to the Athenian law of property. See Thompson 1976: passim. MacDowell disposes of this contention peremptorily: "Athenian law did not recognise rights of families, but rights of individual persons" (1989b: 21).

[228]Schaps advances this premise at length and with vigor (1979: 4–17), and his view has won general acceptance: see Powell 1988: ch. 8; Garner 1987: 83–87; Foxhall 1989: 22; Just 1989: 29.

[229]Dem. 36.14: τρισχιλίας ἐγκαλέσας ἀργυρίου δραχμὰς πρὸς αἷς ἔδωκεν ἐκείνη διοχιλίαις τοῖς τούτου παιδίοις.

(multiple-dwelling house) worth 100 mnai, female slaves, gold jewelry, and the other items of hers that are inside [the house]."[230] Whether interpreted as merely confirming Archippē's ownership of property that is already hers, or as granting her new property, or as conveying assets to her new husband as her *kyrios*, the disposition is impossible under conventional interpretations of Athenian law. Since Archippē's new husband, Phormiōn, was not an Athenian citizen, he could not hold the real property as nominal or actual owner (see above, n. 215). The only other possible owner, Archippē herself, could not own the *synoikia*: even those scholars willing to see Athenian women as possibly indirect beneficial owners of assets do not contemplate their direct ownership of property in their own right.[231]

The solution again appears to lie in the ambiguous duality of Archippē's civil status. As a citizen, she would have had the right to own real estate—vitiated only by modern scholarly insistence on a female citizen's inability to own property directly in her own right. As a foreigner, however, her basic right of property ownership—albeit not of real estate—was recognized by Athenian law, though here again indirectly and not explicitly. The fourth-century statute prohibiting marriage between Athenians and foreigners provided that a male foreigner, on conviction, forfeit all of his property and be sold into slavery; it then proceeded to provide *"the same penalty"* (namely, sale into slavery and loss of property) for female foreigners found in violation of the statute.[232] The text necessarily contemplates a foreign woman's direct ownership of property, a clear indication that whatever the limitations under Athenian law on Athenian women's rights of ownership, these were not applicable to foreign women.

Outside Athens, women clearly had substantial rights to own property directly. In the only other polis for which we have knowledge comparable to what we have for Athens in the classical period, Gortyn on Crete,[233] women had full legal power to hold and manage their own assets in their own name,[234] and even to inherit their own portion from their parent's estate (although only one-half of a brother's interest).[235] They could deal with their property without the inter-

---

[230]Dem. 45.28. See the Greek text, n. 211 above.

[231]Harrison, for example, believes that denial of Athenian women's "ownership" of property is essentially an exercise in semantics ("largely a matter of definition," 1968–71, 1: 236). But he still insists that "there can be no doubt that a woman remained under some sort of tutelage during the whole of her life," and that it was this *kyrios* who had to represent her except for "the most trifling contract" (ibid., 108).

[232]ἔστω δὲ καὶ ἐὰν ἡ ξένη τῷ ἀστῷ συνοικῇ κατὰ ταὐτά. For fuller reference, see above, n. 214.

[233]In the Hellenistic and Roman periods, women are frequently identified as property owners. See Ste. Croix 1970: 273. Even at Athens, I.G. II² 2776 (2nd century A.D.) discloses a number of women as landowners. See Day 1942: 232–33.

[234]See Lex. Gort. 2.45–50; 3.17–37, 40–43; 4.23–27, 48–54; 5.1–9, 17–22; 6.52 to 8.30; 9.1–11). See Willetts 1967: 20, 23. Cf. Thomson 1966: 204; *DHR* 1.457.

[235]Lex Gort. 4.29–48.

vention of a *kyrios*,[236] and there is frequent mention of "maternal" assets separate from "paternal" property.[237] At Tegea, an inscription concerning the return of exiles provides for confiscated property, and recognizes "maternal assets" independent of "paternal."[238] Without recorded resistance or even special notice, Spartan women even entered their own teams in the pan-Hellenic Olympic chariot races—and won.[239] By the third century, most of the wealth in Sparta was said to be under the control of women.[240]

Thus—as assumed in Dem. 59.16 (see n. 214 above)—Athenian legislation dealing with foreign women could not avoid recognizing their possible ownership of property under the laws of their own state. Archippē, therefore, as a foreigner, pursuant to her "Janus-like" duality of citizenship, could be, and apparently was, recognized under Athenian law as direct owner of her own assets. This right of banking wives—or at least the many who were not citizens—to own property directly provided the nexus for perpetuation of the banking *oikos*. In this context, disposition of the bank was inseparable from the marital disposition of the banker's wife. Separation of the widow from the bank's new proprietor would, at the least, have created enormous legal conundra, necessarily disturbing to the "confidence" (*pistis*) critical to a successful bank operation (Dem. 36.57). Athenian bankers had strong property incentive to prefer "a pile of money over pedigree"[241] by joining their wives and slaves in marriage. To this preference the law was accommodating.

It was an accommodation whose significance should not be underestimated: Athens was strongly committed to the uniform imposition of Athenian law wherever possible, especially on noncitizens resident in Attica, but also on all others having any juridical contact with the state. This is clear even in the fragmentary materials surviving from bilateral interstate treaties concluded during the fifth-century period of empire.[242] In the fourth century, all evidence "shows the exclusive application of Athenian law in the courts and observance of it by metics."[243] (These metics would include former slaves who, even after

---

[236]Ibid., 8.47–51, 9.1–7.

[237]Ibid., 4.43–6, 6.31–46, 11.42–45.

[238]S.I.G.³ 306, ll. 4–9, 48–57 = Tod 1948: 202: τὰ ματρῶια, τὰ πατρῶια.

[239]Paus. 3.8.1, 6.1.6.

[240]Plut., *Agis* 7.3–4, 4.1.

[241]Defending the practice of marrying bankers' widows to successors of servile origin, Demosthenes makes this explicit: [τοῖς ἀπὸ τοῦ χρηματίσασθαι ἀξιωθεῖσιν] ἐν πλήθος χρημάτων ἀντὶ τοῦ γένους καλόν ἐστιν ἐλέσθαι (Dem. 36.30).

[242]For such treaties, see Gauthier 1972: Cataldi 1983. The surviving texts of these agreements, too fragmentary to offer much substantive guidance (cf. MacDowell 1978: 220–21), are generally analyzed in political rather than juridical terms. See Cataldi 1983: 345–46 n. 108. On direct conflicts of law, the fullest treatment is Lewald 1946, the continued viability of which (reprinted twice [including a German translation] during the twenty-five years following its initial publication) suggests the dearth of attention to the subject.

[243]Whitehead 1977: 89. Maffi has argued that ethnic groups resident in Athens continued to

obtaining their freedom, did not receive Athenian citizenship, but were legally assimilated to other metics. [244]) Indeed, Lysias shows clearly that the Athenian metic was considered, by the very fact of residence in Attica, to have accepted the applicability of Athenian law. [245]

But this consistent insistence on Athenian substantive provisions occurred in the courts, in the public sphere of men. For Athenian law, adaptation to women's rights, and acceptance of alien legal standards, was far easier in the context of the *oikos*. As we have seen, in many ways the *oikos* itself was alien to the world of law, antithetical to the male world of community. It was fitting, then, that the *trapeza*, mediating between public and private life, be allowed a legal solution that made economic sense—albeit with a clarity explicable not through modern juridical exegesis, but only through an appreciation of Athenian values and concepts.

---

utilize their own law (1972: 177–79). Although Isokrates (19.12–14) does attest to the appeal by two Siphnians resident in Aigina to Siphnian-Kean law (§13), Maffi was unable to offer a single actual Athenian example of such usage.

[244]Harrison 1968–71, 1: 188. Cf. Biezunska-Malowist 1966a: 66–72.

[245]Lysias 22.5: ὡς πεισόμενος τοῖς νόμοις τοῖς τῆς πόλεως.

Chapter 5

BANKING OPERATIONS: "RISK-LADEN REVENUES FROM 'OTHER PEOPLE'S MONEY' "

The Athenian bank is a business operation that produces
risk-laden revenues from other people's money.
—Demosthenes[1]

DEMOSTHENES' CLASSIC DEFINITION captures the inherent tension of the Athenian bank: the coupling of an obligation to repay funds from various external sources with the risk of seeking to profit from, or even lose, these monies in loan and investment activities.

"Other people's money" delivered to a bank was termed a *parakatathēkē*. By the fourth century, the word had acquired clear meaning in banking context: loans were said to be funded from "bank deposits."[2] Like the English word "deposit," however, *parakatathēkē* was not an exclusively technical term. It might describe any placement of property or money entrusted to the care of any person or institution.[3] Herodotos (5.92), for example, tells of the dire consequences arising from a *parakatathēkē* delivered by a friend to the Corinthian tyrant Periander, but mislaid by him. Because of this element of "trust," the word appears to have encompassed, from early times, both the concept of "delivery" and a concomitant fiduciary aspect: at some point the *parakatathēkē* had to be returned or repaid.

This fundamental obligation of repayment, rather than legalistic nuances reflected in terminology,[4] governed the bank's receipt of monies. Deposits

---

[1]Dem. 36.11: ἡ δ᾽ ἐργασία προσόδους ἔχουσ᾽ ἐπικινδύνους ἀπὸ χρημάτων ἀλλοτρίων. "Operation" was an especially appropriate word to describe a business dealing in money, since ἐργασία was commonly extended in Greek usage to describe the income resulting from business endeavors, e.g., the earnings of a slave (Hyp., *Ath.* 22: ἐὰν ἐργασίαν εὕρῃ ὁ οἰκέτης) or even "money-making" itself (Aristot., *E.N.* 1160a16: πρὸς ἐργασίαν χρημάτων).

[2]Dem. 36.5: ἀπὸ τῶν παρακαταθηκῶν τῶν τῆς τραπέζης.

[3]The "Definitions" attributed to Plato (415d) delineate παρακαταθήκη as δόμα μετὰ πίστεως ("gift with trust"). The term came even to have a figurative meaning, as in the concept of holding laws as a trust (Dem. 21.177: ταῦτ᾽ [*sc.* τοὺς νόμους] ἔχεθ᾽ ὑμεῖς οἱ δικάζοντες ἀεὶ παρὰ τῶν ἄλλων ὡσπερεὶ παρακαταθήκην; cf. Aischinēs 21.177). A person entrusted to a guardian was considered a *parakatathēkē*. See Dem. 28.15 (children); Dein. 1.9 (persons under protection of the state).

[4]Although other phrases, such as *thema* and *parathema* ("placements"), were also employed, only in the later Hellenistic period are these terms used with the specialized meaning of "bank

placed with banks are even denominated as "loans" to the *trapezai*. When a bank was leased, the obligation to repay deposits was a lessee's prime concern.[5] Subject to this basic duty, the absence of governmental restrictions or economic monopoly (see above, Chapter 3) resulted in wide variance in the terms on which, and the mechanisms through which, bankers sought funds. Some *trapezitai* on at least some occasions offered a direct return on monies entrusted to them. Other sums earned no monetary yield but provided customers with nonmonetary benefits that required prior delivery of funds to the bank: utilization of financial mechanisms such as payment orders to third parties; participation in business opportunities through the bank, including syndications of maritime loans; and the concealment of wealth, extremely significant in a state where taxes were imposed at extremely high rates, but only on a limited number of the most conspicuously wealthy individuals. Depositors in turn often had more than one motivation. The result of such interplay was a myriad of highly individualized arrangements.

This summary, presented hereafter in detail, conflicts sharply with the highly formalistic characterization of Athenian bank deposits that has prevailed since at least the sixteenth century, an analysis proffering definitional refinements derived not from Athenian evidence but from Roman-law conceptualization set forth, not surprisingly, in Latin vocabulary. According to this schema, deposits are first categorized as "regular" ("depositum merum et purum") and "irregular" ("depositum irregulare," essentially "mutuum"). "Regular" deposits must be retained by the banker, who is obligated to return the exact item(s) delivered and may not utilize them in any fashion; "irregular" deposits may be employed by the banker to produce revenue for the bank.[6] Further refinements are offered: divisions of "irregular" deposits, and identification of special categories (such as the "depositum sequestrum") that are in reality representative of Roman practices.[7]

The entire categorization is artificial, however, and demonstrably in conflict with actual Athenian practice. For example, not a single case is known of any

---

deposit," and even then usage is not entirely consistent. Considerable (and inconsistent) variety in terminology continued even after the classical period (*pace* Bikerman 1939–44: 15). See Korver 1934: 28–39.

[5]The bank's deposits, a prime object of lease (Dem. 36.13), were likely to have been committed in large part to loans and investments (see below, pp. 185–89). Thus the lessee Phormiōn, on "taking the deposits" (τὰς παρακαταθήκας λαμβάνων), endeavored to insure that he would be able to repay those monies by preserving his predecessor's ability to collect certain outstanding loans (Dem. 36.4–6). See below, pp. 129–36.

[6]For classic statements of this formulation, see, for example, Paoli [1930] 1974: 21–22; Beauchet [1897] 1969, 4: 333–37. Cf. Gernet 1981: 350 n. 14.

[7]Cf. Lipsius [1905–15] 1966: 714–15; Caillemer 1876: 525–27. In fact, these terms are often post-classical. "Depositum irregulare," for example, was unknown even to the Glossators. It first appeared in the Middle Ages in the writing of Jason of Maino. See Niemeyer 1889: 110 n. 21; Litewski 1974: 215.

"regular" deposit in money. The bank's obligation to repay a deposit in specie could always be met through the return of other coins having equivalent value; not a single example can be cited of any restriction on a banker's handling of money on deposit.[8] Far from being obligated to return specific coins, the bankers on occasion (as we shall see below) actually received deposits in order to convey equivalent sums through representatives at distant places, thus avoiding physical delivery of the coins deposited. "Regular deposits," a term unknown to the Athenians, were actually nonfinancial transactions involving legal documents and valuable objects. With regard to papers, the *trapezitai* appear to have functioned like modern escrow agents.[9] In the case of precious goods, their role was one of safekeeping (in modern terms, similar, perhaps, to "bailees" under so-called contracts of "bailment"). When thus acting as fiduciaries, the bankers were expected to return the actual item delivered.[10] But this tells us nothing about the terms governing receipt of monetary deposits.

Utilizing this supposed dichotomy between "regular" and "irregular" deposits, however, the prevailing modern scholarly view posits anachronistically that Athenian *trapezitai*, in the fashion of modern bankers, actually differentiated between two forms of "irregular deposits": interest-bearing time deposits ("dépôts de placement"), and demand deposits ("dépôts de paiement") on which they did not pay interest.[11] (This opinion, of course, presupposes absolutely or relatively uniform practice, a similarity of operation not likely to have prevailed among the unregulated Athenian banks). Here again, the very formulation (payment of "interest" on types of "deposits" corresponding to modern categorization) itself violates Attic conceptualization: just as "interest" was unknown to Athenians functioning through polarized concepts of "landed" and "maritime" "yield" (see above, Chapter 3), clearly defined categories of deposit were also alien.

For the Athenians, funds delivered to a bank remained the property of the depositor and had to be repaid, even if the bank in seeking to generate revenues

---

[8]Given the wide variety of coins and their varying exchange rates, determination of "equivalent value" might not be without difficulty. See above, pp. 18–19; below, pp. 149–50.

[9]Cf. Dem. 34.6, 56.15; I.G. II² 2741 (Finley no. 39) ll. 4–6.

[10]But see Dem. 49.31–32, where a deposit of precious bowls, inadvertently given by the bank to a third party, is repaid—after negotiation—at an agreed-on cash price.

[11]For this *opinio communis*, see Isager and Hansen 1975: 95; Bogaert 1986a: 19; 1968: 346–48. Hasebroek (1920: 156–58) proffers the distinction, but relates it, arbitrarily, to the Greek differentiation between φανερὰ οὐσία and ἀφανὴς οὐσία. Of course, the constant changes in modern practices can quickly undo even sophisticated recourse to contemporary practice. Thompson (1979: 225), for example, notes that "modern banks normally distinguish between demand deposits, which bear no interest, and time deposits, which do" and concludes that "some scholars have failed to notice this distinction when discussing Greek banking and have thus fallen into error." But in the years immediately following 1979, "transaction accounts" ("demand deposits" carrying interest payments) quickly became fashionable; the "distinction" disappeared.

had actually suffered losses. But—absent explicit agreement to the contrary—the banker was free to use funds on deposit as he wished, subject always to a paramount fiduciary obligation to return "other people's money": not the specific coins given to him, but their equivalent value. Hence, Demosthenes' characterization of the *trapeza* as a "business operation that produces risk-laden revenues from other people's money."

Obtaining "Other People's Money"

An ancient scandal illustrates the banks' absolute obligation to return funds delivered, the bankers' freedom to use these monies while on deposit, and the often clandestine considerations that generated funds for the *trapeza*. Although the episode preserves the only surviving explicit reference to Athenian bankers paying a yield on funds entrusted to them (W. E. Thompson 1979: 228), these funds are described not as deposits but as "loans," and are subject to repayment at the will of the depositor, "on demand," in stark opposition to the modern view that bankers paid such "interest" only on time deposits.

The Treasurers of Athena, overseers of the monies belonging to the Goddess, and the Treasurers of the Other Gods[12] were imprisoned after burning the Opisthodomos, part of the sacred complex on the Acropolis, in an effort to avoid detection for having delivered sacred monies to certain bankers.[13] The scheme had been well conceived: funds lying in the Opisthodomos were "lent" to the bankers, in order to utilize the confidentiality of bank transactions to prevent anyone outside the scheme from knowing that the Treasurers themselves were so "profiting." On repayment, the Treasurers would have been able to retain the monies earned on the principal sums entrusted, and the Goddess would have had her funds back, without yield, just as if the funds had remained untouched in the Opisthodomos. But the scam was discovered after the banks were unable to make repayment.

This episode establishes clearly that bankers might offer a cash return on

---

[12]On these officials, see Ferguson 1932 (pp. 129ff. for this episode), and Linders 1975. For 377/6 as the possible date of the fire, see Chapter 6.

[13]Scholion to Dem. 24.136: ἔδοξε τοῖς ταμίαις, ὥστε λάθρα τῆς πόλεως δανεῖσαι ταῦτα τοῖς τραπεζίταις, ἵν' αὐτοὶ κερδάνωσιν ἐκ τούτου. ὡς δὲ τοῦτο ἐποίησαν, ἔτυχεν ὕστερον ἀνατραπῆναι τὰς τραπέζας. ἔδοξεν οὖν αὐτοῖς ἐμπρῆσαι τὸν ὀπισθόδομον, ἵνα δόξῃ τὰ χρήματα ὑπὸ τοῦ πυρὸς ἀναλωθῆναι καὶ μὴ ὑπ' αὐτῶν (Dilts 1983–86: 272b). An alternative note (ibid., 272a) explicitly describes the "loan" as having been made to "certain (τισὶ) bankers" who were "unable" to repay the funds (ἀπορησάντων τῶν τραπεζιτῶν). The scheme is remarkably similar to the scandal involving the privately owned Bank of Crete that brought down the Greek government of Prime Minister Papandreou in 1989. In the modern case, government ministers deposited enormous amounts of government funds in the Bank of Crete, with the interest thereon allegedly to be diverted to the officials personally. Here, too, the bank's failure resulted in disclosure of the wrongdoing. See *The New York Times*, Sept. 21, 1989, A14; Sept. 27, 1989, A3.

funds entrusted to them: otherwise the Treasurers could not have hoped both to "profit" themselves and to return the principal intact to the Acropolis, where it had supposedly been lying sacrosanct but clearly producing no revenue (*arga*). But, in conflict with modern insistence that a return could be paid only on funds left for a fixed period,[14] these monies necessarily had to be available "on demand": the Treasurers could not anticipate when the city might need the Goddess's cash.[15]

Furthermore, the monies delivered to the bankers here are not referred to as "deposits" at all, but rather as "loans," in Athenian context an appropriate characterization. Linguistically, the Greeks defined "lending" and "borrowing" by the same term, *daneiz-*. Lending is the active form of the word; borrowing, the reflexive or passive. Thus it was natural to describe the receipt of money *by* a bank as a loan, and the disbursement of money to others also as a loan. The banker Aristolochos is described as "owing" funds to many.[16] The bankers Sōsinomos and Timodēmos and others are said to have failed when they were unable to repay those to whom they were in debt.[17] This terminology should not be surprising, for a "loan" and a "deposit" are not inherently differentiable: the essence of a bank deposit, the absolute obligation of the banker to return the funds, is implicit in the very concept of a "loan."[18] In the absence of governmental regulations defining and limiting the placements that might be accepted by a bank, flexibility in terminology may be expected to accompany flexibility in the actual terms of deposit.

Confidentiality is a recurrent motivation for placement of funds with a *trapeza*. Thus the wealthy Stephanos is said to have acted in concert with various bankers, including Phormiōn and Aristolochos, "to conceal his wealth . . . in order that he might obtain secret returns through the bank."[19] As with the Treasurers' bank placements, secrecy from the state was sought: Stephanos was

---

[14]Distant analogies have been offered to justify the prevailing dogma relating payment of interest to the entrusting of funds for a fixed period, or the alternate view that bankers simply did not pay for funds. Bogaert (1986a: 23–24) offers the comparison of alleged Roman practice; Thompson (1979: 225, 239) appeals to fourteenth-century Bruges as an example of a banking community that depended essentially on noninterest-bearing demand deposits and rarely paid "interest" on "time deposits."

[15]Bogaert himself recognizes this: "S'ils apprenaient que la ville allait avoir besoin de fonds déposés dans l'Opisthodome, ils pouvaient immédiatement les retirer des banques" (1986a: 23–24).

[16]Dem. 36.50: ὁρᾶς τὸν Ἀριστόλοχον τὸν Χαριδήμου· ποτ' εἶχεν ἀγρόν, εἶτά γε νῦν πολλοί· πολλοῖς γὰρ ἐκεῖνος ὀφείλων αὐτὸν ἐκτήσατο.

[17]Dem. 36.50: καὶ τὸν Σωσίνομον καὶ τὸν Τιμόδημον καὶ τοὺς ἄλλους τραπεζίτας, οἵ, ἐπειδὴ διαλύειν ἐδέησεν οἷς ὤφειλον, ἐξέστησαν ἁπάντων τῶν ὄντων.

[18]Bogaert even offers an explanation for describing a "deposit" in Greek as a "loan": "Le scoliaste a voulu souligner le caractère lucratif de l'opération; en effet, δανεῖσαι évoque le paiement d'intérêts, ce qui n'est pas le cas pour παρακαταθεῖναι même en banque (1986a: 24).

[19]Dem. 45.66: τὰ ὄντ' ἀποκρύπτεσθαι . . . ἵν' ἐργασίας ἀφανεῖς διὰ τῆς τραπέζης ποιῆται. Cf. Gernet 1954–60: "par l'intermédiaire de la banque." See below, pp. 138–39.

using the banks as intermediaries to hide his substantial wealth[20] in order to avoid the costly public duties ("liturgies")[21] that lay at the heart of the Athenian tax system.[22] Only through placing funds with bankers in confidence, and obtaining a yield thereon, would Stephanos have been able both to "conceal his wealth" and to obtain "secret returns."[23] Similarly, a family sold or encumbered much of its equipment and furniture, thus frustrating a creditor seeking to collect a judgment (Dem. 47.54). But the family was keeping enough money "in the bank" to pay the judgment, a fact that the wife blurts out as the creditor is seizing her own property (§57). The physical assault by the creditor, leading to stout resistance at the time and counterclaims later, resulted from the creditor's ignorance as to the situs of the family's assets,[24] a likely motivation here for the family's conversion of physical assets into bank deposits.

The interplay of factors motivating placement of monies in a *trapeza* is most strikingly illustrated by the extensive dealings between the bank of Pasiōn and the son of Sopaios, a wealthy Bosporan businessman. In this fullest surviving report of relations between a banker and a customer (Isok. 17), the factor of secrecy is paramount, but the provision of services, including credit enhancement and the giving of personal and business advice, is also important.

The father, Sopaios, was a prominent and powerful figure in the Bosporan kingdom who had sent his son to Athens with money and ships filled with grain to engage in commerce (Isok. 17.3–4, 40). There he became a customer of Pasiōn's bank. His relationship with Pasiōn was so close, the son alleges, that he relied on the banker not only regarding money, but on other matters as well

---

[20]He is described as ἔχων οὐσίαν τοσαύτην ὥσθ' ἑκατὸν μνᾶς ἐπιδοῦναι τῇ θυγατρί. In contrast to this dowry of 100 mnai, Demosthenes claims that from an estate of almost 14 talents his father provided a dowry of only 80 mnai for Demosthenes' mother and 120 mnai for his sister (Dem. 27.5). And such assets would have placed the father among the most affluent residents of Attica: Demosthenes insists that even his guardians recognized these assets as comparable to those of the wealthiest Athenians (οἱ τὰ μέγιστα κεκτημένοι: Dem. 27.7). See Ste. Croix 1953: 45ff.; Schaps 1979: 78. For the considerable variations in dowry values, see Dimakis n.d.: 130–35.

[21]Dem. 45.66: ἵν' . . . μήτε χορηγῇ μήτε τριηραρχῇ μήτ' ἄλλο μηδὲν ὧν προσήκει ποιῇ. He was ultimately unsuccessful. In 322 (to be sure, more than 25 years after Apollodōros's charge), Stephanos's known wealth was sufficient to place him in the liturgical class (as syntrierarch on the tetērēs *Paralia Demotelous*: I.G. II² 1632, l. 29).

[22]See below, pp. 194–201.

[23]Thompson (1979: 226) suggests that Stephanos might have participated "as a partner" in banking "ventures." This still would have involved placing funds with the bankers and obtaining a yield thereon, quite compatible with Athenian banking activity, if not with modern terminology and concepts. See below, pp. 151–60.

[24]ᾤοντο μὲν γὰρ οὐ τοσαῦτα μόνον λήψεσθαι, ἀλλὰ πολλῷ πλείω· τὴν γὰρ οὖσάν μοι ποτὲ κατασκευὴν τῆς οἰκίας καταλήψεσθαι· ἀλλ' ὑπὸ τῶν λῃτουργιῶν καὶ τῶν εἰσφορῶν καὶ τῆς πρὸς ὑμᾶς φιλοτιμίας τὰ μὲν ἐνέχυρα κεῖται αὐτῶν, τὰ δὲ πέπραται.

(§6). Thus when the father fell temporarily into disfavor with the Bosporan king and the king's agents ordered the son to hand over his money and to return to Bosporos, Sopaios's son insists that he instead followed the banker's advice to deliver to the agents only that wealth of which the agents might have knowledge,[25] but to disclaim having funds in the *trapeza*: rather he insisted that he was actually indebted to the bank and to others (§§5–7). Although Sopaios was later restored to favor at Bosporos, permitting his son to reclaim his deposits, the banker then denied holding any such funds, citing the Bosporan's prior insistence that he was in fact indebted to the bank (§§8–11).

The litigation tantalizingly, if fleetingly, raises the veil that otherwise obfuscates the role of the banks in the "hidden" or "parallel" economy (see below, Chapter 6). At the same time, the case explicitly confirms the general prevalence of banking confidentiality: unique among Athenian commercial transactions, banking obligations, we are told, were created without witnesses.[26] Not surprisingly, in view of the other incentives for deposit of the Bosporan's monies, there is no indication that the banker provided a monetary yield on funds. But there is constant reminder of the bank's absolute obligation to return such money to its owner: this commitment implicitly underlies the entire dispute. The banker's sole defense is that he held no deposits; he offers no suggestion of possible circumstances that might absolve him of his obligation to repay monies delivered to the *trapeza*. The amounts involved are enormous: deposits sufficient to secure credit extensions of no less than seven talents (42,000 *dr.*),[27] gold bullion exchanged for currency having a value of about four talents (24,000 *dr.*).[28] These indications of the enormous scale of Athenian banking are confirmed by the overall tenor of the entire presentation: Athenian bankers disposed of enormous resources, relying on their profes-

---

[25]τὰ φανερὰ τῶν χρημάτων (§7). For the fundamental Athenian distinction between "manifest" (φανερά) and "hidden" (ἀφανής) property, see below, pp. 193–94.

[26]§2: τὰ μὲν γὰρ συμβόλαια τὰ πρὸς τοὺς ἐπὶ ταῖς τραπέζαις ἄνευ μαρτύρων γίγνεται. Cf. §53: περὶ τῶν πρὸς τοὺς ἐπὶ ταῖς τραπέζαις συμβολαίων . . . οὐ γὰρ δὴ μάρτυράς γ' αὐτῶν ποιούμεθα. Repayment of a loan, in contrast, generally occurred before an assemblage of onlookers. See Dem. 33.12 (many witnesses to repayment of a 3,000 *dr.* bank loan): ἀποδοθεισῶν δὲ τῶν τριάκοντα μνῶν ἐπὶ τὴν τράπεζαν καὶ τῶν δέκα μνῶν τῷ Παρμένοντι, ἐναντίον πολλῶν μαρτύρων τάς τε συγγραφὰς ἀνειλόμεθα, καθ' ἃς ἐδανείσθη τὰ χρήματα. Cf. Dem. 27.58 (a 3,000 *dr.* payment before numerous observers in the agora), 34.30, 48.46.

[27]§44. For the enormous purchasing power of these sums, see above, Chapter 1, n. 92.

[28]The transaction actually was for 1,000 staters (§40), presumably Cyzicene. The rate of exchange between the Athenian drachma and the Cyzicene stater has been the subject of extended debate. (See Bogaert 1963, 1964b, 1965b, 1977; Guépin 1965; Eddy 1970.) Provision of exchange facilities was the original (and into the fourth century a continuing) function of the Athenian *trapezai*. See above, Chapter 1. Indeed, the Athenian decree regulating the testing of Attic silver currency explicitly provided for the tester to function in the city μεταξὺ τῶν τραπεζῶν and for the text of the law to be inscribed on a stone stele also to be placed μεταξὺ τῶν τραπεζῶν. Stroud 1974: ll. 4–8, 44–46.

sional reputations to handle large sums of money without the presence of witnesses.[29]

Beyond confidentiality and advice, delivery of funds to a bank was a necessary precondition to a customer's use of certain bank-credit mechanisms. For example, in connection with the Bosporan's financing of a cargo ship allegedly owned by a Delian, the Bosporan required surety for seven talents, a "frighteningly large" sum,[30] but one that Pasiōn was able to provide through Archestratos "from the bank" (§43). The son of Sopaios asserts explicitly that this credit enhancement was provided in reliance on his deposits at the *trapeza*,[31] an important item of evidence for banking practice—even though we cannot confirm the truthfulness of the Bosporan's contention that he actually had such funds on deposit or obtained the guarantee from the bank. In a separate transaction, the Bosporan argues that the bank's guarantee of his future payment of principal and yield on 300 staters was "prime evidence" of his having funds at the bank,[32] asserting explicitly that the guarantee would not have been provided in the absence of sums on deposit sufficient to fund the bank commitment.[33]

The amount of the guarantee on the Delian ship, seven talents, has been cited, inappropriately, as evidence that the son of Sopaios received a monetary yield on his deposits with Pasiōn's bank.[34] This argument assumes that the Bosporan deposited only six talents (since this is the sum that he is accused of having taken from the bank, §§11–12), and that the guarantee for seven talents encompassed the original deposit plus "interest" thereon at a rate of 10 percent (presumably for somewhat more than a year). In fact, however, the Bosporan never specifies the amount he claims to have placed in the bank: the actual deposit may have been even larger than the seven talents guaranteed, or the banker might have been willing to extend a portion of the guarantee against the banker's own anticipated earnings on the funds (even if not payable to the Bosporan, who might otherwise have had to seek immediate repayment of his monies in order to obtain the guarantee elsewhere). Although this specific

---

[29]Isok. 17.2: Τὰ μὲν γὰρ συμβόλαια τὰ πρὸς τοὺς ἐπὶ ταῖς τραπέζαις ἄνευ μαρτύρων γίγνεται . . . τοιούτους . . . οἳ . . . χρήματα πολλὰ διαχειρίζουσι καὶ πιστοὶ διὰ τὴν τέχνην δοκοῦσιν εἶναι.

[30]Even the Bosporan's family friend, Philippos, refused to provide it (δείσας τὸ μέγεθος τοῦ κινδύνου, Isok. 17.43).

[31]§44: τῶν δ' ἑπτὰ ταλάντων ἐγγυητὴς μοι ἐγένεθ' ἡγούμενος πίστιν ἔχειν ἱκανὴν τὸ χρυσίον τὸ παρ' αὐτῷ κείμενον.

[32]See §§35–37: (36) ἐμοὶ δὲ μέγιστ' ἔσται τεκμήρια τὰ πρὸς Στρατοκλέα πραχθέντα ὡς ἦν μοι παρὰ τούτῳ χρυσίον. . . . (37) Πασίων' αὐτῷ συνέστησα, καὶ ὡμολόγησεν οὗτος αὐτῷ καὶ τὸ ἀρχαῖον καὶ τοὺς τόκους τοὺς γιγνομένους ἀποδώσειν. The transaction involved more than a talent. See below, n. 167.

[33]§37: Καίτοι εἰ μηδὲν ἔκειτο παρ' αὐτῷ τῶν ἐμῶν, οἴεσθ' ἂν αὐτὸν οὕτω ῥᾳδίως τοσούτων χρημάτων ἐγγυητήν μου γενέσθαι;

[34]Bogaert 1968: 64–66, 346–47; 1986a: 19–20. For the unsubstantiated assumptions underlying this theory, and an alternative explanation for the guarantee, see Thompson 1979: 225–26.

passage therefore cannot reasonably be taken as an additional clear example of a monetary return on deposits, there is, of course, no reason why individual customers, even where deposits were motivated primarily by a desire for bank confidentiality, might not have negotiated cash yields on funds entrusted to bankers. The Treasurers of the Goddess clearly did so.

Even beyond utilization as collateral for complex credit extensions, deposit of funds was a precondition to a bank's provision of payment services to third parties. Because the Greeks did not use paper money or receipts,[35] transfer of funds outside a bank might entail enormous physical effort, inconvenient and possibly costly meshing of personal schedules, complex measures to confirm proof of payment, and significant risk of losing the monies in transit, to the elements or to marauders, problems especially daunting to merchants and traders actively engaged in overseas commerce. Making payments through a bank mitigated or avoided these difficulties. Not surprisingly, then, bank handling of such payments was so routine that standard procedures had been developed: in effectuating third-party transfers, we are told, "all the bankers" were accustomed to make formulaic entries in their records setting forth the name of the person providing the funds, the sum involved, and the name of the recipient (if the person were known to the bank) or the name of the individual who would identify the payee if he were not personally known to the banker.[36]

Since the payee had to present himself personally at the bank, the *trapeza* might retain the funds for an extended period, even in the case of a payee resident in Athens and seeking rapid access to the money. For example, in the purchase of a profumery business (Hyp., *Ath.* 5–9), Epikratēs with difficulty raised the purchase price of 4,000 *dr.* from various sources. Prior to effectuating the purchase, and apparently during the process of gathering the funds, this money was placed in a bank.[37] Even after the funds were delivered to the *trapeza*, and despite the parties' mutual desire to complete the transaction expeditiously, further discussions and meetings were required. Only after these negotiations, execution of a written agreement, and an actual visit to the premises, were the monies paid over to the seller. Beyond offering a payment mechanism, deposit of the funds in the *trapeza* might provide confirmation to the seller that the funds were truly available. Since this money was being

[35]Absence of paper money: Finley 1981: 74; above, Chapter 1. Absence of receipts: below, n. 54.

[36]Dem. 52.4: εἰώθασι δὲ πάντες οἱ τραπεζῖται, ὅταν τις ἀργύριον τιθεὶς ἰδιώτης ἀποδοῦναί τῳ προστάττῃ, πρῶτον τοῦ θέντος τοὔνομα γράφειν καὶ τὸ κεφάλαιον τοῦ ἀργυρίου, ἔπειτα παραγράφειν 'τῷ δεῖνι ἀποδοῦναι δεῖ,' καὶ ἐὰν μὲν γιγνώσκωσι τὴν ὄψιν τοῦ ἀνθρώπου ᾧ ἂν δέῃ ἀποδοῦναι, τοσοῦτο μόνον ποιεῖν, γράψαι ᾧ δεῖ ἀποδοῦναι, ἐὰν δὲ μὴ γιγνώσκωσι, καὶ τούτου τοὔνομα προσπαραγράφειν ὃς ἂν μέλλῃ συστήσειν καὶ δείξειν τὸν ἄνθρωπον, ὃν ἂν δέῃ κομίσασθαι τὸ ἀργύριον.

[37]Hyp., *Ath.* 4–5: ἐκέλευέ με τὴν ταχίστην πορίζειν τὸ ἀργύριον, πρὶν μεταδόξαι τι Ἀθηνογένει. συναγαγὼν δ᾽ ἐγὼ πανταχόθεν καὶ τοὺς φίλους ἐνοχλήσας καὶ θεὶς ἐπὶ τὴν τράπεζαν τὰς τετταράκοντα μνᾶς.

gathered from a number of persons purportedly for the purchase of a business, use of the bank as an escrow holder might insure that the monies actually were expended for the purported transaction.[38]

In any event, a necessary by-product of the bank's involvement in payment arrangements was the generation of deposits. Where their intervention was most valuable—deposit of funds by and payable to active traders not normally resident in Athens—the bankers necessarily obtained extended use of funds. Illustrative is the deposit of 1,640 *dr.* by Lykōn, one of many traders using Pasiōn's bank.[39] Originally from Hēraklea (probably the city in Bithynia, on the coast of the Black Sea), Lykōn delivered the funds to Pasiōn's bank shortly before his departure for Libya. He gave instructions to pay the money to his partner, one Kēphisiadēs, when that businessman, normally resident on Skiros but at that time away on matters of commerce, should return to Athens (Dem. 52.3). This money was destined to remain with the bank for an extended period. When the Athenian representative of Hēraklea, Kallippos, learned that Lykōn had died on the voyage, banking confidentiality forced Kallippos to ask at the *trapeza* whether it had even dealt with Lykōn. Despite his official position, personal prestige, and considerable power (§§1, 5, 11), it was only with difficulty, after announcing Lykōn's death and confirming his own position as representative at Athens of the Hērakleans, that Kallippos was able to obtain information about the funds on deposit. Some five months later, Pasiōn and Kallippos were still unsure whether the funds had been paid out (§§6, 8), an indication of how long such deposits might normally remain in a banker's possession. (In fact, sometime before the representative's further inquiry, but after news of Lykōn's death had already reached Athens, Kēphisiadēs had received the money [§7].)

The prohibition on real-estate ownership by noncitizens (and the resultant lack of a permanent residence for transient businessmen) encouraged delivery to a *trapeza* of monies received in Attica by such visitors, even by residents who were not citizens—and even where third-party payments were not immediately required.[40] Indeed, the Athenian citizen-businessman Timosthenēs, when going abroad for an extended period, deposited with the banker Phormiōn not only cash but also valuable (and portable) personal possessions, in this case cups of Lykian work (Dem. 49.31). And even resident citizen-businessmen who were not engaged in overseas commerce are known to have kept monies at Athenian banks. The father of Demosthenes, for example, himself the proprietor of local sofa and cutlery manufactories, maintained a number of bank

---

[38]Thompson (1988: 830) suggests that the bank's role was to "verify" the transfer of the funds. For the bank's possible involvement in funding part of the purchase price, see below, p. 215.

[39]§3: Lykōn "used the bank [of Pasiōn] just as the other *emporoi.*" Cf. C. Mossé (1983: 60): "Lycon from Heraclea was 'as were all the *emporoi*' a client of Pasion's bank."

[40]Athenian banks, however, seem to have been housed in premises physically no more secure than the typically well-girded Attic private residence (see above, pp. 68–69).

accounts (Dem. 27.9–11). These deposits, in turn, offer further insight into the banks' generation of funds by acting as intermediaries, not in payment orders, but in maritime lending.

DEPLOYING OTHER PEOPLE'S MONEY FOR MARITIME LOANS

Because of the prevailing belief that Athenian bankers took no part in "maritime commercial loans, which all came from individual lenders,"[41] the relation between maritime lending and bank deposits has not been explored. A remarkable concatenation of evidence involving the most famous Athenian estate and the best-attested bank, however, confirms bankers' receipt of deposits directed to maritime lending.

Demosthenes' Inheritance

In seeking to recover monies allegedly looted from the estate of his father, the famous orator Demosthenes catalogues in considerable detail the deceased's assets (Dem. 27.9–11).[42] After noting that his father (also named Demosthenes) left a talent in loans yielding 12 percent (1 percent per month), 8,000 dr. in cash, and disparate items such as workshops, furniture, and jewelry, he adds: "But [he also left] maritime loans: 7,000 dr., a sea-loan (ekdosis) with Xouthos, 2,400 dr. at the bank of Pasiōn, 600 at that of Pyladēs, 1,600 with Dēmomelēs the son of Dēmōn, and also about a talent loaned at 20 percent and 30 percent."[43]

---

[41]Austin 1988: 741. Virtually all contemporary scholars accept this view without reservation: "All the lenders we meet in court speeches are private capitalists and not professional bankers . . . there is not a single known example of Greek bankers' having financed foreign commerce" (Isager and Hansen 1975: 84). Vélissaropoulos notes "l'absence totale de témoignages concernant le financement de l'enterprise maritime au moyen du crédit bancaire" (1980: 303). Ste. Croix agrees: "We have no good evidence of a banker making a maritime loan" (1974: 51 n. 39).

[42]Dem. 27.9–11: ὁ γὰρ πατήρ . . . κατέλιπεν δύ' ἐργαστήρια . . . μαχαιροποιοὺς μὲν τριάκοντα καὶ δύ' ἢ τρεῖς . . . κλινοποιοὺς δ' εἴκοσι . . . ἀργυρίου δ' εἰς τάλαντον ἐπὶ δραχμῇ δεδανεισμένον. . . . καὶ ταῦτα μὲν ἐνεργὰ κατέλιπεν. . . . χωρὶς δὲ τούτων ἐλέφαντα μὲν καὶ σίδηρον, ὃν κατηργάζοντο, καὶ ξύλα κλίνει' εἰς ὀγδοήκοντα μνᾶς ἄξια, κηκῖδα δὲ καὶ χαλκὸν ἑβδομήκοντα μνῶν ἐωνημένα, ἔτι δ' οἰκίαν τρισχιλίων, ἔπιπλα δὲ καὶ ἐκπώματα καὶ χρυσία καὶ ἱμάτια, τὸν κόσμον τῆς μητρός, ἄξια σύμπαντα ταῦτ' εἰς μυρίας δραχμάς, ἀργυρίου δ' ἔνδον ὀγδοήκοντα μνᾶς. καὶ ταῦτα μὲν οἴκοι κατέλιπεν πάντα, ναυτικὰ δ' ἑβδομήκοντα μνᾶς, ἔκδοσιν παρὰ Ξούθῳ, τετρακοσίας δὲ καὶ διοσχιλίας ἐπὶ τῇ τραπέζῃ τῇ Πασίωνος, ἑξακοσίας δ' ἐπὶ τῇ Πυλάδου, παρὰ Δημομέλει δὲ τῷ Δήμωνος υἱεῖ χιλίας καὶ ἑξακοσίας, κατὰ διακοσίας δὲ καὶ τριακοσίας ὁμοῦ τι τάλαντον διακεχρημένον.

[43]Not "in amounts of 200 and 300 dr." For similar construction utilizing as a ratio "κατὰ plus a drachma amount," cf. Dem. 28.4: κατὰ τὰς πέντε καὶ εἴκοσι μνᾶς πεντακοσίας εἰσφέρειν. See the maritime loan at Dem. 35.10, where the yield is described as "225 per thousand," i.e., 22.5% (ἐπὶ διακοσίαις εἴκοσι πέντε τὰς χιλίας). The markedly higher yield is characteristic of maritime loans. See above, pp. 53–58.

As is common in Athenian financial descriptions (see above, pp. 46–58), the orator distinguishes between "maritime" (*nautika d'*) and nonmaritime (here "domestic," *tauta men oikoi panta*) assets. Although he has grouped among "domestic assets" a talent of loans at a nonmaritime yield of 1 percent per month (*epi drakhmēi*), he places separately in the maritime category another talent of loans lent at maritime rates. Although modern readers might find strange the grouping of one talent of loans among furniture and similar items, and the placement of another talent of loans among bank accounts, an Athenian was culturally predisposed to separate sea-related and land-oriented financial assets.[44] But why are bank deposits grouped among maritime loans?

The clause listing maritime loans and bank deposits in juxtaposition has been generally understood to describe an unrelated potpourri of assets (sea financing, bank accounts, money delivered to a relative [Dēmomelēs], various small loans).[45] But in a brief discussion more than 60 years ago Paoli had already suggested that all four of the named individuals were bankers and that all four banks had made maritime loans utilizing the father's deposits (Paoli [1930] 1974: 20 n. 2). Paoli based his interpretation strictly on grammatical considerations ("ragioni sintattiche"),[46] but economic and historical factors, in my opinion, confirm his conclusions.

Since Athenian law did not accord independent legal standing to the *trapeza*, and since Athenians did not usually differentiate between the banker personally and his banking entity (see above, pp. 62–66), Demosthenes had no need to, and did not, endlessly repeat the word "bank" to communicate that maritime loans, utilizing his father's deposits, had been made in the amount of 7,000 *dr.* at the bank of Xouthos, 2,400 at the bank of Pasiōn, 600 at the bank of Pyladēs, and 1,600 at that of Dēmomelēs. This clarity results from the Athenian practice of routinely referring to deposits at a particular bank as monies "with" an individual banker. For example, throughout Isokrates 17 funds on deposit at the bank of Pasiōn[47] are routinely referred to as sums "with Pasiōn,"

---

[44]For the Greek tendency to expand spatial separations and relationships into intellectual and psychological determinants, see Vernant 1983. Cf. Jameson 1990a and 1990b. Lloyd properly emphasizes the extent to which sociological factors ("styles of discourse, converse, reasoning and the various contexts in which they were used") supplement or supersede "purely psychological" factors in such categorization (1990: 9–10).

[45]See, e.g., Korver 1942: 8–22; Davies 1971: 127 (with reference to earlier bibliography at 113); Thompson 1979: 227; Bogaert 1986a: 21. On the passage as an example of the Athenian tendency to organize reality through contrasting opposites, see above, pp. 52–53.

[46]Paoli stresses Demosthenes' utilization of the connective δὲ after the various monetary enumerations but not after ἔκδοσις, necessitating that ναυτικὰ be descriptive also of the additional monetary enumerations. I would also note the stylistic chiasmus in the presentation of the four items: commencing with the amount followed by the παρὰ reference (ἑβδομήκοντα . . . παρὰ Ξούθῳ) and ending with the παρὰ reference followed by the amount (παρὰ . . . χιλίας καὶ ἑξακοσίας), Demosthenes inserts in the middle of the description the two explicit bank references (ἐπὶ . . . ἐπὶ), suggesting that, in the orator's mind at least, there was a linkage among the four items.

[47]Isok. 17.44: πολλὰ χρήματ' . . . ἐπὶ τῇ τούτου τραπέζῃ κεῖταί μοι.

as at §7, where monies "with Pasiōn" (*para toutōi*) describe funds clearly "on deposit with the bank of Pasiōn." Usage is identical at §§8, 36, 37, 39, 44. And in every one of these examples the situs of the bank deposit is described by *para* ("with") followed by the appropriate personal reference, exactly as in the references at Dem. 27.11: *para Xouthōi* for "with Xouthos" meaning "at the bank of Xouthos"; *para Dēmomelei* for "with Dēmomelēs" meaning "at the bank of Dēmomelēs." (For a fuller consideration of this usage and its basis, see above, pp. 63–65.) The grammatical and verbal construction employed to describe the deposit with Dēmomelēs is identical to that used in the description of the monetary relationship with Xouthos (*para Xouthōi . . . para Dēmomelei*). In the case of Xouthos, the use of funds for maritime finance is explicit (*nautika, ekdosis*); for Dēmomelēs, there is independent evidence for his family's deep and continuing involvement in maritime finance.

A mass of evidence corroborates characterization of all four of the individuals named by Demosthenes as bankers. There is also independent support for their reported involvement in maritime lending.

Pasiōn is known to have conducted his banking business at the Piraeus harbor, rather than at the city agora (Dem. 49.22, 52.8, 52.14). All of the merchants engaged in overseas trade (*emporoi*) were said to be his banking clients.[48] He maintained overseas representation at Tenedos (Dem. 50.56) and at Lampsakos (Dem. 50.18); he is known to have disposed of financial resources at Peparethos (Dem. 45.28). He was capable of repaying huge sums at the far reaches of the Black Sea (Isok. 17.19). Through his network of representatives, he was said to have engaged in banking transactions throughout "Hellas" (Dem. 50.56). Whereas his successor Phormiōn owned and/or financed ships (Dem. 45.64)[49] and engaged in maritime trade (Dem. 49.31), Pasiōn himself is known to have traveled by sea for commercial purposes:[50] in the course of his banking business, he undertook to travel great distances by sea, as far as Bosporos, to resolve banking disputes (Isok. 17.19, 17.51). Most strikingly (in view of the fragmentary nature of so much of the evidence), we have independent verification for Pasiōn's utilization of bank deposits in the making of maritime loans: at Dem. 36.5, Pasiōn's bank acts as intermediary on a massive scale between bank depositors and maritime borrowers (see below, pp. 129–36).

[48]Dem. 52.3. Cf. n. 39 above. Despite continuing discussion as to the composition and attributes of the persons involved in Athenian trade (see below, n. 104), there is universal agreement that the word *emporos* "usually designates a trader who takes his wares on board a ship and sells them in a foreign harbor" (Isager and Hansen 1975: 65).

[49]Dem. 45.64: ὑπὲρ τούτου πρεσβευτὴς μὲν ᾤχετ' εἰς Βυζάντιον πλέων, ἡνίκ' ἐκεῖνοι τὰ πλοῖα τὰ τούτου κατέσχον, τὴν δὲ δίκην ἔλεγεν τὴν πρὸς τοὺς Καλχηδονίους. From the text alone it is unclear whether Phormiōn had a creditor's interest (through a maritime loan) or (as has generally been assumed) an ownership interest in the vessels held by the Byzantines. Cf. Chapter 3, n. 16; and n. 123 below.

[50]Commercial "passenger on a sea voyage" is the original meaning of the word *emporos*. Cf. Finley 1935.

Xouthos's status as a banker is confirmed by Demosthenes' charge (29.36) that his guardians conspired with Xouthos to destroy bank records: "As to the loan (*ekdosis*),[51] combining with Xouthos and dividing up the monies, and doing away with the contracts (*syngraphai*), and fashioning everything in whatever way you wished, and destroying the records (*grammata*), as Dēmōn testified against you, you are distorting and seeking to deceive these [jurors]."[52] This information explicitly relates Xouthos to *grammata*—and *grammata* is the technical term for *bankers'* records![53] In contrast to other fourth-century business dealings, where written documentation was extremely rare,[54] banking transactions were routinely recorded, through formulaic written memoranda setting forth the salient information concerning loans and deposits.[55] In business disputes where bankers were not involved, the absence of written records frequently resulted in arguments from "likelihood" (*eikos*); Demosthenes even sought to establish the annual revenues generated by his father's workshops, not through the review of written entries, but by asserting the reasonableness of assuming later results equivalent to those achieved during his father's lifetime.[56] Although Demosthenes is quick to charge the guardians with responsibility for the absence of material where written documentation was reasonably to be anticipated (for example, his father's will [Dem. 27.40–

---

[51]For *ekdosis* as a possible technical term for a deposit with a bank intended to be utilized for maritime lending, see below, pp. 157–60.

[52]περὶ δ' αὖ τῆς ἐκδόσεως, ἐπικοινωνήσαντες τῷ Ξούθῳ καὶ διανειμάμενοι τὰ χρήματα καὶ τὰς συγγραφὰς ἀνελόντες, καὶ πάνθ' ὃν τρόπον ἐβούλεσθε κατασκευάσαντες, καὶ διαφθείραντες τὰ γράμματα, ὡς ὑμῶν ὁ Δήμων κατεμαρτύρει, φενακίζετε καὶ τουτουσὶ παρακρούσασθαι ζητεῖτε. The "authenticity" of this speech is now generally accepted: see MacDowell 1989a; Thür 1972; Behrend 1975: 146.

[53]Cf. Dem. 36.20, 21, 36; 49.43, 44, 59; 52.5, 19.

[54]Bogaert 1968: 384: "Les contrats écrits étaient encore rares, excepté pour le prêt maritime, et les ordres de paiement étaient donnés verbalement." Cf. Isager and Hansen 1975: 92. Even the written receipt itself was unknown (Hasebroek 1923a: 393ff.; Pringsheim 1955: 287–97). (The papyri, however, demonstrate the wide utilization of receipts in the Hellenistic period.) Surprisingly, as Kennedy has observed (1963: 3–7), despite relatively widespread literacy, writing "in fifth- and fourth-century Athens" was "difficult and unnatural."

[55]For these ὑπομνήματα, see Dem. 49.5: οἱ γὰρ τραπεζῖται εἰώθασιν ὑπομνήματα γράφεσθαι ὧν τε διδόασιν χρημάτων καὶ εἰς ὅ τι καὶ ὧν ἄν τις τιθῆται, ἵνα ᾖ αὐτοῖς γνώριμα τά τε ληφθέντα καὶ τὰ τεθέντα πρὸς τοὺς λογισμούς. Cf. Dem. 49.8, 30, 43, 59; Dem. 36.20–21 and 36.

[56]Cf. Thompson 1983: 69–70. Of course, as this speech shows, the Athenians understood the concepts determining the profitability of business operations. Athenians did not need the "double-entry accounting" claimed for them by Costouros (1979). The origin of double-entry bookkeeping may be of great significance for the history of accounting, but its practice is irrelevant to the requirements of ancient business. See Ste. Croix 1956: 34, and Macve 1985: 257. On balance, the limited availability of business records may not have been deleterious to the Athenian judicial process: consider the evidentiary problems in recent American protracted litigation arising from the superabundance of written documentation. But litigational requirements should not be confused with business needs.

41] and the list of debts allegedly included therein [Dem. 27.40–41, 49]), he does not blame the guardians for the absence of these basic business accounts—and on their part, the guardians proffer no relevant records.

Possibly because of their uniqueness in an otherwise verbal business environment, bankers' *grammata* were accorded special significance as evidence in Athenian litigation,[57] a fact likely to have increased the credibility of Demosthenes' dramatic outrage at the guardians' role in destroying these records. Indeed, these book entries may have been critical to a banker's ability to enter into "banking litigation" (*dikai trapezitikai*), which offered expedited "monthly" procedure.[58] In fact, in the same passage in which Xouthos is charged with conspiring to destroy the *grammata*, reference is made to his participation in "doing away" with the *syngraphai*, the written contracts required to render maritime loans legally enforceable in the Athenian commercial maritime courts (*dikai emporikai*),[59] which also offered "monthly" process. But unlike banking records, these agreements were intended to be destroyed: repayment of a loan was always accompanied by the destruction of the document embodying the obligation.[60] Accordingly, destruction of the *syngraphai* created no problem for the guardians. There could have been no justification for destroying bankers' records, however. The entire point of the passage, therefore, arises from Xouthos's position as a banker. Since the *trapezitai* were the

---

[57]Gernet notes "le crédit particulier qui est attribué en justice aux livres des banquiers" (8955b: 176 n. 2). Cf. Harrison 1968–71, 2: 22 n. 7. Bogaert notes that all scholars other than himself have long attributed "preuve absolue" to entries in bankers' books. He correctly includes in this group Guillard, Perrot, Lécrivain, Brescia, Lenschau, Platner, Gneist, Schäfer, Lipsius, Wilamowitz, Calhoun, "et même encore Pringsheim" (1968: 382 n. 461). Bogaert's solitary refusal to attribute independent probative value to bankers' records is critical to his refusal to identify Xouthos as a banker (Bogaert 1965a: 143–44). But his willingness on this one point to contest the (rare) unanimous conclusion of specialists in Greek law is inconsistent with his stated policy, almost invariably adhered to in 1968:, of abstaining from legal issues: "Nous n'avons pas approfondi l'aspect juridique des problèmes, car il est toujours hasardeux, pour un non-juriste, de s'aventurer sur ce terrain semé d'embûches" (1968: 34 n. 30).

[58]These *dikai emmēnoi* are enumerated by Aristotle at *Ath. pol.* 52.2. See Cohen 1973: 12ff. Cf. above, pp. 96–97.

[59]See Cohen 1973: 100–114, 129–36; 1990: 59. The word "courts" seems to me the preferable rendering for δίϰαι in the term δίϰαι ἐμποριϰαί, since their procedural and jurisdictional attributes differ markedly from those of other forms of legal action. Although δίϰη is conventionally rendered in English as "case" (see MacDowell 1976: 84–85), translation as "courts" better conforms to common-law usage. Thus judges "sitting in equity" in common-law jurisdictions are referred to as constituting "courts of equity," notwithstanding the fact that technically they otherwise function as part of the "district court" or the "Court of Common Pleas." And indeed, the δίϰαι ἐμποριϰαί may have been heard before specially qualified juries constituting a physically differentiated "court" (cf. Cohen 1973: 93–95).

[60]This practice necessitated the gathering of many witnesses at the time of payment in order to permit later confirmation of the delivery of funds. Cf., for example, Dem. 27.58, 33.12, 34.30, 48.46. The absence of receipts also mandated that delivery of goods occur in the presence of witnesses. Cf. Dem. 27.21. See below, pp. 178–79.

only Athenians known to utilize "other people's money,"[61] only Xouthos's functioning as a banker can explain the delivery to him of funds that were recorded in journal entries. Recognizing Xouthos as a banker certainly is compatible with his juxtaposition in a listing of funds delivered to at least two other persons known to have been bankers.

Although Pyladēs is not otherwise known, the reference to his bank is explicit at 27.11 (*epi tēi Pyladou*). Thus there is no opening for the circular argument that he could not have been a banker since he is not otherwise known to have been engaged in trapezitic matters.

There is substantial independent evidence, however, for the continuing involvement in varied lending and maritime activities by the fourth individual, Dēmomelēs, the cousin of Demosthenes, who himself is known to have "worked" in maritime lending and on Athenian banking matters.

Dēmomelēs was the brother of Dēmophōn, one of the guardians from whom Demosthenes sought compensation for the destruction of his father's estate.[62] Dēmomelēs' son, Dēmōn (who bore his grandfather Dēmōn's name),[63] was actively engaged in the financing of seaborne trade: he was a principal in the litigation described at Dem. 32, one of the limited number of "private" speeches universally accepted as the true work of Demosthenes. The case involved an alleged fraud in which individuals from Massalia (modern Mar-

---

[61]To explain the undeniable—that Demosthenes' father did deliver funds to Xouthos that were utilized for maritime loans—Bogaert invents a profession otherwise unknown in Athens: the broker who serves as an intermediary in the making of maritime loans (Bogaert 1965a: 143–44). Although Bogaert is unable to find any evidence for the existence of such a functionary at Athens, this "broker," as imagined by Bogaert, functions much as the *trapezitēs* did: he gathered funds from individuals, he arranged and administered commercial loans. But he did so "sans faire de la banque dans le sens propre du terme" (ibid., 144), since Bogaert imagines that he did this for a "commission" and at the risk ("naturellement") of the client. Destruction of his *grammata* then would have had far less impact, since only bankers' entries were entitled to special evidentiary significance. Although Bogaert suggests that the "records" destroyed may merely have been entries in the books of Demosthenes' father, the orator specifically accuses Xouthos of personal involvement in the guardians' conspiracy. But how could Xouthos have had access to the father's accounts, and how could Xouthos be relevant to the disappearance of such accounts? Bogaert's suggestion furthermore contradicts Demosthenes himself, who suggests (27.40–41, 49) that his father's written records (not ongoing business accounts but estate records, also referred to as *grammata* in a nontechnical sense) have not been destroyed but are in the possession of the guardians (§41: καταλειφθῆναι μὲν ὁμολογοῦσιν, αὐτὰς δ' οὐκ ἀποφαίνουσι. ταῦτα δὲ ποιοῦσι τό τε πλῆθος οὐ βουλόμενοι καταφανὲς ποιῆσαι τῆς οὐσίας τὸ καταλειφθέν; 49: οὔτε γὰρ ὡς ὀφείλοντά με κατέλιπεν ὁ πατὴρ ἐν τοῖς γράμμασιν ἀπέφηνεν).

[62]The family's genealogy, beginning with the great orator's paternal grandfather, also named Dēmomelēs, is known with some exactitude. See Schäfer 1885–87, 1: 261ff., and 1858: 56 n. 4 and 292–96; Blass 1887–98, 3: 1, 492–98; Davies 1971: 113–23 and Table 3.

[63]The attribution appears certain: it has been generally accepted since Boeckh ([1842] 1976), with whom Davies concurs (1971: 118). Indeed, in all of the relations here considered, the relationship to the celebrated Demosthenes is certain—unlike the case of the author of the preserved decrees of 329/8 and 325/4 proposed by a Demosthenes who came from a family and deme different from that of the celebrated orator. See Thompson 1974.

seilles) were claiming the cargo that secured Dēmōn's loan. Although modern scholars generally conclude that the cargo probably did belong to the Massaliots,[64] Dēmōn's lending and loan-administration skills had enabled him to prevail, juridically and pragmatically, in all the prior stages of the dispute: he had even been able to take possession of the cargo and had forced his foreign adversary to litigate in Athens, where Dēmōn was objecting on procedural grounds to his opponent's right to pursue the litigation at all (§1). Through one agent,[65] Dēmōn had offered premium wages to the crew if they should succeed in saving the ship (§8); through another agent, after a hearing at Kephallēnia, he had forced the ship to sail on to Athens (§§11, 14),[66] where he personally seized the disputed cargo (§17). His famous relative Demosthenes[67] was deeply involved: indeed, Dēmōn's opponents see reliance on Demosthenes as underlying the various strategems, an involvement far beyond the orator's preparation of Dēmōn's masterful court presentation (§31). Dēmōn in turn admits that he has called on Demosthenes for aid, but claims that the political leader was reluctant to be involved: his public responsibilities now prevented his continued pursuit of a private matter (§32). Still, Dēmōn admits that Demosthenes had agreed to do whatever Dēmōn required ("for it would be terrible not [to do so]").[68]

But his "private activity" (*pragm' idion*) encompassed continuing relationships with bankers and with maritime finance, including his personal involvement as a maritime lender, an important aspect of the political leader's life usually ignored in analyzing his career and his role in the climactic struggle with Macedonia.[69] Banking and maritime litigation, of course, is heavily represented among the surviving private orations attributed to Demosthenes,[70] and

[64]Gernet 1954–60, 1: 113ff.; Isager and Hansen 1975: 149; Vinogradoff 1922: 164. *Contra*: Phōtiadēs 1923: 118.

[65]On the function of the ὁ παρ' ἡμῶν ἐπιπλέων, see Gofas 1989: 428–30. Cf. Dem. 56.7 for an associate who ἐπέπλει ἐπὶ τῆς νεώς.

[66]"Legal realists" might conclude that the creditors' success in forcing the ship to return to Athens from Kephallēnia reflected Athenian power over that island in the 340s. (For the date of Dem. 32, "about 340," see Gernet 1954–60, 1: 117, and n. 78 below.) In 372, the Athenian general Iphikratēs had subjugated Kephallēnia (Xen., *Hell.* 6.2.33), and I.G. II/III² 98 records a treaty highly protective of Athenian interests there. See Isager and Hansen 1975: 142.

[67]Demosthenes, a "blood relative" (οἰκεῖος γένει, Dem. 32.31), was actually Dēmōn's second cousin (see Davies 1971: 117), despite Plutarch's terming Dēmōn the ἀνεψιός of Demosthenes (Plut., *Dem.* 27.6).

[68]"Δήμων," ἔφη, "ἐγὼ ποιήσω μὲν ὡς ἂν σὺ κελεύῃς (καὶ γὰρ ἂν δεινὸν εἴη). . . . ἐμοὶ συμβέβηκεν, ἀφ' οὗ περὶ τῶν κοινῶν λέγειν ἠρξάμην, μηδὲ πρὸς ἕν πρᾶγμ' ἴδιον προσεληλυθέναι."

[69]Scholars tend to attribute to chance the concentration on banking and maritime matters found in the corpus attributed to Demosthenes. Cf. Thompson 1979: 224; Bogaert 1965a: 145.

[70]Of the 33 surviving "private" speeches, 5 focus on disputes relating to maritime finance, and no fewer than 7 relate directly or indirectly to the banker Pasiōn's business. As to the authorship of the seven speeches written for delivery by Apollodōros, the banker Pasiōn's son, see Pearson 1966: 359 (= 1983: 223) and 1969: 19 n. 8 (= 1983: 225 n. 8). Cf. Gernet 1954–60,

speeches generally recognized as the actual work of Demosthenes himself, in particular Demosthenes 36 and 45, reveal close familiarity with banking procedures. This in turn makes less surprising his deep involvement on both sides of the protracted litigation between the banker Pasiōn's son and his successor, Phormiōn.[71] When Deinarchos accuses Demosthenes of having taken bribes to obtain Athenian citizenship for certain persons, two of the six named are bankers, Epigenēs and Konōn (Dein. 1.43).

Demosthenes' family background and personal business activity may indeed have influenced ancient editors to attribute to him court presentations on financial matters now considered the work of others, resulting in the weighting of his extant corpus toward monetary disputes. His contemporary, Hypereidēs, reports that Demosthenes worked actively as a maritime lender, a statement confirmed by Plutarch in his *Life of Demosthenes*.[72] Not surprisingly, he maintained a house in the port of Piraeus.[73] Given the high returns available from maritime finance (see Chapter 3) and his family's long involvement with such lending, Demosthenes' emergence as the "wealthiest Athenian"[74] should not then be dismissed as inherently incredible or necessarily corrupt. Although modern writers have generally accepted his opponents' lurid charges that his wealth "depended almost entirely on speech-writing and *dōrodokia* [bribe-taking],"[75] a complementary (or perhaps alternative) explanation for his financial success would recognize his own lending, his family's intimate involvement in both banking and maritime trade, and the pivotal function of Athenian bankers' maritime loans in the maintenance of confidentiality (or less gently, *apokrypsis ousias*: concealment of wealth). Significantly, despite Demosthenes' recognized wealth, he is said never to have acquired anything that could be attributed to him (*phaneron*):[76] for the Athenians, loans, especially maritime financing, were the quintessence of "unattributable" (*aphanēs*) assets.[77]

Maritime lending by Dēmomelēs, especially through the surreptitious use of other people's money, would thus conform to the family pattern. Indeed, his son, Dēmōn, makes specific reference to unnamed financial associates in his own maritime lending, whom he terms *koinōnoi* ("partners" or "participants,"

3: 11–13; Blass 1887–98, 3: 514–43; Paley and Sandys [1896–98] 1979, 2: xxxix–xlvii; Kennedy 1963: 246.

[71]An involvement criticized by Plutarch (*Dem.* 15.1–2; *Comp.* 3.5) and by most modern readers (cf. Pickard-Cambridge [1914] 1979: 222–23).

[72]Hyp., *Dem.* 17: [. . . καὶ νῦν δὲ ναυ]τικοῖς ἐργάζῃ [τι]σὶν καὶ ἐκδόσεις δί[δως] (Kenyon 1907); Plut., *Comp.* 3.6 (ἀνθρώπου δανείζοντος ἐπὶ ναυτικοῖς).

[73]Dein. 1.69; Hyp., *Dem.* 17; Aesch. 3.209.

[74]Dein. 1.111: πλουσιώτατον ὄντα τῶν ἐν τῇ πόλει. Cf. Hyp., *Dem.* 22.

[75]Davies 1971: 133. In fact, Demosthenes was one of the few Athenians described in antiquity as being unbribable: see Harvey 1985: 98 (but cf. Dein. 1.43).

[76]Dein. 1.70: μηδὲν φανερὸν ἐν τῇ πόλει κεκτῆσθαι. This appears to have been a family practice: his father seems systematically to have kept his property, as far as possible, ἀφανής. See Korver 1942: 21–22.

[77]See below, pp. 201–2.

Dem. 32.21). Although we have no knowledge of who these *koinōnoi* were, in Demosthenes 33, a speech dating from approximately the same period as the dispute involving Dēmōn, the Hērakleidēs bank is explicitly reported as participating with a private individual in financing a maritime loan.[78] In Demosthenes 36, eleven talents from the deposits of Pasiōn's bank are reported as constituting part of the funding for loans (maritime loans, in my opinion; see below), of which the remainder came from the proprietor's private monies. The bank of Pasiōn, of course, is one of the banks specifically enumerated at Demosthenes 27.11. We have, then, indications that Athenian banks participated in maritime loans in conjunction with individual lenders; that Dēmōn, the son of Dēmomelēs, was involved in maritime loans in which he had unnamed participants; that Demosthenes' father deposited funds in at least one bank, that of Pasiōn, which participated in loans only partially funded by bank deposits; and that Demosthenes' father entrusted funds to his nephew Dēmomelēs (in a passage otherwise dealing with bank deposits and maritime lending). Dēmōn's maritime financing may thus have utilized funds entrusted to Dēmomelēs the *trapezitēs* for maritime lending (bank confidentiality then would justify Dēmōn's reticence in identifying his associates).

As was said of Stephanos in a maritime context and in relation to one of the same banks,[79] Demosthenes *père* was utilizing "the bank as intermediary" to obtain preferential returns without public disclosure.[80] Such bank intermediation would offer the bank diversification through the pooling of funds from various sources (a portion possibly of the higher yields available from maritime loans), and would allow a bank depositor the right to return of his money (subject, as a practical matter, to the bank's solvency and to the specific arrangements with a particular banker). Beyond illuminating both the mechanics of bank operations and the deep involvement of Demosthenes' family with the *trapezai* and with maritime commerce, Demosthenes 27.9–11 explains how this patriot and statesman might have become legitimately, rather than through corruption, "the wealthiest Athenian" (as he was termed by contemporaries).

Apollodōros's Inheritance

Pasiōn's use of bank deposits for maritime lending is independently confirmed by evidence preserved in a dispute relating to Pasiōn's own estate. Although the ancient text discussing Pasiōn's assets (Dem. 36.4–6)[81] has long been recog-

---

[78]For the range of meanings of κοινωνός, see Chapter 4, n. 71. Dem. 33 is dated "not earlier" than 341 (Gernet 1954–60, 1: 132); Dem. 32, "about 340" (ibid., 117).

[79]Dem. 45.66: τὰ ὄντ' ἀποκρύπτεσθαι προῄρηται πράττειν, ἵν' ἐργασίας ἀφανεῖς διὰ τῆς τραπέζης ποιῆται. See below, pp. 138–39, 151–60.

[80]It has long been recognized that the senior Demosthenes during his lifetime concealed much of his property, possibly to avoid taxes (Ste. Croix 1953: 55 n. 105), or perhaps to avoid liability for his father-in-law's public debts (Davies 1971: 128–29).

[81]δεῖ δ' ὑμᾶς ἀκοῦσαι καὶ μαθεῖν ἐκ τίνος τρόπου προσώφειλεν τὰ ἕνδεκα τάλανθ' ὁ

nized as highly significant, it has confounded commentators[82] who have sought to ascertain the total wealth of Pasiōn or the "capital" of his bank.[83] Analyzed in the context of Athenian finance's basic maritime/landed differentiation, however, this text clearly confirms the indication in Dem. 27.11 that Pasiōn's bank channeled depositors' funds into maritime commerce.

The passage seeks to explain an apparently inappropriate provision in a lease from Pasiōn that provided for Phormiōn's operation of Pasiōn's banking business. This explanation is offered in a lawsuit against Phormiōn, brought many years after Pasiōn's death, in which Apollodōros, Pasiōn's son, sought damages of twenty talents, alleging various wrongful acts.[84] The lease purportedly listed Pasiōn as a debtor to the bank in the amount of eleven talents. Phormiōn's defender struggles to justify the startlingly paradoxical claim that a wealthy bank owner would entrust his own bank to a lessee (indeed, to his own former slave) on terms that left the owner indebted to the bank, and for a colossal sum:

> He did not owe these [sums] because of lack of means (*aporian*) but because of diligent operation (*philergian*). For (*men*) Pasiōn's landed loans (*eggeios ousia*)[85] were about twenty talents, but (*de*) money had been loaned in addition to this (*pros*

Πασίων ἐπὶ τὴν τράπεζαν. οὐ γὰρ δι' ἀπορίαν ταῦτ' ὤφειλεν, ἀλλὰ διὰ φιλεργίαν. ἡ μὲν γὰρ ἔγγειος ἦν οὐσία Πασίωνι μάλιστα ταλάντων εἴκοσιν, ἀργύριον δὲ πρὸς ταύτῃ δεδανεισμένον ἴδιον πλέον ἢ πεντήκοντα τάλαντα. ἐν οὖν τοῖς πεντήκοντα ταλάντοις τούτοις ἀπὸ τῶν παρακαταθηκῶν τῶν τῆς τραπέζης ἕνδεκα τάλαντ' ἐνεργὰ ἦν. μισθούμενος οὖν ὅδε τὴν ἐργασίαν αὐτὴν τῆς τραπέζης καὶ τὰς παρακαταθήκας λαμβάνων, ὁρῶν ὅτι, μήπω τῆς πολιτείας αὐτῷ παρ' ὑμῖν οὔσης, οὐχ οἷός τ' ἔσοιτ' εἰσπράττειν ὅσα Πασίων γῇ καὶ συνοικίαις δεδανεικὼς ἦν, εἵλετο μᾶλλον αὐτὸν τὸν Πασίωνα χρήστην ἔχειν τούτων τῶν χρημάτων ἢ τοὺς ἄλλους χρήστας, οἷς προειμένος ἦν. καὶ οὕτω διὰ ταῦτ' ἐγράφη εἰς τὴν μίσθωσιν προσοφείλων ὁ Πασίων ἕνδεκα τάλαντα, ὥσπερ καὶ μεμαρτύρηται ὑμῖν.

[82]Despite numerous discussions, especially in recent years but starting in the seventeenth century, the difficulties in this passage have remained unresolved. (For early interpretations, see Beyer, "Über den Sachverhalt" [diss., Berlin, 1968], 41–43 [cited in Bogaert 1986a: 29 n. 54] and Erxleben 1973: 119; for discussions since 1968, see Bogaert 1986a: 35–42.) Frequent efforts have been made to alter the received text in order to resolve cruxes. Already in the nineteenth century, Sandys had athetized ἴδιον, and Blass had eliminated λαμβάνων from the text. Subsequent editors have generally accepted these deletions. Thus Pearson, in 1972, finds ἴδιον a "foolish interpolation" and λαμβάνων "unnecessary" (1972: 211). Gernet (1954–60) omits the words without comment. Recent tendency has been to accept the received text: Bogaert 1986a: 39 n. 109; Thompson 1981: 92 n. 18. See below, nn. 87, 324.

[83]The passage does not purport to summarize Pasiōn's entire estate, and therefore cannot be used to determine Pasiōn's total wealth. Determination of the bank's "capital" presupposes a modern conceptualization and an institutional structure alien to the Athenian *trapeza*. See below, pp. 183–89.

[84]The clearest explanation of this much-discussed claim is in Thompson 1981. Wolff clarifies the procedural aspects (1966: 52–57).

[85]ἔγγειος οὐσία: generally translated "real property" (Murray 1936–39; Gernet 1954–60, "bien-fonds") or "landed property" (Pearson 1972). A better translation is "landed assets" or

tautēi)[86] privately (*idion*)[87] amounting to more than fifty talents. Then among these fifty talents from the deposits of the bank eleven talents were employed (*energa*).

Despite a lack of consensus about many individual points, the passage has been uniformly understood as describing Pasiōn's ownership of real estate with a value of approximately twenty talents, and of loan receivables worth more than fifty talents. This interpretation, however, gives rise to numerous difficulties. How had a former slave (who only late in life attained citizenship and the corresponding right to own real property) been able to accumulate real estate worth twenty talents? Why was there no other indication that Pasiōn had owned such valuable landed property?[88] Moreover, the Greek text required some counterpoint (*men . . . de*) between the two types of property attributed to Pasiōn, but "landed property" and "loan receivables" are complementary rather than contrasting.

This conundrum can now be solved, thanks to the demonstration by Russian scholar V. N. Andreyev (1979: 134–39) that landed *ousia* (*eggeios ousia*) does not mean "real estate" or "landed property," as had always been assumed, but rather "landed loans."[89] As he notes, the basic meaning of *eggeios* is "in or of the land. In translating *eggeios ousia* at Dem. 36.5 as "real property" or "landed property," scholars had treated the text as though it read *eggeios gaia* or *eggeioi ktēseis*, either of which might properly be translated as "landed property."[90] But the words actually present in the text are *eggeios ousia*. For

---

"landed loans," in the sense of "nonmaritime investment," capturing the contrast (μὲν . . . δὲ) between ἔγγειος οὐσία and ἀργύριον ἴδιον, more accurately translating οὐσία, and consonant with the necessary sense of the passage. See below.

[86]Erxleben (1973: 119) argues that the phrase πρὸς ταύτῃ means "at the bank." Thompson (1981: 89–92) adduces convincing reasons for maintaining the traditional translation "in addition to" (see Paley and Sandys [1896–98] 1979: 8). Either interpretation is fully compatible with bank intermediation in maritime financing. The translation "in addition to" confirms the contrast between the two types of assets (ἔγγειος οὐσία and ἀργύριον δεδανεισμένον); the reading "at the bank" confirms the bank's central role in the maritime financing.

[87]Editors generally have followed Sandys in excising the word ἴδιον because of the alleged logical inconsistency in terming as "private" holdings that included outside bank deposits. Thompson (1981: 92 n. 18), however, points out that although "editors have generally condemned the word on *logical* grounds . . . the word makes excellent sense *rhetorically*."

[88]See Davies (1971: 431), who seeks, but never really manages, to explain this total. There is no basis for Bogaert's assumption (1986a: 37) that the 3,000 *dr.* annual revenues mentioned at Dem. 36.38 are entirely from real estate owned by Pasiōn and thus provide the basis for a mathematical projection of the value of Pasiōn's real property.

[89]To some extent, Andreyev's insight was anticipated by E. L. Grace (1968: 33), who had suggested the translation "20 talents invested into land property." Accepting the prior scholarly misconception, which assumed that "landed" loans were defined by real-estate collateral and not by their contrast to "maritime" loans (see Chapter 3), Andreyev actually uses for *eggeios ousia* the term "money lent on the security of real property" (1979: 135). The secured-lending characterization is, of course, entirely absent from the Greek text.

[90]Cf. I.G. IX² 338.9 (Thess.) and C.I.G. 2056 (Odessus).

this term there survive only two examples in ancient Greek:[91] the passage from Demosthenes under discussion, and a fragment from Lysias (frag. 91 [Thal.]).[92] In the Lysias fragment, *eggeios ousia* cannot be translated "landed property." There the orator notes the law's mandate that guardians establish *eggeios ousia* for orphans; in contrast (*de*), "this [guardian] shows us *nautikous* ['yields,' 'loans,' or 'investments'—the substance must be supplied from the context]." Although the argument is not advanced by Andreyev, "maritime property" is not a possible meaning in ancient times for *nautikous*, since the word then would have had to refer to property on or under the sea, an impossible concept prior to the relatively recent oil-generated interest in national ownership rights to the Aegean sea-bed. Observing the frequent use of *eggeios* "in connection with loans and mortgages," Andreyev suggested that the "opposition" of *eggeios ousia* to "maritime loans" in Lysias (frag. 91) requires its translation there as "loans on the security of land." *Eggeios ousia* in Demosthenes 36.6 should accordingly be understood as "money lent on the security of real property" (Andreyev 1979: 135, 139).[93]

When Andreyev's insight is combined with a recognition of the basic landed-/maritime contrast permeating Athenian finance (Chapter 3), the meaning of Demosthenes 36.4–6 is clear: Pasiōn's assets included about twenty talents in "landed loans" (*men*), but (*de*) more than fifty talents in "maritime loans." Because the two types of loans are explicitly contrasted (*men . . . de*) in the Greek text, and because "maritime" loans is the formulaic opposition required in Greek categorization to "landed" loans, the "fifty talents loaned" must be understood as "maritime loans." Fortuitously, the ancient sources provide explicit confirmation of this interpretation. In the only other reference in the entire corpus of surviving ancient Greek writings, *eggeios ousia,* clearly meaning "landed loans," is explicitly contrasted (*de*) to "maritime loans" (*nautikous*) (Lysias, frag. 91 [Thal.]).

There is further confirmation. Not only *ousia* but also *khrēmata*, the plural of the Greek word for "money," have primary meanings, in modern terms, of "property."[94] Aristotle defines *khrēmata* in language that establishes it clearly

---

[91]I found no other use of the phrase ἔγγειος οὐσία in an examination utilizing the Ibycus system to scan the computer-based data bank of ancient Greek texts (nearly 2,900 authors by 1986) developed by the Thesaurus Linguae Graecae (Irvine, California). For the texts covered by the Thesaurus, see Berkowitz and Squitier 1986. A similar computer study of inscriptions and papyri also yielded no other examples.

[92]τοῦ νόμου κελεύοντος τοὺς ἐπιτρόπους τοῖς ὀρφανοῖς ἔγγειον τὴν οὐσίαν καθιστάναι, οὗτος δὲ ναυτικοὺς ἡμᾶς ἀποφαίνει. The impression that Lysias seems to be attempting to convey, that guardians were not permitted to engage in maritime loans, is misleading: Gernet (1924–26, 2: 183 n. 3) observes that the cases of Diogeitōn and Aphobos show that maritime loans were allowed. Finley ([1951] 1985: 235) agrees with Gernet.

[93]Andreyev, of course, uses the prevailing translation for nonmaritime loans: "landed loans" would be more accurate (for the reasons detailed in Chapter 3, n. 24).

[94]Cf. Liddell-Scott-Jones Lexicon, s.v. "οὐσία," "χρῆμα."

as a synonym for *ousia*.[95] Thus *eggeia khrēmata* should be synonymous with *eggeios ousia*, a theoretical expectation actually confirmed by surviving evidence: the Anecdota Graeca preserves a definition of *eggaia khrēmata*[96] that is identical to Andreyev's proposed interpretation of *eggeios ousia*: *eggaia khrēmata* is "that which is lent against the security of real property."[97] In context, this ancient definition seems clearly to preclude any interpretation of *eggeios ousia* other than "landed loans."

The passage at Demosthenes 36.4–6 also offers insight into how bankers handled real-estate assets and loans. It is noted there that since Phormiōn was not yet an Athenian citizen when he leased the operation of the bank and took over the deposits, he would not have been able to execute on the sums that Pasiōn had lent against land and multiple dwellings (*epi gēi kai synoikiais*); accordingly, he preferred to have Pasiōn as a debtor for these sums rather than the other borrowers to whom he had lent. "Therefore Pasiōn was written down in the lease as owing eleven talents." Since the eleven talents are explicitly included among the fifty talents that we interpret as consisting of "maritime loans," a further issue arises: considering the fifty talents as sea finance conflicts with the assumption "obvious to everyone" (Andreyev 1979: 135) that these eleven talents of bank deposits had been utilized for real-estate loans.[98] This assumption arises from Phormiōn's stated desire to be able to execute on monies lent against land and buildings. But an assumption that these fifty talents of loans were made in reliance upon real-estate security conflicts with yet another generally held assumption, the shibboleth that loans secured by real property were "beyond the reach" (in the words of another Soviet scholar) of Athenian bankers, since "most of them did not have the right of *egktēsis* [power to own Attic real property]" (Gluskina 1970: 43).

Both assumptions are, at best, overly simplistic. Although the noncitizen Phormiōn assumed operation of the bank only after these loans had been funded,[99] Pasiōn had been well established as a banker long before he became a

---

[95]χρήματα λέγομεν πάντα ὅσων ἡ ἀξία νομίσματι μετρεῖται (*E.N.* 1119b26).

[96]Alternative spellings of *eggeios* and its cognates are frequent. Cf. the manuscript readings of ἔγγεια and ἔγγυα at Pollux 3.84. On instability in Attic vowel usage as early as the fifth century B.C., see Browning 1969: 32–33.

[97]*Anecdota Graeca* (Bekker) 251.26: ἔγγαια χρήματα· ὑποθήκῃ διδόμενα. Again Andreyev in 1979 follows the prevailing interpretation of "landed loans" as financing secured by real property. The Greek text here is compatible with "landed loans" as collateralized by any type of secured interest (ὑποθήκη).

[98]Just as Andreyev failed to define "landed loans" through their antithesis to "maritime loans," he did not relate the other part of the contrast (the fifty talents denominated as ἀργύριον δεδανεισμένον: "money loaned") to a maritime context. His own suggestion that the eleven talents of deposits actually constituted part of the twenty talents utilized for real-estate lending is impossible, since the Greek text states unequivocally that the eleven talents were included among the fifty (ἐν οὖν τοῖς πεντήκοντα ταλάντοις τούτοις ἀπὸ τῶν παρακαταθηκῶν τῶν τῆς τραπέζης ἕνδεκα τάλαντ' ἐνεργὰ ἦν).

[99]Phormiōn entered into the lease of the bank in 371/70 (Dem. 36.37; cf. Dem. 49.42–43), but

citizen.[100] Demosthenes 36.6 itself discloses the mechanism through which any Athenian banker, even a noncitizen, could easily engage in real-estate lending: the use of intermediate loans to an Athenian citizen, here described as the retention of Pasiōn as debtor.[101] But Phormiōn's desire to be able to execute on real property does not prove that the underlying loans were used to fund real-estate obligations.[102] Athenian creditors, not surprisingly, sought to have available, through legal right and financial practicality, multiple sources of repayment. Legal incapacity to collect a loan through any potential source of repayment might imperil the viability of a financing otherwise sound. A new operator, undertaking the lease of a *trapeza*, would obviously want to retain every possible means of repayment: by seeking to preserve the right to execute against landed assets, Pasiōn does not thereby establish that the loans being accepted were "landed," rather than "maritime." (Indeed, as we have seen in Chapter 3, the very category "landed loans" is defined by yield on investment, not simplistically by the nature of security.) Without the negotiated arrangement with Pasiōn, Phormiōn would have been fully responsible for repayment of the bank deposits, but less able than his predecessor to collect the loans funded by these deposits.

Whether making "landed" or "maritime" loans, Athenian lenders sought to be able to collect if necessary from either the marine or real-estate assets of the borrower(s). In a financing involving maritime cargo destined for the Pontic region, for example, Chrysippos takes steps to monitor his collateral and to "follow" the proceeds:[103] if monies generated by the sale of ship-borne cargo were to be invested by the debtor in real property, Chrysippos would wish to be able to execute against that asset. Since it is now clear that many Athenian citizens were actively involved in the conduct of Athenian trade,[104] a maritime creditor had to be able to foreclose on real property in Attica.[105] Indeed,

---

became a citizen only in 361/60 (Dem. 46.13; cf. Dem. 36.6 and 47).

[100]He was naturalized shortly before his death in 370/69 (Dem. 46.13). But he had been a prominent *trapezitēs* more than two decades earlier. Cf. Chapter 4, n. 205.

[101]§6: εἵλετο μᾶλλον αὐτὸν τὸν Πασίωνα χρήστην ἔχειν τούτων τῶν χρημάτων ἢ τοὺς ἄλλους χρήστας, οἷς προειμένος ἦν.

[102]Roman maritime law made explicit provision for real property as collateral for sea finance: Justinian, *Digest* 22.2.6; Ashburner 1909: 218. Maritime law appears to be the only area in which basic provisions of Athenian law survived into Roman times, and indeed into the modern period. See McFee 1951: 36; Colombos 1959: 29–35; Sanborn 1930.

[103]Dem. 34.8: τὰ χρήματα ἐξετάζειν καὶ παρακολουθεῖν.

[104]See M. V. Hansen 1984, confirming the findings of Isager and Hansen 1975: 71–72. Although Hasebroek is often cited for the view that Athenian citizens were not personally active in trade as *nauklēroi* or *emporoi*, even he acknowledged that there must have been some direct citizen involvement in trade (Hasebroek 1978: 106, 159). In recent years, however, even the neo-Hasebroekian Erxleben has acknowledged relatively numerous examples of citizens acting as *emporoi* or *nauklēroi* (1974: 462–77), and thus as potential maritime borrowers owning Athenian real-estate.

[105]There is no basis for the old canard that "maritime loans made to *emporoi* and *nau-*

maritime trade is known to have been financed through loans to persons who owned real estate at Athens (for example, Pasiōn's bank's loans to Menexenos),[106] or who provided guarantors owning Attic real estate.[107] In the sole surviving text of an actual contract for maritime financing (Dem. 35.10–13), explicit provision is made for execution against the borrowers' real property in the event of a deficiency (*ekdeia*) after sale of maritime collateral.[108] Such maritime financing might properly be characterized as a loan with a right of collection "against land and dwellings" (*epi gēi kai synoikiais*).

Legal and practical considerations would have encouraged retention of Pasiōn as an intermediate debtor, without regard to the nature of the underlying loans. Because the *trapezai* did not have independent legal status (see above, Chapter 4), Pasiōn's name would often have appeared on written loan documentation, such as the debtor's promise to repay the funds advanced. In the total absence of any concept of "negotiable paper," which would have permitted transfer of notes through endorsement by one creditor to another,[109] any attempt by Phormiōn to execute in his own name on these loans would have been extraordinarily complicated at best, more likely ineffective, since the debtor owed no money to Phormiōn. This would have been true whether the collateral was "maritime" or "landed."

Amendment of the documentation would have been difficult. In the case of maritime loans, the papers might well have been deposited with a third party

---

klēroi . . . serve to emphasize the poverty of traders, being forced to borrow to pay for their cargoes" (Millett 1983: 46) and therefore being unlikely to own real estate. To the contrary, the ability to borrow confirms not a trader's "poverty" but his own capacity to contribute the considerable equity generally required in sea finance. For this ability to provide capital, see below, pp. 152–53. Some traders were even themselves lenders to others: see below, n. 173. There are, of course, many legitimate reasons for borrowing other than "poverty": "leverage," for example, through which a trader, by utilizing a loan or increasing the amount borrowed, might increase the size of his cargo and thus enlarge his potential profit without adding to his physical labor and personal risk (see Thompson 1983: 65–66).

[106]Among the series of maritime-related financings described in Isok. 17, Pasiōn's bank allegedly provided funds to Menexenos (§12; see above, pp. 39–40). Menexenos's family owned substantial real estate and was deeply involved in the litigation over the assets of Dikaiogenēs, a large estate consisting primarily of real property (Isaios 5.43), much of it subject to creditors (§21). Cf. Mathieu and Brémond [1929–42] 1963, 1: 74 n. 1; Davies 1971: 145ff.

[107]In the maritime financing described at Dem. 33.7, for example, the bank of Hērakleidēs obtains the guarantee of the unnamed speaker who is clearly an Athenian citizen (M. V. Hansen 1984: 82; Erxleben 1974: 476). Since he was himself a financier, although self-described as committing only "moderate" assets to maritime trade (Dem. 33.4), his ownership of at least his own residence seems likely. Dem. 32.29 also envisions the possible involvement of citizen guarantors in maritime-finance disputes.

[108]Dem. 35.12: καὶ ἐάν τι ἐλλείπῃ τοῦ ἀργυρίου, ὃ δεῖ γενέσθαι τοῖς δανείσασι κατὰ τὴν συγγραφήν παρὰ ᾿Αρτέμωνος καὶ ᾿Απολλοδώρου ἔστω ἡ πρᾶξις τοῖς δανείσασι καὶ ἐκ τῶν τούτων ἁπάντων, καὶ ἐγγείων καὶ ναυτικῶν, πανταχοῦ ὅπου ἂν ὦσι.

[109]Payment orders, which the *trapezai* routinely utilized, were "nonnegotiable." See above, Chapter 1, n. 66.

(see Dem. 34.6, 56.15) and thus would not be readily available for revision. Real-estate collateral (even that securing a maritime loan) would likely have been evidenced by *horos*-stones placed on the property.[110] Such *horoi* generally specified the creditor by name.[111] Even if he had been a citizen, Phormiōn still would not have been a named creditor on a *horos*-stone attesting to a debt to Pasiōn.

Even between the parties, there were practical obstacles to a transfer of assets. The maturity of Pasiōn's son Apollodōros, who was legally an adult, would have inhibited arrangements allowing Phormiōn to succeed Pasiōn, even as a guardian, upon the latter's death. Because of the intermingling of "personal" and "bank" assets (see above, pp. 64–65), it is generally recognized that even a banker's loans made entirely from personal funds were likely to have been recorded on the bank's books.[112] In view of the special evidentiary importance granted to banking records (see above, n. 57), altering the *trapeza*'s books to provide for payment to Pasiōn would have been inadvisable, lest adversaries later charge, even in unrelated matters, that the bank's records had been compromised. Rather than seek approval from potentially adverse borrowers for changes in existing documentation, or opening the way to later charges that loan papers and bank records were "altered," the parties to the bank lease utilized an appropriate alternative: Pasiōn recognized his responsibility for repayment of the eleven talents in deposits. Pasiōn's continued liability to the bank for repayment of these loans also insured his maximum cooperation if Phormiōn ultimately had to execute on borrowers' real-property assets. As a practical solution to a business problem, this procedure was equally appropriate to deposits incorporated in "maritime" or in "landed" loans.

MARITIME FINANCE

Few detailed studies have been made of any aspect of trapezitic lending.[113] In the late nineteenth and early twentieth centuries, exaggerated claims were

---

[110]The utilization of real-estate debt for purposes unrelated to property acquisition has long been assumed. The "wide prevalence of indebtedness" evidenced by the *horoi* was explained by Finley as a manifestation of "short-term" borrowing for a transient "social-personal need" (1981: 74).

[111]Finley [1951] 1985: 10; Paoli [1930] 1974: 194 n. 2.

[112]Bogaert 1968: 365 n. 362. Maintenance of a single set of books for the bank's accounts and for the personal transactions of the individual banker was consistent with Athenian juridical characterization of the banker and his bank as a single legal entity. In his collection efforts after his father's death, Apollodōros did utilize "his father's written records" (τάλαντ' εἴκοσιν εἰσπέπρακται ἐκ τῶν γραμμάτων ὧν ὁ πατὴρ κατέλιπεν: Dem. 36.36). In collecting loans made to Timotheos, he used "the bank's records" (τὰ γράμματα ἀπὸ τῆς τραπέζης: Dem. 49.43–44). But it is not clear whether he was actually collecting bank debts, or funds independently lent by Pasiōn, or loans funded from a combination of sources. In any event, jurors as a practical matter may well have accorded to all of Pasiōn's records the special position technically reserved for bank entries.

[113]The author of the standard work on Greek banking, Bogaert, has emphatically disclaimed

made, with little analysis of the evidence, for either the overall importance or the total insignificance of Athenian banks as lenders.[114] A few scholars initially assumed, without detailed investigation, that Athenian banks were actively involved in maritime finance;[115] others noted the summary nature of these assertions and rejected their conclusions, but again without significant independent study.[116] In 1965, Bogaert in a brief treatment found no "indisputable proof" that Athenian bankers made maritime loans.[117] This conclusion, highly compatible with the dominant "primitivist" view of the ancient economy,[118] has since been repeatedly accepted without independent verification, even by those who found the conclusion "strange."[119] In the past twenty-five years, therefore, an assertion about an absence of evidence has become a commonplace that categorically denies to the *trapezai* any role in the finance of maritime commerce.[120]

Yet the ongoing involvement of Athenian banks in sea finance is easily demonstrated. The litigation between the banker Pasiōn and a Bosporan merchant, arising from the complex business dealings between the bank and a customer deeply involved in maritime commerce, chronicles a virtual portfolio

---

the adequacy of his research insofar as it relates to provision of credit by banks, noting the need for thorough investigation: "On n'a pas encore étudié convenablement la part des banques dans l'octroi du crédit" (1968: 367).

[114]Compare, for example, the positive assertions of Goldschmidt (1889: 393–94) and Glotz (1910: 363–65) with the negative conclusions of Pöhlmann 1925: 2:530–31.

[115]Beauchet [1897] 1969, 4: 276, 334; Pringsheim 1916: 29; Knorringa [1926] 1961: 88; Ziebarth 1929: 86.

[116]See, for example, Breccia 1903: 294; Calhoun [1926] 1968: 103.

[117]For this absence of "preuve indubitable," see Bogaert 1965a: 141; reprise, 1986a: 47–48.

[118]For this "new orthodoxy," see Chapter 1, n. 1. The "primitivist" Millett sees the very existence of maritime loans (and *a fortiori* sea finance by banks) as an "embarrassment" insofar as they are "examples of productive borrowing in a society supposedly dominated by a profoundly unproductive mentality" (1983: 44). Cf. Goldsmith 1987: 260 n. 45.

[119]"Strange": Isager and Hansen (1975: 84), who explicitly state that their chapter on Athenian banking "is based on Bogaert" (p. 88). Musti (1981: 116) wonders whether the number of bank loans at Athens must not have been greater ("non dovessero essere più numerosi"), but still is explicit (p. 110 n. 9) in accepting Bogaert's view of Athenian banking. Erxleben finds Bogaert's presentation too "einseitig" ("one-sided"), but confirms his conclusion: "Es gibt kein direktes Zeugnis, das ein von einem Trapeziten gewährtes Seedarlehen bewiese" (1974: 490–91). Thompson, however, sees correctly that there was no inherent barrier to Athenian banks' involvement in maritime finance (1979: 224–41; cf. also Thompson 1983: 55 n. 12), but concludes that "they were an insignificant factor in maritime lending" since "banks were insignificant as providers of credit in all aspects of the Athenian economy" (1979: 241).

[120]Gluskina 1974: 126: "Das Kreditieren des Seehandels nicht gänzlich in den Händen der *trapezitae* befand." Cf. Austin and Vidal-Naquet 1977: 149: bank funds "not invested . . . in maritime loans." See n. 41 above. Ironically, Bogaert himself during this period became even more tentative in his conclusion: "Ceci ne veut pas dire que jamais un trapézite athénien n'aurait risqué l'argent de sa banque dans un prêt maritime . . . mais nous n'en avons aucune preuve" (1986a: 27).

of bank loans encompassing a broad spectrum of sea finance (see above, pp. 38–40). In the matters arising from a loan of 3,000 *dr.* to a ship-owner from Byzantion, Herakleidēs' bank is seen to have had an ongoing participation in maritime finance (see above, p. 40, and below, pp. 166–68). In denying personal responsibility for repayment of a bank loan, the prominent military and political leader Timotheos alleges that the advance was made to a third party solely in connection with the financing of maritime trade, and then proceeds to explain how such financing was normally handled by Athenian banks (see above, pp. 37–38). Individuals deposited funds in banks specifically for utilization in maritime lending. Despite efforts by both bankers and clients to maintain secrecy,[121] at least two extensive series of transactions became known (to ancient tax-collectors and claimants, and even to modern scholars) through the notorious protracted litigation generated by family feuds involving the estates of Pasiōn and Demosthenes. In these transactions (see above), the *trapezitai* acted as intermediaries in utilizing bank deposits for the making of maritime loans.

In a lawsuit ancillary to the dispute about Pasiōn's assets, Apollodōros attacks Stephanos's involvement with various Athenian bankers, especially his relationship with Phormiōn in matters relating to maritime commerce. Apollodōros explicitly alludes to the role of the Athenian *trapeza* as an intermediary in providing profitable investment opportunities for monies otherwise concealed by their owners (Dem. 45.64–66). Stephanos is accused of acting in concert with the bankers "to conceal his wealth in order that he might obtain secret returns through the bank" (*dia tēs trapezēs*; Gernet 1954–60: "par l'intermédiaire de la banque").[122]

In fact, Stephanos, like Demosthenes' father, appears to have been providing funds to the bank for investment in maritime commerce. A man of significant wealth (see above, n. 20), he was deeply involved with bankers and with maritime commerce. Prior to his complex association with the banker Phormiōn, he had enjoyed a notoriously close business and personal relationship with the banker Aristolochos (Dem. 45.63); the intensity of these bank dealings generated the charge that Stephanos was responsible, with others, for Aristolochos's subsequent financial ruin (Dem. 45.64). Stephanos was personally active in maritime commerce and finance. It was he who sailed to the

---

[121]On the role of "confidentiality" in Athenian banking, see below, pp. 202–7.

[122]Dem. 45.66: τὰ ὄντ' ἀποκρύπτεσθαι . . . ἵν' ἐργασίας ἀφανεῖς διὰ τῆς τραπέζης ποιῆται. Although it has been suggested that this phrase refers to profitable "information" obtainable through the bank (see Thompson 1979: 226), such interpretation is entirely inconsistent with the presence of the word ἐργασίας with its specific financial notation of monetary income. See n. 1 above. Moreover, the usage is exactly parallel with that in Dem. 33 (§8), where Parmenōn is known to have been the actual lender of 10 mnai, which were advanced "through" an unnamed speaker. Identical linguistic construction (τάς τε δέκα μνᾶς ἃς δι' ἐμοῦ ἔλαβεν) should describe compatible practice.

Hellespont as the banker Phormiōn's representative when the Byzantines were "holding that man's ships."[123] There against the Kalchēdonians he argued a case necessarily involving maritime and financial considerations. In the light of Apollodōros's accusation that Stephanos's bank relationships offered him the opportunity to "obtain secret returns" on hidden capital through bank intermediation, we might conjecture that these ships, their voyage, or their cargo had been financed partially with Stephanos's funds through the intermediation of Phormiōn's bank (*dia tēs trapezēs*). Apollodōros's close association of the two phenomena (Stephanos's travel on Phormiōn's behalf and Stephanos's alleged secret returns on capital) might have been intended to invite the jury to conclude that Stephanos had a secret financial interest in these ships. Their clandestine business relationships might then suggest additional motivation for Stephanos's allegedly perjured testimony on behalf of Phormiōn.

For our study, importance lies in the accusations themselves, again juxtaposing maritime activity and bank finance, not in their validity (which we cannot determine). If bankers were known to have no involvement with maritime finance, the jury could be expected to dismiss the accusations as absurd, thus seriously damaging Apollodōros's credibility in a case focusing on banking matters. As an heir to Athens's most prominent banking business, he had terminated one lease for the bank, had entered into another, and had spent many years heavily involved in complex litigation largely relating to the collection of bank-related claims. His credibility on banking matters thus would have been high. It is extremely unlikely that he would sacrifice this credibility, key to success in Athenian courts, by asserting charges that presuppose a close involvement of Athenian banks with maritime finance—unless the *trapezai* were in fact active in sea lending.

Economic factors explain the evidence for bankers' concentration on marine loans. Yet the prevailing insistence on the absence of *trapezai* from maritime finance has ignored these considerations while utilizing seriously flawed cliometric data and artificial definitions of a "maritime loan" to reach a false conclusion. In arguing against bank funding of sea trade, Bogaert emphasizes (somewhat anachronistically in view of the limited technology available to the Athenians) the need for lenders' expertise in such matters as weather forecasting, but ignores the need for bankers' attributes, such as credit skills and funding resources. Indeed, financing sea commerce was the natural focus for an Athenian banker's technical abilities and business orientation.

---

[123]Dem. 45.64: ὑπὲρ τούτου πρεσβευτὴς μὲν ᾤχετ' εἰς Βυζάντιον πλέων, ἡνίκ' ἐκεῖνοι τὰ πλοῖα τὰ τούτου κατέσχον, τὴν δὲ δίκην ἔλεγεν τὴν πρὸς τοὺς Καλχηδονίους. From the text alone it is unclear whether Phormiōn had a creditor's interest through a maritime loan (as Erxleben believes [1974: 491–92]) or an ownership interest in the vessels being held by the Byzantines (as has generally been assumed). See Chapter 3, n. 16.

A Natural Channel for Bank Activity

Although Demosthenes cites risk-taking as a central characteristic of the *trapeza* (a business generating "risk-laden revenues from other people's money"), Bogaert attributes the alleged absence of bankers from maritime lending to the substantial risks inherent in maritime lending and to bankers' lack of expertise in sea operations.[124] As to risk, Demosthenes' insistence on risk absorption as a central characteristic of the *trapeza* is preferable to Bogaert's assumption that bankers necessarily avoided potentially dangerous financing; as to expertise, the bankers were in fact uniquely qualified to make maritime loans.

Among the not-inconsiderable dangers of fourth-century maritime lending, the possible loss of the ship to sea hazards was of the greatest significance: often, if not always, the lender was entitled to receive principal and yield only if the security underlying the loan—vessel or cargo—survived the journey. But there is no reason to assume that this risk deterred banks from making maritime loans. It is axiomatic that no lending—not even modern loans to governments of developed nations—is without risk. Sound credit procedures require that the possibility of loss be reasonably quantifiable, that the return be commensurate with the exposure to loss, and that the area of activity, whether maritime finance or house mortgages, be reasonably appropriate for the lender. All three of these requirements are satisfied by bank financing for sea commerce.

Fourth-century maritime loans have long been recognized as carrying quantifiable risk; indeed, ship financing has repeatedly been cited as constituting the earliest known form of insurance.[125] The fundamental principle of insurance is simple: the risk, which is in a single case a great uncertainty, becomes, over a sufficiently large number of cases, a virtual certainty. At Athens, hundreds of ship cargoes were required annually to satisfy Attica's enormous need for food and other items.[126] Virtually all of these cargoes were dependent on

---

[124]Bogaert 1986a: 27: bankers abstained from maritime loans "probablement à cause d'un manque d'expérience des choses maritimes et des risques très lourds de ce genre de prêts, car tous ies risques maritimes étaient portés par le bailleur de fonds." Cf. his fuller exposition in Bogaert 1965a.

[125]Ste. Croix 1974: 42; Finley [1951] 1985: 87, and 1985: 141; Ziebarth 1929: 52; Knorringa [1926] 1961: 92, "loan combined with assurance"; Calhoun 1930: 579–84; Oertel 1928: 1624–25. Cf. Roover 1945: 172–200; Civiletti 1934: 115–37; Besta 1936. Trenerry (1926: chs. 2, 3) tries to establish the "bottomry bond" as a rudimentary form of insurance practiced among ancient Phoenicians, Hindus and Babylonians. Cf. Passamaneck 1974: 2, 26 n. 5.

[126]Because of the primitive condition and high expense of overland transport, virtually all of this trade would necessarily be by sea. See Chapter 3, n. 38. Epigraphical and archaeological evidence suggests that in the fourth century, a single ship might typically carry about 3,000 medimnoi of grain (Casson 1971: 183–84). On Kocevalov's estimate (1932: 321–23) that in the fourth century, 800,000 medimnoi of grain were imported each year into Athens, more than 250 shiploads (500 potential financings including outbound cargo, on an "each way" basis [ἑτερόπλουν]) would have been required for this product alone. Ste. Croix (1974: 44) estimates even larger grain imports already by the middle of the fifth century. Cf. Ste. Croix 1972: 46–49,

loans.[127] These financings, together with the additional loans generated by the Piraeus's dominant position as an entrepôt for the eastern Mediterranean,[128] provided creditors with an opportunity to absorb over many transactions the risk of a total loss from the sinking of a single ship.

The high rates of return on maritime lending compensated for the hazards inherent in ship financing. These elevated yields therefore represented not a barrier to involvement by banks, but market-established rates appropriate to the danger anticipated. Through the extensive experience engendered by the vast scale of shipping activity at the Piraeus—repetitive seasonal cycles of transport financed by thousands of loans—fourth-century maritime lenders likely would have developed a reasonable ability to quantify the possibility of loss. At the Piraeus, in a market free of governmental regulation and private monopolies (see Chapter 3), changes in anticipated rate of loss would likely be reflected in revised charges for loans. The continuation at Athens of significant maritime lending over an extended period suggests the functional feasibility of such market adjustments—although, obviously, the profit experience of specific creditors would likely vary with the lenders' own capacities, experience, and organization.

Creditors' willingness to negotiate agreements relieving borrowers of responsibility in the event of loss of the security underlying the loan suggests that this credit risk was perceived as manageable. No law, regulation, or immutable economic factor required lenders to assume this obligation (and there is evidence that, in some cases at least, agreements provided for borrowers' continued liability even if vessel or cargo or both were lost: see below, pp. 163–66). But valid considerations encouraged the setting of rates high enough to

---

217–18. Isager and Hansen (1975: 63) assume "a minimum of six hundred shiploads of grain" annually, and argue for total annual grain import significantly in excess of 800,000 medimnoi. For similar elevated estimates of total imports, see Gomme 1933: 28–33 (1,200,000 medimnoi per year); and Gernet 1909: 273–93. Cf. Segrè 1947. Even the lowest scholarly estimate of the grain requirement (400,000 medimnoi, "enough to feed around 90,000 people," in certain years: Garnsey 1985: 74; cf. above, Chapter 3, n. 15) would still have required almost 300 one-way trips (150 trips from and to Athens, ἀμφοτερόπλουν). And this covers only grain. Many other items were imported to Athens by sea. For a summary list, see Hopper 1979: 92. Garland (1987: 85) suggests that nongrain imports to Piraeus were probably equal in number of shiploads to those required for grain.

[127]Dem. 34.51: οὔτε ναῦν οὔτε ναύκληρον οὔτ' ἐπιβάτην ἔστ' ἀναχθῆναι, τὸ τῶν δανειζόντων μέρος ἂν ἀφαιρεθῇ. See n. 168 below. For the enormous amount of credit required to fund this trade, see n. 170 below.

[128]See Burke 1990: 11. The harbor served as a redistribution center for goods destined eventually for a further location: ἐμπόριον ἐν μέσῳ τῆς Ἑλλάδος τὸν Πειραιᾶ . . . τοσαύτην ἔχονθ' ὑπερβολὴν ὥσθ' ἃ παρὰ τῶν ἄλλων ἓν παρ' ἑκάστων χαλεπόν ἐστιν λαβεῖν, ταῦθ' ἅπαντα παρ' αὐτῆς ῥᾴδιον εἶναι πορίσασθαι (Isok. 4.42). Cf. Xen., Por. 5.3. The Piraeus's position as the "leading commercial centre in the eastern Mediterranean" (Garland 1987: 95) continued until well beyond Athens's political eclipse by Macedonia, in fact until the rise of Rhodes beginning in the third century B.C. Cf. Adam 1989: 284.

justify relieving borrowers of this liability. Obtaining repayment from a merchant victim of a sea calamity, or his heirs, would require costly, complex, and time-consuming legal efforts, as the Lakritos case (Dem. 35) illustrates. Even if a judgment were obtained, collection of the debt might still be difficult, or ultimately impossible.[129] In commercially appropriate cases—in particular, those involving borrowers who lacked substantial assets independent of the security for a particular loan—an increase in yield, with waiver of borrowers' liability in the event of maritime disaster, might be the only economically justifiable form of financing.

To minimize the effects of a single disaster, each loan theoretically should be apportioned over the largest available network of lenders.[130] Significantly, in every Athenian maritime financing known to us in any detail, more than one lender is present. Banks, of course, through their depositors, represent a diversity of funding sources. Bankers further limited their exposure to a single devastating loss by cooperating with independent lenders in formal participations (as the banker Hērakleidēs did in Dem. 33), by utilizing bank deposits in conjunction with the proprietors' own money (Pasiōn in Dem. 36), and by raising funds for maritime lending through deposits specially directed to this field (Dem. 27).

The absence of statistics prevents modern scholars from determining the actual percentage of fourth-century ships that failed to survive a journey from or to Athens. A rough estimate of the degree of risk perceived can be made, however, by observing the rate of return on maritime and nonmaritime loans. Maritime yields of 20 to 30 percent (plus repayment of principal)[131] are compatible only with a relatively low perceived risk of a vessel's loss on any individual journey. In addition to returning at least a reasonable anticipated profit to the lenders, these rates had to cover all other expenses, contingencies, and perils: the lenders' cost of money (in payments to others and in opportunities foregone), possibly substantial expenditures for monitoring collateral and similar administrative costs,[132] an allowance for potential loss or fraud, expenses relating to currency exchange, and costs associated with market adversities (including commercial difficulties adversely affecting the value of the security, such as sudden shifts in commodity prices or absence of demand at

[129]On the problems of locating heirs and litigating in foreign *fora* likely to be sympathetic to debtors, see Thompson 1988: 834–35.

[130]In modern practice, this is termed "syndication," and it is not unusual for large loans to be funded by several, in some cases even scores, of institutional lenders. Rather than reflecting a prohibitive risk, such dispersion of funding is considered appropriate "risk management."

[131]For Athenian conceptual differentiation between maritime and nonmaritime loans, and calculation of the actual yields thereon, see above, pp. 52–58.

[132]Because of the relatively vast distances involved and the complexity of business arrangements, these costs could be quite high, especially since agents often accompanied the security, and representatives might have to intervene in distant localities. Dem. 32 offers good insight into these challenges and expenses. See Gofas 1989.

distant emporia, as detailed in Dem. 34 and 56). A fear of widespread losses would have resulted in yields not of a percentage of the sums advanced, but of many times the amounts loaned. The relatively modest level of anticipated return should warn against the modern tendency to exaggerate the danger of shipwreck in antiquity.[133]

In any event, there is absolutely no suggestion in our sources that Athenian bankers were inherently risk-averse. To the contrary, there is considerable confirmation of Demosthenes' characterization of the bankers as engaged in a "risk-laden business." Unlike bankers of later times and other places, the Athenian *trapezitai* could not generate revenues by providing funds, with relative safety, to the government. Because of their perceived lack of commitment to repay loans, the city-states, including Athens itself, did not enjoy a favorable credit standing and consequently were able to borrow funds only "short term, accompanied by heavy security, [at] high interest, and [in] strange forms."[134] For their part, the governments seldom sought true loans (although they sometimes extracted additional taxes or "gifts" in the guise of borrowing).[135] Nonmaritime loans from the *trapezai* were clearly fraught with danger. Bankers utilized deposits for speculative real-estate investments (Dem. 36.50),

[133]The recent success of underwater archaeologists in locating dozens of wrecks in the Mediterranean (for a sample catalogue, see Gianfrotta and Pomey 1981: 328–41, 359–61, and Casson 1971: 214–16) has exacerbated a tradition of frequent passing reference to sea transportation's "high risks" (e.g., Millett 1983: 36), extended discussions of the legal and financial implications of these perils (e.g., Paoli [1930] 1974: 77–84, "rischi derivanti dal mare"), and sensational treatments of piracy (the jacket for Ormerod's *Piracy in the Ancient World* [1987] promises "the exciting story of the ancestors of Kidd and Bluebeard"). Cf. Ziebarth 1929: 100–117. But these archaeological finds and literary references encompass more than two thousand years of history and a vast geographical area. Modern studies tend to ignore ancient mariners' skill and adaptability: for a more balanced view, see Rougé 1981: 11–23. Far removed from random and mindless destruction, ancient piracy should itself be recognized as "a form of commercial enterprise" (Gofas 1989: 429). In fact, the loss of a ship in fourth-century Hellas seems akin to the crash of an aircraft at the present time: an occurrence whose infrequency results in enormous public attention. For example, in Dem. 34, the sinking of a freighter is the occasion of widespread grief throughout the vast southern Russian area encompassed by the Bosporan kingdom (34.10), and the fate of a survivor (who by chance did not travel on the ship) is said to have been common knowledge among the general populace (πάντες). But the very notoriety of this incident suggests the relative rarity of such losses.

[134]Andreades [1933] 1979: 172; cf. 171–76. Despite occasional modern suggestions that the Athenian bankers provided substantial funds to the state (e.g., Calhoun [1926] 1968: 104–5; Hasebroek 1920: 162), there is not a single case known of a loan to the state from any Greek banker.

[135]On the rarity of true public loans as "un moyen ordinaire de financement" in the fifth and fourth centuries, see Migeotte 1984: 361–62. In accord: Andreades [1933] 1979: 168–71. The "loan" from the goddess's treasury on the Acropolis (I.G. I³ 369) at an interest rate slightly in excess of 1% per year—in fact, a mere transfer of funds from one entity under the city's control to another—illustrates the formalistic nature of such financing at Athens. Loans to governments from private persons in the Hellenistic period appear to have been somewhat more frequent. See the survey in Gatti 1967.

for politically motivated loans to impecunious borrowers (Dem. 49.16–17; cf. §§6, 22, 29), and for start-up credits for speculative business enterprises such as silver mines (Dem. 40.52). Bogaert (1968: 355) believes that they frequently made unsecured loans, at "great risk" ("risques grands"), to borrowers whose limited credit standing was low. Bank failures were not unknown.[136]

A certain Aischinēs was a credit risk of such notoriety that "in the Piraeus people are of the opinion that it seems to be much less risky to 'sail to the Adriatic'[137] than to deal with this fellow; the money he borrows he considers to be his own much more than what his father left to him."[138] But the banker Sōsinomos lent this habitué of the harbor, target of maritime lenders' jibes, money to establish a profumery business—at the incredibly high landed interest rate of 36 percent per year, and apparently without security.[139] Bankers willing to provide merchants notorious in the Piraeus with unsecured business loans more risky than "sailing to the Adriatic" would certainly not have avoided the risk of secured loans for voyages to the same sea, or to waters considered less dangerous.

Athenian bankers not only would have been willing to engage in maritime financing, they also had a unique capacity to make and collect such loans. They routinely provided loan-related fiduciary services to persons engaged in overseas trade,[140] maintained representation in important foreign *emporia*, personally engaged in maritime trade, and were themselves frequently of foreign origin. Hence, the great disquiet (above, n. 119) expressed by those scholars who have felt compelled, despite their awareness of the close connections between bankers and marine activity, to accept allegedly scientific studies asserting the total absence of bank lenders from sea commerce.

Athenian bankers were very active in the Piraeus. Monetary exchange services, the original function of the banks and still in the fourth century an important part of their activity (see Chapter 1), were so prevalent in the Piraeus that Nikophōn in his resolution on the testing of coined silver explicitly required

---

[136]See below, Chapter 6; Thompson 1988: 831; Bogaert 1974.

[137]Apparently a proverbial nautical allusion to maritime danger, reflected in the extraordinarily high yields for voyages to the Adriatic from Athens. See Lysias 32.25.

[138]Lysias, frag. 38 (Gernet) 4–5: οἱ ἐν τῷ Πειραιεῖ διάκεινται, ὥστε πολὺ ἀσφαλέστερον εἶναι δοκεῖν εἰς τὸν Ἀδρίαν πλεῖν ἢ τούτῳ συμβάλλειν· πολὺ γὰρ μᾶλλον ἃ ἂν δανείσηται αὐτοῦ νομίζει εἶναι ἢ ἃ ὁ πατὴρ αὐτῷ κατέλιπεν.

[139]Lysias, frag. 38.1–2: Οὗτος ὀφείλων ἀργύριον ἐπὶ τρίσι δραχμαῖς Σωσινόμῳ τῷ τραπεζίτῃ καὶ Ἀριστογείτονι προσελθὼν πρὸς ἐμὲ ἐδεῖτο μὴ περιιδεῖν αὐτὸν διὰ τοὺς τόκους ἐκ τῶν ὄντων ἐκπεσόντα. "Κατασκευάζομαι δ'" ἔφη "τέχνην μυρεψικήν. ἀφορμῆς δὲ δέομαι." On ἀφορμή, see below, pp. 184–89. The banker's valuation of the risk, as reflected in the elevated charge, proved correct: the lender who provided Aischinēs with the funds to pay off the banker's loan wound up in litigation.

[140]For safekeeping of maritime loan agreements, for example, see Dem. 34.6, 56.15. This task might be critical in maritime lending: the banker Kittos's secure possession of the loan agreement in Dem. 34 is explicitly cited as a barrier to the fraud alleged (§32).

that the text of this decree be set up also in the Piraeus. In the *deigma*, the building in which commercial activity in the *emporion* was centered, bankers' tables complemented the displays of merchandise.[141] Polyainos reports (6.2.1–2) that when Alexander of Pherai made a surprise raid on the Piraeus in 361, bankers' funds were seized. The first *trapezitai* known to us by name, Antisthenēs and Archestratos, conducted their banking business in the port.[142] Decades later, in the middle of the fourth century, the Piraeus banker Chariōn was immortalized by a gravestone on which he is pictured holding a book-roll, presumably bankers' records (Clairmont 1970: 58, with pls. 26–27). The most famous Athenian banker, Pasiōn, operated his business from his home in the Piraeus (Dem. 49.22, 52.8, 52.14): Timotheos, about to set sail, was thus able to obtain a loan by personally "approaching Pasiōn in the harbor,"[143] paralleling Apatourios's arrangement "in the *emporion*" of his loan from the bank of Hērakleidēs (Dem. 33.6). And bankers not only made loans, but themselves engaged directly in maritime trading. Indeed, Pasiōn's successor, the banker Phormiōn, is sometimes cited by scholars as the only person in Athens known to have owned more than a single merchant ship;[144] in an entirely separate context, he is described as the "partner" (*koinōnos*) of Timosthenēs, who was engaged in maritime trade on his own account (*kat' emporian idian*).[145]

Non-Athenians were well represented among both bankers and traders, offering a natural nexus for bankers' finance of overseas commerce.[146] Thus the bank owner Apollodōros explicitly notes his father's ability to make loans throughout "Hellas" (Dem. 50.56): we know that Pasiōn had ties with Lampsakos (Dem. 50.18), was involved in business at Peparēthos (Dem. 45.28), and utilized Kleanax and Epēratos as his representatives at Tenedos (Dem. 50.56). In contrast, prohibitions on ownership of land by noncitizens imposed an immediate barrier to loans by noncitizen bankers secured by real property. Although mechanisms were developed to circumvent this limitation (see pp. 133–36 above), bank confidentiality (a prime desideratum in trapezitic transactions; see below, Chapter 6) was innately incompatible with the

---

[141]Polyain. 6.2.2; Xen., *Hell.* 5.1.21–22. Cf. above, Chapter 2, n. 38; Chapter 3, n. 35.

[142]Garland 1987: 68; Musti 1990: 582. The elusive Antimachos mentioned by Eupolis (frag. 127 K = Edmonds i 342) may be an earlier example, but not even his nationality is known.

[143]Dem. 49.6: προσελθὼν τῷ πατρὶ τῷ ἐμῷ ἐν τῷ λιμένι.

[144]See above, Chapter 3, n. 16. The possibility of a single individual controlling a large number of merchant ships and their cargoes was not inconceivable to the Athenians: see Athēnaios 12.554e for an imaginary example.

[145]Dem. 49.31. A "Phormiōn" appears as witness to the maritime loan documented at Dem. 35.10 and as the *emporos*-borrower in Dem. 34. For possible identification of this "Phormiōn" with his homonym, the banker, see Chapter 4, n. 103; below pp. 176–78.

[146]Recent studies have shown that many citizens did engage in maritime trade (see above, n. 104). Although there is no basis for the shibboleth that virtually all bankers at Athens were noncitizens, many were in fact foreigners (see above, Chapter 4, n. 44).

public disclosure inherent in real-estate financing: the stones marking a lien on landed property explicitly revealed the creditors' and debtors' interests to all within sight. Maritime finance, variable in duration and dependent on pledges of mobile vessels, could be furnished without overt disclosure. Although lenders need not themselves be technically proficient in a particular field in order to evaluate and deal with its credit risks, close involvement in maritime matters and milieu—and "use" of the banks by the commercially oriented persons active in the *emporion*—certainly would have given *trapezitai* the business knowledge appropriate to sea financing.[147] But sophisticated lending skills were also needed.

In practice maritime finance in the fourth century was extraordinarily complex.[148] A single ship might carry many "traders" (*emporoi*), and each of these *emporoi* might have separate cargo securing separate loans:[149] at least thirty merchants were on board the cargo ship whose sinking is the focus of the litigation at Demosthenes 34.[150] The vessel itself might be securing a separate loan from still other lenders,[151] and the ship owner might have subjected part or all of his own cargo to further lien(s) from yet other financier(s). Each of these lenders would normally require the borrower to provide substantial equity subordinate to each borrowing (see above, n. 105). This capital might itself be borrowed, possibly against yet other collateral. The resulting complexity is illustrated by the transaction about which we know most, the voyage from Athens to the Crimea (Dem. 35), the subject of the only maritime loan agreement surviving from antiquity.[152] The vessel used for this transaction carried

[147]Although Bogaert argues (1965a: 142) that lenders would have needed skills in weather forecasting and special knowledge of diplomatic conditions to judge "des dangers de la route à suivre, de la frequence des tempêtes selon la saison; il devait connaître les lois commerciales, les zônes infestées de pirates, les ports où un droit de représailles contre le navire était à craindre, etc.," Thompson (1983: 67) more reasonably notes that lenders should be able to evaluate "the character of the borrower, business conditions of the moment, and the chances of war." To supplement their own knowledge or skills, or for convenience, bankers might utilize mariners working in the *emporion*, as the *trapezitēs* Hērakleidēs did in Dem. 33 (see below). Athenian law and practice was especially receptive to bankers' use of agents (see above, Chapter 4).

[148]With excellent insight, Montgomery (1986: 43–61) has argued that the alleged underrepresentation of Athenian citizens in trade resulted essentially from the complexity of fourth-century overseas commerce, not from citizens' ideological distaste for commerce.

[149]Cf. Dem. 35.31–32. Dem. 56.24 is explicit: οἱ ἐπιβάται τὰ ἑαυτῶν χρήματα ἀπέστελλον. In Dem. 32, representatives are on board acting for two separate creditor groupings claiming the same cargo (32.5–8), and the ship itself was separately financed (§14)! See n. 250 below.

[150]We know that at least thirty *free* persons died in this shipwreck. Since the captain-*nauklēros* appears to have been a slave (see Schäfer 1885–87, 3: 2, 305ff., "früher Dions Sklave"; and for later discussion, Cohen 1973: 121 n. 48), it seems unlikely that these persons were crew members: they may not all have possessed their own cargoes, however.

[151]See Dem. 32.14 and 56.6. In the latter case, the goods selected for transport to the Piraeus were hypothecated to other creditors. Cf. Gernet 1954–60, 3: 133 n. 4.

[152]For the agreement and its terms, see above, pp. 54–55; for its uniqueness, see below, n. 211.

numerous merchants and agents pursuing their own separate undertakings: retainers of a certain Apollōnidēs of Halikarnassos, a "partner in the ship," were on board (§33);[153] a loan had been made to the ship operator secured by the vessel and by goods being transported to the Pontos (§§32–33); freight was being carried from Pantikapaion to Theodosia (in the Crimea) under arrangements unrelated to the loan documented in Demosthenes 35 (§34). So disparate were the transactions that in addition to crew members, eight other persons offer depositions (§§20, 34) concerning cargo transported from Mendē to the Pontic area, other goods on board when the vessel was sailing along the Crimean coastline, and various financing arrangements covering diverse freight. The preserved contract clearly anticipates multiple cargoes independently owned: decisions on jettison must be taken by majority vote of persons on board (§11).

As creditors recognized,[154] skill and diligence were needed to avoid ruinous losses. Maritime lenders faced a daunting set of challenges: the initial credit decision, the subsequent monitoring of collateral, control of the funds resulting from sale of the collateral, protection of position if the goods were not immediately saleable on favorable terms upon arrival at destination, continuing observance of the actual progress of the transaction. Each of these complexities was inherent in every maritime financing. The (presumably) exceptional situation—where the borrower purposely sought through fraud to avoid repayment—would require yet additional professional skills. In fact, the lender at Demosthenes 35.1 suggests anticipation of legal defenses and the ability to collect from "forgetful" debtors as further skills needed by creditors.[155]

In an *emporion* experiencing numerous arrivals and departures, a sound credit decision necessarily depended on accurate information about the borrowers and the particular transaction. This the Athenian banking relationship tended to provide: bankers such as Pasiōn are reported to have done business with virtually all of the *emporoi* (see above, p. 17), thereby minimizing the possibility of isolated advances to unfamiliar maritime borrowers. For Pasiōn, initial dealings arise out of preexisting relationships with other clients; thus the son of Sopaios was introduced to him by Pythodōros "the Phoenician" and thereafter "used" Pasiōn as his banker (Isok. 17.5). "Use" of a banker (*khratai*) is the term applied in our sources to an intensive relationship extend-

---

[153]κοινωνεῖν δὲ καὶ αὐτὸν τῆς νεὼς Ὑβλησίῳ. The *nauklēros* Hyblēsios illustrates the varied functions often performed by a single individual in fourth-century maritime undertakings: besides his ownership interest in the vessel, he personally sailed on the voyage and was himself a borrower. For the prevalence of such multiple roles, see Gofas 1989: 425–30, esp. n. 1. For the lender, this lack of specialization—with its inherent conflicts and potential for confusion—increased the need for professional loan administration. For the Greek κοινωνός as "partner" or "participant," see above, Chapter 4, n. 71.

[154]Cf. Dem. 56.1: ὁ δανειζόμενος ἐν παντὶ προέχει ἡμῶν [sc. τῶν δανειζόντων].

[155]οὗτοι γὰρ δεινότατοι μέν εἰσι δανείσασθαι χρήματα ἐν τῷ ἐμπορίῳ, ἐπειδὰν δὲ λάβωσιν καὶ συγγραφὴν συγγράψωνται ναυτικήν, εὐθὺς ἐπελάθοντο καὶ τῶν συγγραφῶν καὶ τῶν νόμων.

ing well beyond the mere maintenance of depository accounts or use of currency-exchange facilities (see above, pp. 65–66). Even in advising customers, Athenian bankers would be likely to obtain information useful for decisions regarding loans.

Absence of such intimate knowledge could be disastrous: Androklēs claims total ignorance of the borrowers who failed to repay him.[156] But even lenders with adequate personal information about would-be borrowers would need reliable information about their anticipated commercial activities. When each confirmed for the other that they had placed substantial collateral on board a vessel (Dem. 32.4), a *nauklēros* and an *emporos* allegedly defrauded lenders who had advanced funds on the same collateral. The debtor in Demosthenes 34 delivers entirely insufficient collateral, but then succeeds in effectuating a number of loans, each secured by the same cargo, a clear multiple encumbrance—all of which goes undetected by the lender (§6). Although this creditor did recognize the need to monitor the collateral once it arrived on the outward journey to the Bosporos (§8), he lacked personnel to convey his instructions to his associates, who were resident at the port of delivery. Instead, because of his reliance on the ship's captain, his associates allegedly never received his instructions to "examine and follow" the proceeds of the collateral after arrival.[157] In contrast, when an Athenian bank financed maritime trade through loans to pay freight charges for the importation of bulk items such as timber, its standard procedure was to require the goods to remain in the harbor under bank supervision, and through bank personnel to collect all revenues resulting from sale of the collateral until the advance was repaid in full (Dem. 49.35).

While commerce could not have functioned if all borrowers actively sought to defraud their creditors—and the Athenians clearly recognized the necessity in commercial activity for a reputation for integrity[158]—professional skills and experience were vital in lending to sea merchants and maritime operators who, personally or through agents, were accompanying aboard ship the property constituting security for the loans, and were thereby in a position to react directly to the manifold vagaries of marine transport in antiquity.[159] *Trapezitai* were alone at Athens in conducting a business that generated lendable funds, honed lending skills, and demanded a high level of financial organization.

The bank loan to the ship owner Apatourios (Dem. 33) was in concept relatively simple: the ship itself, rather than portions of a variegated cargo,

---

[156]ἐγὼ αὐτὸς οὐδ' ὁπωστιοῦν ἐγνώριζον τοὺς ἀνθρώπους τούτους (Dem. 35.6).

[157]Dem. 34.8: τάχιστα ἐξαιρεθῇ τὰ χρήματα ἐξετάζειν καὶ παρακολουθεῖν.

[158]Dem. 36.44: πίστις ἀφορμὴ πασῶν ἐστι μεγίστη πρὸς χρηματισμόν. Although the Romans made *Graeca fides* a synonym for dishonest dealing, there is absolutely no basis for attributing to the ancient Greeks an abnormal predilection for litigation or sharp practices. See Cohen 1973: 133; J. W. Jones 1956: 232.

[159]For these representatives and their procedures in the fourth century, see Gofas 1989: 425–28. Cf. Meyer-Termeer 1978: 65 n. 32.

served as security, and the vessel was present at the Piraeus, not in some distant port. Nonetheless, the use of financial guarantees and monetary participation for this relatively simple transaction suggests the likely complexity of other, inherently more difficult financings. Significantly, in the Apatourios dispute, the bank recovered its loan promptly and in full,[160] whereas the individual guarantor some years later was still involved in litigation arising from the non–bank creditors' clumsy efforts at self-help (Dem. 33.9). (And the Hērakleidēs bank, which failed shortly after effectuating this loan,[161] may not have been the most capable of banking operations!) The experiences of Dēmōn, son (and successor?) of the banker Dēmomelēs (see above, pp. 126–29), further illustrate the diligence and organization demanded of maritime lenders—and the unlikelihood of direct sea lending by the aristocratic but essentially uninvolved capitalist so often pictured in secondary studies (see below). On making a maritime loan, Dēmōn had placed on board ship an agent who was later able to obtain control of the ship, partly by offering premium wages to the crew if they should succeeed in saving the vessel (Dem. 32.8). He thus protected the collateral that Dēmōn claimed. Even so, Dēmōn had to send Aristophōn from Athens to Kephallēnia (§11), where Aristophōn succeeded, against opposition, in forcing the ship to sail to Athens (§14), thus preserving the Athenian creditors' position. There Dēmōn himself was required to seize the cargo (§17), possibly because of his adversary's desire to establish Dēmōn's personal liability for the appropriation.

The variety of coins circulating in the fourth century, the absence of standardized exchange values, and the danger of accepting worthless imitations of precious metals generated currency risks that enormously complicated the challenge of maritime lending.[162] Here, too, the bankers' concurrent activity in monetary exchange provided them with advantages for maritime lending, supplementing their already unique capacity, through lending skills and depositary resources, to meet the intricate demands of financing overseas trade. This commerce, necessarily involving distant locations, was greatly affected by variations in the relative values of different currencies. Even in a single limited area, exchange ratios might vary enough in a few months to affect significantly

---

[160]Dem. 33.12: πραθείσης τῆς νεὼς τετταράκοντα μνῶν, ὅσουπερ ἡ θέσις ἦν.

[161]Dem. 33.9. Thompson (1979: 236–37) assumes, plausibly but without proffering evidence, that the bank's failure was unexpected.

[162]Surviving fourth-century coin hoards from even relatively provincial areas reveal a remarkable variety of coinages, many from outside the area, and the simultaneous presence of coins of varied standards. For Thessaly, for example, see T. R. Martin 1985: 41–59; for Olbia, see Ziebell 1937: 75. The profusion of counterfeit coins is suggested by governmental laws and treaties seeking to deal with the problem: at Mytilene and Phokaia (Tod 1948: 112 = I.G. XII 2.1; Gauthier 1972: 381–82); and at Athens (Stroud 1974). If Stroud is correct in his interpretation of the Athenian legislation as requiring acceptance of even foreign imitations of Athenian coins in good silver, the need for money-changing expertise was even greater. But see Chapter 1, n. 46.

the calculation of claims for legal damages arising from expenditures on a single trireme.[163] In the Bosporos, an area critical to Athenian food-supply,[164] numismatic evidence suggests that the Cyzicene stater, not the Athenian drachma, was the standard currency.[165] The number of drachmas required to purchase a single stater appears, not surprisingly, to have been much higher (perhaps a third greater) in the Bosporos than at Athens.[166] In view of the critical importance of commerce from the Black Sea, Athenian maritime finance could not have been, and was not, restricted to loans denominated in drachmas.[167] Even a trading voyage intended to originate and terminate in the Piraeus might require a lender to recover his monies in a foreign locus (as allegedly happened in Dem. 56), and the difference in currency might bring disaster to a lender unable to deal with deviations in coinage values. This enormous variation in exchange ratios, however, offered considerable opportunity for profit to Athenian bankers who could charge appropriate rates for credit accommodations for the Bosporos market (such as that reported at Isok. 17.35–37), but could minimize through their exchange operations the cost to the bank if such guarantees had to be funded. Here, too, the bankers, with their expertise in currency exchange and their stock of foreign specie, were uniquely positioned to provide maritime loans.

[163]Thus Apollodōros (Dem. 50.30) emphasizes his recordation of exchange rates and charges: ἡ τιμὴ τίς ἦν καὶ νόμισμα ποδαπόν, καὶ ὁπόσου ἡ καταλλαγὴ ἦν τῷ ἀργυρίῳ.

[164]According to Strabo (7.4.6), Leukōn, king of Bosporos, sent 2,100,000 medimnoi from Theodosia to Athens, a daunting volume even if delivered over a period of years. See Hopper 1979: 90–92. Demosthenes (20.31) reports that as much grain came from the Pontic region as from all other sources combined.

[165]Not a single Athenian coin has been found in coin hoards from the Black Sea coast (Isager and Hansen 1975: 165). In contrast, Cyzicene staters have been found with relative frequency in hoards dating to the fourth century in southern Russia (IGCH 1001; IGCH 1011; IGCH 1012; IGCH 1013; IGCH 1045). Staters have also been found in the Piraeus (IGCH 47), and Cyzicene coins are known to have been held by Athenians (Lysias 12.11; 32.6, 9). There are several references to Cyzicene staters in the accounts at Athens of the Treasurers of Athena (I.G. I² 30–31, 5–6; 302d, 12, 54–55; 305.15) = I.G. I³ 18/30; 370; 378.

[166]The drachma/stater exchange rate ranged from as high as 28 drachmas to the stater in the Bosporos to about 21 drachmas in Athens (Isager and Hansen 1975: 164–66). Specific exchange values of the Cyzicene stater have been much debated. See n. 28 above. On the fluctuating value of the Roman denarius against "local" bronze coinages at different sites within the empire, see Gara 1976; Lo Cascio 1981: 77–78; Bellinger 1956: 147ff.

[167]For example, the son of Sopaios, a Bosporan who resided in Athens, after arriving with two ships of grain, obtained a bank guarantee to facilitate a borrowing from Stratoklēs, denominated in staters (Isok. 17.35–37). After his family had already resided in Attica for over thirty years, Lysias kept in his money-box a wide variety of currencies: at least three talents in silver (presumably Athenian drachmas), 400 Cyzicene (staters), and 100 Persian *darics* (and four silver cups!). See Lysias 12.11.

Intermediation

> The resources required for trade are provided by lenders:
> without lenders, not a ship, not a ship-owner, not a traveler
> could put to sea.
> —A fourth-century litigant speaking to an
> Athenian jury[168]

Overseas trade has always been entirely dependent on the availability of financing.[169] For Athens, each year's food supply alone required loans amounting to millions of drachmas.[170] The high level of activity at the Piraeus harbor throughout the fourth century confirms that sufficient funding was forthcoming.[171] But from whom if not from the bankers? Not from the government, which—aside from regulations intended to make grain available for local consumers—entirely avoided involvement (see above, pp. 42–44). Only two other significant sources of credit have been suggested: a money-lending class of *rentiers*, wealthy Athenian landowners whose business activity was limited to providing loans passively to the marginal creatures engaged in trade;[172] or the persons engaged in trade themselves (or their friends and

[168]Dem. 34.51: αἱ γὰρ εὐπορίαι τοῖς ἐργαζομένοις οὐκ ἀπὸ τῶν δανειζομένων, ἀλλ᾽ ἀπὸ τῶν δανειζόντων εἰσίν, καὶ οὔτε ναῦν οὔτε ναύκληρον οὔτ᾽ ἐπιβάτην ἔστ᾽ ἀναχθῆναι, τὸ τῶν δανειζόντων μέρος ἂν ἀφαιρεθῇ. An assertion necessarily compatible with reality, even if possibly overstated: a blatantly false claim would have been immediately recognized from the jurors' personal knowledge, destroying the speaker's credibility. Even Ste. Croix, who treats this statement "with skepticism," finds it "very likely that many if not most merchants" would have operated with borrowed funds (1974: 43). In accord: Hasebroek 1978: 7–10, 36–37; Millett 1983: 46.

[169]Even today's "foreign direct investment" is ultimately dependent on financing that is often generated on local capital markets. See McCulloch 1979: 93. Cf. R. W. Jones 1978: ch. 12; Ragazzi 1973.

[170]Casson (1984: 26) has estimated that financing for 100 shiploads of grain (400 tons per ship) would have required 4,000,000 *dr*. In fact, persuasive arguments have been made for the import of as many as 600 shiploads of grain, although the actual amount of a "shipload" has been estimated at only 120 tons (3,000 medimnoi) (see above, n. 126). The range of financing suggested by these figures is roughly compatible with Isager and Hansen's estimate of total trade as amounting to at least 2,300 talents (13.8 million *dr.*) per year (1975: 52).

[171]"The system must have worked: the Athenians, after all, did not starve" (Thompson 1978: 417). Only through borrowed money were Athenians able to realize "on which side Athens' bread was buttered, or rather, that without the traders and shipowners there would be scant bread to butter" (Casson 1984: 33).

[172]Since at least the late nineteenth century (cf. Clerc 1893: 396–97; Francotte 1900: 192), this group has been identified as the primary source of trade financing. In his classic exposition, Hasebroek insisted on a fundamental division in the polis between *rentiers*, generally citizens living on income derived from capital investments and property, and the noncitizens actively involved in trade and production (1978: 22, 28, 35). Maritime loans were explained as finance provided by these citizen-*rentiers*, themselves uninvolved in business activities, to the poor but

family).[173] Although both groups did provide funding for maritime loans "through the bank" (*dia tēs trapezēs*, Dem. 45.66), for different reasons neither group was able directly to furnish any significant portion of the needed financing.[174]

Individuals engaged in trade have long been portrayed as abjectly poor, an image in sharp conflict with suggestions that they (sometimes aided by their families and acquaintances) were able to provide the millions of drachmas of financing required annually for hundreds of shiploads. The conventional view is of

> merchants and shipowners [who] were invariably without any capital worth mentioning of their own. They were always in difficulties, they had no reserves to fall back upon, they possessed nothing that might serve as security for a loan but their ship or the goods that borrowed money had enabled them to buy." (Hasebroek 1978: 7–8)

Although recent studies have modified this picture somewhat, pointing out that some merchants even lent money to others,[175] there is absolutely no indication that traders possessed any great pool of excess capital. Any funds available to merchants or ship owners, or to persons associated with them, would first have been needed to meet maritime lenders' equity requirements. To obtain financing of 3,000 *dr.*, for example, the borrowers at Demosthenes 35 were required to contribute an equal amount of capital. For a loan of 2,000 *dr.* at Demosthenes 34, equity of 2,000 *dr.* was required (and the same debtor had to furnish substantial, although for us not precisely determinable, capital to obtain a further advance of 4,500 *dr.*). A single trader often was unable and/or unwilling to provide the equity necessary to support even a modest sea loan: partnerships or participations were frequently utilized for borrowing even relatively small amounts.[176] Furthermore, prudent business planning and profit moti-

---

commercially active noncitizen traders (pp. 7–10, 36–37, esp. p. 7 n. 4). Hasebroek's conceptualization was anticipated by, and essentially derived from, Weber's analysis (see esp. [1909] 1924: 32–33). Despite the often high heuristic value of Weber's conceptualizations, they are frequently, as here, of limited usefulness in explaining actual historical phenomena: see Aron 1950: 232–36; Veyne 1971: 173–75.

[173]Bogaert 1965a: 142: "La plupart des bailleurs de fonds dans le crédit maritime étaient des commerçants en activé ou retirés des affaires." Cf. Millett 1983: 47–50; Isager and Hansen 1975: 83–84.

[174]Proponents of maritime financing by either group have seen clearly the impossibility of the other sector playing a significant role. Thus Millett (1983: 52) eliminates the *rentier*: "The complexity of maritime credit made it an unsuitable field for casual lenders without practical experience in trading." Hasebroek eliminates the traders (1978: 7–8).

[175]See especially Isager and Hansen 1975: 73–74; M. V. Hansen 1984: 88, 92 (n. 74). Cf. the much earlier similar observations of Oertel 1928: 1624–25.

[176]The sole surviving written contract governing a maritime loan (Dem. 35.10–12) involves dual lenders and dual borrowers, as does the agreement purportedly quoted in Dem. 56. At least

vation would dictate that any excess funds available to individual traders or ship owners be utilized in their own ventures, either to provide equity for additional voyages or to reduce the ratio of debt incurred for present ventures.

In contrast, substantial monies were available for maritime investment by individuals having no personal involvement in overseas commerce. Indeed, the fifth century had seen a revolutionary expansion in liquid wealth, permitting fourth-century Athens—despite the loss of imperial power—to maintain a high level of material prosperity, manifested above all by the booming commerce of the Piraeus. Whereas in the sixth century, residents of Attica disposed of virtually no wealth "which could not be measured in terms of agricultural produce" (Davies 1981: 38), by the end of the Peloponnesian War and the beginning of the fourth century there had been a total transformation in liquidity. Wealthy residents could accumulate cash for investment in maritime trade from many new sources: industrial workshops, silver mines, rents for houses and real estate in Attica,[177] investments in property outside Attica, and reinvestment of continuing profits from financing trade.[178] Prevailing opinion correctly asserts that much of this money was used to fund overseas commerce.[179] But the funding was not done directly. The complexity of maritime trade, which required knowledgeable, highly organized, personally involved lenders,[180] effectively precluded an independent role for *rentiers*. Furthermore, many of these investors needed the anonymity of working through others: much money for investment was being generated from the "invisible" (*aphanēs*) economy, avoiding taxes and creditors and Athenian laws requiring grain to be imported into Attica despite more favorable market conditions elsewhere (see Chapter 6). Only in this desire for confidentiality did the Athenian investor resemble modern passive investors who are able to "clip coupons" from unregistered bonds. To meet the myriad needs of inactive and

---

two borrowers appear in Dem. 32 (Protos and Fertatos, §17) and Dem. 52 (Megakleidēs and Thrasyllos, §20). None of these loans amounted even to a talent. Ships themselves were owned in partnership: see the deposition of Apollōnidēs, co-owner of the vessel in Dem. 35 (§33).

[177]For the legal basis and implications of such leasing, see Thür 1989; for its extent, consider the significant value of real estate held for commercial lease in even middle-class families (A.H.M. Jones [1957] 1977a: 89, 151–52 n. 61).

[178]For detailed consideration of these "new sources of personal wealth," see Davies 1981: 41–66. Cf. Mossé 1973: 42–49.

[179]See M. V. Hansen 1984: 71. But rather than seeking the profit motivation and mechanisms through which such investment might be effectuated, scholars have instead tended to treat these investments as though they were implementations of *noblesse oblige* social policy or as childlike satisfaction of gambling urges. Says Ste. Croix: "The important social function of the maritime loan was to spread the considerable risks of commerce over the much larger and richer landowning class" (1974: 43). Cf. Calhoun's description of "The Capitalist" in fourth-century Athens: "Then, as now, people who had a little money to invest were tempted by the promise of large and quick returns, and, if they thought at all of the risk involved . . . it did not deter them from employing their capital in this way" ([1926] 1968: 50).

[180]See above, pp. 144–50.

undisclosed lenders, and of borrowers working in trade, not finance, intermediaries were needed. "Through the bank" an intermediary was often present.[181]

Even in making landed loans *trapezitai* are known to have acted in conjunction with private lenders (for example, the banker Sōsinomos cooperated with Aristogeitōn in lending Aischinēs the money to conduct a profumery business; Lysias, frag. 38.2). The disputes concerning the estates of Demosthenes senior and of Pasiōn (see above) showed how *trapezitai* joined with other persons in funding maritime loans. Pointedly, the poseur satirized by Theophrastos is described as sending his slave off to his bank at the very moment that he is boasting of his maritime lending: his empty account betrays the falsity of his braggadocio.[182] But the most detailed surviving description of the interplay among banks, individual investors, and persons engaged in maritime trade is provided by the actions of Hērakleidēs' bank in the financing described in Demosthenes 33.

Apatourios, a ship owner from Byzantion, arrives at the Piraeus, where creditors attempt to seize his ship because of his delinquency on a loan for 4,000 *dr.* With Parmenōn, an exile from Byzantion, he seeks funds by approaching, in the *emporion* itself, an unnamed individual who for a number of years had traveled the seas on business, developing an especially close relationship with Byzantines. Having accumulated "some money," this mariner has retired from sea travel and has been "working" with these funds for the past seven years.[183] But how does our retired mariner, and self-styled modest financier handle this funding request? He arranges with the bank that he "uses" (see above, pp. 65–66), that of Hērakleidēs, to provide 3,000 *dr.*, taking himself as guarantor (since the mariner did not personally have any cash available).[184] The exile, Parmenōn, had previously agreed to provide the remaining 1,000 *dr.* Thus 4,000 *dr.* was raised, with the bulk coming from the *trapeza*. The bank's loan transaction is merely the factual background to a dispute between Parmenōn and the ship owner, resulting in an arbitrator's judgment and a court action that also involves the mariner. There is no opportunity or motivation, therefore, for special pleading by the *trapeza*: it is not even a party to the proceedings through which information concerning this transaction is pre-

---

[181]Although procedures at later times and distant places offer no guidance for practice at Athens, it is of interest that at Ephesos, in Egypt, and in Rome, three of the areas for which ancient banking practices are best attested, bankers were involved in the making of maritime loans as intermediaries. See Rougé 1966: 348–60, esp. 349, 355.

[182]Theophr., *Char.* 23.2: ὁ δὲ ἀλαζὼν τοιοῦτός τις οἷος . . . ἐν τῷ διαζεύγματι ἑστηκὼς διηγεῖσθαι ξένοις ὡς πολλὰ χρήματα αὐτῷ ἐστιν ἐν τῇ θαλάττῃ, καὶ περὶ τῆς ἐργασίας τῆς δανειστικῆς διεξιέναι ἡλίκη, καὶ αὐτὸς ὅσα εἴληφε καὶ ἀπολώλεκε, καὶ ἅμα ταῦτα πλεονάζων πέμπειν τὸ παιδάριον ἐπὶ τὴν τράπεζαν, ‹οὐδὲ› δραχμῆς αὐτῷ κειμένης.

[183]§4: οὔπω δὲ ἔτη ἐστὶν ἑπτὰ ἀφ' οὗ τὸ μὲν πλεῖν καταλέλυκα, μέτρια δ' ἔχων τούτοις πειρῶμαι ναυτικοῖς ἐργάζεσθαι.

[184]§7: Ἐμοὶ μὲν οὖν οὐκ ἔτυχεν παρὸν ἀργύριον, χρώμενος δὲ Ἡρακλείδῃ τῷ τραπεζίτῃ ἔπεισα αὐτὸν δανεῖσαι τὰ χρήματα λαβόντα ἐμὲ ἐγγυητήν.

served. Yet there is no suggestion that there was anything unusual in the bank's participation in maritime lending, in the mariner's "use" of the *trapeza*, or in the borrowers approaching the bank for a sea-related loan—each of which would have been most exceptional if banks did not generally engage in ship finance. Again, forensic considerations argue for the basic reliability of the speaker's presentation of bank involvement as routine: the mariner, who speaks to the jury, himself a defendant in the litigation, would have destroyed his credibility if he had presented a summary wildly at variance with the everyday reality of bank and harbor activity, a reality about which the jurors would have been quite knowledgeable.

Indeed, the bank's skill in handling this financing suggests considerable experience in maritime lending. Utilizing the services of the mariner, the *trapeza* takes the ship itself as collateral,[185] requires the participation of one private lender, and obtains the guarantee of another. As a result, through the sale of the security (§12), the bank obtains repayment of its loan without complication; the other parties are left many years later still embroiled in protracted litigation.[186]

Although the banker Hērakleidēs supplied most of the monies for the loan, he did not ultimately appear as a named creditor. The loan transaction instead was completed as a "purchase" (*ōnē*) in which the mariner became the stated "owner" of the ship, and the persons actually providing the funds were not named or otherwise mentioned as lenders.[187] We even know why the true suppliers of funding were not explicitly parties to the transaction: a disagreement had occurred between the two Byzantines, after the bank loan had already been funded but before Parmenōn had actually expended the last 700 of the 1,000 drachmas to which he was committed. "Parmenōn therefore did not *himself* wish to enter into the legal obligation."[188]

For the creditors, this shift to a "dummy" lender was advantageous. If

---

[185]Bogaert erroneously asserts (1986a: 28) that the bank loan was not secured by the ship. This is clearly incorrect: the *trapeza*'s funds were used to repay an earlier loan collateralized by the vessel, and were ultimately repaid from the proceeds of the sale of the ship (§12). In fact, the mariner explicitly claims to have actually delivered to the bank's "guarantors" the security (documentation): διηγησάμην τοῖς ἐγγυηταῖς τῆς τραπέζης τὴν πρᾶξιν, καὶ παρέδωκα τὸ ἐνέχυρον (§10).

[186]The Greek practice of destroying a loan agreement on repayment meant that if professional bankers were measurably more successful than other lenders in obtaining repayment of maritime loans, less evidence of their maritime lending would survive. The actual contract in Dem. 33 is reported as having been destroyed upon repayment of the underlying bank loan (§12), and the text of the preserved court speech accordingly cannot quote from or incorporate this συγγραφή.

[187]§8: ὠνὴν ποιοῦμαι τῆς νεὼς καὶ τῶν παίδων, ἕως ἀποδοίη τάς τε δέκα μνᾶς ἃς δι' ἐμοῦ ἔλαβεν, καὶ τὰς τριάκοντα ὧν κατέστησεν ἐμὲ ἐγγυητὴν τῷ τραπεζίτῃ. For the form of financing, see below, pp. 166–68.

[188]§§7–8: ὡμολογηκὼς δ' εὐπορήσειν αὐτῷ δέκα μνᾶς, καὶ τούτων δεδωκὼς τὰς τρεῖς, διὰ τὸ προειμένον ἀργύριον ἠναγκάζετο καὶ τὸ λοιπὸν διδόναι. αὐτὸς μὲν οὖν διὰ τοῦτο οὐκ ἐβούλετο ποιήσασθαι τὸ συμβόλαιον, ἐμὲ δ' ἐκέλευεν πρᾶξαι (emphasis added).

Parmenōn were not explicitly mentioned as a lender, the borrower, Apatourios, would have more difficulty in asserting, as a defense to nonrepayment, claims arising from his disagreement with Parmenōn. If the bank were not explicitly named as a lender, the *trapeza* might avoid (as it in fact did) direct involvement in any resultant litigation and thus avoid possible forced disclosure, before the magistrate or otherwise, of the sources of its funds. Since the money had already been disbursed (the bank's share entirely and Parmenōn's participation partly), the creditors realistically could not refuse to complete the funding: otherwise, in failing to honor their agreement, they would, at the least, have placed in question their legal right to return of the funds already advanced.

The shift in form of transaction had the affect of "changing the creditors,"[189] thus entirely masking—certainly to third parties, possibly even from Apatourios, the borrower—the true identities of the lenders.[190] The creditors' disappearance is so complete that even the liquidators ("guarantors") of Hērakleidēs' bank (which failed shortly after this loan was made) were entirely unaware of Parmenōn's participation: the mariner has to point out to them, when he delivers the "security" (*enechyron*) for the loan, that they are not entitled to all of the proceeds; 1,000 of the 4,000 drachmas actually came from Parmenōn.[191] As a result of the change in form of documentation, the mariner was disadvantaged in his later effort to avoid liability through a plea against jurisdiction (*paragraphē*) in the maritime courts. To succeed in this plea, the mariner had to establish an absence of legal relationship with Apatourios.[192] In fact, of the three persons involved in the financing, the mariner was the only one who had not supplied monies; through his "purchase" of the vessel, however, he was the only one named in the documentation as having a legal relationship with Apatourios.

If the Hērakleidēs financing had been mentioned merely in passing—the manner of citation for most allusions to maritime lending at Athens—the lender would have seemed to have been not the bank, but the *trapeza*'s client, the mariner, the sole "owner" of the vessel under the form of financing utilized. No mention would have been made of the banker's involvement. Analogously, at least eight other cases are known of maritime "lenders" who actually were bank customers.[193] Since we are able to identify relatively few maritime lend-

---

[189]§9: Τὸν μὲν τρόπον τοῦτον ἀπήλλαξεν τοὺς χρήστας Ἀπατούριος οὑτοσί.

[190]The mariner might have suggested to Apatourios that in order to complete the funding he had obtained new financiers, a possible pretext for the change in form of loan.

[191]§10: παρέδωκα τὸ ἐνέχυρον, εἰπὼν αὐτοῖς ὅτι δέκα μναῖ ἐνείησαν τῷ ξένῳ ἐν τῇ νηί.

[192]On jurisdictional requirements in the *dikai emporikai*, see Cohen 1973: 96–157; Kussmaul 1985: 33–39. On the *paragraphē*, see most recently Katzouros 1989; Talamanca 1975; Wolff 1966; Schönbauer 1964.

[193]See Thompson 1979: 234 n. 56. Similarly, Apollodōros's advance to Nikostratos of 1,000 *dr.* was actually funded by the banker Theoklēs (Dem. 53.9).

ers or bankers (see above, pp. 31–32), and relatively fewer bank customers, this concatenation itself argues for substantial bank involvement in sea finance: it is highly unlikely that the Hērakleidēs financing, the maritime loan whose context is best known, represented a unique occurrence, the only case in which a bank customer appeared as lender of record for a loan in which the funds actually came from the *trapeza*.

Demosthenes 33 also illustrates the practice of intermediation in maritime finance. Whereas the banker functions as an intermediary in using depositors' monies, in whole or in part, for funding the bulk of this maritime loan, the mariner himself functions as an intermediary of record for the banker and for Parmenōn. Although none of the funds loaned were in fact his own, the mariner, in describing his role with regard to Parmenōn's money, refers to the loan funds as provided "through me,"[194] the same formulation (the preposition "through" governing a noun in the genitive case) used at Demosthenes 45.66 to describe Pasiōn's bank's actions on behalf of Stephanos, who was there accused by Apollodōros of making money clandestinely "through the bank."

The distinguished French scholar Gernet long ago assumed, albeit without citing any example, that depositors must have been able to share with the *trapezitai* in the profits generated from the banks' use of their funds.[195] In similarly arguing that grammatical considerations compelled the conclusion that all four of the individuals named at Demosthenes 27.11 were bankers who had made maritime loans utilizing Demosthenes' father's deposits (see above, pp. 121–29), Paoli suggested that the word *ekdosis* specifically denominated a bank deposit intended to be utilized for maritime finance.[196] This word, whose basic notation is a "giving out" or "giving up," occurs in many contexts clearly unrelated to banking.[197] In this it is similar to such terms as "deposit" (*parakatathēkē*; see above, pp. 111–12) and reflects the absence generally at Athens of a specialized vocabulary of technical terms applicable solely to financial instruments.[198]

But *ekdosis* does appear in a number of bank-related contexts where "maritime loan" or "maritime finance" is referred to simultaneously through an-

---

[194]§8: τὰς δέκα μνᾶς ἃς δι' ἐμοῦ ἔλαβεν.

[195]Gernet 1981: 350 n. 14: "Money is conceived of as virtual credit: when deposited with a banker . . . it can be put to work, and as in modern practice, the banker invests it on his own (and often agrees to a fifty-fifty share with his client)."

[196]Paoli [1930] 1974: 22 n. 1. The same suggestion was made, apparently independently, at about the same time by Ziebarth (1929: 86).

[197]For its broad spectrum of meanings, ranging from the "giving up" of persons, as in the delivery of a bride into marriage (Plato, *Laws* 924d) or the surrender of suppliants (Herod. 1.159), to the "giving out" or publication of a book (Dion. Hal., *Amm.* 1.10; Ail. Tact. Praef. 4), see Van Groningen 1963: 1–14. For its financial denotations, see Korver 1934: 95–97.

[198]For the Athenian tendency to use economic and business terms without precision, see nn. 215, 219 below.

other term or phrase.[199] In such passages, reference to *ekdosis* would be redundant unless it conveyed a meaning beyond reiteration of the fact of a maritime loan. The 7,000 drachmas delivered to the banker Xouthos by Demosthenes' father are identified as a maritime loan (*nautika d'*), but are then further described as an *ekdosis* (Dem. 27.11). (At Demosthenes 29.36 the same monies are again described as an *ekdosis*, in a context replete with references to bankers' contracts and records.[200]) Lykōn, a customer of the banker Pasiōn, is described as having put out an *ekdosis* to Akē. The reference comes in the context of litigation about Lykōn's own bank deposits. In this case there is no redundant reference to maritime finance, although the context makes clear that the loan was in fact a sea financing.[201]

In Lysias 32.6, in meeting with his wife and brother before departing for military service, Diodotos "disclosed maritime loans (*nautika*), seven talents and forty mnai, which had been given out (*ekdedomena*)" or "maritime loans (*nautika*) funded from bank deposits (*ekdedomena*)." Although the presence of a separate word for "maritime loans" accompanied by a form of the word *ekdosis* might otherwise be attributed merely to periphrastic construction, Diodotos's business activity was precisely the same as that of the mariner in Demosthenes 33 who, we know, lent in his own name funds actually supplied by the banker Hērakleidēs. Both Diodotos and the mariner are described as working in the *emporion* at maritime lending.[202] The mariner, however, claims to be working partly with his own funds (although he is not able to contribute a single drachma from his own monies to financing the ship owner Apatourios). Significantly, perhaps, despite the great detail in which Diodotos's assets are described in the Lysias speech, there is no indication that the monies employed by Diodotos are entirely his own.

In his speech against Demosthenes, Hypereidēs charges, depending on the proper interpretation of *ekdosis*, either that Demosthenes himself "makes maritime loans (*nautikois*) and gives maritime loans (*ekdoseis*)" or that he "makes

---

[199]To denote maritime financing, Athenian writers utilize descriptive phrases such as "maritime yield" (ναυτικὸς τόκος) or employ, unsystematically, adjectival and adverbial uses of "maritime" (ναυτικός, ναυτικά, ναυτικόν as a substantive). The earliest direct appearance of the phrase ναυτικὸν δάνεισμα ("maritime loan") occurs in a papyrus published in 1957 (P. Vindob. G 19792 = SB VI 9571) dating from the middle of the second century A.D. Ναυτικὸν δάνεισμα, however, does appear in certain late sources that are largely compendia of citations from earlier writers (the lexicographers Pollux [3.84, 3.115], Harpokratiōn [s.v. ἔκδοσις and the *Anecdota* (Bekker I, 283)].) The lexicographers tend to treat ἔκδοσις as synonymous with "maritime finance."

[200]περὶ δ' αὖ τῆς ἐκδόσεως, ἐπικοινωνήσαντες τῷ Ξούθῳ καὶ διανειμάμενοι τὰ χρήματα καὶ τὰς συγγραφὰς ἀνελόντες . . . καὶ διαφθείραντες τὰ γράμματα. See the discussion above, pp. 124–26.

[201]Dem. 52.20: ἐκεῖνος γὰρ τετταράκοντα μνᾶς ἔκδοσιν ἐκδοὺς εἰς Ἄκην Μεγακλείδῃ κ.τ.λ.

[202]Lysias 32.4: ἐργασαμένου δὲ Διοδότου κατ' ἐμπορίαν πολλὰ χρήματα. Dem. 33.4: μέτρια δ' ἔχων τούτοις πειρῶμαι ναυτικοῖς ἐργάζεσθαι.

maritime loans (*nautikois*) and provides funding through bankers' deposits (*ekdoseis*)."²⁰³ Demosthenes' close involvement, through family and clients, with Athenian banking has already been chronicled. His utilization of bankers for the making of sea loans would be merely a duplication of his father's practice (which the orator himself describes in Dem. 27.11). By contrast, it is difficult to accept the image of the Athenian political leader and statesman as personally engaged in making maritime loans late in life, when even as a young man he had insisted that he had no time for "private matters," not even those involving courtroom speeches (Dem. 32.32). Even without reference to *ekdosis*, Hypereidēs could not have hoped to convince his audience—who knew directly Demosthenes' all-consuming personal involvement with affairs of state and politics—that Demosthenes busied himself personally in conducting a maritime-finance business. But the explanatory use of the word *ekdosis*, if it referred to the making of loans through intermediaries, would have made the charge credible.

With the exception of the Diodotos citation, I have been able to find no examples where *ekdosis* is employed in a maritime-financing context other than with reference to persons known to be closely involved with Athenian bankers.²⁰⁴ The evidence, however, is insufficient to permit a firm conclusion that the Athenians recognized *ekdosis* as a verbal formulation specifically denoting maritime loans funded from bank deposits. We may conjecture that the inherent obligation of repayment, the tendency to consider bank deposits as akin to loans, may have resulted in the depositor generally being entitled to return of his money without regard to the bank's success in obtaining repayment of any specific maritime loan. But actual practice would have been subject to individual negotiation and may have involved the same variability of terms and motivations that accompanied a banker's general receipt of deposits (see above, pp. 114–21). Although the relatively high return on sea finance would have allowed a banker to offer enticing terms, individual arrangements would have varied with the banker's need for funds, the customer's need for confidentiality, terms offered by competitors, general economic conditions, and—possibly most important—the banker's reputation for solvency and integrity.²⁰⁵ And regardless of the terms negotiated, maritime investors were always ultimately dependent on the financial strength of the individual banker to whom funds

²⁰³Dem. 17: ναυ]τικοῖς ἐργάζῃ χ[ρήμα]σιν καὶ ἐκδόσεις δί[δως]. In financial context, the term ναυτικοῖς ἐργάζεσθαι (literally, "to work with maritime matters") is generally translated as "to make maritime loans." Thus, at Dem. 33.4, the mariner is said to be "making loans on adventures overseas" (Loeb translation of ναυτικοῖς ἐργάζεσθαι). But the translator (in the Loeb series) of this passage is forced to render ναυτικοῖς ἐργάζῃ as "you engage in sea commerce" to avoid the redundancy of "makes maritime loans and gives maritime loans." The possibility of Demosthenes actually "engaging in sea commerce" as a *naukleros* or *emporos* seems even more remote than his merely "making loans" on his own and for his own account.

²⁰⁴Source analysis by the Ibycus computer system has confirmed this.

²⁰⁵See above, p. 148 and note 158. Cf. Isok. 17.2.

were delivered: although Stephanos was accused of obtaining clandestine profit, he was in fact involved not only with the highly successful banker Phormiōn but also with Aristolochos, whose bankruptcy ruined many customers (Dem. 36.50, 45.63–64).

Denial of the Role of Bankers in Sea Finance

With evidence so abundant for bankers' substantial participation in maritime finance, why have scholars in recent years unanimously insisted on their absence from sea commerce? As practitioners of the emerging "sociology of knowledge" might anticipate, the nineteenth-century assumptions about trapezitic involvement in sea lending coincided with the then-prevalent orientation toward "modernism" in ancient historical studies: with the ascendancy of "primitivism," the mere existence of maritime loans became an "embarrassment,"[206] only exacerbated by any suggestion that banks provided this financing systematically through sophisticated methods. The absence of careful scholarly studies of lending activity, perhaps itself a reflection of prior disinterest in "mundane" subjects among students of the "higher culture" long represented by classical studies,[207] fostered the easy acceptance of assertions compatible with primitivistic expectations. But two intellectual considerations seemed to confirm the absence of bankers from maritime lending: (1) legalistic studies that assumed that the "maritime loan" represented a narrowly defined institution,[208] having fixed characteristics juridically established, thus permitting scholars to disregard, as not constituting "maritime loans," even the overt cases of maritime finance by banks; and (2) econometric studies, allegedly objective and scientific, that claimed that the absence of bankers from maritime lending was numerically certain.

Overly Narrow Definitions of "Maritime Loan"

Modern scholarship has treated the Athenian "maritime loan" as an established juridical category whose legal effectiveness was dependent on the presence of certain provisions. Although the nature and number of these requirements is

[206]Millett 1983: 44. See above, n. 118.

[207]Traditional scholarship was determined to see the Greeks as a people whom "business could not make dull," to paraphrase Matthew Arnold. General works on Greek civilization have entirely ignored fiscal matters: see van Effenterre 1979: 19 n. 1. For the determined avoidance of "unsavory" aspects of the Athenian economy, see below, pp. 191–92.

[208]For examples of its continuing characterization as an "institution": *OCD* s.v. "bottomry loans" (Heichelheim); Millett 1983: 186 n. 1; Humphreys 1978: 150; Finley [1951] 1985: 56, 83–87.

variously stated,[209] two criteria are universally insisted upon: (1) a maritime loan must necessarily ("obligatoirement") be collateralized by security of ship or sea cargo, free of other encumbrance (Vélissaropoulos 1980: 306); and (2) a maritime loan must necessarily contain a provision freeing the borrower from the obligation of repayment if this security is lost at sea (the so-called "ship survival" clause).[210] Modern interpretation, however, conflicts with the ancient sources,[211] which offer examples of "maritime" loans that do not conform to the contemporary definition. Although the legal characteristics of the "maritime loan" were supposedly derivative from legislation, regulations, or custom,[212] or a combination thereof, Athenian evidence makes clear that the

[209]Paoli ([1930] 1974: 59), for example, sets forth six "essential elements" ("elementi essenziali") without which a maritime loan "would not exist" ("non esisterebbe"). For Beauchet ([1897] 1969, 4: 279–93), the "essential elements" ("éléments essentiels") were only four in number, but these four corresponded, with only slight variance, to the four criteria essential for "le prêt à la grosse" under the French Commercial Code as in effect in 1897! Cf. Amit 1965: 136–37.

[210]Cf. Millett: "This is the crucial point about maritime loans that makes them different from all other types of loan transaction: if as a result of shipwreck or piracy the ship and its cargo were lost, the borrower was freed from all obligation to repay the loan" (1983: 36).

[211]Many efforts have been made to justify prevailing interpretation of fourth-century practices by reference to Hellenistic and Roman sources—usually without regard to the methodological problems inherent in explaining earlier phenomena by later material not explicitly or implicitly relating to prior historical periods. Beyond Athenian material from the fourth century, however, there survives very little evidence relating to maritime loans. Cf. Ste. Croix 1974: 53, 54: for "the Hellenistic period (roughly the last three centuries B.C. in the eastern Mediterranean world) . . . there is very little evidence . . . ; there are scattered references to maritime loans in the sources for the Roman Principate and Later Empire (covering the first few centuries of the Christian era)." Despite the recent publication of a second-century A.D. document relating to maritime financing of trade with India (Harrauer and Sijpesteijn 1985), for the Roman period there has not survived a single "true maritime loan document" ("eine eigentliche Seedarlehensurkunde," Thür 1987: 229). In accord: Casson 1990: 202. Taubenschlag (1936: 276) has emphasized the extreme rarity of evidence for maritime finance in Greek sources from Egypt. Far from offering explanations for the relatively well-attested fourth century B.C., such snippets of evidence are more likely themselves to be illuminated by a better understanding of the Athenian data. By way of example: with the exception of the mortgage document pertaining to India and of a "receipt" dated to A.D. 38 possibly relating to a maritime loan (Tab. Pomp. 13; Sbordone and Giordano 1968), from the entire ancient period, only two papyri (from the second centuries B.C. and A.D., respectively) have survived relating to sea finance. One (SB III 7169), examined in the context of scholarly "requirements" for maritime loans, presents "plusieurs anomalies quand on le compare aux prêts à la grosse athéniens du IVe siècle" (Bogaert 1965a: 147); that is, far from buttressing the conventional interpretation of Athenian maritime commerce, the document offers substantial contradictions, explained by Bogaert as derivative from the peculiarities of Ptolemaic circumstance. The other (SB VI 9571) is skillfully explicated by its initial editor (Casson 1986: 16–17) not through conclusory modern dogma but by reliance on information from fourth-century Athenian texts (Dem. 32.14; 33.6, 12; 34.6; 35.9, 32; 56.3, 6, 15): the fourth-century material is far more extensive, and in context far clearer, than the fragmentary papyrus.

[212]The purported legal basis for this alleged definitional rigor is seldom articulated. In the rare

Athenians accepted as "controlling" (*kyria*) "whatever arrangements either party willingly agreed upon with the other."[213] Enforceability of sea-loan agreements was governed not by requirements as to the substance of contractual covenants, but primarily by the procedural standards applicable to "maritime cases" (*dikai emporikai*).

Maritime loans did constitute for the Athenians a category recognizably separate from other finance, as shown by summary allusions in Athenian court speeches, without explanation, to "maritime yield" (*nautikos tokos*) or "maritime financing" (*nautika*).[214] But the distinct meaning of "maritime loan" was not determined by legal requirements. In actual usage, "maritime loan" was defined essentially through contrast to "landed loan," and in particular through the differing methods of calculating yield on "landed loans" and "maritime loans." This distinction is compatible with the Athenian tendency to use commercial terms with relative imprecision, and often even inconsistency,[215] and with the Hellenic tendency to conceptualization through antithesis (see above, pp. 46–52). Nonetheless, considerable ingenuity has been exhibited, ultimately without success, in the effort to reconcile Athenian evidence with the modern insistence on the rigorously defined "maritime loan."

If "maritime loan" had constituted for the Athenians a technical term carrying legal signification, fourth-century Athenian courtrooms and modern scholarly publications might have avoided much disputation about the criteria for admission of cases to the "commercial maritime" category (*dikai emporikai*).

---

instances where it is, the explanation is couched in generalities. Heichelheim writes vaguely of "elaborate regulations" (*OCD* s.v. "bottomry loans"); Paoli, even less specifically, alludes to legislation "in alcuni luoghi" and "consuetudine commerciale" elsewhere ([1930] 1974: 15–16).

[213]τοῖς νόμοις τοῖς ὑμετέροις [sc. Ἀθηναίοις] οἳ κελεύουσι, ὅσα ἂν τις ἑκὼν ἕτερος ἑτέρῳ ὁμολογήσῃ κύρια εἶναι (Dem. 56.2), implying absolute governmental noninvolvement in the conditions and terms of maritime finance. Cf. Dem. 42.12, 47.77; Hyp., *Dem.* 13. On the effect of fraud or improper influence on requisite volition, see Wolff 1968: 484 n. 3; Maschke 1926: 162; Simônetos 1939: 193ff.; J. W. Jones 1956: 222.

[214]As a substantive, ναυτικά itself simply connotes "maritime (matters)." The meaning of "maritime financing" is always obtained from the context, a further indication that the Greek word lacked legally effective technical significance. Thus, for example, Xenophon has the Spartan commander Kallikratidas, in a military setting, refer to "naval warfare" as (τὰ) ναυτικά (Xen., *Hell.* 1.6.5). But in the context of financial arrangements, Xenophon's reference to ναυτικά at *Poroi* 3.9 takes the meaning of "maritime financing."

[215]In a volume entirely devoted to Greek usage of various economic terms, especially those relating to credit, Korver concludes that the Greeks generally were exceedingly "vague" not only in their manner of expression but also in their conception of economic phemonena (see 1934: esp. 151). Cf. Fine 1951: 61–95. D. Cohen (1983: 6) observes that "Athenian theft statutes are formulated in such a way that they do not expressly define the relevant concept (e.g., theft, hierosulia), but rather presuppose a definition and a conception of the law that, given the nature of the legal system, cannot reside anywhere else but in the collective consciousness of the judges who happen to be sitting in court on a particular day."

Loans for sea commerce are the subject of all known cases raising this issue of admissibility. Yet—although the Greek litigants argue extensively about the nature of their contractual relationships and about the convoluted jurisdictional criteria for classification of a case as emporic, including the requirement of *syngraphai* ("written contracts")—there is not the slightest indication that the parties had not been free, regarding commercial terms, to arrange their loan relationships as they wished, or that there existed in fourth-century Athens a legally cognizable category of "maritime loans."[216] In fact, Athenian governmental and legislative involvement with maritime trade and finance was minimal (see above, pp. 42–44). The maritime-loan document preserved at Demosthenes 35.10–13,[217] the sole surviving text of an actual Athenian maritime-loan agreement, provides explicitly that as to the matters covered in the agreement "nothing else [will] have greater validity than [this] contract,"[218] a provision possible only if Athenian law did not delineate the terms required of "maritime loans."

One requisite of the orthodox view of maritime loans is that they be "made . . . upon security of a ship, or its cargo or both" (Ste. Croix 1974: 41). At Demosthenes 50.17, however, we have a clear case of a loan specifically denominated by the ancient source as "maritime" (*nautikon*), but indisputably lacking security of ship or cargo. Apollodōros, while serving as trierarch of an Athenian warship in the northern Aegean, claims to have effectuated two borrowings, one for 1,500 *dr.* from a certain Archedēmos, and another at 800 *dr.* on a "maritime" basis from Nikippos the *nauklēros* ("operator/owner of a cargo ship"),[219] "who happened to be at Sēstos."[220] The maritime loan was at

---

[216]Nor in the extensive modern scholarship on the subject is there any suggestion that definition of "maritime loan" was relevant to admission to the "maritime" courts—although the existence of a legal "obligation" was at the heart of the jurisdictional requirements. See most recently Kussmaul 1985: 33–39. Bianchini (1979: 247) emphasizes the probatory function of the συγγραφή, properly denying it status as an "elemento costitutivo del prestito a cambio marittimo."

[217]This document is now generally accepted as genuine. See Chapter 3, n. 4.

[218]κυριώτερον δὲ περὶ τούτων ἄλλο μηδὲν εἶναι τῆς συγγραφῆς. The speaker further interprets this clause specifically as giving the contract priority over laws and decrees (§39). The same provision of overriding effect was found in the contract (not preserved) that is the subject of litigation in Dem. 56 (see §26 of that speech). Cf. IG XII 7.67, 27 and 76.

[219]My characterization of *nauklēros* is intended to be descriptive, not definitive. The Athenians, here, too were not precisely consistent in employing business appellations. See Finley (1935: 320–36), who demonstrates that terms such as *nauklēros* and *emporos* were "used in one way and in other cases differently." Cf. Adam 1989: 286 n. 7; and n. 215 above. Because of this verbal inexactitude, various efforts to establish rigid categories for retail and wholesale trade functions have been unsuccessful. See, for example, Hasebroek 1923a; Knorringa [1926] 1961: esp. pp. 46–47, 51–52, 96–98, and 113–18; Paoli 1924: 45–63, and [1930] 1974: 23–24. Indeed, much of the merchant population at Athens in the fourth century used Greek only as a second language. Xenophon states explicitly that non-Greeks constituted a large portion (πολλοί)

a "yield" of "one-eighth" (12½ percent), with the principal and interest to be repaid if and when the ship returned to Athens. This financing is of extraordinary evidentiary value since in the entire corpus of Demosthenes this is the only *loan*[221] whose provisions are described in detail and which is termed by an Athenian, rather than a contemporary scholar, as "maritime."

But the loan carries a provision fatal to the orthodox formulation: the ship operator/owner is the lender! Ship and cargo, far from being the debtor's collateral, belong to this lender. The borrower is operating a warship and thus has no "cargo" to pledge.[222] Instead of recognizing that the prevailing scholarly definition of a "maritime loan" is in conflict with this ancient evidence, commentators have even gone so far as arbitrarily to brand as "impossible"[223] the text's explicit characterization of the loan as "maritime." Indeed, one scholar has even offered the war-vessel as collateral,[224] thus appropriating, as security for a private debt, a ship that actually belonged not to the borrower but to the Athenian state![225] (Since the lender is identified in the text as an Athenian citizen, he would presumably have been wary of accepting a state-owned trireme as collateral for a loan to its commander.)

In the fourth century, there were sound economic reasons for including in at least some maritime-loan contracts a provision requiring repayment only if the ship and/or its cargo arrived safely at the destination anticipated.[226] We know

---

of the commercially oriented metic population— "Lydians, Phrygians, Syrians, and every-other-kind of non-Greek" (*Por.* 2.3). Xenophon's claim is confirmed by other evidence: Gauthier 1972: 123–24 and n. 55. Cf. I.G. II² 1956; Pope 1935: 67–68; Launey 1949, 1: 67–69.

[220]δανεισάμενος ἐγὼ ἀργύριον παρ' Ἀρχεδήμου μὲν τοῦ Ἀναφλυστίου πεντεκαίδεκα μνᾶς ἐπίτοκον, ὀκτακοσίας δὲ δραχμὰς παρὰ Νικίππου τοῦ ναυκλήρου ναυτικὸν ἀνειλόμην, ὃς ἔτυχεν ὢν ἐν Σηστῷ, ἐπόγδοον, σωθέντος δὲ τοῦ πλοίου Ἀθήναζε ἀποδοῦναι αὐτὸ καὶ τοὺς τόκους.

[221]All other references are to "maritime contracts" (Dem. 33.3; 35.1, 17, 32, 45), "maritime operations" (Dem. 33.4), "maritime assets" (Dem. 35.12), or "maritime yield" (Dem. 56.17)—from which the presence of a "maritime loan" may be inferred. The only other direct references to "maritime financing" (Dem. 27.11; 35.42, 47) provide no information about lending arrangements and provisions.

[222]Even the ship's tackling, claimed by Apollodōros as his own (although normally supplied by the state, Dem. 50.34), was not pledged as collateral for the loan: it is later offered to Polyklēs as security for a separate loan (Dem. 50.55).

[223]See above Chapter 3, n. 95.

[224]Ste. Croix 1974: 50: "We might have been tempted to think that [this] loan, on security of Apollodorus' trireme, was not a genuine bottomry transaction either, since there is no other evidence to suggest that such loans were secured on any except merchant ships."

[225]The trierarch was responsible not only for commanding the trireme but also for meeting the ship's operating costs for a year. See Rhodes 1981: 680; Morrison and Coates 1986: 118–24. But the Athenian state built the ship and provided it for the trierarch and crew (Andreades [1933] 1979: 322). Cf. Xen., *Por.* 3.14. The public funds for such construction were handled through the ταμίας τῶν τριηροποιϊκῶν. See Dem. 22.17, 20; I.G. II² 1627.73; Rhodes 1972: 121–22.

[226]On the difficulty of enforcing obligations in the event of a sea calamity, see pp. 141–42, and n. 129 above. In commercially appropriate cases—in particular, those involving borrowers who lacked substantial assets independent of the security for a particular loan—an increase in

from Demosthenes 32.5 that, at least in the western Mediterranean, such clauses were commonly utilized.[227] But Demosthenes 56 seems to provide clear evidence that the provision was not universal. In this case, a vessel traveling from Egypt to Athens was carrying goods belonging to various merchants, most or all of which would have been encumbered under maritime-financing arrangements.[228] Other cargo on board belonged to the ship's *naukvēros*, Parmeniskos, and his colleague resident in Athens, Dionysodōros,[229] who had borrowed funds in Egypt for the journey to Athens and had also borrowed in Athens 3,000 *dr.* secured by the ship (§3) under a contract that explicitly established the boat's safe arrival at Athens as a condition to the borrower's obligation for repayment of the loan (§36). According to the defendants, the vessel, disabled in transit, was unable to complete the journey to Athens, and had to terminate its voyage at Rhodes (§§12, 20, 40). Parmeniskos and Dionysodōros refused to pay the 3,000 *dr.*,[230] relying on the destruction of the ship; the lenders sued, alleging that the ship technically had not been "destroyed." Resolution of this litigation depended on interpretation of the "ship-survival" clause.[231]

But the loans covering other cargo on board did not give rise to similar litigation, as would have been anticipated if the contracts covering these loans had contained similar exculpatory clauses. To the contrary, the defendants actually repaid principal and interest to maritime lenders who had loaned on the one-way journey from Egypt to Athens (§§26–30).[232] Rather than asserting

---

yield (τόκος) might have compensated for waiver of liability in the event of maritime disaster.

[227]οὐσῶν δὲ τῶν συγγραφῶν, ὥσπερ εἰώθασιν ἅπασαι, σωθείσης τῆς νεὼς ἀποδοῦναι τὰ χρήματα. This text exemplifies the applicability of the "ship-preservation" language (σωθείσης τῆς νεώς) to loans secured by cargo, as in this litigation, and not merely to advances secured by the vessel itself. The loan contract at Dem. 35 specifies σωθέντων δὲ τῶν χρημάτων Ἀθήναζε (§11).

[228]For the ubiquity of financing arrangements for sea commerce, see above, n. 168.

[229]Cf. §24: οὐ τῶν ἁπάντων ἀγωγίμων οὔθ᾽ οὗτος ἦν κύριος οὔθ᾽ ὁ κοινωνὸς αὐτοῦ, ἀλλ᾽ οἱ ἐπιβάται τὰ ἑαυτῶν χρήματα ἀπέστελλον. See Dem. 34.6, 35.18. Cf. Thompson 1978: 413 n. 48.

[230]Although the parties reached a settlement providing for partial repayment (§§13–14), the plaintiffs refused to release the borrowers from further liability, and the debtors then refused to pay anything (§§15–16). The speaker asserts that Dionysodōros in fact never contemplated any loan repayment, offering partial compensation only because he was confident that the lenders would refuse the proposal (§13).

[231]The issue was whether or not the vessel had been "preserved to Athens" (σωθείσης τῆς νεὼς εἰς τὸν Πειραιᾶ, §22), i.e., "able to reach Athens." See Meyer-Laurin 1965: 13–14.

[232]By the time the speech was delivered (323/2), Egypt was already under Greek domination. From this Hellenized Egypt we possess an important and relevant papyrus, the text of an actual maritime loan contract, albeit from the first half of the second century B.C., first published by Wilcken in 1925. It specifically provides for the financing (by persons resident in Egypt) of a voyage to Somalia and back, but it does not free the borrowers from obligation for repayment if the ship or its cargo should be lost. P. Berol. 5883 and 5853 = SB III 7169 (see Wilcken 1925). Cf. Fraser 1972, 1: 187; 2: 275 n. 216 and 321 n. 435. It has been conjectured that the clause

freedom from liability on their other loans, the defendants hired boats to transport from Rhodes to Athens at least a portion of their own cargo (§§21, 24). And they made arrangements for continued shipment from Rhodes to Athens of yet other cargoes on board belonging to third parties (§24).[233]

In short, a multitude of maritime loans and legal commitments are honored as though the damage to the ship had no affect on these arrangements.[234] The simplest and most reasonable explanation is that the various other agreements contained no exculpatory language relating to the ship's destruction. If contractual provisions had been identical, how would the defendants not have seen the inherent conflict in their asserting "destruction" of the ship in one case but accepting the vessel's "preservation" in others? And why would the plaintiffs not have at least alluded to the inconsistency of the defendants' behavior, instead of merely claiming that the arrangements with the other creditors are irrelevant to their own claims?[235]

The formalistic approach also denies status as a "maritime loan" to financing where "the ship was not about to sail out on a voyage" (Ste. Croix 1974: 52). Ste. Croix asserts that the financing of Apatourios the *nauklēros* by the banker Hērakleidēs is not a "maritime loan," not because he questions whether a bank was the lender or whether the borrower was engaged in maritime trade, but merely because the "form of transaction, a sale with option of redemption (*onē* or *prasis epi lysei*) is unknown, as far as I am aware, in bottomry transactions," and because "the ship was not about to sail out on a voyage," a supposed requirement for a "true" maritime loan.

Even if the transaction were indeed a "sale with option of redemption," it would be inappropriate to draw any conclusions from that fact: not only is this

---

must have been contained in a missing part of the papyrus (see Bogaert 1965a: 150). But in light of the extensive text surviving on every line of this lengthy (but fragmentary) document and the liberal restorations of supposedly lost letters, words, and clauses suggested by papyrologists (including the original editor), it is significant that even recent editors offer no emendation on this point. Cf. Annexe no. 21 in Vélissaropoulos 1980: 356–57.

[233]Gernet (1954–60, 3: 143 n. 1) has noted that this transit may have been provided pursuant to an obligation of the ship operators to provide transportation without exculpation by maritime damage. This continued obligation of merchants and ship operators to meet their contractual obligations without regard to the hazards of sea travel is inconsistent with a universal freedom from repayment of sea loans in the event of maritime losses.

[234]Although the plaintiffs assert that the defendants selected out for further shipment only those items whose prices had risen at Athens (§24), the increase would have had to have been enormous to exceed prices in Rhodes by an amount sufficient to justify transportation costs, further sea risks, and repayment of the underlying loans—if the debtors were in fact free of repayment obligation as to those goods in the event of exculpatory maritime occurrences!

[235]§26: περὶ δὲ τῶν δανειστῶν . . . ἔστι μὲν οὐδὲν πρὸς ἡμᾶς τοῦτο. Despite the plaintiffs' stated concern that they might appear to have funded the illegal transportation of grain to a market other than Athens (§§6, 13), they actually were not in a position different from that of the other lenders and debtors: the text of the written contract providing for transportation to Athens, frequently alluded to (there are at least 48 references to συγγραφή in the speech: Carey and Reid 1985: 200 n. 50), would have exonerated them from any such false inference.

legal form totally unknown in maritime context, but the term does not occur in any surviving fourth-century materials in any context.[236] Indeed, almost nothing is known about such transactions. The *concept* of "sale with option of redemption" itself is "almost imperceptible" in surviving literary sources (Andreyev 1979: 137), although the existence of something like "sale with right of redemption" in real-property transactions is suggested (but not described) by the presence of similar phrases on certain surviving mortgage (*horoi*) stones.[237] But our ignorance as to the nature of Athenian secured lending makes necessarily circular any argument based on the known characteristics of categories of collateral.[238]

Moreover, in suggesting that the transaction was, even in form, essentially a "sale" rather than a loan, Ste. Croix misreads the facts. When the initial arrangements were made, Apatourios was the owner of the vessel: there is no suggestion in the text that the loan from the bank was not initially a direct hypothecation. Subsequently, in connection with funding of the remaining 1,000 *dr.* by Parmenōn, the owner agreed to the "sale" of the ship, but this alteration clearly could have no effect on the prior secured position of the bank (see above, n. 185). In fact, because of a dispute occurring after partial funding of the 1,000 *dr.*, Parmenōn did not wish to provide the rest of the money but felt compelled to do so lest he endanger repayment of the portion he had already advanced.[239] Before the rest of this money was paid out, *but after the bank's funds had already been provided*,[240] the form of transaction was altered. The ship now would no longer "belong" to Apatourios, and repayment would presumably be the only manner in which the borrower could recover "ownership" of his vessel. But whatever the implications of this form, the altered arrangement could not disregard the bank's prior loan and prior lien position, and obviously could not change the economic reality of bank participation in maritime lending.[241]

[236]Harrison 1968–71, 1: 256; Isager and Hansen 1975: 155 n. 31.

[237]Πεπραμένου, πεπραμένης, or πεπραμένων ἐπὶ λύσει (Finley [1951] 1985: nos. 11–101 and App. 3), "sale on condition of release" (Finley's translation, ibid., p. 31). Cf. E. M. Harris 1988: 351.

[238]In the only full discussion of these characteristics, E. M. Harris (1988) denies that ὠνή differed substantively or even procedurally from the alternative form of hypothecation (ὑποθήκη) otherwise utilized in ship financing. Although Apatourios's original loan seems to have been secured only by the vessel (§6: ὀφείλων ἐπὶ τῇ νηὶ τῇ ἑαυτοῦ τετταράκοντα μνᾶς), the ὠνή covered both ship and slaves (§§8, 10). This dual security allowed specific provision for sale of the slaves if the loan were not fully repaid from the proceeds on disposition of the ship (§10: εἴ τις ἔνδεια γίγνοιτο, τὰ ἐλλείποντα ἐκ τῶν παίδων εἴη). Maritime finance clearly did not treat creditors' interests as necessarily "substitutive," but rather as collateral for repayment of the loan. See Chapter 6, n. 132.

[239]Dem. 33.7: διὰ τὸ προειμένον ἀργύριον ἠναγκάζετο καὶ τὸ λοιπὸν διδόναι.

[240]§7: ἤδη δὲ τῶν τριάκοντα μνῶν πεπορισμένων, ἔτυχεν προσκεκρουκώς τι τούτῳ ὁ Παρμένων.

[241]E. M. Harris (1988: 365) notes that even after the alteration in form, the transaction was still referred to "as a loan (§12: ἐδανείσθη) which it undoubtedly was."

Even more formalistic is the contention that "the ship was about to sail out on a voyage." By this logic, if the loan was not made in anticipation of sailing, it cannot be a "maritime loan." In truth, as Thompson has already shown, the loan actually may well have been made in anticipation of a journey by sea: Apatourios obviously contended that the loan was related to the transportation of goods from or to Athens, for the ship owner brought the litigation as fitting the commercial maritime category (*dikai emporikai*). These suits were limited, *inter alia*, to disputes relating to maritime commerce to or from Athens. And his opponent does not object to the case's pendency as an emporic case on the basis that a sea voyage from Athens was not anticipated; rather, he alleges termination of the agreement and release by the *nauklēros* (Dem. 33.3, 33.12).[242]

Again, however, only irrelevant formalism would place definitional importance on the stage in the trade cycle at which a bank loan occurs. Provision of funds at the end of a journey to permit payment to prior creditors is no less vital to maritime trade than finance for an anticipated voyage. This is true because of the fungibility of money, the serial impact on all further stages of exchange arising from the availability or absence of credit at any stage, and the consequent importance of the availability of financing at every point in an economic process. For example, at Demosthenes 56, a loan of 3,000 *dr.* is secured by a ship that is contractually obligated to journey between Athens and Egypt, returning to Athens. At variance with Demosthenes 33, where the ship is already in Athens and an effort is made by the borrower to remove it from the Piraeus, the borrowers in Demosthenes 56 allegedly never returned the ship to Athens. A return to Athens would have brought the ship at Demosthenes 56 to the point in the maritime finance process where Hērakleidēs' bank made its loan. Since these loans were dependent not on the value of cargo but on the worth of the ship, the borrower in both cases required a source for repayment of the original loan. Financing for a vessel setting out on a journey might normally be repaid from fees earned from the cargo carried, but receipt of these fees was itself dependent on favorable market conditions. The reason cited in Demosthenes 56 for halting the ship at Rhodes is a fall in the price of grain at Athens.[243] Such a decline might have resulted in the borrowers' inability to meet loan obligations secured by their own hypothecated grain. Furthermore, the loan against the ship itself possibly was to be serviced from transportation charges, which might have gone unpaid because of the price decline's adverse effect on the financial position of *emporoi* transporting goods on board the vessel. In the Zēnothemis case (Dem. 32), market prices fell, and individual *emporoi* were unable to repay their creditors from the value of the goods transported.[244] The persons associated with the *nauklēros* here also attempted

---

[242]Thompson 1979: 235 n. 71, citing Cohen 1973: 100–114.

[243]Dem. 56.25: τὰς γὰρ τιμὰς τὰς ἐνθάδε ἀνεικέναι ἤκουον.

[244]Dem. 32.25–26, with reference to Prōtos.

to halt the ship at Kephallēnia and prevent it from sailing to the Piraeus.[245] On arrival in Athens, the ship owner's creditors immediately sought to seize the vessel.[246] Again, this is the point in the trade cycle at which the *nauklēros* in Demosthenes 33 was forced, in crisis, to obtain financing from Hērakleidēs' bank, a trauma that the ship owners in Demosthenes 56 avoided.

Similarly, at Demosthenes 34.22–23, a loan was allegedly arranged at Bosporos to refinance cargo caught in a "buyer's market" (*aprasia tōn phortiōn*). The source of this loan is unclear. The possibility of bank credit should not be ruled out, however, in view both of the evidence in Demosthenes 33 for bank provision of financing for the repayment of prior maritime credit, and of the extensive evidence in Isokrates 17 for a relationship between Athenian bankers and Bosporan merchants that was already close some decades earlier. Indeed, the Athenian banker Pasiōn allegedly agreed to arbitration in Bosporos for a dispute involving return of bank deposits and repayment of maritime financing (Isok. 17.19).

A bank is fully involved in maritime finance both when it lends to a ship owner to permit repayment of prior debts relating to a completed journey and when it lends for repayment of prior debts relating to a forthcoming trip. Each type of loan would be made when the ship is in port, and each loan would depend on the ship owner's ability to repay the loan. The loan made by Hērakleidēs' bank, if made in the absence of an anticipated "stream of income" from transportation fees and in spite of the existence of unpaid prior creditors, would have involved clearly troublesome credit risks. As a practical matter, the risk of a ship's sinking is inherent in a maritime loan. Vessels are mobile, regardless of legal agreements. Apatourios's efforts to move the vessel away from Athens would have endangered Hērakleidēs' bank's collateral whether or not the movement conformed with loan documentation.

Loans such as that from Hērakleidēs' bank were critical to maritime commerce. A ship performed no economic function while held by creditors, as in Demosthenes 32; Athens would not be fed through vessels kept at Rhodes (Dem. 56) because of inability to pay creditors at the Piraeus. In providing loans secured by trading vessels, Athenian banks would be confirming the collateral value of those ships. Ultimately, banks and others would be able to extend credit collateralized by ships only if the vessels were known to have economic value wholly apart from the income immediately anticipated through transportation fees from the next journey.

---

[245]These efforts were unsuccessful: see n. 66 above. In contrast to the result at Kephallēnia, Dem. 56 relates to events in the late 320s, when Athenian influence on Rhodes was minimal.

[246]Dem. 32.14: τὴν ναῦν οἱ ἐπὶ τῇ νηὶ δεδανεικότες ἐνθένδ' εὐθέως εἶχον.

Flawed Cliometrics

The absence of Athenian banks from maritime lending is allegedly proven by cliometric analysis: according to Bogaert, a data base comprising the entire body of surviving references confirms this absence without a single exception. Among those providing maritime loans, he finds a variety of persons ("des métèques et des citoyens athéniens, des commerçants actifs ou retirés et des propriétaires fonciers"), but not a single banker ("mais aucun trapézite," 1986: 27). Hence, the allegedly scientific conclusion that Athenian bankers did not provide maritime loans.

This negative generalization, however, is garbed in a false cloak of mathematical objectivity. The selection and interpretation of the relevant citations is actually highly subjective, and the fragmentary nature of the evidence defies arithmetical organization. The complexity of maritime financing and its relationship to the "unseen economy" of tax evasion and creditor avoidance often obfuscates the identity of the actual source(s) of funds (see above, pp. 155–57, and below, pp. 202–7). Although loans were provided almost invariably by *groups* of financiers, under Athenian procedure legal action could be brought only by a single plaintiff against a single defendant,[247] necessarily tending to obscure the identity of lenders other than the single named party. Some surviving references to sea finance represent not single loans but an indeterminable number of financings about which virtually nothing is known. Problems inherent in the evaluation of such data mirror those encountered in the flawed efforts to derive numerical conclusions as to who was involved in overseas trade (see above, pp. 29–30). Thus Bogaert in 1968 claims that "we know of at least" eighteen maritime loans mentioned in Athenian court cases.[248] In 1974, however, Erxleben (1974: 462–71) analyzes at least twice as many examples of sea finance, including several that he terms "doubtful" ("unsicheren"). By 1986, Bogaert—although insistent on eliminating a number of loans identified by Erxleben—now finds a total not of eighteen but of twenty-eight

---

[247]Gernet 1954–60, 1: 147: "Les règles de la procédure exigent qu'une δίκη soit inscrite sous le nom d'un seul demandeur et d'un seul défendeur." Cf. ibid., 4: 131–32. The rule may have applied only in business litigation. In any event, this is the reason for the otherwise puzzling failure by Lykōn to sue Thrasyllos as well as Megakleidēs in the commercial lawsuit described at Dem. 52.20 (cf. E. M. Harris 1989: 343). Despite the absence at Athens of joint liability for associates' separate actions, all principals, even those not parties to the suit, might be affected, if only indirectly, by any resultant judgment. For this reason, perhaps—contrary to usual practice—more than one party from each side is allowed to speak in the actual litigation relating to maritime loans (most strikingly in Dem. 34, where a number of individual lenders participate in the proceedings [but without identifying themselves by name]). A ruling against a plaintiff in any of these cases would probably have allowed all defendants to object to any further action by any lender through a *paragraphē* citing the prior adverse adjudication (Harrison [1968–71, 2: 119–20], who notes the difficulty of determining "what exactly constituted a bar by previous δίκη").

[248]Bogaert 1968: 373, up from the fifteen maritime loans cited at Bogaert 1965: 141.

maritime loans (1986: 27, 47–48). "Eliminating all doubtful cases," Millett in 1983 finds "at least" thirty-seven references to maritime loans in various sources.[249]

These variations suggest, of course, that identification of a "maritime loan" is ultimately subjective. Thus, for example, Erxleben interprets as a maritime loan an advance of 12,000 *dr.* secured by a cargo ship (Lysias 32.25; Erxleben 1974: 462). Bogaert objects that the yield reported by Lysias is much higher than that of any maritime financing on his own list, and that the language in Lysias is "very general," possibly descriptive of property arrangements other than financing (Bogaert 1986: 47–48). In the interpretation of such sketchy information, there is always the danger that one might fail to recognize (or falsely assume) that a maritime loan is being mentioned. Many of the loans are mentioned in highly abbreviated references that often provide no information as to the source of the financing: these summary citations have then been taken, improperly, as further confirmation of the absence of *trapezai* from maritime finance. But bankers should not be arbitrarily ruled out as providers of credit in situations where nothing is known as to the source of the funding, often not even the names of the lenders.[250] Even where creditors are identified by name, we seldom have any information as to their occupations—but no reason automatically to assume that they are not bankers or funded by bankers. In these cases, analysis of context and of other available information is often helpful, albeit subjective. Negative generalization, however, has eschewed such ancillary aid. In neither his 1968 nor his 1986 study does Bogaert attempt to analyze any of the data cited to establish the absence of bank financing from maritime loans. But the following examination of each of the loans contained in Bogaert's original list of eighteen[251] reveals that in no case can trapezitic involvement be ruled out; in a number of situations, in fact, bank financing seems certain.

BANK LENDERS EXPLICITLY PRESENT: DEMOSTHENES 27.11, 33.4, 33.6–8; ISOKRATĒS 17.42

Since Demosthenes 27.11, 33.4, 33.6–8, and Isokratēs 17.42 appear in contexts concerning bank loans made either for explicitly maritime purposes or to persons engaged in sea commerce, these references are strange "proof" for the absence of Athenian banks from maritime lending. Demosthenes 27.11 deals explicitly with deposits at the banks of Pyladēs and Pasiōn, and sets forth a number of maritime loans provided by no less than four separate bankers.

[249]Millett 1983: 41, 188 nn. 13, 14.

[250]For example, in Dem. 32, the only information about the providers of one maritime loan is their description as "οἱ ἐπὶ τῇ νηὶ δεδανεικότες" ("those who have lent on the ship"; §14), and the lenders against cargo are described only as "τοὺς τούτῳ δανείζοντας" and "τοὺς ἐκείνῳ [sc. δανείζοντας]" (§4).

[251]Source: Bogaert 1968: 373 n. 408.

Demosthenes 33.4–8 describes how the bank of Hērakleidēs, apparently involved in sea finance on a recurring basis, made a loan to a ship owner secured
by his vessel. Isokratēs 17 provides numerous examples of bank loans for
maritime finance. (These situations are discussed in detail above; see pp. 121–
29 [Dem. 27]; pp. 166–68 [Dem. 33]; and pp. 38–40 [Isok. 17].)

BANK LOANS LIKELY: DEMOSTHENES 32.4, 32.14; HYPEREIDĒS, AGAINST
DEMOSTHENES COL. 17

Demosthenes 32.4 and 32.14, and Hypereidēs, *Against Demosthenes* col. 17,
contain references to maritime lending by Demosthenes and his relative Dēmōn, son of the orator's cousin Dēmomelēs. Dēmōn's father himself was a
bank proprietor involved in making maritime loans; Demosthenes' father employed banks as intermediaries for deposits utilized for maritime loans (see
above, pp. 126–29). The two sons appear to have continued their fathers'
practices. Dēmōn, possibly a banker, may in any event have utilized bank funds
in making maritime loans (see above, pp. 128–29). Even more than his
businessman-father, Demosthenes would have needed intermediaries in making the maritime loans attributed to him by Hypereidēs. Much earlier in his
political career, he already had been unable to devote any time to "private
matters."[252] Just as Demosthenes provided his kinsman Dēmōn with technical
expertise and presentation skills in litigation relating to sea commerce, the
orator could have used Dēmōn for the actual making and administration of
maritime loans: Dēmōn's own experience as a lender confirms the need for
professional skills and organization in ship finance (see above, p. 149). As we
have seen, Hypereidēs describes Demosthenes' activity in maritime finance by
the very term (*ekdosis*) used by Demosthenes himself in reporting his father's
maritime financing through the banker Xouthos (Dem. 27.11). These passages
certainly cannot be taken as positive evidence for the absence of bank involvement in sea financing by these scions of a family known to have been active in
maritime lending through banks.

In Demosthenes 32, mention is made of additional loans secured by the very
cargo that was supposedly encumbered by Dēmōn's loan (§§4, 8), and by the
ship (§14).[253] The identity of these lenders is unknown. There is, however, no
reason to assume that they were not bankers or persons utilizing bank funds. In
fact, evidence does survive indicating that at least two *groups* provided the
funds for the further loans against cargo, and that the lenders were from

---

[252]Dem. 32.31–32. See the discussion above, p. 127.

[253]Erxleben (1974: 467) does include the ship loan in his catalogue; Bogaert appears to have
omitted it from the 1968 canon, but he includes it in his 1986 list. There is no basis for
Pringsheim's suggestion (1916: 13–14) that a "maritime loan" could not be secured by the
vessel alone. For another example of such a loan, see Dem. 33.6–8 and the discussion above, pp.
166–68.

Marseilles (ancient Massalia), although the loan was made in Syracuse.[254] This limited information obviously does not rule out possible participation by bankers, and the fact of sea commerce to Athens funded in Syracuse from Massaliot monies further attests to the complexity of fourth-century maritime finance, and the consequent need for professional lenders.

BANK LOANS POSSIBLE: DEMOSTHENES 35.8–11, 35.23, 35.32, 34.6, 52.20, 50.17, 56.3, 56.17, AND LYSIAS 32.6

In none of the remaining examples (actually culled from only a half-dozen cases)—Demosthenes 35.8–11, 35.23, 35.32, 34.6, 52.20, 50.17, 56.3, 56.17, and Lysias 32.6—can bank lending be ruled out. In several, bank funding is strongly suggested by linguistic or factual considerations. Because our information is derived from court presentations, little is known about the creditors: litigation about loans usually generates data about borrowers—justifications for not repaying loans, accusations of their improper behavior, refutations of debtors' explanations. The identities and situations of the creditors are usually irrelevant. Once the money has been advanced, a lender's role is complete.[255] The only factor focusing attention on creditors is a public consideration: the law permitting maritime lenders resident at Athens to provide funds for trade in grain only if the cereals were to be transported to Athens.[256] This requirement does evoke some discussion of a creditor's actions, motives, and residence, but little specific information about personal characteristics. Because of his tie to the "unseen" economy and consequent need for confidentiality, a banker would likely avoid identification as the eponymous claimant actually bringing a lawsuit. Furthermore, because blatantly unsuccessful plaintiffs were subject to fines, tactical considerations argued for naming as plaintiff the least vulnerable, presumably often the least wealthy, creditor—who for this reason was also least likely to have been a principal source of the actual financing. Thus there is an inherent fallacy in methodology that assumes that a creditor is not a banker unless the text identifies him as such.

[254]Dem. 32.4: χρήματ᾿ ἐν ταῖς Συρακούσαις ἐδανείζεθ᾿ οὗτος κἀκεῖνος. ὡμολόγει δ᾿ ἐκεῖνος μὲν πρὸς τοὺς τούτῳ δανείζοντας . . . οὗτος δὲ πρὸς τοὺς ἐκείνῳ. . . . (8) καὶ τὰ χρήματ᾿ ἐκεῖθέν ἐστι.

[255]The speaker at Dem. 56.1 emphasizes the creditors' limited obligation—to provide the money at the beginning of the transaction—and heavy dependence on the borrowers' future behavior: λαβὼν γὰρ ἀργύριον φανερὸν καὶ ὁμολογούμενον, ἐν γραμματειδίῳ δυοῖν χαλκοῖν ἐωνημένῳ καὶ βυβλιδίῳ μικρῷ πάνυ τὴν ὁμολογίαν καταλέλοιπε τοῦ ποιήσειν τὰ δίκαια. ἡμεῖς δ᾿ οὐ φαμὲν δώσειν, ἀλλ᾿ εὐθὺς τῷ δανειζομένῳ δίδομεν τὸ ἀργύριον. The concept of "lenders' liability," by which the creditor is legally answerable for improper administration or collection of a loan (frequently asserted in the United States during the 1980s) is not a recognizable factor in Athenian cases. Dēmōn's behavior in seeking to prevent an alleged fraud (Dem. 32), however, does augment the usual skimpy information about lenders—and permits his possible identification as a banker!

[256]Dem. 35.50–51; 34.37; 56.6, 11; Lykourgos, Leōkratēs 27. See above, Chapter 3.

At Demosthenes 35.23, there is a fleeting reference to a maritime loan of 1,100 *dr.* made by one Aratos.[257] He is identified only as being from Halikarnassos, a city in Asia Minor; otherwise we know absolutely nothing of him. Since his being a Halikarnassian is his sole known characteristic, the only possible basis for assuming him not to be a banker is his origin in Asia Minor. Similar obscurity cloaks the source of the loan at 35.32: we know nothing of its provider, one Antipatros, except that he is from Kition (presumably the town on the south coast of Cyprus). Both lenders are non-Athenian; both lenders are assumed not to be bankers. Now consider the third loan listed by Bogaert from Demosthenes 35: Androklēs, a lender identified as an Athenian citizen in the loan agreement (§10). *Mirabile dictu*, precisely because he is a citizen, he is classified with "people who are taken as non-bankers because they are Athenian."[258] In fact, a considerable portion of the bankers at Athens, either by birth or by naturalization, were Athenian citizens (see above, p. 70, n. 44, pp. 88–89), but many were not. Place of origin or naturalization seems an irrelevant basis for concluding that a person was or was not a banker, and in the case of these loans in Demosthenes 35 it is a highly contradictory one. Indeed, in a fourth example in this same speech (§22), not mentioned by Bogaert in his original survey, a maritime loan is attributed to an unnamed individual of unknown origin. Of him we know only that he was young.[259] Youthful bankers are not unknown; the banker Phormiōn, for example, was already of considerable importance when still a youth, *and* a slave (see above, Chapter 4, n. 101). Nonetheless, we are told, without other justification, that "the guileless youth of Demn. 35 can hardly be a banker."[260]

Deeper analysis of even this limited source material can yield far more sophisticated conclusions. Androklēs (the Athenian citizen), who delivers the speech, does identify himself as a maritime trader (*emporos*) (§49). This characteristic, however, does not *ipso facto* eliminate the possibility of a trapezitic source for his funds, or of his personally being engaged in banking. The *emporos* Timosthenēs is reported to have had as his "partner and close associate" the banker Phormiōn (Dem. 49.31). Strikingly, a certain "Phormiōn from the Piraeus" appears as one of the three "witnesses" to Androklēs' loan agreement.[261] Should this "Phormiōn" be identified with the banker? And is he the actual source of Androklēs' funds?

Androklēs clearly needed financial assistance: he asserts to the jurors his own

---

[257]Ἄρατος Ἁλικαρνασσεὺς μαρτυρεῖ δανεῖσαι Ἀπολλοδώρῳ ἕνδεκα μνᾶς ἀργυρίου ἐπὶ τῇ ἐμπορίᾳ, ἣν ἦγεν ἐν τῇ Ὑβλησίου νηὶ εἰς τὸν Πόντον.

[258]Thompson 1979: 234, summarizing accepted opinion.

[259]ἀμελήσαντες τῶν γεγραμμένων ἐν τῇ συγγραφῇ δανείζονται παρά τινος νεανίσκου, ἐξαπατήσαντες ὡς οὐδενὶ οὐδὲν ὀφείλοντες. No exact age is conveyed by the term νεανίσκος: like νέος, it could easily accommodate men up to the age of 30. See Garland 1990: 200; Forbes 1933: 60–61.

[260]Thompson 1979: 234.

[261]§13: Μάρτυρες Φορμίων Πειραιεύς, Κηφισόδοτος Βοιώτιος, Ἡλιόδωρος Πιθεύς.

poverty, claiming that it would be "outrageous and shocking and shameful" for
those who had provided financing for the Athenian grain market now to be sent
to prison because of their inability to pay the relatively small fine imposed by
Athenian law on a litigant not obtaining a minimal portion of the jurors'
ballots.[262] Since the total loan was only 3,000 *dr.*, this penalty (the *epōbelia*[263]) would have been only 500 *dr.*, an inconsequential sum for an individual utilizing his own funds in maritime lending, especially someone like
Androklēs, who appears to be engaged in such financing on an ongoing
basis.[264] His claim of indigence would have been credible only if the jurors
realized that the party named as creditor in a maritime-loan contract had not
necessarily utilized his own funds. Androklēs' appeal, in fact, parallels the
mariner's presentation of his own modest resources in Demosthenes 33 (§4),
where the nominal lender shows that he actually provided no part of the 4,000
dr. loan (which was largely funded by the bank of Hērakleidēs and, in lesser
amount, by an individual lender, Parmenōn).

In Demosthenes 35, a participating creditor also appears, Nausikratēs from
Karystos on the island of Euboia. Once again, we have no independent knowledge of Nausikratēs, no basis for concluding that he is or is not a banker, and no
indication of what portion of the funds he might have provided. Despite Nausikratēs' inclusion in Androklēs' plea of poverty, Androklēs' reference to the
number of creditors is inconsistent: in close juxtaposition, and seemingly at
random, he alludes to the creditors sometimes in the first-person singular and
sometimes in the plural.[265] Androklēs does, however, clearly identify himself
as the individual who brought the suit.[266] If Nausikratēs were not a banker but

---

262§46–47: μὴ ἱκανὸν εἶναι ἡμᾶς ἀποστερεῖσθαι ἃ ἐδανείσαμεν χρήματα ὑμῖν, ἀλλὰ
καὶ εἰς τὸ δεσμωτήριον παραδοθῆναι ὑφ' ὑμῶν προσοφλόντας τὰ ἐπιτίμια, ἐὰν μὴ
ἐκτίνωμεν. καὶ πῶς οὐκ ἂν δεινὸν εἴη καὶ σχέτλιον καὶ αἰσχρὸν ὑμῖν, ὦ ἄνδρες δικασταί, εἰ οἱ δανείσαντες ἐν τῷ ἐμπορίῳ τῷ ὑμετέρῳ χρήματα ναυτικὰ . . . ἀπάγοιντο
εἰς τὸ δεσμωτήριον;

263The amount of the penalty is known (one obol per drachma). The circumstances governing
its imposition are still in controversy: was it imposed only if a plaintiff failed to obtain at least
one-fifth of the votes in procedures involving a *paragraphē* (the better view, in my opinion), or
upon a plaintiff's mere failure to prevail? See Harrison 1968–71, 2: 183–85; Cohen 1973: 76–77,
84, 87; Wolff 1966: 87ff.

264Androklēs, like the mariner in Dem. 33, is solicited for the loan (§6) in the commercial
harbor (ἐν τῷ ἐμπορίῳ: §1, 42). Appeals to the jurors based on insouciant lack of experience are
commonplace in Athenian litigation—cf. for example the pleader in Hyp., *Ath.*, who, in a similar
situation, contrasts the cleverness of the persons defrauding him with assertions of his own
inexperience (§26, col. 12). Androklēs does characterize the borrowers as skilled at fraud (§§1–
2), but he never suggests that he himself was inexperienced in maritime finance.

265Cf. the singular in §3 (χρήματα δανείσας, μοι) with the plural in §5 (ἡμᾶς τε τοὺς
δανείσαντας). Inconsistent use of the first-person singular and plural characterizes the entire
presentation by Androklēs.

266Λακρίτῳ τουτῳὶ εἴληχα τὴν δίκην ταύτην (§3). For the requirement that lawsuits on
behalf of multiple lenders be brought in a single name, see n. 247 above. Strategic considerations

participated in the funding along with a bank lender, the pattern would be identical to that in Demosthenes 33, where the mariner was named in legal documentation, but where funding came from Parmenōn and the banker Hērakleidēs.

In this case, it is the banker Phormiōn who is involved. Despite the obvious danger in facilely identifying as a single individual two Athenians bearing the same name, there are other good reasons to conclude that Phormiōn the banker and Phormiōn "from the Piraeus" are the same person. At the time that Phormiōn "from the Piraeus" witnessed the maritime-loan contract,[267] his homonym was still active in the banking business.[268] We know of a trierarch named Phormiōn who in 347/6 provided oars (I.G. II² 1622, line 472) and sometime before 334/3 was the principal contributor to the ship *Nemeas Lysikleidou* (I.G. II² 1623, line 245). He died sometime before 325/4, when his son settled his accounts from a final trierarchy on *Homonoia Archeneo* (I.G. II² 1629, ll. 645–56). Strikingly, the trierarch's deme-identification ("from the Piraeus") is the same as that of the witness to the loan contract. The usually cautious Davies (1971: 436) finds "obvious" the identification of Phormiōn the witness and Phormiōn the trierarch. But can we further equate Phormiōn the trierarch and Phormiōn the banker? This identification is no less likely. The substantial benefactions to Athens attributed to Phormiōn the trierarch and his son are at the

---

probably affected the choice of defendant in this case: although the brothers Artemōn and Apollodōros are the borrowers named in the contract (and only Artemōn is said to have died, §3), the lawsuit is against a third brother, Lakritos—who appears to have had the financial ability to pay a judgment and was present in Athens. Although Lakritos's financial capacity and physical presence may have motivated his being named as defendant, the case against him has appeared deeply flawed, to both modern and ancient commentators. See Libanios (Hyp. to Dem. 35), defending the authenticity of the speech's attribution to Demosthenes: πρὸς δὲ τὴν παραγραφὴν ἀσθενέστερον ἀπήντηκε διὰ τοῦ πράγματος τὸ πονηρόν. Cf. Isager and Hansen 1975: 174–75; Gernet 1954–60, 1: 176.

[267]Gernet (1954–60, 1: 179) judges 351 as a likely date for delivery of the speech; the contract, of course, was signed earlier. Isokratēs, mentioned as Lakritos's teacher (§15), was still alive when the case was heard (§40). He died in 338. The contract presumably was entered into before 340, when Athens's war against Macedon made maritime trade on the Pontos commercially impractical (cf. Philochoros, frag. 162).

[268]Despite the termination in 362 of his lease for Pasiōn's bank, Davies correctly concludes that Phormiōn "probably" continued to be active as a banker but assumes that "the only evidence for this [continued activity] is indirect, namely (Dem. 45.64–66)" (1971: 435). In fact, approximately a dozen years after termination of the lease, Demosthenes confirms Phormiōn's continuing banking activity (36.49): he claims that a judgment against Phormiōn might result not in the destruction of Phormiōn's assets alone, but in his bank's destruction, and consequent losses to depositors, an illogical suggestion if Phormiōn were not then engaged in banking. A further reference to Phormiōn as a banker comes in the same speaker's allusion to Phormiōn's continuing ability to provide funds far beyond his personal resources (Dem. 36.57). Apollodōros later charges that Stephanos has acted in concert with Phormiōn "in order that he might obtain secret returns through the bank" (Dem. 45.66; above, pp. 115, 138). Aischinēs (2.165) explicitly characterizes Phormiōn as a *trapezitēs* at the time of his litigation with Apollodōros.

exalted level appropriate to the wealthy banker. There is also chronological accord. All known dates relating to Phormiōn the trierarch and Phormiōn the witness are fully compatible with the career of Phormiōn the banker born about 400 (above, Chapter 4, n. 101) and known still to be alive when the contract witnessed by "Phormiōn from the Piraeus" was entered into (sometime before 340).[269] Phormiōn the banker, of course, had extremely close ties to the Piraeus and was personally active in maritime commerce (see above, pp. 76, 139, and 145). He likely would have continued to reside in the Piraeus after his marriage to Archippē, widow of the banker Pasiōn (who was himself a resident of Piraeus), and would have conducted his banking business there. Almost inconceivably if the banker and the trierarch were not the same person, the trierarch's son bore the name Archippos.[270] Archippos's career also is chronologically compatible with his being the banker's son born in the 360s to Archippē.[271] Here, too, Davies finds "a very plausible dovetail" between trierarch and banker.[272]

Moreover, the "Phormiōn" engaged in maritime trade with the Pontos in Demosthenes 34 also can be identified with the banker who is independently attested as involved in sea commerce (Dem. 45.64, 49.31). Indeed, his bank had a long history of activity in the Pontos, and his predecessor, Pasiōn, had committed to travel personally to Bosporos on banking business (Isok. 17.51), although he ultimately sent "Kittos" as his representative. The Phormiōn of Demosthenes 34 is even reported to have utilized the services of the banker Kittos (§6), generally believed to be a relative of his homonym "Kittos" (see Isok. 17 passim), who was engaged in the banking business with Pasiōn. Although discussions of Demosthenes 34 routinely warn readers not to confuse the Phormiōn of the speech with the banker,[273] only two arguments have been advanced against identifying the two Phormiōns: the belief that the Phormiōn

[269]Phormiōn the banker is known to have been alive after 340 when the law regulating trierarchic contribution was amended (see Hyp., frag. 134 [Blass] = frag. 43 [Kenyon]).

[270]Phormiōn is known to have had two sons by Archippē: Dem. 36.32, 45.4.

[271]Archippē died in February 360 (Dem. 50.60). Since Pasiōn had died in 370/69 (Dem. 46.13), her sons by Phormiōn were born in the 360s. Archippos was syntrierarch on the ship *Delphis Epigenous* sometime between 336 and 334/3 (I.G. II² 1623, ll. 300–301). He also served as syntrierarch on *Eukarpia Epigenous* prior to 334/3 (I.G. II² 1623, ll. 103–4) and was chorēgos in the men's dithyramb (for the tribe Hippothontis) in 331/30 (I.G. II² 2318, ll. 335–36). He is possibly the [–ι]ππος Πε[ι]ραι(εύς) listed as principal trierarch for the vessel *Aktis Lysikleous* (323/2) (I.G. II² 1631, ll. 544ff.).

[272]Davies 1971: 436. Although former slaves are not otherwise known to have received patronymics after obtaining citizenship, Phormiōn the trierarch does have a patronymic Κτησιφῶντος. There are, however, other examples of naturalized citizens receiving patronymics (cf. Χαιρέφιλος Φείδωνος Παιανιεύς and Χαρίδημος [Φι]λοξένου Ἀχαρνεύς). As for the mid-fourth-century grave-stele (I.G. II² 6060a, p. 880) with its reference to Φορμίων Ὀφέλωνος Πειραιεύς, it should be noted that even within a small deme, homonymity does not necessarily imply relationship.

[273]See, for example, Ste. Croix 1974: 50.

of Demosthenes 34 was not an Athenian citizen,[274] and the assumption that Phormiōn the banker could not have been alive at the late date (about 330[275]), when Demosthenes 34 is believed to have been delivered.

The two passages sometimes cited to deny Athenian citizenship to the Phormiōn of Demosthenes 34 are far from dispositive. At §50, the unlikely claim is advanced that the Athenian courts had decreed the death penalty for a citizen who had defaulted on a loan, "the son of a general." But the citation does not establish, or even imply, that Phormiōn the defendant in Demosthenes 34 was not a citizen: the assertion (that Athenian courts had dealt savagely in the past with defaulting citizens, even of patriotic background) would certainly be appropriate in support of an effort to collect money from a citizen who had served Athens as trierarch. Nor does the statement (§12) that Phormiōn "epedēmēsen" establish that Phormiōn was a metic noncitizen: the word, in this context, means only "came home" (Gernet 1954–60: "fut arrivé"; Murray 1936–39: "reached Athens").[276]

If the banker is to be identified with the trierarch, as discussed above, he is attested as still alive shortly before 325/4. The *trapezitēs* indisputably was alive after 340 (Hypereidēs, frag. 134). Since Phormiōn the banker appears to have been only 65 or slightly older in 330 (above, Chapter 4, n. 101), there is no implausibility in his appearing in a commercial context about that time.

Phormiōn's function as a "witness" to the maritime loan contract should not be confused with the passive role of modern witnesses to commercial agreements, whose principal, often exclusive task is to confirm in writing the fact of execution of a written contract (often only the authenticity of a signature). The Athenian witness orally makes confirmatory declarations (*martyrei*) as to the contents of the document, and the making of these declarations is noted at the end of the writing. The banker thus did not merely sign his name: he signalled the correctness of the documentation at the time of the writing.[277] This was at least potentially a partisan role. Even in the modern world, witnesses are usually not chosen at random: corporate executives will have their signatures attested generally by other company executives, in the United States often by the corporate "Secretary." In Athens, to a far greater extent, a witness was likely to be a person deeply involved in the transaction. Prior to the first decade of the fourth century, written contracts were unknown, and agreements were entirely oral, their contents to be established by oral attestation from wit-

[274]See, for example, M. V. Hansen 1984: 73.

[275]The speech is generally dated to 327/6 (Gernet 1954–60, 1: 151; Isager and Hansen 1975: 169), but perhaps was delivered as early as 334/3 (Doherty 1927: 14).

[276]Cf. the inquiry at Dem. 52.8 as to whether Kēphisiadēs "had returned to Athens" (Murray 1936–39, εἰ ἐπιδεδημηκὼς).

[277]There are no "signature lines" for the contract and no execution by the parties. The witnesses' presence in the formulation of the maritime contract is noted after all of the provisions: Μάρτυρες Φορμίων Πειραιεύς, Κηφισόδοτος Βοιώτιος, Ἡλιόδωρος Πιθεύς.

nesses.[278] The fourth century saw gradual transition to documentation, resulting finally, late in the century, in reliance on unwitnessed written agreements, presaging later Hellenistic practice.[279] The maritime contract at Demosthenes 35 represents a stage in the progression from the oral method: "The witnesses, the oral method, are still trusted, perhaps trusted more than writing, [which] had only just acquired legal status."[280] Reflecting the importance of human testimony, issues of authenticity at this time generally focused on the reliability of witnesses, not of the written text.[281] This again reflects the potentially partisan role of the deponents. Indeed, reliance on three witnesses to the writing parallels procedure for privately arranged arbitration, including that arising from maritime finance: selection of a representative of each of the two disputants, and a third person acceptable to both of the parties or selected by the other two arbitrators.[282] If Phormiōn were the actual provider of even a portion of the funds loaned, he would be an obvious choice as witness: in his banking capacity, he would be knowledgeable about the details of the financing and thus able to confirm the arrangements; his credibility as a banker would be useful if he were ultimately needed to testify in court. In any event, the banker's intimate involvement in this case certainly provides no confirmation for claims that bankers were completely absent from maritime lending.[283]

Almost nothing is known about the lenders mentioned at Demosthenes 34.6, but the financial activities described there take place in an environment suffused with bank involvement. The parties to the loan that is the subject of litigation (2,000 *dr.* lent on maritime cargo) are bank customers: a copy of the maritime loan contract has been delivered to the *trapezitēs* Kittos (§6). A "Phormiōn" appears again, this time as the borrower; as discussed above, his identification with the banker is likely. The plaintiff in the case, Chrysippos, again is not alone: reference is made to a group of "associates," who have been identified (in Doherty's words) as "interested" parties.[284] If Chrysippos were a banker,

---

[278]See Pringsheim 1955. The earliest known written contract appears to be the συγγραφαί reported at Isok. 17.20.

[279]See Thomas 1989: 41–45. The earliest known unwitnessed written contract appears to be that utilized in Hyp., *Ath.* (in the 320s).

[280]Thomas 1989: 29. Cursive script had not yet been developed, further reinforcing the traditional reliance on oral witnessing for authentication. For other cases of oral confirmation of written contracts, see Harvey 1966: 610.

[281]See, for example, Aristot., *Rhet.* 1.15.1375b. Cf. Calhoun 1914 and Bonner 1905: 80.

[282]See Dem. 33.14–19, where Apatourios selected Aristoklēs of Oē; Parmenōn named the mariner; and they both agreed on their fellow Byzantine, Phōkritos. On such private δίαιτα, see Meyer-Laurin 1965: 41–45; Steinwenter 1925: 63ff.

[283]A banker may also have been present as the party with whom the written documentation was deposited. The holders of maritime contracts in Dem. 34 (§6) and 56 (§15) were bankers. Although we have no information as to the trade of Archenomidēs (Dem. 35.14), there is no basis for assuming that he is not a *trapezitēs*.

[284]§32: οἵδε μὲν πρὸς σὲ δύο συγγραφὰς ἐποιήσαντο ὑπὲρ τοῦ συμβολαίου. Gernet

these likely would be his customers, for whom he would be acting as intermediary. As usual, our sources contain absolutely no information about these "participants" (§12).[285] Nor do we learn much about Chrysippos: he is apparently resident at Athens and he claims to have made other maritime loans,[286] neither of which establishes that he is not a banker. The other lenders' attributes are also unknown. There is a reference to one Theodōros, a Phoenician, who allegedly extended to Phormiōn a loan of 4,500 *dr.* (§6); absolutely nothing is known about him. There are other "lenders who lent" against cargo only for the journey out from Athens (§§8, 22); we learn nothing about them. Chrysippos claims that the ship operator himself lent 1,000 *dr.* (§6), but, if true, this seems likely to have been merely a postponement of freight charges rather than an actual cash advance.[287]

In litigation arising from the relationship of Pasiōn's bank with its customer Lykōn, specifically Kallippos's claim to certain deposits after the customer's death (Dem. 52.20), the word *ekdosis* is used to describe a maritime financing provided by Lykōn to a third party.[288] Although this loan is mentioned only to demonstrate (through Lykōn's reliance on others in resolving a dispute relating to the *ekdosis*) that Lykōn had no specially close relationship with Kallippos, *ekdosis* is the very word purported to have the specialized meaning of "a bank deposit intended to be utilized for maritime finance" (see above, pp. 157–60). Since this supposed technical signification arises from the use of *ekdosis* in descriptions of bank loans for maritime purposes, there is no reason to assume that Pasiōn's *trapeza* played no role in the financing of the *ekdosis* itself. Pasiōn himself and his successor Phormiōn both had deep involvement with sea commerce (see above, pp. 44, 145). Lykōn is described as having a close relationship with the bank, which was "used" by maritime merchants generally.[289] The deposit in dispute was left with the bank by one sea merchant for delivery at a later date to another maritime businessman. In light of the pervasive secrecy in which maritime finance was conducted, the bank owner's detailed knowledge of the *ekdosis* is itself significant, and somewhat improbable if the bank

---

translates οἵδε μὲν as "mes associés." See Doherty 1927: 78. The multiple copies were presumably held for the benefit of these persons.

[285]§12: ἐπειδὴ δὲ ἀνεκοινώσατο τοῖς νῦν παροῦσιν αὐτῷ καὶ συνδικοῦσιν. These persons, otherwise unknown, would appear to be the same persons mentioned in §32, referred to inexactly by Doherty as Chrysippos's "partners in the suit" (1927: 74).

[286]§§1, 38. Persons known to be bankers, of whom the most prominent is Pasiōn, of course utilized their own funds for the making of maritime loans. See above, pp. 64–65.

[287]See Thompson 1980: 140.

[288]ἐκεῖνος γὰρ τετταράκοντα μνᾶς ἔκδοσιν ἐκδοὺς εἰς Ἄκην Μεγακλείδη τῷ Ἐλευσινίῳ καὶ Θρασύλλῳ τῷ ἀδελφῷ αὐτοῦ, μεταδόξαν αὐτῷ μὴ ἐκεῖσε πλεῖν μηδὲ κινδυνεύειν, ἐγκαλέσας τι τῷ Μεγακλείδη περὶ τῶν τόκων ὡς ἐξηπατημένος διεφέρετο καὶ ἐδικάζετο, βουλόμενος τὴν ἔκδοσιν κομίσασθαι. The passage also illustrates the nature of maritime τόκος. See above, Chapter 3.

[289]§3: τῇ τραπέζῃ τῇ τοῦ πατρὸς ἐχρῆτο, ὥσπερ καὶ οἱ ἄλλοι ἔμποροι. For the combined business and social involvement inherent in "using" a bank, see above, pp. 65–66.

were uninvolved in the arrangements. Although the borrowers of the *ekdosis* had sought to return the principal, Lykōn had insisted on yield as well, whereupon his adversaries withheld all payment in an effort to effectuate settlement.[290] Lykōn's unyielding stance is understandable if in fact he was already entitled to return of principal—as a bank depositor who had utilized the *trapezitēs* Pasiōn as an intermediary for maritime lending by *ekdosis*. Although the actual nature of the bank's involvement is necessarily conjectural, the passage offers no substantiation at all for the absence of *trapezai* from maritime lending.

Demosthenes 50.17 concerns a maritime loan for 800 *dr.* borrowed by Apollodōros, the bank owner involved in the litigation at Demosthenes 52 and himself the son of the banker Pasiōn. The loan was obtained from Nikippos the *nauklēros* (ship owner/operator) while Apollodōros was serving as trierarch of an Athenian warship in the northern Aegean and needed funds to pay his crew.[291] Although the *nauklēros* is named as the source of the loan, the circumstances suggest that the loan may in fact have depended on a guarantee of repayment by the bank. Nikippos advanced the funds when he was in Sēstos on his way to Athens. The loan was to be repaid on his ship's arrival there.[292] But by whom? Not by Apollodōros, who remained in Sēstos until his trierarchic term expired, and then stayed on in the northern Aegean for several additional months (§§18–23). In fact, we are told specifically that Apollodōros at this time was relying upon his father's contacts at Lampsakos, perhaps the bank's representatives (*xenoi*), to aid in recruiting and paying additional crew members.[293] Again, a maritime loan to a bank owner on sea duty, known to be utilizing bank contacts to meet the need for skilled mercenaries, is far from conclusive evidence that banks played no role in marine loans.

Lysias 32.6 tells of Diodotos, who, immediately prior to his departure for military service in 409, reviewed his assets with his wife and brother, revealing 46,000 *dr.* in maritime loans, a huge sum obviously representing a number of individual loans.[294] Commentators have struggled to explain how one individual, about whose business activities almost nothing is known,[295] could have come to generate receivables of such magnitude. An obvious explanation, not incompatible with anything in the text, is that, like the mariner in Demosthenes 33, Diodotos was advancing funds not his own. Like the mariner, who is known

---

[290]Thompson 1987: 601 n. 4.

[291]On this loan, see above, pp. 163–64, and Chapter 3, n. 95.

[292]§17: παρὰ Νικίππου τοῦ ναυκλήρου ναυτικὸν ἀνειλόμην, ὃς ἔτυχεν ὢν ἐν Σηστῷ, ἐπόγδοον, σωθέντος δὲ τοῦ πλοίου Ἀθήναζε ἀποδοῦναι αὐτὸ καὶ τοὺς τόκους.

[293]§§17–18: ναυτικὸν ἀνειλόμην . . . καὶ πέμψας Εὐκτήμονα τὸν πεντηκόνταρχον εἰς Λάμψακον, δοὺς αὐτῷ ἀργύριον καὶ γράμματα πρὸς τοὺς ξένους τοῦ πατρὸς τοῦ ἐμοῦ, ἐκέλευσά μοι αὐτὸν ναύτας μισθώσασθαι ὡς ἂν δύνηται ἀρίστους.

[294]Thompson (1983: 67) suggests that "about a dozen" loans would be required "to absorb such a large amount of capital."

[295]Cf. Davies 1971: 152.

to have used the banker Hērakleidēs as the source for his maritime funding, and like Androklēs in Demosthenes 35, who may have used the banker Phormiōn as the source for his maritime funding, Diodotos is described as working in the *emporion* at maritime matters (see above, n. 202). Perhaps significantly, here too Diodotos's activities are described by a form of the word *ekdosis*,[296] again a possible reference to maritime loans funded indirectly by bank depositors' monies.

Demosthenes 56.3 and 56.17[297] actually deal with a single transaction: the borrowers, instead of repaying the 3,000 *dr.* loan described in §3, are accused of using these same funds to earn "maritime yields" from others (§17). But the transaction does not confirm bankers' absence from maritime finance. To the contrary, the situation is similar to the one with which we have become familiar: nominal lender, undisclosed actual financing source, banker intimately involved but in a role unclear to us, and possibly also unclear to the borrowers or even to the jurors. Here the contract is in the name of a certain Pamphilos, although at least part of the funding is provided by another person, Dareios,[298] whose identity is entirely undisclosed in the loan papers, and indeed in the litigation itself.[299] Dareios, who speaks in the legal proceedings without revealing his identity, describes himself as a "partner in this loan"[300] without further explanation. The jurors presumably needed no explanation: they were aware, as we have become through the analysis of other maritime loans, that sea finance often involved groups of lenders of undisclosed professional background and funding sources, utilizing a lender of record who may or may not have provided part of the actual monies advanced.[301]

But the jurors do learn of the involvement of an unnamed banker. The borrowers had offered to repay principal and a portion of the yield, but the offer was rejected because it was tied to a demand for a complete release of the debtors. But Dareios was willing "as to the money that you might repay to make the contract ineffective in the presence of the banker," leaving the debtors

---

[296]ναυτικὰ δὲ ἀπέδειξεν ἐκδεδομένα.

[297]Although a number of other maritime loans (omitted from Bogaert's original catalogue) are referred to in this speech (§§28–30), we have absolutely no information as to their source of financing—but of course, we also have no indication that bankers were not involved.

[298]His name is known only through its mention centuries later by an ancient commentator, who does not disclose the source of this attribution. See Libanios's Hypothesis to Dem. 56: Δαρεῖος καὶ Πάμφιλος Διονυσοδώρῳ δανείζουσι τρισχιλίας δραχμάς. Libanios, however, omits the name of the other borrower, Parmeniskos.

[299]§6: ἐν μὲν οὖν ταῖς συνθήκαις δανειστὴς ἐγράφη Πάμφιλος οὑτοσί· ἐγὼ δ' ἔξωθεν μετεῖχον αὐτῷ τοῦ δανείσματος.

[300]§1: κοινωνός εἰμι τοῦ δανείσματος τούτου. For modern readers lacking the jurors' knowledge of Athenian life, the phrase clearly cries for elucidation. Carey and Reid note the "abruptness and obscurity" of the phrase: "Whose partner? What loan? Why τούτου?" (1985: 198).

[301]The speaker here also asserts (§4) the possibility of imprisonment for inability to pay the *epōbelia*. See above, n. 263.

liable for the remainder.[302] Although this reference to "the banker" is generally explained on the assumption that a *trapezitēs* was holding the contract,[303] the text makes no mention of an agreement in the hands of a banker. If he were a fiduciary entrusted with a written contract, the banker would be called on only to surrender the document, not to "make the contract ineffective" in part. Although bankers, because of their credibility, were clearly desirable as witnesses, in this case we know that many witnesses had already been carefully gathered and that an additional group of citizens on their own had joined the negotiations (which were apparently being conducted in public).[304] The only way in which "the banker" could make the contract partially ineffective would be through his acceptance of the repayment of a portion of the amount outstanding. If the banker were in fact the principal lender, or if he were serving as an intermediary for depositors, Dareios's proposal is easily explicable. Just as the mariner in Demosthenes 33 (§10) involves the bank administrators ("guarantors") in the resolution of the ship financing for Apatourios, the banker's involvement would be necessary here if he represented a major portion of funding. Although we are left to speculate as to the banker's actual role, once again this episode— with its clear allusion to trapezitic involvement—cannot fairly be cited as positive evidence for the absence of bankers from maritime lending.

THE BANKERS' OWN MONEY

Demosthenes' characterization of Athenian banking as dependent on "other people's money" is confirmed by Biōn, a contemporary philosopher who poses the conundrum: Why do bankers lack money even though they have it? The answer: they have only other people's money, not their own.[305] Yet despite the general reliance of bankers on "outside" funding, at least one *trapezitēs* is known to have employed substantial personal monies in lending activity: Pasiōn made more than fifty talents of loans, largely with his own money but also utilizing eleven talents of bank deposits (see above, pp. 129–36). In the unregulated Athenian banking community, there was no requirement that bankers possess even a minimum of personal money; there was likewise no law or

---

[302]§15: κατὰ μὲν τἀργύριον ὃ ἂν ἀποδῷς, ὁμολογήσομεν ἐναντίον τοῦ τραπεζίτου ἄκυρον ποιεῖν τὴν συγγραφήν.

[303]Isager and Hansen 1975: 78; Carey and Reid 1985: 217.

[304]§13: μάρτυρας πολλοὺς παραλαβὼν προσῄει, φάσκων ἕτοιμος εἶναι ἀποδιδόναι τὸ δάνειον καὶ τοὺς τόκους τοὺς εἰς Ῥόδον. §14: τῶν ὑμετέρων πολιτῶν τινὲς παραγενόμενοι ἀπὸ ταὐτομάτου συνεβούλευον ἡμῖν τὸ μὲν διδόμενον λαμβάνειν, περὶ δὲ τῶν ἀντιλεγομένων κρίνεσθαι.

[305]Telēs 36.7–8 (ed. Hense²): πῶς δὲ οἱ τραπεζῖται, φησὶν ὁ Βίων, χρημάτων [sc. σπανίζουσιν], ἔχοντες αὐτά; οὐ γὰρ αὐτῶν ὄντα ἔχουσιν. Biōn was a student under Theophrastos at the Peripatos (and at the Academy under Xenokratēs).

administrative provision precluding *trapezitai* from intermingling their own funds with bank monies.[306] Clients' demands and the proprietor's skills and desires alone determined the amount of the proprietor's funds, if any, required to operate a *trapeza*.

The Athenians applied the term *aphormē* to such nondeposit monies as might actually be employed at a *trapeza*. Although the basic meaning of *aphormē* is "starting point," easily extended to denote "something to start with,"[307] and hence the initial operating monies needed for a business, in practice the word came to denote the funding necessary for continuing operations, in Athenian terms a "provision for functioning" or for "earning a living,"[308] akin to Anglo-American "working capital" or the French "capital de roulement."[309] In a banking context, it constituted the business's operating requirements not met from customers' deposits. Far from "equity capital," *aphormē* itself might be borrowed.[310] Since deposits were—in Athenian formulation—themselves "loans" to the banker, monies borrowed to meet the *trapeza*'s operating needs and monies borrowed to fund loans would be entirely fungible. Where operating funds were derived from the proprietor's own resources (including reinvested cash flow), the Athenians referred to "private (*idia*) *aphormē*."[311]

Although modern studies often treat this operating money as though it were "equity capital" contributed to an institution, and thus something separate from the private assets of the bank owner,[312] in reality *aphormē* was indis-

---

[306]See above, pp. 64–66. Modern government regulators of banks have adopted widely variant standards as to the amount of capital required of, or appropriate to, financial institutions. Although officials of the various "developed" countries have now agreed on unified international criteria scheduled to take effect at the end of 1992, U.S. regulators in 1990 were calling for yet higher capital levels for American institutions (*Wall Street Journal*, October 9, 1990, p. C1).

[307]See, for example, Thuc. 1.90. The related verb ἀφορμάω has a literal meaning of "to start from a certain place." See Homer, *Od.* 2.375, 4.748; Sappho, *Supp.* 6.7.

[308]See schol. to Euripides, *Medea* 342: ἣν ἡμεῖς προβολὴν καλοῦμεν εἰς τὸ ζῆν, οἱ Ἀττικοὶ ἀφορμὴν λέγουσι.

[309]For the extension of meaning from "starting point" to "working capital," see the compendium of uses in Korver 1934: 22–25.

[310]Cf. Aristot., *Ath. pol.* 52.2: κἄν τις ἐν ἀγορᾷ βουλόμενος ἐργάζεσθαι δανείσηται παρά τινος ἀφορμήν. Lysias, frag. 38.2 (Πρὸς Αἰσχίνην): κατασκευάζομαι τέχνην μυρεψικήν· ἀφορμῆς δὲ δέομαι, καὶ οἴσω δέ σοι ἐννέ' ὀβόλους τῆς μνᾶς τόκους. A *trapeza* functioning through borrowed operating funds would be leveraged in the extreme.

[311]See Dem. 36, §12 (προσμεμισθωκὼς ἰδίαν ἀφορμήν) and §13 (παρέδωκεν ἰδίαν ἀφορμήν). Cf. Dem. 36.11 (ἰδία τις ἀφορμὴ τούτῳ πρὸς τῇ τραπέζῃ = χρήματα τῇ τραπέζῃ ἴδια); Dem. 36.14.

[312]Davies (1971: 432) refers to ἀφορμή as "the indispensable reserve capital of the bank." Erxleben (1973: 125–26) speaks of the bank's capital ("Gesamtkapital") carefully, separating it from the owner's "Eigenkapital," which consisted of Pasiōn's personal assets ("Privatvermögen"). His analysis is divided between sections entitled "Das Kapital der Bank des Pasion" and "Das Privatvermögen des Pasion." Pearson speaks of "a private investment of Pasion in the bank" (1972: 215). Bogaert (1986a) has separate analyses: "le capital de la banque de Pasion-Phormion" (35–42) and "la fortune personnelle de Pasion"—as if these were two distinct items! Cf. Hasebroek 1920: 166; Gluskina 1970, 3: 35; Thompson 1981: 84.

tinguishable from the personal resources and personal obligations of the banker. These personal monies therefore should not be confused with institutional "bank capital" in a modern sense. Since the *trapeza* was not recognized as an independent entity for legal purposes, it could possess no assets apart from those of its proprietor, and could incur no liabilities of its own. As a corollary, the *trapeza*'s lack of independent juridical standing subjected all of the assets of a wealthy bank proprietor to the bank's obligation to repay deposits.

So long as the owner himself operated the banking business, this intermingling of funding sources, and concomitant personal liability for bank obligations, presented no legal or economic complexities. But when an Athenian bank owner entered into a leasing or rental arrangement (*misthōsis*) providing for someone else to operate the bank, thus separating ownership from operation, the "business" did not thereby obtain an independent legal existence: its assets and liabilities still belonged to its owner. Since at lease end these assets and liabilities (or products of these arising in the course of operations) would be returned to the owner, identification of the precise items delivered pursuant to *misthōsis* was vital. Since the financial assets and liabilities of the bank, the essential elements of transfer, routinely were carefully recorded in the books of the *trapeza*,[313] a lengthy document was not required (in fact, the "lease" preserved at Dem. 45 [§31] is exceedingly brief). But the owner's use of personal monies might not have generated the same systematic entries. Ineluctably intertwined with banking operations, quite possibly fully integrated with the owner's other business and personal undertakings, these items might easily become the subject of innocent confusion, or the material for purposeful fraud. Not surprisingly, therefore, an essential issue in Apollodōros's suit against Phormiōn (Dem. 36) is whether personal monies belonging to Pasiōn, in addition to "other people's money" (deposits), were delivered to Phormiōn as part of the *misthōsis* of Pasiōn's bank. Although we have no means of ascertaining the "truth" underlying this particular litigation, there is no dispute about the central presupposition of the opposing claims: an Athenian bank could operate with or without "owner's money" dedicated to the business. Phormiōn does not deny that banks did sometimes function with owners' capital; he argues only that this *trapeza* on transfer to the lessee had none.

Despite frequent scholarly reference to the leasing arrangements between Pasiōn and Phormiōn,[314] the mechanism and implications of a bank's *misthōsis* have been largely ignored. The standard source compilation on Greek banking does not even list the subject in its indices, although it duly references more than 300 other terms relating to banks.[315] The basic work on Athenian leasing

---

[313]Bankers' books were proverbially detailed; see Chapter 4, n. 55; above, pp. 119, 125. For the purposeful omission of transactions from banking books, see Chapter 6, n. 99 and text there.

[314]See, for example, Isager and Hansen 1975: 89 n. 18; Calhoun [1926] 1968: 121–22; Osborne 1988: 312.

[315]The Greek index to Bogaert's *Banques et banquiers* (1968) does not cite μίσθωσις; Bogaert's French index, although many times longer, has no listing for "loyer," "bail" or "location."

entirely ignores leases of *trapezai*.[316] Legal works are no more helpful.[317] Yet understanding of the juridical and economic significance of *misthōsis* clarifies the nature of the Athenian bank itself.

The essence of *misthōsis* is that the owner grants the right to use certain assets in return for a payment (*misthos* means "fee," by extension "wages").[318] In its earliest form, land appears to have been the object of the transaction: an owner would allow someone to work a portion of his farm holdings in return for a fixed proportion of the yield from the land.[319] By the end of the fifth century, the rent was invariably payable in cash, not in crops; leases might cover not only land but also buildings; elaborate lease documents were sometimes employed.[320] Although *misthōsis* thus developed as a mechanism for temporarily entrusting tangible assets, not for transferring a functioning business, bankers found in it a ready model for the lease of a *trapeza*.

Phormiōn's lease of Pasiōn's bank illustrates this adaptation. The document preserved at Demosthenes 45.31 provides for a fixed net rental (payable in money) independent of the actual results of the operation, still due annually (as in the original lease of agricultural land), but with special provisions relating to the banking business:

> Pasiōn has leased the bank to Phormiōn on the following terms: Phormiōn is to pay to Pasiōn's children a rental for the bank of two talents, forty mnai per year, over and above daily operating expenses; Phormiōn is prohibited from engaging in banking independently, unless he should obtain the consent of Pasiōn's children. Pasiōn owes to the bank eleven talents for the deposits.[321]

---

[316]In its index of source material, Behrend 1970 does not cite Dem. 36, 45, or 46, the principal sources for information on the leasing of bank assets. (Behrend, however, essentially treats only epigraphical materials, mainly leases from public bodies.) Osborne, in his section on "the leasing of private property," mentions the lease of Pasiōn's bank, but only in passing ("the property of Pasion's family is too complex to describe in detail"); see Osborne 1988: 312. Cf. Kussmaul 1969: 37–61.

[317]The index to volume 1 of Harrison's *Law* (1968), for example, does contain references to μίσθωσις of property and of mines, but there is no citation in the indexes to either volume to μίσθωσις of banks or of any other business. Even the index to Pollux (ed. Bethe, repr. 1967, Stuttgart) includes only two references to μίσθωσις, and both of these (6.178 and 8.31) are to μίσθωσις οἴκου. Even the full discussions of μίσθωσις οἴκου by Harrison (1968–71, 1: 105–7, 293–96) and MacDowell (1989b: 12–15) make no reference to the lease of a bank.

[318]Frisk 1960–72, s.v. There is no basis for the assertion that μισθός came to carry the meaning of "rent" (Schulthess, in *RE* 15.2085). Cf. von Herrmann 1958: 99.

[319]See Behrend 1970: 40–49. Cf. Wolff 1961: 134.

[320]See Osborne 1988: 291–92; MacDowell 1978: 141; I.G. II² 2490–2504. Cf. Chapter 1, n. 14.

[321]ΜΙΣΘΩΣΙΣ ΤΡΑΠΕΖΗΣ. Κατὰ τάδε ἐμίσθωσε Πασίων τὴν τράπεζαν Φορμίωνι· μίσθωσιν φέρειν Φορμίωνα τῆς τραπέζης τοῖς παισὶ τοῖς Πασίωνος δύο τάλαντα καὶ τετταράκοντα μνᾶς τοῦ ἐνιαυτοῦ ἑκάστου, χωρὶς τῆς καθ᾽ ἡμέραν διοικήσεως· μὴ ἐξεῖναι δὲ τραπεζιτεῦσαι χωρὶς Φορμίωνι, ἐὰν μὴ πείσῃ τοὺς παῖδας τοὺς Πασίωνος. ὀφείλει δὲ Πασίων ἐπὶ τὴν τράπεζαν ἕνδεκα τάλαντα εἰς τὰς παρακαταθήκας.

Although the lease, as recorded in the preserved manuscript text of Demosthenes,[322] does not specify the assets and liabilities constituting "the bank," Demosthenes himself identifies the two items transferred: (1) the *ergasia* ("operation") of 'the bank, an all-encompassing term that would incorporate all specific assets, such as loans receivable, cash on hand, and ongoing business activity;[323] and (2) the deposits, which are actually an intangible obligation of repayment to third parties, constituting the basic, and possibly only, liability connected with the business. Thus Phormiōn is described simply as "leasing the operation (*ergasia*) of the bank and taking its deposits (*parakatathēkai*)."[324] In a later *misthōsis* of the bank, Apollodōros and Pasiklēs are reported to have "leased the deposits and the *ergasia* relating to them."[325] By characterizing the lease of the *trapeza* as a lease of its *ergasia*—the business's entire means, both tangible and intangible, of earning revenues—the parties are effectively specifying the delivery for the rental term of all the bank's assets. These assets, like the deposits, would be identified with specificity in the bank's detailed records. Only the *aphormē*, if present, would not necessarily be reflected in the bank's records. For this, separate specification might be made in the legal documentation.[326] Both parties in fact agree that in the *misthōsis* of Pasiōn's bank, explicit provision was made for *aphormē*; they disagree only about the content of this provision.

The lessee claims that in delivering the bank "operation," the owner had transferred no personal funds; to the contrary, he retained 11 talents from bank deposits, partial funding for loans that he removed by agreement from the

---

[322]The authenticity of this document was long ago convincingly established by Drerup (1898: 223ff.). Cf. Gernet 1954–60, 2: 152 n. 1. Although the generally well-esteemed manuscript S "Parasinus 2934" omits the text of the alleged lease, S in fact omits all testimonia. For a similarly brief lease of a bank during the mediaeval period, see di Tucci 1935: 85.

[323]For the nature of *ergasia*, see n. 1 above.

[324]Dem. 36.6: μισθούμενος οὖν ὅδε τὴν ἐργασίαν αὐτὴν τῆς τραπέζης καὶ τὰς παρακαταθήκας λαμβάνων. Although all manuscripts contain λαμβάνων, editors since Blass have uniformly eliminated it from the text without justification other than its absence from a reference later in the speech at Dem. 36.13 (see n. 325). Pearson (1972), for example, finds λαμβάνων "unnecessary." To the contrary, the emendation is "unnecessary": "taking" is fully compatible with the process of "leasing"—since lessees "leased deposits" (Dem. 36.13), they would be obligated to return them, and could properly be characterized as initially "taking" them.

[325]Dem. 36.13: τὰς παρακαταθήκας καὶ τὴν ἀπὸ τούτων ἐργασίαν αὐτὴν ἐμισθώσαντο.

[326]This is confirmed by Hyp., *Ath.*, a dispute focusing on the alleged failure by a seller of a business to identify the liabilities assumed by the buyer. The purchaser argues that the legal documentation should have included a discrete specification of the obligations incurred. See §§6–12, esp. §7 (εἰ δὲ πριαίμην ὠνῇ καὶ πράσει, ὁμολογήσας αὐτῷ τὰ χρέα ἀναδέξεσθαι, ὡς οὐθενὸς ἄξια ὄντα, δ[ιὰ] τὸ μὴ π[ρο]ειδέναι, ἐπάξειν μοι ἔμελλεν ὕστερον τοὺς χρ[ῆσ]τας καὶ τοὺς πληρωτὰς τῶν ἐράνων ἐν ὁμολογίᾳ λαβών) and §§10, 12 (τὰ δὲ πολλὰ τῶν χρεῶν καὶ τὰ μέγιστα οὐκ ἐνεγέγραπτο ἐπ' ὀνομάτων, ἀλλ' ἐν προσθήκης μέρει ὡς οὐδὲν ὄντα, "καὶ εἴ τῳ ἄλλῳ ὀφείλει τι Μίδας" . . . τούτους δ' οὐκ ἐνέγραψεν ἐν ταῖς συνθήκαις, ἀλλ' ἀπεκρύψατο).

operation. Accordingly, the lease provided that "Pasiōn owes to the bank 11 talents for the deposits." Under this version, the "bank" as leased had the following footings (disregarding possible miscellaneous items, which would be minor, and "contra" items, including cash):[327] assets consisting of loans receivable from third parties and the 11 talents receivable from Phormiōn, *less* the 50 talents in loans retained by Phormiōn; liabilities equal to the bank's deposits. The bank's assets and liabilities were in balance because the amount due from Phormiōn was the number of drachmas necessary to equalize assets and liabilities. The lessee would be obligated to return the banking business to its owner, at expiration of the lease, in the same balanced position—but without any *aphormē*.

The owner's son, however, claims that at the time of entry into the lease, the business had *aphormē*. He, too, claims that it was dealt with in the lease documentation, but he asserts that the true documentation has been destroyed, and that the lease provided by the lessee is fraudulent.[328] On Apollodōros's formulation, [total loans receivable plus cash] = [deposits plus *aphormē*]. Both characterizations of the lease are consistent with the original concept of *misthōsis* as merely giving the lessee the right to *use* an item. The bank remained the property of its owner. The farmer utilizing an owner's land to produce crops—and paying a fixed monetary rent for that use—did not by that sole act relieve the owner of liability to a lender for repayment of a loan secured by the land.[329] Similarly, the lessee utilizing an owner's bank to produce revenues—and paying a fixed monetary rent for that use—would not thereby relieve the owner of liability to depositors for repayment of monies entrusted to him. But during the term of the lease, the lessee would be primarily responsible for producing the cash required to meet obligations associated with the business, including repayment of deposits. There is no evidence to suggest, and no reason to assume, that the lessor was liable for repayment of bank deposits delivered

[327]Any other assets and liabilities would be immaterial: as Apollodōros asks rhetorically, ἔστιν οὖν ὅστις ἂν τοῦ ξύλου καὶ τοῦ χωρίου καὶ τῶν γραμματείων τοσαύτην ὑπέμεινε φέρειν μίσθωσιν; (Dem. 45.33). Cf. above, pp. 67–69. In any event, under either of the parties' suggested scenarios, such other elements would be in rough equivalence. In the absence of the renting of *aphormē*, any cash on hand would be balanced by an obligation to return deposits.

[328]Dem. 45.32–33; 36.18. For a reconstruction of Apollodōros's likely argument, proceeding from these fundamental contentions, see Thompson 1981: 87–89.

[329]Of course, the landowner would have no personal liability if Greek secured lending were merely "substitutive," as asserted, diffidently, by Finley ([1951] 1985: 110–15). Under this formulation, a creditor's sole right on default is to retain the asset pledged, without regard to the relation between the amount of the debt and the value of the pledged asset(s), and without further claim against the debtor for any deficiency. But even Finley acknowledged that loans on collateral other than land, such as maritime finance, and on land itself by the fourth century, followed the contrary "collateral" pattern (ibid., 87). See below, Chapter 6, n. 132. Harris (1988: 372) notes that "a debtor who remained on a piece of land pledged as security was exactly like a lessee who had rented property from its owner."

after he had ceased to operate the bank. Nor would the owner have obtained ownership of assets added to the *ergasia* during the lessee's term of operation: his compensation was explicitly limited to a previously negotiated, fixed periodic payment. The prohibition on Phormiōn's independent banking activity is compatible with the economic requirements of the transaction: because Athenian businesses were not recognized as independent juridical persons, chaos would have resulted if a single lessee were able independently to conduct outside banking transactions during the period of his rental of an existing bank operation. The same economic considerations would have militated for recognition of the direct liability of slaves for banking debts incurred in their autonomous operation of a banking business, and for recognition of slaves as parties and witnesses in "banking cases" involving *trapezai* operated by unfree persons pursuant to lease arrangements (see above, pp. 94–98).

Chapter 6

THE BANKS' ROLE IN THE ECONOMY

WIDESPREAD DEPENDENCE on credit is universally recognized as characteristic of Athenian life.[1] Hence the importance of the banks, for whom lending was a central function. The banks' role in providing maritime credit (see Chapter 5) was critical to the financing of trade by sea, a crucial desideratum for a society so dependent on the import of food. Even in the absence of statistics, the pervasive presence of the *trapezai* is confirmed by frequent passing references in courtroom presentations to bank activity: in speeches carefully constructed to be persuasive, the casual involvement of banks in personal and business life is routinely mentioned, allusions that, if untrue or misleading, would be destructive to the litigants' forensic aims, since this background material and related presuppositions were within the general knowledge of the jurors themselves (see Chapter 2). The speaker in Demosthenes 47 claims that he had funds on deposit "at the bank"; the statement has no relevance to the questions in dispute, but his credibility, key to success in an Athenian courtroom, would be adversely affected—unnecessarily—if individuals did not normally maintain such accounts. Yet insistence on the "primitive" nature of the Athenian economy has led modern scholarship to a quite different, and erroneous, prevailing view—an insistence that the *trapezitai* were mere pawnbrokers and money changers (see Chapter 1) and that the undeniable ubiquity of credit at Athens arose from social values embedded in Athenian culture that mandated the profuse extension of loans on a "friendly" basis, free of interest and other monetary considerations. This explanation posits the Athenian as *homo politicus*, a special type of human being motivated by considerations of public service and communal pride—in sharp contrast to *homo oeconomicus*, the mediaeval or modern "economic man" motivated by financial self-interest.[2] This mythical Athenian, instead of seeking profit through interest-bearing or profit-generating bank deposits, supposedly preferred to keep his money inertly at home, protected in strongboxes or buried in the ground. The purported proof

---

[1]Millett 1983: 42: "The easy availability of credit was essential to the smooth functioning of Athenian society; loan transactions of one type or another are a pervasive feature at all levels of Athenian private life." Athens in the fourth century provides a disproportionately high percentage of the hundreds of separate loans identifiable from classical Greek antiquity.

[2]For the *locus classicus* of this view, see Weber 1921: 756. The concept permeates the important works of Erb (1939) and Hasebroek (1931, 1978). For the fullest discussion of the impact of this differentiation on modern scholarship, see Humphreys 1970a and 1978: 159–74 ("Homo politicus and homo economicus").

of this eschewing of banks: the relatively small proportion of bank deposits reported in inventories of Attic estates,[3] a phenomenon that is actually a confirmation of the *importance* of Athenian banking: clandestine trapezitic relationships were a primary means of shielding personal wealth from disclosure through testamentary transfers.[4]

In reality, the Athenians were no more altruistic than other human beings, and much evidence has survived to confirm their efforts to obfuscate their assets and avoid creditors and taxes. Furthermore, the reality of economic life, and the banks' role therein, must be analyzed through Athenian, not alien, concepts. The tax evasion, creditor avoidance, and profit motivation endemic in other societies were not unknown to Athens: indeed, the basic Athenian tendency to organize and perceive reality through complementary opposites led to the division of the Athenian economy into "invisible" and "visible" spheres. The banks' relatively minor presence in the "visible" economy contrasts with their apparent dominance of the alternative market.

THE "INVISIBLE ECONOMY"

For the Athenians, "invisible" (*aphanēs*) assets formed a separate sphere that functioned in counterpoint to the market of "visible" (*phanera*) commerce. Yet this "hidden economy" has received little attention from modern scholars, for a number of reasons: primitivist assumptions denying the very existence of an economy did not encourage the complicating recognition of a parallel commercial system, especially one that performed specialized functions; the inherent secrecy of undisclosed assets did not provide source materials easily accessible to ancient or modern observers; and tax evasion and the defrauding of creditors do not teach the moral lessons for which the classics have been cultivated in the high culture of the Western world.[5] Assuming underlying impropriety, scholars

[3]See Thompson 1979: 229–30, 1988: 833. Cf. Thiel 1922: 50; Bolkestein 1958: 119 and 124.

[4]Formal estate procedures were utilized primarily to dispose of real estate: "In ancient Greece an inheritance was primarily real, rather than financial" (MacDowell 1978: 108). Individuals with large real-property holdings functioned in the "visible economy," where banks were relatively inactive (see below). Hidden assets would not have passed through public testamentary proceedings. When the courts became involved through family disputes in the handling of personal assets—which otherwise would have been transferred without official involvement—the result was complex and protracted litigation, with no satisfying resolution, as in the proceedings relating to the estates of Demosthenes and Pasiōn (Chapter 5). The dominance of realty in estate inventories explains the Athenian tolerance for the long time periods required to close an estate. Hagnias's estate remained in dispute for half a century, and testimony focused on information relating back almost 100 years (Isaios 11; Dem. 43).

[5]On this past ethical orientation, see Connor 1989: 533–36; Todd 1990b: 161; Bernal 1987: 4. For classical studies' resolute avoidance of ancient sexual attitudes and behaviors, see Halperin, Winkler, and Zeitlin 1990: 7–8; Forberg [1824] 1966: 7; Halperin 1990: 2–3. Cf. Dover 1978: vii. For ancient history's general avoidance of Greek financial and business topics, see Chapter 5, n. 207; for its discovery of women only in the last quarter-century, see Peradotto and Sullivan 1984: 4; Clark 1989: 1.

have eschewed study of the "invisible" economy.[6]

In recent years,[7] however, contemporary economists have come to attribute to such "underground" or "parallel" markets[8] various legitimate economic functions. Rather than an immoral challenge to legitimate authority,[9] the underground economies' circumvention of governmental inefficiencies or absurdities, ranging from counterproductive or repressive systems of taxation to restrictions on the free operation of commerce, is now recognized as critical in many societies to even minimal effective functioning of the overall economy.[10]

---

[6]For example, Hasebroek's suggestion (1920: 156–58) that all loans at the *trapezai* and much deposit activity constituted "invisible" assets was rejected by Bogaert with the explanation that "il faudrait considérer tous les Athéniens ayant de l'argent en banque ou chez des particuliers comme des fraudeurs fiscaux, ce qui est naturellement injuste à leur égard" (1968: 349). Similarly, although Bogaert is aware of bankers' heavy involvement in the clandestine economy (see 1986b: 16), in analyzing their role in the economy he ignores the unseen market, which leads to the false conclusion that "dans le financement du commerce, dans le crédit commercial, leur action a été fort limitée" (1968: 411).

The one exception: the brilliant French scholar Louis Gernet, who—although he never worked extensively on ancient banking itself—saw clearly, even in passing, the significance of this dimension: "the term ['invisible'] introduces a new world that is not without mystery. The person who symbolizes this new world is the banker, and he is already an energetic participant in it" (1981: 348).

[7]In the United States it was not until 1958 that the first systematic effort was made to compute the approximate amount of income not reported to the taxing authorities (Cagan 1958); only in 1977 did Gutmann refine Cagan's methodology to produce a mature estimate of the "subterranean economy" in the United States (approximately 10% of gross national production in 1976; Gutmann 1977). During the mid-1970s, Italian scholars started serious investigations of "hidden labor": see Bergonzini 1973; Deaglio 1974; Frey 1975. In the United Kingdom as late as 1979–81, the Board of Inland Revenue was only beginning to estimate the magnitude of the unobserved economy (House of Commons, 1980, Q 4637; 1981–82, QQ 4658–60). Even in 1989, the phenomenon could be characterized as a "neglected part of the German economy" (Langfeldt 1989: 197). Cf. Langfeldt and Lehment 1980.

[8]Contemporary economists use a multitude of terms ("underground," "clandestine," "black," "subterranean," "hidden," "parallel," and many others) to describe phenomena that in practice are unified only by being "unobserved." The modern Greek term is παραοικονομία: a major aim of proposed tax reform in Greece is to reduce the size of this parallel economy and the tax avoidance (φοροδιαφυγή) that it spawns (see "Νέα φορολογική μεταρρύθμιση," Καθημερινή, June 10, 1990, p. 57).

[9]Even where models of quantitative policy consider on a macroeconomic scale the social costs of illegality, with its adverse effect on values and order, countervailing attention is paid to determining the socially optimal dimensions desirable for the underground sector (Frey 1989: 111–26). Cf. Tinberger 1952, and Theil 1968.

[10]An Italian economist, for example, lauds the parallel market: "The so-called underground economy in Italy [is] a masterpiece of my countrymen's ingenuity, a second Italian miracle which has saved the country from bankruptcy" (Martino 1980: 2). Underground economic activity is sometimes seen as merely a rational response to the malfunctioning of the official economy. Already in 1981, Connolly had observed that although conventional Marxist theory tacitly assumes the state's rational capacity for policy-making and the availability to it of accurate economic data, Marxist economists "underplay . . . the extent to which citizens . . . quietly obstruct the performance of the political economy" (1981: 136). These clandestine markets appear in every differentiated economy (see Feige 1989: 9; Rosenvallon 1980).

At Athens, the "invisible" economy performed a societal function beyond the amelioration of oppressive taxation and the facilitation of private economic arrangements: it reflected the Athenian penchant for shaping perception and organizing activity through complementary opposites. Precisely because this differentiation of "visible" and "invisible" assets was grounded in Athenian cognitive concepts of bipolarity and their attendant societal values,[11] modern scholars have been entirely unsuccessful in abstract efforts to find distinct qualities inherent in specific objects that would render them predictably either "invisible" or "visible."[12] Athenian antithesis permitted not a spectrum of objects and a variety of categories, but only a counterpoised opposition of the two types of assets. Where Anglo-American law easily contrasts "real property" and "personal property," but still allows for items sharing certain characteristics of both ("fixtures"), the Greek antithetical universe permitted only two divisions: "disclosed property," characterized as *phanera ousia*, and "other property," categorized as *aphanēs ousia*. Even the differentiation between realty and personalty tended to be expressed in terms of this antithesis.[13] Yet since we know of real estate whose ownership had been carefully hidden, and of items of personal property with dominion unambiguously "disclosed,"[14] the Athenian categorization is manifestly unsatisfactory to modern analysts accustomed to classification along a spectrum that provides special place for incompatible exceptions and for objects of blended nature.[15] To the Athenians, however, consistency lay in the universality by which objects were organized

[11]For the philosophical treatment of this polarity between "visible" and "invisible" qualities, see Schuhl 1953.

[12]A number of researchers have focused on the object's capacity to appear as ἀφανής or φανερά: Büchsenschütz 1869: 38; Boeckh [1842] 1976: 633; Hermann and Blümner 1882: 96; Busolt and Swoboda 1920–26, 2: 1213 n. 2. For the inadequacy of these efforts, but without a clear alternate formulation, see Bongenaar 1933: 234–39; Koutorga 1859: 6–11, Schodorf 1905: 90ff.; and Weiss 1923: 173, 464, 491. For other inconclusive efforts to attribute innate characteristics to these terms, see Gabrielsen 1986: esp. 101 n. 7.

[13]Harpokratiōn, s.v.: ἀφανὴς οὐσία καὶ φανερά. ἀφανὴς μὲν ἡ ἐν χρήμασι καὶ σώμασι καὶ σκεύεσι, φανερὰ δὲ ἡ ἔγγειος· Λυσίας ἐν τῷ πρὸς Ἱπποθέρσην. (Fragments of this speech are preserved in P. Oxy. 13, no. 1606 [Gernet and Bizos 1924–26, 2: 252ff.].) The separation of realty from all other assets, and its characterization as φανερὰ οὐσία, was so pervasive that the mere act of selling real property might be seen as the conversion of "visible" into ἀφανὴς οὐσία: Dem. 5.8 (cf. Plut., *Orators' Lives* 850d; Aischinēs 1.96–97, 101–3. See Lysias, frag. 79 (= Gernet and Bizos 1924–26: 24.2) and below, n. 67.

[14]Owners of real estate are said to have refused rental income solely in order to keep their holdings ἀφανής: Lysias 32.23; Dem. 28.7. Cf. the χωρίον whose ownership Theopompos was charged with concealing (Isaios 11.47). See Wyse [1904] 1967: 712; Thompson 1976: 57–59; Humphreys 1983a: 221ff. For "visible" personalty, see Dem. 43.5ff.; Lysias 19.31; below, n. 17.

[15]Gabrielsen (1986: 101) characterizes the ancient evidence as "hardly credible." For modern frustration in seeking to organize the source material through non-Athenian categories, see Beauchet [1897] 1969, 3: 13–21; Lipsius [1905–15] 1966: 677; Weiss 1923: 173, 464, 491. For the modern tendency "to divide each difficulty into as many parts as necessary the better to solve it," extolled by Descartes, see Lévi-Strauss and Eribon 1991: 112.

by reference to antithetical grouping. It was the persistence of the counter-poised categories, not the "true" nature of the objects, that determined classification of particular items. Because ownership of land was difficult to conceal, real property became identified with "visible" wealth;[16] because control of intangibles was relatively easy to hide, financial assets came to be seen as the essence of "invisible" property. But even bank deposits might be revealed by their owners or otherwise become attributable to them, and thus become "visible."[17] Yet with further obfuscation they could be returned to the universe of invisible wealth (*aphanēs ousia*),[18] a world congenial to bankers, but not to taxes, creditors, and governmental controls.

Tax Considerations

Taxes at Athens were imposed at high rates, but only on a relatively small number of persons appearing to own the largest amounts of property. Efforts to avoid ascription into this expensive minority provided motivation and funding for the "invisible" economy and the bankers who acted as its treasurers. The Athenian system, in fact, constitutes the quintessence of "progressive" taxation:[19] only a limited number of the wealthiest individuals residing at Athens paid any direct imposts, but these select few incurred costs perceived as intolerable. Fourth-century Athens had desperate need of revenues: the long-term decline in income from the silver mines (which were state-owned) exacerbated the loss in the Peloponnesian War of the empire and the revenues derived from

[16]Although MacDowell goes too far in claiming that "land and buildings are always counted as visible" (1962: 146), realty was indeed the form *par excellence* of φανερὰ οὐσία (Gernet 1956: 345; Gabrielsen 1986: 110).

[17]At Isok. 17.11, the depositor—after changed circumstances free him of concern over possible seizure of his assets—determines to withdraw his bank deposits and function "visibly" (φανερῶς ἤδη πράξω περὶ τῶν ἐμαυτοῦ). Money on deposit at the bank of Hērakleidēs is described at Dem. 48.12 as ἀργύριον . . . φανερὸν ἐπὶ τῇ τραπέζῃ τῇ Ἡρακλείδου. See Dem. 45.30 (τῶν δ' ἐπὶ τῆς τραπέζης ὄντων, ἃ πάντες ᾔδεσαν). Cf. Hyp., *Dem.* 9 (χρέα φανερά); Lysias 12.83 (τὰ χρήματα τὰ φανερά); Isaios 11.43–44 (χρέα δ' ἐπὶ τόκοις ὀφειλόμενα . . . καὶ οὔπω λέγω περὶ τῶν ἄλλων, ἃ κατελείφθη μὲν οὗτοι δ' οὐκ ἀποφαίνουσιν, ἀλλὰ τὰ φανερὰ καὶ τὰ ὑπὸ τούτων ὁμολογούμενα).

[18]See, for example, Isok. 17.7. (At first the son of Sopaios had made his assets openly known; Isok. 17.41.) This obfuscation of assets even developed special nomenclature: ἀφανίζειν or ἀποκρύπτεσθαι τὴν οὐσίαν. See Isaios 11.47; Dem. 28.3, 45.66. Cf. Cloché 1941: 35–36; Chapter 4, n. 90 above.

[19]For the rich, the tax burden constituted a "bleeding of the wealthy" (Andreades [1933] 1979: 359), a "redistribuzione a favore delle masse popolari" (D'Albergho in Gera 1975: 13). But for the society as a whole, tax obligations were "lenient" when "compared with the taxation of modern days" (Thomsen 1964: 256 [writing in Denmark in 1964]). Cf. Littman 1988: 805–7. Even those who believe that the *eisphora* was for a time imposed at an equal percentage on a large portion of propertied residents recognize that the associated *proeisphora* affected only the wealthiest. See Ste. Croix 1953: 58–62.

tribute-paying dependencies.[20] The resultant tax burdens generated frequent complaints, even claims of financial ruin from the minority subject to these exactions.[21] Xenophon pities a youth who thinks that his wealth will free him of financial worries: the state will oppress him with ordinary and extraordinary taxes—and if his resources prove at all inadequate for meeting these public burdens, it will punish him "just as though he were caught robbing it of its own property."[22] Because fiscal obligations were exclusively placed on the wealthy, the term "taxpayers" (the *triērarchoi* or the *leitourgountes*) became in popular usage interchangeable with "the rich" or "the well-off."[23]

Although it is often said that the Athenians had a strong aversion to imposing "direct taxes" on their own citizens,[24] state revenues in fact were dependent on the liturgy, "that form of taxation-cum-personal service"[25] which obligated those citizens appearing to have the greatest wealth to finance and perform such obligations as paying for and commanding a warship for a year, underwriting the cost of and producing a dramatic or choral performance, or training and supporting a group of relay-runners.[26] Since the liturgical system provided only for recurring expenses relating to ongoing state functions, an extraordinary levy (the *eisphora*) was utilized from time to time to meet other needs, but this too was a tax directly related to individual capital.[27]

[20]On the long-term depression in silver production (which had been entirely disrupted by the war), see Hopper 1953: 215–16, 250–52; Ober 1985: 28–29. For the resultant adverse effect on state revenues, see Hopper 1968. During some periods of the fourth century, Athens did receive some revenue from outlying areas: the inscription discovered in the Athenian agora in 1986 and dating to 374/3 (Shear 1987) discloses a tax of "one-twelfth" on grain production from Lemnos, Imbros, and Skyros.

[21]Dem. 1.8–9, 24.197–98, 38.26, 47.54, 50.8–9, 52.26; Isaios 4.27, 6.60–61, 7.40; Isok. 8.128, 12.145; Lysias 7.31–32, 12.20, 18.7, 18.21, 19.9, 19.29, 19.57–59, 20.23, 28.3, 29.4, 30.26; Xen., *Hell.* 6.2.1, *Symp.* 4.30–32; Hyp., frag. 134; Aristot., *Pol.* 1309a15ff.; Antiphanes, frag. 204, II 98K; Dem. Phal., frag. 136 Wehrli = Plut., *Mor.* 349a; Diod. 13.47.7, 52.5, 64.4; Anaximenes 2 (p. 22, ll. 5ff., ed. Hammer). See Davies 1981: 82–84; Christ 1990: 150–57; Wyse [1904] 1967: 396.

[22]Xen., *Oik.* 2.6–7: ἔτι δὲ καὶ τὴν πόλιν αἰσθάνομαι τὰ μὲν ἤδη σοι προστάττουσαν μεγάλα τελεῖν, ἱπποτροφίας τε καὶ χορηγίας καὶ γυμνασιαρχίας καὶ προστατείας . . . καὶ τριηραρχίας καὶ εἰσφορὰς τοσαύτας σοι προστάξουσιν ὅσας σὺ οὐ ῥᾳδίως ὑποίσεις. ὅπου δ' ἂν ἐνδεῶς δόξῃς τι τούτων ποιεῖν, οἶδ' ὅτι σε τιμωρήσονται Ἀθηναῖοι οὐδὲν ἧττον ἢ εἰ τὰ αὐτῶν λάβοιεν κλέπτοντα κ.τ.λ.

[23]Aristot., *Pol.* 1291a33–34: τὸ ταῖς οὐσίαις λειτουργοῦν, ὃ καλοῦμεν εὐπόρους. See Xen., *Ath. pol.* 1.13; Dem. 21.151, 153, 208; Isok. 8.128; Lysias 27.9–10. For the converse, see Dem. 18.102, 108, where all but the 300 richest are seen as "poor" (πένητες, ἄποροι). For further examples and fuller discussion, cf. Hemelrijk 1925 (German summary, pp. 140–42).

[24]See, for example, Andreades [1933] 1979: 126–30; Thomsen 1964: 11; Vannier 1988: 12.

[25]Davies 1971: xx. For terminology associated with the "liturgy," see N. Lewis 1960 and 1965.

[26]For a summary of the system, see Christ 1990: 148–51. Cf. Lauffer 1974: 147ff.; MacDowell 1978: 161–65; Gera 1975: 92–98; Costanzi 1927: 53. See also the so-called "Trierarchic Law" (I.G. I³ 236 [= Oliver 1935; S.E.G. 10.142]).

[27]See Ste. Croix 1953: 31. Cf. also Mossé 1979b. The theory that it was a tax on income,

These liturgies were expensive. The least costly obligation (a Panathenaic chorus) required 300 *dr.*,[28] an amount virtually equal to the entire annual income of a contemporary skilled workman (see Chapter 1, n. 92 above). The most expensive—and not rare[29]—commitment, the individual maintenance of a warship for a year, cost about a talent (6,000 *dr.*),[30] probably a quarter to a third of the entire (known) net assets of many members of the liturgical class. Even for these relatively wealthy persons, individuals with capital of not less than two talents,[31] imposts on this scale were highly significant, often constituting "the major part of a man's income" (Davies 1981: 82). Nor was the obligation, like modern estate taxes, a one-time spoliation. The obligations recurred annually, and were imposed on all residents of Attica, not on citizens alone.[32] The only general relief accorded by law was an exemption from performing a liturgy in two successive years.[33]

Even beyond these exactions, a further tax, the *eisphora*, was levied on property held by residents of Attica, assessed at intervals to provide funds for a specific undertaking such as a naval campaign.[34] Although the provisions for its collection and other technical aspects of its administration remain unclear

---

advanced *inter alios* by Rodbertus (1867: 453–58), has long been unanimously rejected.

[28]Dem. 21.155. There is a single reference (I.G. II² 417) to an *eutaxia* liturgy that supposedly cost only 50–100 *dr.*, but it is never mentioned again and "was probably short-lived" (Davies 1981: 9).

[29]Trierarchs normally numbered 300. Xen., *Ath. pol.* 3.4; Dem. 18.102–9; Aischinēs 3.222; Dein. 1.42; Hyp., frag. 134, 159 (Jensen = 160, 173 [Sauppe]). See Davies 1981: 19–24. Gabrielsen (1989) argues that the law of c. 340 permitted a higher number but increased the financial burdens for the 300. But cf. Gabrielsen 1987: 7.

[30]Dem. 21.155. Trierarchies for a total of seven years are reported to have cost a total of seven talents (Lysias 21.2). The cost of three trierarchies required 8,000 *dr.* (Lysias 19.29 and 42), but these appear to have been syntrierarchies, for which the 8,000 *dr.* represent only a portion of the total expense. The 2,000 *dr.* reported at Dem. 21.80 for a syntrierarchy was one-third the total cost, according to the scholiast (Dilts 1983–86: 262). Lysias 32.24 and 27 report an expenditure of 4,800 *dr.*.

[31]Demosthenes (27.64) claimed in 363 that estates originally worth as little as one talent, after doubling through capable management, had become liable for liturgies. After surveying the evidence, Davies concludes (1971: xxiii–xxiv) that persons with property worth less than three talents were free of liturgical obligation. Cf. Ruschenbusch 1985: 237–40.

[32]See Katayama 1970. Cf. Whitehead 1977: 80–82.

[33]Dem. 20.8, 28; 50.9. See Gabrielsen 1987: 7–8. MacDowell has suggested (1990: 372) that after 357, persons responsible for maintaining a ship for a year (the trierarchs) continued to be exempt from successive liturgies, although under Peisandros's law (Dem. 47.21) they received financial assistance from a contributor class (συντελής), which aided in meeting the high expense of a sole or joint trierarchy.

[34]On the *eisphora* system, see Thomsen 1964; Brun 1983: 3–73; Gera 1975: 31–84. For imposition of the tax on metics as well as citizens, see I.G.² II–III 244.26 and the fragment from Hypereidēs preserved at Pollux 8.144. Cf. Whitehead 1977: 78–80 and 1986a: 146. There is some evidence for annual imposition of the *eisphora* from 347/6 to 323/2. See Thomsen 1964: 239–43.

(and highly disputed),[35] it too was imposed on a limited number of residents in amounts based on their known property.[36] This supplemental impost itself is known in individual cases to have amounted to thousands of drachmas.[37] And from the 300 individuals who could be identified as the wealthiest,[38] the state required a contribution of *proeisphora*, in effect tax-anticipation payments (but without any state commitment that sums advanced would be recovered). From his own assets, the wealthy contributor of *proeisphora* paid immediately the total amount of *eisphora* due from a number of other taxpayers. In return, he was given the right, with other advance payers, to recover his excess payment from the various obligors. While some contributors of *proeisphora* might have suffered only small or limited losses, the potential expense was enormous, as one hapless bank owner who provided *proeisphora* in 362 reminisced some years later: "I never did recover [the funds advanced], because at that time I was away in your service as trierarch, and later, when I returned, I found that the money from those with resources had already been collected by others, and only those without money were left."[39] Even men fortunate enough to collect all or most of the taxes advanced would still have absorbed the interest or opportunity cost of funds prior to eventual reimbursement; they would never recover the inconvenience and cost of collection. And in those periods when there was no general *eisphora*, wealthy individuals might be called upon to provide contributions (*epidoseis*) for arms, grain, public sacrifices, repair of theaters, and the like—in form voluntary, but in fact, by the fourth century, a further compulsory extraction.[40]

Since these charges were imposed only upon those who appeared to own the largest amounts of property, the system provided direct motivation for the masking of assets and the growth of the "invisible" economy. For a wealthy man, the decision to maintain his assets in visible form was a determination to

[35]See, for example, the early studies of Momigliano (1931) and Schwahn (1933). For a summary of the multitudinous divergent interpretations through 1964, see Thomsen 1964: 14–37. Cf. recent work by Rhodes (1982), MacDowell (1986), and Ruschenbusch (1978, 1985, and 1987). For the number of taxpayers subject to the *eisphora*, ranging upward from 1,200, see Ober 1989: 128–29 nn. 58 and 59.

[36]Dem. 21.157, 27.7–9. See MacDowell 1990: 375–76; Gabrielsen 1986: 99–100.

[37]See Lysias 21.3 (payments of 3,000 *dr.* and 4,000 *dr.* in the late fifth century); Lysias 19.43 (4,000 *dr.* paid by two individuals in the late 390s); Dem. 27.37 (1,800 *dr.*, mid-fourth century).

[38]See Isaios 7.60; Aischinēs 3.222; Dein. 1.42; Hyp., frag. 154; Dem. 18.103, 18.171, 21.153, 37.37, 42.4, 42.5, 42.25, 50.8–9. For various (highly disputed) aspects of this grouping, see Wallace 1989.

[39]Dem. 50.9: Καὶ οὐκ εἰσεπραξάμην, διὰ τὸ τότε μὲν ἀποδημεῖν ὑπὲρ ὑμῶν τριηραρχ-ῶν, ὕστερον δὲ καταπλεύσας καταλαβεῖν τὰ μὲν εὔπορα ὑφ' ἑτέρων προεξειλεγμένα, τὰ δ' ἄπορα ὑπόλοιπα.

[40]See Isaios 5.38. Littman 1988: 802: "Although the voluntary nature of these public contributions prevailed in the fifth century, the institution of *epidoseis* was formalized in the fourth [century] and became virtually compulsory."

undertake the burden of taxation.[41] Those who wished to avoid liturgies and special assessments on capital might use their bankers to hide their property.[42] In effect, the state, by imposing on a limited number of persons specific functions to be performed or particular amounts to be paid, and by then providing a legal process (the *antidosis*, "exchange") through which an individual might force another to take his place, made of taxation the stereotypical "zero-sum" competition (*agōn*) that permeated Athenian life.[43] Although officials initially assigned liturgies and other obligations to specific individuals,[44] the *antidosis* allowed a named taxpayer to insist that another (allegedly wealthier) man undertake the obligation.[45] In this court contest, losers were almost certain to be those who had maintained their assets in more visible form and so could be shown to have the larger estates. The tax system thus offered wealthy residents of Attica considerable incentive to place or keep their property in the "invisible" economy; there, financial assets—deposits and loans—constituted the least traceable form of unseen property. But skill at hiding assets could have no adverse effect on state revenues: one person's success (in avoiding taxes) was attained at another's cost (in paying those taxes).[46]

The mere existence of the *antidosis* and the abundance of surviving evidence

---

[41]Lysias 20.23 makes explicit the connection between "invisible" assets and tax avoidance: ἐξὸν αὐτῷ τὴν οὐσίαν ἀφανῆ καταστήσαντι μηδὲν ὑμᾶς ὠφελεῖν εἵλετο μᾶλλον συνειδέναι ὑμᾶς, ἵν᾽, εἰ καὶ βούλοιτο κακὸς εἶναι, μὴ ἐξείη αὐτῷ, ἀλλ᾽ εἰσφέροι τε τὰς εἰσφορὰς καὶ λητουργοίη. Cf. Dem. 28.3: Δημοχάρης . . . οὐκ ἀποκέκρυπται τὴν οὐσίαν, ἀλλὰ χορηγεῖ καὶ τριηραρχεῖ καὶ τὰς ἄλλας λητουργίας λητουργεῖ.

[42]Which Stephanos is specifically accused of having done: ἐπὶ τῷ τὴν πόλιν φεύγειν καὶ τὰ ὄντ᾽ ἀποκρύπτεσθαι προῄρηται πράττειν, ἵν᾽ ἐργασίας ἀφανεῖς διὰ τῆς τραπέζης ποιῆται, καὶ μήτε χορηγῇ μήτε τριηραρχῇ μήτ᾽ ἄλλο μηδὲν ὧν προσήκει ποιῇ (Dem. 45.66).

[43]"Zero-sum competition"—that form of contest in which winners gained rewards and honors only at the expense of losers, who incurred corresponding shame or penalties—may be seen as the social expression of the conceptual system based on complementary opposition. Anonymous Iamblichi states the rule explicitly: "People do not find it pleasant to give honor (τιμᾶν) to someone else, for they suppose that they themselves are being deprived of something" (*Fragmente der Vorsokratiker* 2.400). Cf. Plato, *Laws* 1.626b: πάντα δὲ τὰ τῶν νικωμένων ἀγαθὰ τῶν νικώντων γίγνεσθαι. See Gouldner 1965: 45–55; Winkler 1990: 178; above, pp. 46–47.

[44]See Aristot., *Ath. pol.* 61.1; Dem. 14.16, 39.8, 50.44, 50.66; the Ikarion decree found in 1983 (Bingen [1972–76] 1984: no. 75 [with fig. 109], ll. 2–3, 5—cf. Whitehead 1986c). For further analysis of the selection mechanism, see Rhodes 1982: 3–4, and Jordan 1975: 61–67.

[45]On the ἀντίδοσις, see Gabrielsen 1987; Christ 1990: 160–68. Cf. Goligher (1907), who at 514–15 provides bibliographic reference to numerous earlier studies. Through the procedure termed σκῆψις, an individual (a minor, for example) might claim that he was not liable for liturgical payments. For such exemptions, see Harrison 1968–71, 1: 234–36.

[46]In contrast to the systems prevalent in the modern world, where a change in the value of a resident's total property or income results in a difference in overall taxes due, the Athenian state received the same revenues or services without reference to overall economic conditions and without regard to the identity of the particular taxpayers ultimately liable.

for the actual utilization of the complex judicial procedures governing it[47] is very much at odds with the romantic notion that Athenian taxpayers gloried in paying governmental charges and contended in *agonistic* fervor to advance ever-greater sums.[48] Some individuals, from political motivation, may have "voluntarily" undertaken fiscal obligations[49] and then sought public credit for so doing.[50] Other persons may have sought honor and glory (in Athenian terms, *lamprotēs* and *philotimia*) by undertaking public benefactions costing more than the minimum anticipated.[51] Such (rare) actions occur today in some countries, but often—as in ancient Athens—even these benefactions, on analysis, prove to be motivated in fact by the exigencies of the state revenue system.[52] The speaker of Lysias 3 is not atypical: although he boasts (§47) of the many liturgies he has performed for his country, he actually undertook them only after exhausting all possibilities for tax avoidance, including protracted litigation to avoid these payments.[53] The bank owner Apollodōros claims patriotically to have spent far more than the minimum in performing a naval liturgy—and then sues to recover a large part of that expenditure from his successor![54] In fact, some trierarchs actually managed to spend absolutely nothing on the obligation that allegedly had been undertaken only to obtain exemption from other state obligations.[55] As embarrassingly detailed in De-

[47]See Harrison 1968–71, 2: 236–38; Lipsius [1905–15] 1966: 590–99; MacDowell 1978: 162–64.

[48]For extreme assertions of this ardor, see Guiraud 1893: 531; Finley 1985: 150–52. Roberts (1986: 369) even sees this aristocratic competition as conflicting with democratic values. See Christ (1990: 152–60) for a recognition that "the problem of liturgy avoidance in Athens was more serious than scholars have allowed" (p. 148).

[49]An ἐθελοντής as trierarch was allowed even after Periander's legislation of 357: Dem. 18.99, 21.161. Cf. I.G. II² 1623, ll. 309–11.

[50]Rhodes (1986), for example, shows how liturgical expenditure was used to gain political support and influence. Cf. Sinclair 1988: 188–90; Manville 1990: 22–23.

[51]On "the close association of *philotimia* with the expenditure of money," see Whitehead 1983: esp. 64ff. For χάρις, the gratitude allegedly anticipated from the citizens in return for public benefactions, see Dover 1974: 292–95; Ober 1989: 226–40.

[52]Consider the alleged manipulation of the modern Greek tax system through the establishment of the Alexander Onassis Foundation and the threat in 1982 to abort construction of the Onassis Cardiac Surgery Center. Death duties were avoided, while control was maintained over assets important to the operation of the underlying private business. See Davis 1986: 205–6, 254–55. Cf. Limperopoulos 1983: 187.

[53]§47: μὴ περιίδητε ἐκ τῆς πατρίδος ἀδίκως ἐκπεσόντα, ὑπὲρ ἧς ἐγὼ πολλοὺς κινδύνους κεκινδύνευκα καὶ πολλὰς λῃτουργίας λελῃτούργηκα. He gives no details as to these benefactions, but the truth is revealed at §20: δίκας ἰδίας ᾔσθετο κακῶς ἀγωνισάμενου ἐξ ἀντιδόσεως. On the extensive judicial procedures employed in this effort to evade taxes, see Carey 1989: 101–2.

[54]Dem. 50. Far from being typical, even his initial expenditure at best reflected a "naive enthusiasm [that] both his commander and his successor seem to have exploited shamefully" (Morrison and Coates 1986: 127).

[55]Dem. 21.155: αὐτῶν ἐνίοις τῇ ἀληθείᾳ τὸ μηδὲν ἀναλῶσαι καὶ δοκεῖν

mosthenes 51, the mass of trierarchs appears to have sought to expend as little as possible and to evade even the minimal obligations imposed by law.[56] Even those liturgists seeking special commendation from the state are said to have neglected their ships, but not the speeches lauding their patriotism.[57]

The most fulsome propagandists for *lamprotēs* and *philotimia* personally sought to avoid fiscal obligations. Isokratēs, whose *Panathēnaikos* encomium is a paean to Athenian patriotism, congratulated himself on having performed liturgies "more extensively and better" than required by law.[58] Yet he, too, did so only after unsuccessfully claiming that he was not really among the elite group of wealthy individuals subject to tax, and after losing in his efforts through *antidosis* to have another person undertake his responsibilities.[59] In his turn, the very symbol of Athenian patriotism, Demosthenes, charged Meidias with having financed a public chorus only after losing a legal action brought to avoid this tax (while Demosthenes himself undertook the same burden "voluntarily" [*ethelontēs*]—but only after state and deme officials had fallen into bitter recriminations upon their extended failure to find anyone to undertake the liturgy).[60] Demosthenes further contrasts his own voluntary maintenance of a ship with Meidias's avoidance of trierarchic service (until a new system introduced in 357 effectively forced him to contribute to the maintenance of the fleet).[61] But Demosthenes was himself heir to a long tradition of tax avoidance. Although his father's estate, as ultimately revealed in the extensive litigation chronicled in Demosthenes 27–31, clearly placed the elder Demosthenes among those liable for liturgical contribution,[62] Demosthenes *père* seems systematically to have kept his property "invisible,"[63] and successfully to have avoided the performance of even the smallest liturgy.[64] His son, the statesman,

---

λελειτουργηκέναι καὶ τῶν ἄλλων λειτουργιῶν ἀτελεῖς γεγενῆσθαι περίεστιν.

[56]Dem. 51.7: σκεψάμενοι γὰρ τὸν ἐξ ἐλαχίστου τριηραρχεῖν βουλόμενον, μεμισθώκασι τὴν λῃτουργίαν. Cf. §4 (failure to provide ships on a timely basis).

[57]Dem. 51.2: τῆς τριήρους ἀμελήσαντες τοὺς ῥήτορας παρεσκεύασαν.

[58]Isok. 15.145: εἰς δὲ τοὺς . . . εἰσφέροντας καὶ λειτουργοῦντας οὐ μόνον αὐτὸν παρέχεις ἀλλὰ καὶ τὸν υἱόν, καὶ τρὶς μὲν ἤδη τετριηραρχήκατε, τὰς δ' ἄλλας λειτουργίας πολυτελέστερον λελειτουργήκατε καὶ κάλλιον ὧν οἱ νόμοι προστάττουσιν. "But his self-praise diminishes in credibility when confronted with the fact(s)": Gabrielsen 1987: 38.

[59]Isok. 15.4–5: ἀντιδόσεως γενομένης περὶ τριηραρχίας . . . καὶ καταλαζονευομένου περί τε τοῦ πλούτου καὶ τοῦ πλήθους τῶν μαθητῶν, ἔγνωσαν ἐμὴν εἶναι τὴν λειτουργίαν. Τὴν μὲν οὖν δαπάνην οὕτως ἠνέγκαμεν. Cf. Bonner 1920: 194.

[60]Dem. 21.13: οὐ καθεστηκότος χορηγοῦ τῇ Πανδιονίδι φυλῇ, τρίτον ἔτος τουτί, παρούσης δὲ τῆς ἐκκλησίας ἐν ᾗ τὸν ἄρχοντα ἐπικληροῦν ὁ νόμος τοῖς χορηγοῖς τοὺς αὐλητὰς κελεύει, λόγων καὶ λοιδορίας γιγνομένης, καὶ κατηγοροῦντος τοῦ μὲν ἄρχοντος τῶν ἐπιμελητῶν τῆς φυλῆς, τῶν δ' ἐπιμελητῶν τοῦ ἄρχοντος.

[61]Dem. 21.151–56, esp. 154, 156.

[62]See Ste. Croix 1953: 55; Davies 1971: 128.

[63]See Korver 1942: 21–22. He owned no land; his only real property was the house, which also served as a workshop (Dem. 27.24–25).

[64]Although Demosthenes skillfully implies that the family was accustomed to meet such

although sufficiently rich to be tagged the "wealthiest Athenian,"[65] in his turn is said never to have acquired anything that could be attributed to him (*phaneron*).[66]

The Primacy of Financial Assets

In this sphere of invisible property, financial assets held a primacy similar to that of real estate in the complementary world of visible resources.[67] Although money "loom(s) large among the attested instances" of invisible wealth,[68] coins were still inherently tangible, in contrast to the bankers' deposits (*parakatathēkai*) and "loans" (*chrea*), which had absolutely no corporeality. Loans and deposits are recognized as the archetypes of unseen assets and as ultimately different from all other forms of property because they alone could not be physically seized.[69] This is strikingly shown by the Greek expression for a credit unaccompanied by security (which would provide tangibility): a mere "naked loan" is termed an obligation "in the sky" (*meteōron*),[70] whereas landed assets constitute "visible" property *par excellence*. Thus, at Isaios 8.35, a broad variety of assets, all expressed in monetary value, all termed *phanera*, are contrasted with the single other asset, a not-inconsiderable sum identified as "loans" (*daneismata*).[71] Similarly, the businessman Diodotos delivers cash to his closest relatives, but "reveals" the existence of various loans (Lysias 32.5–6).[72] At both Demosthenes 38.7 and Andokidēs 1.118,

---

obligations (Dem. 27.64, 28.19), his explicit statement as to the liturgies performed by his relative Dēmocharēs (Dem. 28.3) sharply contrasts with the absence of similar claims for his father.

[65]Dein. 1.111: πλουσιώτατον ὄντα τῶν ἐν τῇ πόλει. Cf. Hyp. *Dem.* 22.

[66]Dein. 1.70: μηδὲν φανερὸν ἐν τῇ πόλει κεκτῆσθαι.

[67]For real estate as the prime form of φανερὰ οὐσία, and monetary assets as its counterpoised equivalent in the world of ἀφανὴς οὐσία, see, for example, Lysias, frag. 79 (= Gernet and Bizos 1924–26: 24.2): Εἰ μὲν γὰρ ἀγροὺς κατέλιπεν ᾿Ανδροκλείδης ἢ ἄλλην φανερὰν οὐσίαν . . . περὶ ‹δὲ› ἀργυρίου καὶ χρυσίου καὶ ἀφανοῦς οὐσίας. See above, pp. 193–94, and nn. 13 and 14.

[68]Gabrielsen 1986: 102. It is Demosthenes' money that Deinarchos brands μηδὲν φανερόν (1.70): see Wyse [1904] 1967: 516. Cf. Aristoph., *Ekkl.* 602.

[69]On the legal implications of this differentiation, see Gernet 1981: 347–48.

[70]See Dittenberger 1915–24: 364.42.46 (Ephesos, 3d century): οἱ τὰ μετέωρα ἐγγυώμενοι. Cf. S.E.G. 1.363.9 (Samos, 3d century): δικαστήριον τὸ διαλῦσον τὰ μετέωρα συμβόλαια. Sokrates was accused of being τὰ μετέωρα φροντιστής (Plato, *Apol.* 18b).

[71]ἐκέκτητο οὐσίαν, ἀγρὸν μὲν Φλυῆσι, καὶ ταλάντου ῥαδίως ἄξιον, οἰκίας δ᾿ ἐν ἄστει δύο, τὴν μὲν μίαν μισθοφοροῦσαν . . . χιλίας εὑρίσκουσαν, τὴν δ᾿ ἑτέραν . . . τριῶν καὶ δέκα μνῶν· ἔτι δὲ ἀνδράποδα μισθοφοροῦντα καὶ δύο θεραπαίνας καὶ παιδίσκην καὶ ἔπιπλα . . . , σχεδὸν σὺν τοῖς ἀνδραπόδοις ἄξια τριῶν καὶ δέκα μνῶν· σύμπαντα δὲ ὅσα φανερὰ ἦν, πλέον ἢ ἐνενήκοντα μνῶν·χωρὶς δὲ τούτων δανείσματα οὐκ ὀλίγα.

[72]αὐτῷ δίδωσι καὶ πέντε τάλαντα ἀργυρίου παρακαταθήκην· ναυτικὰ δὲ ἀπέδειξεν ἐκδεδομένα ἑπτὰ τάλαντα καὶ τεττᾱράκοντα μνᾶς . . . , δισχιλίας δὲ ὀφειλομένας ἐν Χερρονήσῳ κ.τ.λ.

debts are specifically contrasted with "visible" assets.[73] And at Demosthenes
42.5, the thought is expressed that an asset "once becoming a loan will disap-
pear."[74] Even where other cash holdings are generally known (*phaneron*), an
individual's bank deposits might be kept in confidence.[75]

Clandestine Finance

The tale of Theophēmos's violent efforts to execute on a judgment illustrates the
complex interplay of tax burdens, creditor avoidance, bank deposits, and the
invisible economy. Seeking to collect over 1,200 *dr.*, Theophēmos attacked a
judgment-debtor's home. But instead of the ample personal property that he
had anticipated, he was able to carry off only a small amount of furniture. The
debtor explains that "through liturgies and capital-tax payments (*eisphorai*)
and my liberality to the state, part of my property had been pledged as security
for loans, and the rest had been sold."[76] (In other words, his wealth had been
transferred from the visible to the invisible sphere, for protection from such
onslaughts by creditors). In their frustration, the raiding party allegedly even
maltreated the women of the house. But the debtor, protected by his bankers
from taxation and creditors, was able to plead self-righteously: "Theophēmos
should have followed me to the bank to recover his judgment, instead of seizing
property"; "my wife told them that the money was waiting for them at the
bank."[77] But these assertions are made only much later: by this time, the assets
might have been further transferred or transformed. Perhaps the statements
actually reflect some aspect of the truth—since they are made in court in a suit
charging Theophēmos's associates with perjury! In any event, they reflect a
story intended to be credible to the jurors: a claim that a person believed to be
wealthy, overwhelmed by taxes and assailed by creditors, kept little tangible

---

[73]Dem. 38.7: ἐγὼ δ᾽ οἶδ᾽ ἀκούων ὅτι τὴν οὐσίαν Ξενοπείθης καὶ Ναυσικράτης ἅπασαν
χρέα κατέλιπον, καὶ φανερὰν ἐκέκτηντο μικράν τινα· And. 1.118: τὰ ὀφειλόμενα opposed
to φανερὰ οὐσία.

[74]χρέως γενόμενον ἀναφανήσεται. On money itself as "invisible property" in Lysias 32.4
(τὴν μὲν ἀφανῆ οὐσίαν ἐνείμαντο, τῆς δὲ φανερᾶς ἐκοινώνουν), see Wyse [1904] 1967: 516.

[75]Isok. 17.7: ἐδόκει βέλτιστον εἶναι τὰ μὲν φανερὰ τῶν χρημάτων παραδοῦναι, περὶ δὲ
τῶν παρὰ τούτῳ [sc. Πασίωνι τῷ τραπεζίτῃ] . . . ἔξαρνον εἶναι. At §2, Isokrates' client
offers the jurors subtle word-play on bankers' avoidance of the "visible" sphere: after noting
how bankers incur obligations "without witnesses," he promises to make "*phaneron*" the way
in which he was deprived of his own deposits:Ὅμως δὲ καὶ τούτων ὑπαρχόντων ἡγοῦμαι
φανερὸν πᾶσι ποιήσειν ὅτι ἀποστεροῦμαι τῶν χρημάτων ὑπὸ Πασίωνος.

[76]Dem. 47.54: ᾤοντο μὲν γὰρ οὐ τοσαῦτα μόνον λήψεσθαι, ἀλλὰ πολλῷ πλείω· τὴν γὰρ
οὖσάν μοι ποτὲ κατασκευὴν τῆς οἰκίας καταλήψεσθαι· ἀλλ᾽ ὑπὸ τῶν λητουργιῶν καὶ τῶν
εἰσφορῶν καὶ τῆς πρὸς ὑμᾶς φιλοτιμίας τὰ μὲν ἐνέχυρα κεῖται αὐτῶν, τὰ δὲ πέπραται.

[77]Dem. 47.52: Ὁ δὲ Θεόφημος ἀντὶ τοῦ τὴν καταδίκην ἀπολαβεῖν ἀκολουθήσας ἐπὶ
τὴν τράπεζαν, ἐλθών μου τὰ πρόβατα λαμβάνει. §57: Ἔτι δὲ ἔφη τὸ ἀργύριον αὐτοῖς
κείμενον εἶναι ἐπὶ τῇ τραπέζῃ.

property but held large deposits "at the bank" (*epi tēi trapezēi*). As a practical matter, invisible banking assets were not as accessible to third parties as this pleader suggests. Even the prominent Kallippos, *proxenos* of the Herakleōtes, inquiring at a bank as to possible deposits belonging to a deceased Herakleōte, was dismissed by a slave functionary with the derisive, "And what business is it of yours?"[78]

Bankers also made loans in secrecy. A prominent example is the loan transaction in which the banker Hērakleidēs supplied the bulk of the monies but did not appear as a named creditor (see above, pp. 155–57). Through the process of bank intermediation (*dia tēs trapezēs*), *trapezai* shielded the identity of depositors whose "invisible" assets funded maritime loans (see above, pp. 151–60). In a lawsuit indirectly relating to bank assets, the bank owner Apollodōros alludes to the role of the Athenian *trapeza* as an intermediary in providing profitable investment opportunities for monies otherwise concealed by their owners (Dem. 45.64–66; see above, pp. 115–18). Through a number of banks, Demosthenes' ubiquitous father was able to invest in maritime loans and to obtain preferential returns without public disclosure (see above, pp. 121–29).

When silent payments were required to settle political disputes or to forestall prosecutions, bankers frequently provided the funds, anonymously. When a *trapezitēs* merely approached a prominent leader who was planning a politically explosive prosecution, it was widely assumed— "Here we go again!"[79] —that money was being delivered to settle a claim in which the banker himself had no involvement. Hence the ridiculous position forced on Demosthenes, who had been insulted by Meidias during the festival of Dionysos, and was approached shortly thereafter by the banker Blepaios. In order to defuse expectations that Meidias was buying freedom from prosecution for his gross violation of Athenian propriety and law, Demosthenes felt it necessary, even amidst a crowd of spectators, to "let my cloak drop so that I was left almost nude in my tunic," thus showing by his half-nakedness that he was not accepting secret payments from the *trapezitēs*,[80] a testimonial to the general populace's association of bankers and clandestine arrangements. Only occasionally, in exceptional circumstances, did the actual arrangements underlying this public perception became publicly known. In the most spectacular example, the sacred Opisthodomos, part of the Acropolis complex, was actually burned

---

[78]Dem. 52.5–6: τύχης δὲ συμβάσης τοιαύτης τῷ Λύκωνι τούτῳ ὥστε . . . ἀποθανεῖν, ἔρχεται ἐπὶ τὴν τράπεζαν Κάλλιππος οὑτοσὶ εὐθὺς ἐρωτῶν . . . 'ἆρα καὶ ἐχρῆτο ὑμῖν '; ἔφη ὁ Φορμίων· "ἀλλὰ πρὸς τί ἐρωτᾷς;"

[79]MacDowell's translation (1990: 213) of τοῦτ᾽ ἐκεῖνο. (see Greek text below, n. 80).

[80]Dem. 21.215: προσελθόντος μοι Βλεπαίου τοῦ τραπεζίτου τηλικοῦτ᾽ ἀνεκράγετε ὡς, τοῦτ᾽ ἐκεῖνο, χρήματά μου ληψομένου, ὥστε με, ὦ ἄνδρες Ἀθηναῖοι, φοβηθέντα τὸν ὑμέτερον θόρυβον θοἰμάτιον προέσθαι καὶ μικροῦ γυμνὸν ἐν τῷ χιτωνίσκῳ γενέσθαι φεύγοντα ἐκεῖνον ἕλκοντά με. For acceptance of money by other citizens, see Dem. 21.20.

down by the Treasurers of Athena in a desperate effort to avoid disclosure of their secret bank deposits of public monies supposed to be lying in their trust untouched on the sacred hill. When the *trapezai* were unable to repay the deposits, the Treasurers resorted to arson in a vain attempt to keep their bank activity secret. The ensuing investigation revealed their wrongdoing, resulting in their imprisonment—and confirming the popular association of banking with the unseen economy.[81]

Athens was threatened with serious diplomatic contretemps when Satyros, the king of Pontos, sought the return of funds which had been brought to Athens by the son of an important royal associate who had later fallen into disfavor (Isok. 17.3ff.). Because the enormous sums were all that had been salvaged from the family's wealth, the son was reluctant to hand over the funds.[82] But since Athens was highly dependent for food on imports from the Pontic kingdom,[83] the son's outright refusal to return the monies would have resulted in the Athenians' returning *him* to Pontos[84]—as required by traditional notions of *xenia* and practical political considerations.[85] In the world of disclosed assets, no satisfactory resolution was available. But in the parallel economy of invisible assets, a Solomonic solution was provided by the son's banker: "Agree to do everything that the king has ordered; hand over the monies that are visible (*phanera*); but as to the funds on deposit at the bank, not only deny their existence, but even reveal (*phainesthai*) that you are in debt on yield-bearing obligations to the bank and others."[86] The son claims that he did so. After a reconciliation between his father and the king, the Pontian was now free to withdraw his deposits from the bank and return them to the "visible" world.[87] But when he seeks to recover these funds, the banker claims that the son's earlier assertions had been true: there were no net funds on deposit at the bank,

[81]Scholion to Dem. 24.136. See above, pp. 114–15.

[82]Isok. 17.6: Ἡγούμην δ᾽ εἰ μὲν προοίμην ἅπαντα τὰ χρήματα, κινδυνεύειν, εἴ τι πάθοι ἐκεῖνος, στερηθεὶς καὶ τῶν ἐνθάδε καὶ τῶν ἐκεῖ, πάντων ἐνδεὴς γενήσεσθαι.

[83]Later in the century, Demosthenes claimed that the Athenians consumed more imported grain than any other people, and that Pontos supplied as much of this grain as all other exporters combined (Dem. 20.31–33). See Garnsey 1985: 63–64, 1988: 97. At the time of the litigation over the alleged bank deposits, the Bosporan king was already an important benefactor of the Athenians, favoring them with grain at times of scarcity (Isok. 17.57). An Athenian decree of 346 honors later Bosporan rulers with the privileges previously granted to Satyros (τὰς δωρειάς, ἃς [ὁ δῆμ] ος ἔδωκε Σατύρωι; ll. 22–23, Tod 1948: 167 (= Dittenberger 1915–24: 206; I.G. II² 212+). Cf. Burstein 1978; Gajdukevič 1971: 96ff.

[84]Isok. 17.5: ἐπιστέλλει δὲ τοῖς ἐνθάδ᾽ ἐπιδημοῦσιν ἐκ τοῦ Πόντου τά τε χρήματα παρ᾽ ἐμοῦ παραλαβεῖν καὶ αὐτὸν εἰσπλεῖν κελεύειν· ἐὰν δὲ τούτων μηδὲν ποιῶ, παρ᾽ ὑμῶν ἐξαιτεῖν. §9: εἰ μὲν αὐτοῦ μένειν ἐπιχειροίην, ἐκδοθήσεσθαί μ᾽ ὑπὸ τῆς πόλεως Σατύρῳ.

[85]For the conflict between the idealized and practical implications of relationships such as that between the Athenians and Satyros, see Herman 1987: 118–28. Cf. Seibert 1979: passim.

[86]Isok. 17.7: προσομολογεῖν πάντα ποιεῖν ὅσα Σάτυρος προσέταττε, καὶ τὰ μὲν φανερὰ τῶν χρημάτων παραδοῦναι, περὶ δὲ τῶν παρὰ τούτῳ κειμένων μὴ μόνον ἔξαρνον εἶναι, ἀλλὰ καὶ ὀφείλοντά με καὶ τούτῳ καὶ ἑτέροις ἐπὶ τόκῳ φαίνεσθαι.

[87]Isok. 17.11: φανερῶς ἤδη πράξω περὶ τῶν ἐμαυτοῦ.

only loans.[88] Although the actual facts underlying the parties' dispute cannot be determined—indeed, we can only speculate as to who prevailed in the litigation[89]—the case provides unique information about otherwise hidden business and trapezitic practices, and insight into the scale and functioning of banking in the unseen economy. Unlike similar situations where the parties' mutual interests and fears might have kept the dispute out of court and the transactions secret, this litigation could be safely and openly pursued through an Athenian tribunal, even though it exposes the "unseen" economy of Athens: the Bosporan plaintiff had sought to evade not Athenian taxes, but Bosporan claims, and his family's reconciliation with the ruler of the Pontic kingdom left him free to claim the funds without fear of the Bosporan authorities.

Thus we glimpse bank activity that would otherwise have remained unseen and undisclosed. The Bosporan's deposits were significant enough to secure loans of no less than seven talents (42,000 *dr.*; §44); he had exchanged gold bullion for currency having a value of about four talents (24,000 *dr.*).[90] These sums represented enormous purchasing power, many thousands of days of skilled labor.[91] Yet in argumentation based on proofs from "probability" and "plausibility,"[92] as was usual in Athenian courts, there is no suggestion that these huge amounts were incredibly beyond the normal scope of trapezitic operations (although this argument would have significantly aided the banker's defense). To the contrary, we are told explicitly that Athenian bankers, because of their reputation for integrity, were able, in secrecy, to obtain and work with large amounts of currency.[93]

This link at Athens between banking and the hidden economy was fostered by business procedures: the unique lack of witnesses for banking obligations,[94] and the special legal recognition accorded to banking records.[95] All other Athenian commercial transactions required witnesses, even for written obligations;[96] the simple written receipt was unknown.[97] These considerations

[88]Isok. 17.10: ἔξαρνος γίγνεται πρὸς αὐτοὺς μηδὲν ἔχειν τῶν ἐμῶν.

[89]If sustained, the charges, which resemble "a plot devised by a writer of cheap fiction" (Calhoun [1926] 1968: 121), would have greatly harmed the bank. Yet we know of Pasiōn's business still flourishing at a much later date. Cf. Mathieu and Brémond [1929–42] 1963, 1: 68.

[90]§40. For the value of the 1,000 "staters" actually exchanged, see above, Chapter 5, n. 28; for the implications of this significant transaction, see Chapter 1, n. 88.

[91]For the high purchasing power of these monies, see Chapter 1, n. 92.

[92]See, for example, §§31, 36, 53 (τεκμήρια), 46, 54 (εἰκός).

[93]Isok. 17.2: Τὰ μὲν γὰρ συμβόλαια τὰ πρὸς τοὺς ἐπὶ ταῖς τραπέζαις ἄνευ μαρτύρων γίγνεται . . . τοιούτους . . . οἳ . . . χρήματα πολλὰ διαχειρίζουσι καὶ πιστοὶ διὰ τὴν τέχνην δοκοῦσιν εἶναι.

[94]Ibid.: τὰ μὲν γὰρ συμβόλαια τὰ πρὸς τοὺς ἐπὶ ταῖς τραπέζαις ἄνευ μαρτύρων γίγνεται. Cf. §53: περὶ τῶν πρὸς τοὺς ἐπὶ ταῖς τραπέζαις συμβολαίων . . . οὐ γὰρ δὴ μάρτυράς γ' αὐτῶν ποιούμεθα.

[95]For these ὑπομνήματα, see above, p. 119. See also above, Chapter 5, n. 57.

[96]Unwitnessed written agreements were unrecognized and unenforceable until very late in the fourth century. See Thomas 1989: 41–45; above, pp. 178–79.

[97]See Hasebroek 1923: 393ff.; Pringsheim 1955: 287–97.

evoked, in nonbanking transactions, strong dependence on third-party witnesses, and a correspondent lack of confidentiality. In contrast, funds delivered to a *trapezitēs* were known only to the banker, or at most to the group of family members who helped in the operation of the *trapeza* (see above, pp. 70–82). Indeed, the widespread use of bankers to effectuate and monitor business transactions seems an effort to obtain the advantages of bankers' commitment to secrecy.[98] Although bankers normally did maintain written records of their transactions, the verb *aphanizein* ("to erase") came to refer to banking transactions that were omitted even from the banks' internal records.[99]

In foregoing written references to the deposit of funds, the *trapezitai* themselves ran no financial risk. To the contrary, in the event of dispute the banker could rely on his records—with their high evidentiary significance—to establish the absence of deposits, and thus to avoid a claim for return of funds. (The banker's defense in Isokrates 17 is based on this contention.) But loans engendered more complex considerations. To forestall later denials by debtors, lenders needed witnesses who could confirm that the requisite monies had actually been advanced to the borrowers.[100] This public procedure necessarily rendered visible (*phaneron*) funds that had been held as "invisible" assets.[101] Since borrowers would seek similar public knowledge of repayment, return of monies generally occurred before an assemblage of onlookers: the bank loan of 3,000 *dr.* in Demosthenes 33, for example, was repaid before a large crowd, which also witnessed the destruction of the relevant loan documentation.[102] This publicity provided prime motivation for the making of maritime loans "through the bank." For persons seeking to keep their assets unseen, direct loans were not feasible. But bankers used as intermediaries would keep assets "invisible." Identification of a banker as "the lender" revealed nothing as to the true source of funds. Because of the bankers' intermingling of trapezitic funds with depositors' money, even the limited use of depositors' money could not be assumed by spectators observing the disbursement or repayment of bankers' loans.

[98] In the complex dealings in maritime loans, bankers are ubiquitously present. For *trapezitai* as witnesses, and as holders of documents, see above, Chapter 5, n. 283. Cf. I.G. II² 2741 (Finley no. 39) ll. 4–6.

[99] Cf. Bogaert 1986b: 16; Lipsius 1916: 185; Andreades [1933] 1979: 341. See Dem. 45.66 (ἐργασίας ἀφανεῖς); Isaios 11.47.

[100] Cf., for example, Dem. 34.30 (witnesses to borrowing of money); Dem. 27.21 (witnesses to delivery of goods).

[101] Thus at Dem. 56.1, the lender notes that in exchange for ἀργύριον φανερὸν καὶ ὁμολογούμενον, the creditor received only paper documentation (ἐν γραμματειδίῳ δυοῖν χαλκοῖν ἐωνημένῳ καὶ βυβλιδίῳ μικρῷ πάνυ τὴν ὁμολογίαν καταλέλοιπε).

[102] §12: ἀποδοθεισῶν δὲ τῶν τριάκοντα μνῶν ἐπὶ τὴν τράπεζαν καὶ τῶν δέκα μνῶν τῷ Παρμένοντι, ἐναντίον πολλῶν μαρτύρων τάς τε συγγραφὰς ἀνειλόμεθα, καθ' ἃς ἐδανείσθη τὰ χρήματα. As the speaker in Dem. 34 noted, ὅταν δ' ἀποδιδῶσιν, πολλοὺς παρίστανται μάρτυρας, ἵνα ἐπιεικεῖς δοκῶσιν εἶναι περὶ τὰ συμβόλαια (§30). Cf. Dem. 27.58 (payment of more than six talents before numerous observers in the agora); 48.46 (presence of witnesses usual).

Where *trapezitai* held documents, the public would know nothing about the actual source of funds—especially since the loan documents were destroyed at the time of the repayment. Where individuals did make loans with their own funds and in their own names,[103] the public acknowledgment inherent in such financings could be followed by the return of the repaid funds to the *aphanēs* sphere—by deposit with a banker![104]

THE STRUCTURE OF CREDIT

Contemporary scholarship has attributed to fourth-century Athens—incorrectly (see Chapter 1)—an embedded "economy" incapable of commercial transactions separated ("disembedded") from social and political relationships. In an "embedded economy," all financial dealings would be handled entirely through sociopolitical relationships (hierarchical dependencies, extended kinship arrangements, and similar connections),[105] not by business transactions in market context. But the ubiquity of loans among apparently unrelated persons, recognized even by the strongest partisans of the "embedded" model,[106] itself belies this conceptualization. To account for this apparent inconsistency, these frequent financings have been explained as almost entirely "friendly loans" (*eranoi*, singular *eranos*), supposedly an interest-free form of social help from family or friends.[107] This explanation conflicts with the ancient evidence, however, which reveals a far more complex credit structure, in which *eranoi*—not necessarily either "interest-free" or from family and friends—combined with explicitly profit-oriented loans from bankers and private persons to supply credit to the residents and businesses of Attica.

[103]In addition to the maritime loans placed through his various bankers, Demosthenes' father, for example, had outstanding about two talents of other loans. See Dem. 27.9–11.

[104]The secrecy of the invisible economy is highly incompatible with conceptualization of Athens as a model "village" community, a perception borrowed inappropriately by Finley from Peter Laslett's work on English village life before industrialization. (Cf. Finley 1973: 17–18; 1983: 28–29.) As Ober has noted, "The polis of Athens was very much larger than a village, and the Athenian state was not constituted as a federation of villages" (1989: 31). Athens is far better conceived as an "imagined community," *imagined* "because the members of even the smallest nation will never know most of their fellow-members, meet them, or even hear of them" (Anderson 1983: 15–16).

[105]Economic functions are sometimes assumed to be embedded in either exclusively social or basically political controls. For assumed political dominance, for example, see Rahe 1984.

[106]For example, Millett 1983: 43; Finley 1985: 198 ("vast amount of moneylending").

[107]Finley 1981: 68: "A familiar and very common device all over the Greek world . . . a friendly loan . . . resorted to by everyone." Cf. Finley [1951] 1985: 85. Herman 1987: 94: "The majority of loan transactions in fourth-century Athens—and hence, presumably, in the whole of the ancient world—involved interest-free loans." This dogma of the universally available, interest-free, socially motivated loan has become generally accepted, even among those who have criticized other extreme contentions as to the primitive nature of the Athenian economy: see, for example, Thompson 1976: 53.

Actual ancient references to *eranoi* loans are invariably vague. Furthermore, these brief allusions to this form of credit are difficult to separate from two other homonymous institutions: the *eranos* as a reciprocal contribution (for example, to a joint meal), and the *eranos* as a mutual-aid society. As a result, throughout much of the nineteenth and twentieth centuries, specialists in Greek legal and economic history have disputed polemically—without reaching consensus— the various murky and somewhat contradictory references to *eranoi*.[108] Only in recent years, as insistence on a primitive Athenian economy has become dogma, has the doctrine of the interest-free *eranos* loan been proffered as a definitive explanation for the otherwise paradoxical prevalence of widespread credit in a supposedly "embedded" culture.

The earliest—and long-persisting—signification of *eranos*, however, was merely as a reciprocal contribution. Homer describes *eranoi* as joint meals to which each of the participants contributed his appropriate share.[109] From such transient mutual arrangements, the term *eranos* came to be applied to estab- lished associations;[110] on eight of the *horoi*-stones attesting to mortgage debts at Athens, the creditor is an *eranos*.[111] Finally, the word *eranos* appears as a specific type of loan with discernible characteristics permitting courtroom speakers to allude to such financing by name without having to explain its nature.

Yet there is no actual evidence that the absence of interest differentiated *eranoi* loans from other types of credit. Not a single allusion to an *eranos* loan carries any positive indication that the financing was interest-free. The al- legedly gratuitous nature of these loans is merely a scholarly inference based on a couple of equivocal comments by Theophrastos, themselves subject to variant interpretation but neither dealing with the presence or absence of a financial yield to providers of *eranoi*.[112] And, despite modern suggestions, there is

---

[108]See Boeckh [1842] 1976: 245–46 (with reference at n. 416 to earlier discussions); Lipsius [1905–15] 1966, 2: 729–35; Ziebarth, s.v., in *RE* 6: 328–30; Finley [1951] 1985: 100–106; J. W. Jones 1956: 171–72; Vondeling 1961 (emphasizing the social, not the credit, aspects of the term); Gluskina 1974; Longo 1983.

[109] *Od.* 1.226. Cf. *Od.* 11.415; schol., *Od.* 1.226. See Athēnaios 8.24; *Etymol. mag.*, s.v. "ἔρανος"; Hesiod, *Works* 722. In philosophical argument, Plato utilized the contributory con- cept of the *eranos* in metaphorical extension: see *Symp.* 177c.

[110]Aristot., *E.N.* 8.9.5 (1160a19–20): ἔνιαι δὲ τῶν κοινωνιῶν δι᾽ ἡδονὴν δοκοῦσι γίνεσ- θαι, θιασωτῶν καὶ ἐρανιστῶν· αὗται γὰρ θυσίας ἕνεκα καὶ συνουσίας. (For the textual reading, see Finley [1951] 1985: 275 n. 1.)

[111]There are also two such references on non-Attic *horoi*, one from Lemnos and the other from Amorgos (Finley nos. 30–32, 42, 70, 110). Finley struggles unconvincingly to show that these references are not to established but to "ad hoc" associations of lenders ([1951] 1985: 100–103). It is only through this idiosyncratic interpretation that he is able to claim (p. 100) that the *eranos*, as "a certain kind of club," is the "latest [signification] to put in its appearance."

[112]See Beauchet [1897] 1969, 4: 262 text and n. 3. At *Charactēres* 1.5, Theophrastos alludes to τοὺς δανειζομένους καὶ ἐρανίζοντας. The reference is so elliptical and uninformative that editors since Salmasius have conjectured a lacuna (which Navarre, Foss, and others have sought variously to fill). In any event, the passage provides absolutely no information for differentiating

nothing inherently "friendly" or noncommercial about an *eranos* loan. To the contrary, Aristotle actually states explicitly that "where a loan is involved, there is no friend, for if a man is a friend he does not lend but gives."[113] Yet *eranoi* loans are clearly not intended as gifts: to secure repayment, they were often collateralized by valuable property.[114] Lawsuits were pursued against defaulting borrowers.[115] Not surprisingly, therefore, *eranoi* appear prominently not only in social milieus, but also in business situations. In these commercial contexts (in contrast with the lack of evidence for interest-free *eranoi*), two other differentiating characteristics are well attested: group funding of *eranoi* by persons having some prior relationship to the borrower, and a provision for repayment in installments. Although a loan funded entirely by a single person is never denominated as an *eranos*,[116] even those which are clearly interest-free, a number of passages referring to "gathering together" or "collecting" *eranoi* confirm the associational nature of the *eranos* loan.[117] Although *eranoi* loans were often sought from or gathered by friends,[118] on other occasions the groups providing *eranoi* seem to have been the creditors and customers of functioning businesses.[119] In the case of the businessman Midas, who was a slave, the numerous *eranoi* loans he received could not have origi-

---

between the two terms. At *Charactères* 17.9, Theophrastos satirizes the "fault-finding" individual as capable of complaining because an *eranos* loan brings an obligation not only of repayment but of gratitude: ἐράνου εἰσενεχθέντος παρὰ τῶν φίλων καὶ φήσαντός τινος· "ἱλαρὸς ἴσθι," "καὶ πῶς;" εἰπεῖν "ὅτε δεῖ τἀργύριον ἀποδοῦναι ἑκάστῳ καὶ χωρὶς τούτων χάριν ὀφείλειν ὡς εὐεργετημένον;" A lender's expectation of gratitude as well as repayment does not prove, or even suggest, that a creditor was satisfied with gratefulness in lieu of interest.

[113]*Problems* 29.2 (950a28): οὐ δὲ τὸ χρέος, οὐ φίλος· οὐ γὰρ δανείζει, ἐὰν ᾖ φίλος, ἀλλὰ δίδωσιν. Cf. *Problems* 29.6 (950b28).

[114]Finley acknowledges this with understatement: "*Eranos*-loans were not infrequently backed up by hypothecation" ([1951] 1985: 85). Cf. his discussion (ibid., pp. 100–106) of the numerous *eranos* loans secured by real-estate encumbrance.

[115]The δίκαι ἐρανικαί were even included by Aristotle among the δίκαι ἔμμηνοι (*Ath. pol.* 52.2). Cf. Pollux 8.37. Harpokratiōn joins the δίκαι ἐρανικαί with the explicitly commercial δίκαι ἐμπορικαί (s.v. "ἔμμηνοι δίκαι"). Two adversarial actions involving *eranoi* are preserved by name: Harpokratiōn mentions a speech attributed to Lysias (*Against Aristokratēs, Concerning Guarantee of an Eranos*, frag. 16 Thalheim), and Dionysios Halikarnasos (Dein. 12) mentions a speech of Deinarchos (*Against the Children of Patrokles, Concerning an Eranos*). For what little is known specifically of the δίκαι ἐρανικαί, see Beauchet [1897] 1969, 4: esp. 267–68.

[116]There is not a single known example of such a loan (see Beauchet [1897] 1969, 4: 259–60). Sometimes, however, an individual appeared as representative of an entire group, as in Hyp., *Ath.* 11, where an *eranos* loan is described as ἐπὶ τοῦ Δικαιοκράτους ὀνόματος. For similar examples on the *horoi*-stones relating to *eranos* loans, see Finley [1951] 1985: 90, 277–78 nn. 12, 13.

[117]Antiphon, *Tetralogies* I β §9; Dem. 21.101, 53.11, 59.3; Lysias, frag. 38; Hyp., *Ath.* 11 (νεοσύλλογοι).

[118]See Theophr., *Char.* 15.7, 17.9, 22.9; Antiphon, *Tetralogies* I β §9.

[119]The *eranos* loans in Hyp., *Ath.*, and at Lysias, frag. 38, are presented in the context of financing by business customers. Indeed, in the Hypereidēs speech, the *eranoi* loans are said to

nated in traditional Athenian concepts of friendship. And beyond the collective origins of *eranoi*, the lexicographer Pollux focuses also on periodicity of payment as a characteristic—but offers no suggestion that *eranoi* loans were interest-free.[120] In the commercial context of loans for a fragrance business, the speaker in Hypereidēs, *Against Athēnogenēs*, alludes explicitly to an *eranos* "on which three installments are left."[121] In a similar business setting, in the litigation against a certain Aischinēs (Lysias, *frag.* 38), the operator of a fragrance business is accused of failing to pay "the remaining installments" of an *eranos* loan.[122]

In contrast to the absence of evidence for interest-free *eranoi* loans, we do know of bank loans that did not carry interest: the various advances made to Timotheos by his banker Pasiōn.[123] Similarly, Pasiōn's son, Apollodōros, provides funding without interest to Nikostratos (Dem. 53.12). Although explicitly interest-free, and motivated by the relationship, allegedly "friendly" between the parties, this loan is not characterized as an *eranos*: it is not part of a mutual contribution and is not payable in installments.[124] The bank owner's advance is to be repaid from an *eranos* loan to be collected in the future: there is no indication that this *eranos* is to be interest-free.[125]

Apollodōros's complex financial arrangements with Nikostratos illustrate the structure of credit and the interrelationship in Athenian life of various forms of financing, including bank loans and *eranoi* transactions. Dealings between Apollodōros and Nikostratos were extensive. For forensic purposes (to emphasize Nikostratos's subsequent "ingratitude"), Apollodōros stresses the social

---

be the source of the business's entire inventory: καὶ τῶν ἐράνων εἰς μὲν . . . ἐνεγέγραπτο . . . οἱ δ' ἄλλοι, ἐφ' οἷς εἰλήφει πάντα ὁ Μίδας, νεοσύλλογοι δ' ἦσαν. §11.

[120]Pollux 8.144: ἔρανοι, ἐρανισταί, κοινὸν ἐρανιστῶν, ἐρανικαὶ δίκαι, ἐρανικὸς νόμος, ἐράνου φορά, ἐράνου καταβολή· κατενεγκεῖν τὸν ἔρανον, πληρώσασθαι τὸν ἔρανον, ἐκλιπεῖν τὴν φοράν. ἐοίκοιεν δ' ἂν τοῖς ἐρανισταῖς καὶ οἱ συμμορῖται, καὶ τὸ παρ' Ὑπερείδῃ μετοικικῆς συμμορίας ταμίας.

[121]§11: καὶ τῶν ἐράνων εἰς μὲν οὖν, Δικαιοκράτης, ἐνεγέγραπτο, οὗ ἦσαν λοιπαὶ τρεῖς φοραί.

[122]Ὅσους δ' ἐράνους συνείλεκται, τὰς μὲν [lac. indic.] ὑπολοίπους φορὰς οὐ κατατίθησιν.

[123]Apollodōros, in his action for repayment (Dem. 49, Πρὸς Τιμόθεον ὑπὲρ Χρέως), seeks only return of principal (τὸ δοθὲν [§2]; τὰ ἑαυτοῦ κομιεῖσθαι [§3]). He states explicitly Pasiōn's expectation that in lieu of interest he might receive special consideration in the future ("if he should need something") from this political leader (ἀλλὰ καὶ ἄλλου εἴ του δέοιτο πρὸς Τιμόθεον πρᾶξαι ὑπάρξειν αὐτῷ). According to Apollodōros, the loans were unsecured and without any definite repayment date (§2: οὔτε ἐπ' ἐνεχύρῳ . . . σωθέντος δὲ ἐπὶ τούτῳ ἐγίγνετο, ὁπότε βούλοιτο εὐπορήσας ἡμῖν ἀποδοῦναι). Beauchet ([1897] 1969, 4: 231–32) cites these advances as examples of what he terms the ἄτοκον χρέος. Bogaert (1968: 356) calls them "prêts personnels sans interêts."

[124]This credit had a specified date for repayment, one year (§12: ἐνιαυτὸν ἀτόκῳ χρῆσθαι τῷ ἀργυρίῳ).

[125]Apollodōros merely says: συλλέξας δὲ ἔρανον, ὥσπερ αὐτὸς φής, λῦσαί μοι (§12).

aspects of their relationship: they were of the same (relatively young) age, they knew each other well even before they became neighbors, and thereafter they became even closer.[126] But the relationship had a heavily commercial dimension: Apollodōros's civic, military, and "other" interests kept him away from Athens, and in his absence Nikostratos managed Apollodōros's agricultural establishment.[127] This was not a mere accommodation of good fellowship on Nikostratos's part: when the bank owner was suddenly called away, he "ordered" Nikostratos to "take care of and to manage affairs at home."[128] While attempting to carry out this charge by pursuing three runaway agricultural slaves (two of whom apparently belonged to Apollodōros), Nikostratos was captured on the Saronic Gulf and sold into slavery.

Despite Apollodōros's presentation of his own subsequent efforts on his agent's behalf as a benefactor's aid to an ultimately unappreciative friend, the bank owner had at least some potential legal responsibility for Nikostratos's plight. Indeed, litigation might have established Apollodōros's responsibility for all of Nikostratos's expenses (including the cost of buying his freedom and travel monies), a total of almost 3,000 *dr.* But far from obtaining the ransom monies on some kind of "friendly" basis from his friends and relatives, or from Apollodōros, Nikostratos actually received the 2,600 *dr.* for his emancipation from certain "foreigners" (*xenoi*), and on draconian terms: a written contractual obligation calling for repayment within thirty days or additional penalties of 100 percent of the money advanced.[129] To his chagrin, his relatives and close friends provided no money: his brother had claimed an inability even to find the funds to visit Nikostratos.[130]

On Nikostratos's return to Athens, faced with the need to repay the ransom money promptly to the foreigners, he asked Apollodōros for aid. The bank

126§4: Νικόστρατος γὰρ οὑτοσί γείτων μοι ὢν ἐν ἀγρῷ καὶ ἡλικιώτης, γνωρίμως μέν μοι εἶχεν καὶ πάλαι, ἐπειδὴ δὲ . . . ἐγὼ ἐν ἀγρῷ κατῴκουν, . . . καὶ μᾶλλον ἀλλήλοις ἤδη ἐχρώμεθα. For ἐχρώμεθα as combining business and personal interaction, see above, pp. 65–66.

127§4: οὗτός τε αὖ ἐμοὶ οὐκ ἄχρηστος ἦν πρὸς τὸ ἐπιμεληθῆναι καὶ διοικῆσαι, καὶ ὁπότε ἐγὼ ἀποδημοίην ἢ δημοσίᾳ τριηραρχῶν ἢ ἰδίᾳ κατ' ἄλλο τι, κύριον τῶν ἐν ἀγρῷ τοῦτον ἁπάντων κατέλειπον.

128§5: τούτῳ δὲ προσέταξα ἐπιμελεῖσθαί τε τῶν οἴκοι καὶ διοικεῖν.

129§10: οἱ ξένοι . . . οἱ δανείσαντες τὰ λύτρα, καὶ ἐν ταῖς συγγραφαῖς εἴη τριάκονθ' ἡμερῶν αὐτὸν ἀποδοῦναι ἢ διπλάσιον ὀφείλειν. The word *xenos* has a wide range of possible meanings, including "foreigner," "stranger," "guest-friend," and "host." See Bolkestein 1939: 87–88; Whitehead 1977: 10–11; Herman 1987: 10–11. In view of Nikostratos's detention as a slave far from Athens, "foreigners" here seems the most appropriate translation. See Gernet 1954–60: "étrangers." Murray (1936–39) uses "strangers." *Pace* Herman (1987: 93), these *xenoi* clearly were not "guest-friends": the harsh terms of the loan, and the threat of fresh servitude for Nikostratos if he did not repay the loan promptly (§11: ἵνα μὴ . . . αὐτὸς ἀγώγιμος γένωμαι), are incompatible with the concept and practice of ritualized friendship.

130§6: δι' ἀπορίαν ἐφοδίων οὐ πεπορευμένος εἴη ἐπὶ τοῦτον πέμποντος τούτου αὐτῷ ἐπιστολάς. §7: κατηγορῶν τῶν ἑαυτοῦ οἰκείων ἐδεῖτό μου βοηθῆσαι αὐτῷ.

owner offered a gift of the travel money (which he had previously advanced) and 1,000 *dr.* "as an *eranos* loan" toward repayment of the 2,600 *dr.*, which did not replace, but rather depended on, bank finance. The *trapezitēs* Theoklēs lent Apollodōros the 1,000 *dr.*, and it was this bank money which Apollodōros ultimately provided as a "gift" (*dōron*) to Nikostratos (§9). But when the remainder of the funds were not forthcoming—and the "foreign" creditors were pressing him—Nikostratos sought from Apollodōros the remaining 1,600 *dr.*, which he would repay by "gathering together an *eranos.*"[131] Since Apollodōros had no further cash available, and since Nikostratos was unable to obtain the remaining funds from other participants or from further real-estate financing secured by his own farm (which was already mortgaged),[132] Apollodōros provided a *synoikia* (multiple-dwelling residential building) as security for a loan from the Athenian citizen Arkesas. We do not know whether Arkesas was a banker (as implied by Apollodōros's description of their initial meeting)[133] or merely a private citizen lending his own funds. We do know, however, that Arkesas charged interest at the rate of 1-1/3 percent per month on the 1,600 *dr.* borrowed.[134]

Despite the allusions in this episode to an *eranos* loan to be raised from a

[131]§11: πόρισον τὸ ἐλλεῖπον τοῦ ἀργυρίου. . . . Συλλέξας τὸν ἔρανον, ἐπειδὰν τοὺς ξένους ἀπαλλάξω, σοὶ ἀποδώσω ὃ ἄν μοι χρήσῃς.

[132]This effort to obtain additional financing on a property already mortgaged is a persuasive indication that the owner of pledged assets retained an interest in the excess value (in Greek terms, in the ὅσῳ πλείονος ἄξιον [Dem. 31.6]). The fact that such secondary financing required the approval of the senior creditor (for sound reasons of credit administration, a common provision in modern institutional debt instruments) establishes nothing concerning the owners' rights on foreclosure: "The rights of the debtor *vis-à-vis* the creditor [cannot] be inferred from what is known about the rights of one creditor *vis-à-vis* other creditors" (E. M. Harris 1988: 353). Such right to excess value does, however, conflict with the theory of substitutive security advanced diffidently by Finley ([1951] 1985: 110–15, where he himself noted the general uncertainty surrounding the subject and his own inability to discuss the point at length [p. 111]). Indeed, Finley was uncharacteristically tentative in suggesting that real-estate hypothecation "normally" (ibid., p. 115) utilized "substitution" (the right and obligation of a creditor to retain the asset pledged in settlement of the debt, without regard to the relation between the debt and the value of the pledged assets). Even Finley recognized that collateral security was used for real estate at Athens by the early fourth century (see Finley 1953b: 481 n. 17) and that maritime lending always utilized collateral (with the creditor's ensuing right to pursue the borrower for any deficiency after disposition of the security, and an ensuing obligation to credit the borrower with any excess; see Finley [1951] 1985: 87).

[133]Arkesas is described as having been "introduced" to Apollodōros by Nikostratos (᾿Αρκέσαντι Παμβωτάδῃ, ὃν αὐτὸς οὗτος προὐξένησεν: §13). Gernet (1954–60, 3: 92 n. 2) notes that the verb προξενεῖν is the equivalent of συνιστάναι, the somewhat ("plus ou moins") technical term used in Dem. 49 to denote an introduction to a banker. The same verb is employed in Isok. 17 to describe the introduction of Apollodōros's father, the banker Pasiōn, to his wealthy Bosporan client (§4: συστήσαντος δέ μοι Πυθοδώρου τοῦ Φοίνικος Πασίωνα ἐχρώμην τῇ τούτου τραπέζῃ).

[134]§13: Τίθημι τὴν συνοικίαν ἑκκαίδεκα μνῶν ᾿Αρκέσαντι Παμβωτάδῃ, ὃν αὐτὸς οὗτος προὐξένησεν, ἐπὶ ὀκτὼ ὀβολοῖς τὴν μνᾶν δανείσαντι τοῦ μηνὸς ἑκάστου. It is not clear who actually paid this interest: Apollodōros had offered to provide the property as security for an

group of participants, and despite Nikostratos's rebuke of his family and friends for their failure to assist him, it is important to note that the actual financing comes initially at an exorbitant rate from "foreign" lenders (about whom we know nothing), and later at Athens from Theoklēs the banker and from the Athenian Arkesas (who may have been a banker; see n. 133), with the cooperation of the bank owner Apollodōros. (Furthermore, Nikostratos appears to have had ongoing involvement with the bank of Pasiōn: note his later close cooperation with the banker Phormiōn in the protracted litigation relating to Pasiōn's *trapeza*.[135]) Although Apollodōros claims to have provided at least part of the funding purely as a gift, he actually provided no money from his own funds (except apparently for travel expenses): all other monies are supplied from commercial sources, at negotiated commercial rates. These transactions reflect the complexity of credit in a financially sophisticated society, not the "embedding" of loans in purely sociopolitical webs.

The progress of Aischinēs from retail merchant to perfume wholesaler[136] further illustrates the complexity and market orientation of business credit. Because Aischinēs was wont to pontificate about justice and moral virtue (and had been a pupil of the great ethical philosopher Sokratēs),[137] a creditor presents the jurors with Aischinēs' history of improper credit dealings—and thus allows us rare insight into various types of borrowings available at Athens, and their interrelation. Initially, Aischinēs had been financed by the banker Sōsinomos and by Aristogeiton at the high interest rate of 3 percent per month. Claiming to face bankruptcy because of these elevated charges, Aischinēs prevailed on the litigant in Lysias, frag. 38 (about whose identity and profession we know nothing) to provide working capital for a "perfume business" at the reduced interest rate of 1½ percent per month.[138] Once the business was established, nearby merchants provided Aischinēs with further financing—which resulted in more lawsuits. He gathered *eranoi* loans, with disastrous results for the lenders. Maritime creditors in the Piraeus refused to deal with him because of his failure to repay prior loans. In its size, the hoard of creditors assailing his house resembled a funeral procession.[139] Here, too, we see the

---

interest-free loan (§12), but his enumeration of his various alleged kindnesses to Nikostratos does not include such payment.

[135] Dem. 53.14: ἐπιβουλεύει μοι μετὰ τῶν ἀντιδίκων, καὶ πίστιν αὐτοῖς δίδωσιν· ἔπειτ' ἀγώνων μοι συνεστηκότων πρὸς αὐτούς, τούς τε λόγους ἐκφέρει μου εἰδώς.

[136] Lysias, frag. 38, §5: αὐτὸν δὲ ἀντὶ καπήλου μυροπώλην ἀπέδειξεν.

[137] §2: τουτονὶ Αἰσχίνην Σωκράτους γεγονότα μαθητὴν καὶ περὶ δικαιοσύνης καὶ ἀρετῆς πολλοὺς καὶ σεμνοὺς λέγοντα λόγους.

[138] §§1–2: Οὗτος ὀφείλων ἀργύριον ἐπὶ τρίσι δραχμαῖς Σωσινόμῳ τῷ τραπεζίτῃ καὶ Ἀριστογείτονι προσελθὼν πρὸς ἐμὲ ἐδεῖτό μὴ περιιδεῖν αὐτὸν διὰ τοὺς τόκους ἐκ τῶν ὄντων ἐκπεσόντα "Κατασκευάζομαι δ'" ἔφη, "τέχνην μυρεψικήν· ἀφορμῆς δὲ δέομαι, οἴσω δὲ σοι ἐννέ' ὀβόλους τῆς μνᾶς τόκους." For the signification of τέχνη, see above, Chapter 4 passim, esp. n. 3; for ἀφορμή as akin to "working capital," see above, p. 184.

[139] §§3–5: οὐχ οἱ μὲν κάπηλοι οἱ ἐγγὺς οἰκοῦντες, παρ' ὧν προδόσεις λαμβάνων οὐκ ἀποδίδωσι, δικάζονται αὐτῷ συγκλήσαντες τὰ καπηλεῖα. . . . Ὅσους δ' ἐράνους συν-

same intermixture of bank loans, *eranoi* loans, and financing (or refusal of credit) from private persons acting from commercial motivation. Failure to repay these loans results in litigation, not in the informal sanctions of the embedded economy.

Another legal case involving the perfume business demonstrates the impossibility of the traditional interpretation of the *eranos* loan as a gratuitous accommodation among Athenian "friends," and further illustrates the interaction of the banks with other sources of financing. The speech attributed to Hypereidēs in the suit *Against Athēnogenēs* involves debts contracted not by an Athenian citizen or resident alien, but by a slave, Midas, who operated a retail perfumery outlet.[140] When the slave was sold, the buyer agreed to assume the business's liabilities, which unexpectedly (the purchaser claims) amounted to the enormous total of five talents, consisting of both conventional loans (*chrea*) and *eranos* loans.[141] But clearly a slave—who for most purposes was a nonperson in the Athenian political, social, and legal universe—could not have obtained *eranos* financing if the *eranos* loan has been correctly understood as a gratuitous gesture from family and friends participating in a traditional network of mutual obligations. In this case, however, all the loans appear to have been obtained in the normal course of business, from prepayments by customers and from others having a commercial relationship to the business.[142] In contrast to the conventional loans (*chrea*), the *eranoi* are explicitly described as gathered from multiple sources, and (explicitly in one case) as having installments still to be paid.[143] The *chrea* have no associational source or periodicity of payment, thus seeming to confirm these factors (and not social relations or absence of interest) as essential in differentiating *eranos* loans from other kinds of financing.

εἴλεκται, τὰς μὲν [lac. indic.] ὑπολοίπους φορὰς οὐ κατατίθησιν, ἀλλὰ . . . διαφθείρονται. Τοσοῦτοι δὲ ἐπὶ τὴν οἰκίαν ἅμα τῇ ἡμέρᾳ ἀπαιτήσοντες τὰ ὀφειλόμενα ἔρχονται ὥστε οἴεσθαι τοὺς παριόντας ἐπ᾽ ἐκφορὰν αὐτοὺς ἥκειν τοῦ τεθνεῶτος· οὕτω δ᾽ οἱ ἐν τῷ Πειραιεῖ διάκεινται ὥστε πολὺ ἀσφαλέστερον εἶναι δοκεῖν εἰς τὸν Ἀδρίαν πλεῖν ἢ τούτῳ συμβάλλειν· πολὺ γὰρ μᾶλλον ἃ ἂν δανείσηται αὐτοῦ νομίζει εἶναι ἢ ἃ ὁ πατὴρ αὐτῷ κατέλιπεν.

[140]On several separate occasions, Midas is explicitly characterized as personally having contracted the debts: §6, ὅσον μέντοι ὀφείλουσιν ἀργύριον; §10, "καὶ εἴ τῳ ἄλλῳ ὀφείλει τι Μίδας" (purportedly the actual language of the purchase agreement); §20, ὀφείλοντα Μ[ίδαν]. For slaves' legal rights in commercial dealings, see the discussion above, pp. 96–98.

[141]§7: τοὺς χρήστας καὶ τοὺς πληρωτὰς τῶν ἐράνων ἐν ὁμολογίᾳ λαβών; §14: τοὺς ἐράνους [καὶ τὰ χρέα; §19: τὰ χρέα καὶ τοὺς ἐράνους.

[142]The seller describes the business as having some financing provided by suppliers and by others having dealings with the operation: ὅσον ὀφείλουσιν ἀργύριον, μύρου τέ τινος τιμὴν Παγκάλῳ καὶ Προκλεῖ καὶ εἴ τι ἄλλο κατέθετό τις ἐπὶ τὸ μυροπώλιον τῶν προσφοιτώντων (§6). The business's inventory was represented as sufficient to repay these loans: πολλῷ πλείω φορτία ἐστὶν τούτων ἐν τῷ ἐργαστηρίῳ, μύρον καὶ ἀλάβαστροι καὶ ζμύρνα, καὶ ἀλλ᾽ ἄττα ὀνόματα λέγων, ὅθεν πάντα ταῦτα δ[ιαλυθ]ήσεται ῥᾳδίως (§6). This inventory had been entirely or largely funded by *eranos* loans (cf. §11: οἱ δ᾽ ἄλλοι [sc. ἔρανοι], εφ᾽ οἷς εἰλήφει πάντα ὁ Μίδας).

[143]§11: καὶ τῶν ἐράνων εἷς . . . οὗ ἦσαν λοιπαὶ τρεῖς φοραί.

The role of the *trapeza* in the Athēnogenēs case appears tantalizingly similar to that of Theoklēs' bank, which actually funded the anticipated *eranos* loan to Nikostratos (Dem. 53.8–9; see above, pp. 212–13). The purchaser from Athēnogenēs gathers the purchase price of 4,000 *dr.* from every possible source, including his friends, but the funds are actually deposited "at the bank."[144] Was the bank lending money to those who were participating in funding the purchase price, just as Theoklēs' bank provided the purchase price for Nikostratos's freedom (see above)? Although we know nothing about the source of the non-*eranoi* loans incurred by Midas the slave-businessman, again this silence in itself does not preclude bank financing. As always, silence and shadow are part of clandestine business operations.

BANK FAILURES AND ECONOMIC HISTORY

Spectacular bank failures, mentioned parenthetically in murky references, illuminate the shadowy significance of the *trapezai*: Attica's dependence on the banks for vital economic functions, the financial risks of trapezitic operations, the secrecy enveloping bank transactions. The insolvencies are pervasive, yet never clearly explained. A sacred building on the Akropolis was torched to hide the loss, due to bank failures, of funds improperly and secretly entrusted to bankers (see above, pp. 114–15). Investigations were undertaken, but the imprisonment of the Goddess's officials still leaves us, as it presumably left the ancient investigators, ignorant as to the extent and time of the bank failures, the amounts involved in the embezzlements, the relationships among the bankers, even the identity of the *trapezitai*. Aristolochos's bank fails: there is fleeting reference to real-estate speculation, to many depositors losing funds, to insolvency, but there is no "hard" information.[145] Hērakleidēs' bank makes a maritime loan, seemingly in the normal course of clandestine business activity; yet in the short time before the advance is repaid, we learn of the bank's unexpected demise and of liquidators ("guarantors") winding up the business in an orderly, almost routine manner (see above, pp. 154–56).[146] The banker

---

[144]§5: συναγαγὼν δ᾽ ἐγὼ πανταχόθεν καὶ τοὺς φίλους ἐνοχλήσας καὶ θεὶς ἐπὶ τὴν τράπεζαν τὰς τετταράκοντα μνᾶς.

[145]Dem. 36.50: ὁρᾶς τὸν Ἀριστόλοχον τὸν Χαριδήμου· ποτ᾽ εἶχεν ἀγρόν, εἶτά γε νῦν πολλοί· πολλοῖς γὰρ ἐκεῖνος ὀφείλων αὐτὸν ἐκτήσατο. Cf. Dem. 45.63–64: ταῦτ᾽ ἴσασι πολλοὶ τῶν ἐνθάδ᾽ ὄντων ὑμῶν. ἐπειδὴ δ᾽ ἀπώλετ᾽ ἐκεῖνος καὶ τῶν ὄντων ἐξέστη . . . τῷ μὲν υἱεῖ τῷ τούτου πολλῶν πραγμάτων ὄντων . . . Ἀπόληξις καὶ Σόλων καὶ πάντες ἄνθρωποι μᾶλλον βοηθοῦσι.

[146]For the unanticipated demise of the bank, see Thompson 1979: 236–37. Nothing is known about the functioning of these liquidators: see Endenburg 1937: 15–18, 185–87. Contrary to the pervasive indications of Athenian bankers' freedom from governmental regulation (see Chapter 3), Bogaert has suggested that these "guarantors" (ἐγγυηταὶ τῆς τραπέζης) were quasi-governmental personages whom bankers were obligated to obtain, responsible for payment of potential shortfalls on insolvency (Bogaert 1974: 525). But he is able to offer only the practice of the Middle Ages as evidence!

Sōsinomos appears, charging high interest on a dangerous loan. This financing is repaid without apparent difficulty—but the banker's subsequent insolvency is revealed in a later passing reference.[147] Through all this upheaval, some banks survive from generation to generation, passing over decades from the original owners to their successors, via testament and through lease: in the well-attested case of Pasiōn, from the bankers Antisthenēs and Archestratos, to Pasiōn, to his sons, on lease to Phormiōn, then to Xenōn, Euphraios, Euphrōn and Kallistratos, an attested history of at least half a century.[148]

Yet such continuity appears not to have been the norm. Demosthenes marvels at Apollodōros's lack of gratitude to Phormiōn, who "preserved the bank" and paid a large rental, whereas "the other bankers," who were not obligated to pay rent but worked for themselves, "all failed."[149] Demosthenes also alludes to Phormiōn's many kindnesses to Pasiōn's family, expressing amazement that Apollodōros through litigation was now attempting to destroy his benefactor—the likely result if Apollodōros prevailed, just as Sōsinomos, Timodēmos, "and the other bankers, when it was necessary to settle with their creditors, had to surrender all their goods."[150] Demosthenes proceeds to warn the Athenians of the dire consequences for Attica if a financier of Phormiōn's importance should be harmed:

> For he has been shown as having provided funds to you greater than he or anyone else has [personally] accumulated. His funding capability (*pistis*) among his collaborators provides for that much money and more by far, through which he makes

[147]For Sōsinomos's loan at 36% annualized interest to a certain Aischinēs, a credit risk of such notoriety that "in the Piraeus people are of the opinion that it seems to be much less risky to 'sail to the Adriatic' " (Lysias, frag. 38.2), see above, pp. 144, 213–14. On his bank's failure, see Dem. 36.50.

[148]On the longevity of Pasiōn's bank, see above, pp. 129–36, 183–89.

[149]Dem. 36.51: οἱ μὲν γὰρ ἄλλοι τραπεζῖται μίσθωσιν οὐ φέροντες, ἀλλ᾽ αὐτοὶ ἑαυτοῖς ἐργαζόμενοι, πάντες ἀπώλοντο, οὗτος δὲ μίσθωσιν φέρων δύο τάλαντα καὶ τετταράκοντα μνᾶς ὑμῖν ἔσωσε τὴν τράπεζαν.

[150]Ibid., §§49–50: τὸν σώσαντα μὲν ἐξ ἀρχῆς τὰ πράγματα . . . τοσαῦτα δ᾽ αὐτὸν τοῦτον ἀγάθ᾽ εἰργασμένον . . . τοῦτον οἴεται δεῖν ἑλὼν τηλικαύτην δίκην ἀδίκως ἐκβαλεῖν. οὐ γὰρ ἄλλο γ᾽ ἔχοις οὐδὲν ἂν ποιῆσαι. εἰς μὲν γὰρ τὰ ὄντ᾽ εἰ βλέπεις ἀκριβῶς, ταῦθ᾽ εὑρήσεις ὧν ἔστιν, ἐάν, ὃ μὴ γένοιτο, ἐξαπατηθῶσιν οὗτοι. ὁρᾷς τὸν Ἀριστόλοχον . . . καὶ τὸν Σωσίνομον καὶ τὸν Τιμόδημον καὶ τοὺς ἄλλους τραπεζίτας, οἵ, ἐπειδὴ διαλύειν ἐδέησεν οἷς ὤφειλον, ἐξέστησαν ἁπάντων τῶν ὄντων. (Rennie's suggested alteration of ἁπάντων to ἅπαντες is unjustified: the manuscripts are unanimous in reading ἁπάντων; the later reference in §51 to πάντες ἀπώλοντο is explicitly limited to bankers who were obligated to pay rentals.) The surrender of property (ἐκστῆναι τῶν ὄντων) is a well-attested procedure in insolvency (Dem 34.25, 37.49, 45.64; Aristoph.. Ach. 615 and schol.; Pollux 8.145), but no information has survived as to its procedural or substantive distinction, if any, from other descriptive terms for bankruptcy (ἀνασκευάζεσθαι, ἀνατρέπεσθαι, ἀπόλλυσθαι). Caillemer ([1877–1919] 1962–63) has suggested that διαλύειν carries the technical signification "to liquidate the bank," but there is no basis for an interpretation beyond the basic "to satisfy completely" or "to repay depositors."

himself useful to you. Don't throw [this] away! Don't allow this piece of filth to bankrupt him![151]

All these elements—the economic importance of the banks, their elusive sources of funds, the risk inherent in their activities—are consonant with the picture of Athenian banking presented consistently by Demosthenes and our other sources. In Athenian finance, nothing is absolutely clear; little is dated; less is quantified for public knowledge. Athenian bank insolvencies are the predictable result of the dangers inherent in their business operations and their freedom from governmental or other regulation. As Demosthenes insists,[152] the public is entitled to be angry at bankers who fail: a moral outrage that would be improperly addressed to individual *trapezitai* if in fact most bank insolvencies resulted from systemic financial crises or generalized commercial emergencies. But the villains, yet more worthy of contumely, are the persons supposedly causing the financial failures—identified as individual borrowers who use their favorable reputations to obtain loans, which they then are unable or unwilling to repay, thus causing bank insolvencies.[153] Demosthenes focuses not on the spectacular and public periodicity of bust and boom, but on clandestine business errors affecting specific bankers. Aristolochos's bank was "destroyed" by shadowy individuals—Stephanos and "men like him;"[154] in the background is a suggestion of unwise real-estate speculation by the banker (Dem. 36.50). The speaker in Demosthenes 33 narrates in microtomic detail the economic circumstances surrounding a disputed loan from the banker Hērakleidēs—but he passes in silence the causes of the bank's collapse. And these two cases are the best attested of Athenian bank failures. Such idiosyncratic, and veiled, causes of individual bank failures may properly be analyzed as structural: the risks inherent in Athenian banking result in the foreseeable failure of some banks on a recurring basis through lenders' inability to collect funds advanced to specific borrowers in confidential transactions. Where banks

---

[151]Ibid., §§57–58: τοσαῦτα γάρ, ὦ ἄνδρες Ἀθηναῖοι, χρήμαθ' ὑμῖν ἀνεγνώσθη προσηυπορηκώς, ὅσ' οὔθ' οὗτος οὔτ' ἄλλος οὐδεὶς κέκτηται, πίστις μέντοι Φορμίωνι παρὰ τοῖς εἰδόσι καὶ τοσούτων καὶ πολλῷ πλειόνων χρημάτων, δι' ἧς καὶ αὐτὸς αὐτῷ καὶ ὑμῖν χρήσιμός ἐστιν. ἃ μὴ προῆσθε, μηδ' ἐπιτρέψητ' ἀνατρέψαι τῷ μιαρῷ τούτῳ ἀνθρώπῳ. For παρὰ τοῖς εἰδόσι as "among his collaborators," rather than the literal "with those who know him," see Pearson 1972: 246: "παρά with the dative indicates where the credit is recognized." For *pistis* as "funding capacity," rather than the literal "credit," cf. Paley and Sandys ([1896–98] 1979: ad loc.), who observe that Phormiōn "was enabled, as a capitalist in the enjoyment of extensive credit in the commercial world, to advance [large] sums of money."

[152]Dem. 49.68: ἡδέως δ' ἂν ἔγωγε πυθοίμην ὑμῶν εἰ ὀργίζεσθε τοῖς ἀνεσκευασμένοις τῶν τραπεζιτῶν. . . . δικαίως ὅτι ἀδικοῦσιν ὑμᾶς.

[153]Ibid.: διὰ τούτους τοὺς ἄνδρας αἱ τράπεζαι ἀνασκευάζονται, ὅταν ἀπορούμενοι μὲν δανείζωνται καὶ οἴωνται διὰ τὴν δόξαν πιστεύεσθαι δεῖν, εὐπορήσαντες δὲ μὴ ἀποδιδῶσιν, ἀλλ' ἀποστερῶσιν.

[154]Dem. 45.64: ἀπώλετ' ἐκεῖνος καὶ τῶν ὄντων ἐξέστη, οὐχ ἥκισθ' ὑπὸ τούτου καὶ τῶν τοιούτων διαφορηθείς.

were heavily involved in a single industry, as the operations of Pasiōn and Hērakleidēs appear to have been with sea finance, joint funding of a single unsuccessful transaction or individual borrower might adversely affect more than one bank (although the fragmented nature of the commercial maritime market would have mitigated the overall impact of any single difficulty). Similarly, where bankers jointly were involved in a related transaction (as with the receipt of illicit deposits from the Treasurers of Athena), difficulties would strike more than a single banker. But the industry continued: ancient evidence provides a model of individual bank operations and individual bank difficulties, continuing throughout the fourth century. At least fifteen years separate the failures of Aristolochos (not later than 350/49)[155] and Hērakleidēs (not earlier than 336),[156] but the same operational business risks, in shadowy concealment, appear to have undone them both.

A modern attempt has been made once again, through "cliometric" methods, to create an appearance of clarity and certainty in the underlying data, and thereby to justify a conclusion that contradicts the impression derived from forensic evidence. Bogaert claims that "the majority" of Athenian bank failures can be directly attributed to "commercial crises" affecting the overall economy.[157] In a society supposed by prevailing scholarly dogma entirely to lack anything resembling a differentiated economy, the banks are here seen as buffeted by macroeconomic waves that allegedly can be dated with remarkable specificity: two crises occurring in rapid succession, in 377/6 and again shortly thereafter in 371.[158] Such a phenomenon is said to be consonant with the alleged general malaise of the Greek city-states in the fourth-century, a formulation of political and social collapse often encountered in summaries of Greek history after the Peloponnesian War.[159] The complementary spectre of economic crisis is raised by specialist works on fourth-century Athenian society

---

[155]Aristolochos became insolvent prior to delivery of Dem. 36 (see §50). This speech can be dated with exactitude to 350/49: see Gernet 1954–60, 1: 204 n. 3.

[156]Only in 341 did Athens and Byzantion resume normal trading relations, when the two states entered into a treaty of alliance. The speaker had only become active in commerce some seven years earlier (Dem. 33.4). His presentation, then, cannot be dated earlier than 334. The bank failure occurred two years before his presentation (§5).

[157]Bogaert 1986a: 29: "Nous avons déjà montré ailleurs que la plupart des banqueroutes athéniennes tombent dans deux périodes de crise politique et économique. . . . [R. Bogaert, Hellenische Poleis I 522–27]." Bogaert 1986b: 19: "In meinen Studien habe ich gezeigt, daß die Mehrzahl der athenischen Bankrotte durch wirtschaftliche Krisen bedingt waren."

[158]Bogaert 1974: 523: "Ins Jahr 377/376 . . . wäre also der Bankkrach datiert. . . . In dieses Jahr [371] kann die zweite attische Bankkrise datiert werden."

[159]For example, cf. Cary (1963: xv), who alludes to the "consciousness of political failure" in the fourth century and concludes that "the age of Pericles . . . was the beginning of a slow but long decline. . . . They [the Greeks] proved unequal to the task of putting their own house in order." See Mossé 1973: passim; Pečirka 1976; David 1984.

bearing rubrics such as "The Domestic Crisis at Athens in the Fourth Century: Financial and Military Difficulties."[160]

Yet even if we posit a sharp deterioration in the social and financial position of Athens after the Peloponnesian War,[161] by the 370s, the alleged decade of banking crisis, Athens was experiencing not a period of depressed collapse but rather an impressive economic success—a period of material well-being that continued at least until 330.[162] After its incredible diplomatic and military success (in 378/7) in reconstituting its naval confederation and political alliance, Athens during the next decade enjoyed a remarkable prosperity—secure grain supplies, expanded commercial activity in the *emporion*, the beginning of a revival of mining, and the welcome resultant increase in critical silver supplies.[163] During this era of expansion, macroeconomic waves of *trapezitic* collapse would have been, at the least, paradoxical. Not surprisingly, then, the evidence for pervasive bank calamities in 377/6 and again in 371 proves, on analysis, nonexistent.

There is, in fact, absolutely no ancient evidence of a financial crisis in 371. Modern insistence on a systemic banking collapse in this year is based entirely on an unfounded and contorted interpretation of a single passage, Demosthenes 36.50–52.[164] There, in commenting on Pasiōn's gratitude (in contrast to his

---

[160]A section (pp. 303–32) of Mossé [1962] 1979. Cf. Musti 1981: 125–34. See Mossé 1972: 137: "Il est tentant—et je l'ai fait moi-même—de parler d'une crise de l'économie athénienne au IV siècle, et d'expliquer par cette crise l'incontestable malaise social qui entraine la cité vers son déclin." By 1972, however, Mossé ("ayant repris l'ensemble de ces problèmes depuis quelques années") was reluctant to accept such a facile explanation (ibid.).

[161]See Strauss 1986: 42–69. Cf. Meiggs 1972: 257.

[162]In *Athens in Decline* (1973), which deals with "the crisis that the city-state was undergoing" in the fourth century, Mossé pays special attention to the prosperity enjoyed by Athens after 380, especially after "the reopening of the Straits route from 378 onwards" (1973: 42–49). For the longevity of this economic blossoming, see ibid., pp. 90–91. Indeed, in 341, Demosthenes was able to declare (9.40) that Greece as a whole was now far more prosperous than ever previously.

[163]On the "Second Athenian Confederation," see Cargill 1981; Accame 1941; Marshall 1905. For the political history of the period, see Seager 1974, and Momigliano 1934. On the *emporion*, see above, Chapter 3, n. 35. On the reopening of the mines, see Crosby 1950, and Hopper 1953, 1968.

[164]§§50–52: ὁρᾷς τὸν Ἀριστόλοχον . . . καὶ τὸν Σωσίνομον καὶ τὸν Τιμόδημον καὶ τοὺς ἄλλους τραπεζίτας, οἵ, ἐπειδὴ διαλύειν ἐδέησεν οἷς ὤφειλον, ἐξέστησαν ἁπάντων τῶν ὄντων. σὺ δ' οὐδὲν οἴει δεῖν σκοπεῖν οὐδ' ὧν ὁ πατὴρ σοῦ πολλῷ βελτίων ὢν καὶ ἀμείνων φρονῶν πρὸς ἅπαντ' ἐβουλεύσατο· ὅς, ὦ Ζεῦ καὶ θεοί, τοσούτῳ τοῦτον ἡγεῖτο σοῦ πλείονος ἄξιον εἶναι καὶ σοὶ καὶ ἑαυτῷ καὶ τοῖς ὑμετέροις πράγμασιν ὥστ' ἀνδρὸς ὄντος σοῦ τοῦτον, οὐ σὲ τῶν ἡμίσεων κατέλιπεν ἐπίτροπον καὶ τὴν γυναῖκ' ἔδωκεν καὶ ζῶν αὐτὸν ἐτίμα, δικαίως, ὦ ἄνδρες Ἀθηναῖοι· οἱ μὲν γὰρ ἄλλοι τραπεζῖται μίσθωσιν οὐ φέροντες, ἀλλ' αὐτοὶ ἑαυτοῖς ἐργαζόμενοι, πάντες ἀπώλοντο, οὗτος δὲ μίσθωσιν φέρων δύο τάλαντα καὶ τετταράκοντα μνᾶς ὑμῖν ἔσωσε τὴν τράπεζαν. ὧν ἐκεῖνος μὲν χάριν εἶχεν, σὺ δ' οὐδένα ποιεῖ λόγον. On the text, see n. 150 above.

son Apollodōros's hostility) toward Phormiōn for preserving the bank while paying substantial annual rents, the orator alludes to a number of bankers who became insolvent even without having to make lease payments:

> You [Apollodōros] see Aristolochos the son of Charidēmos . . . and Sōsinomos and Timodēmos and the other bankers who—when it was necessary to settle with their creditors—had to surrender all their property. But you think that it is not necessary to consider any of those factors which your father, being better by far than you and calculating better, devised in regard to the entire situation. Your father who (by Zeus and the gods!) considered this man to be so much more worthy than you—for yourself and for himself and for your matters—that he did not leave you, even though you were an adult, as guardian of [your younger brother's] half [of the property], and he gave [him] his own wife, and while alive he honored him. Justly, men of Athens! For the other bankers, not making lease payments, but themselves working for themselves, all perished, but this man carrying a lease of 16,000 *dr.* saved the bank for you. For which Pasiōn had gratitude, but you make no account of it.

Since Pasiōn had not yet leased his bank to Phormiōn in 372, and since Pasilamon died in 370/69, Bogaert (1974: 523) has argued that a "bank crisis" must have occurred in 371. Although this "chronology" has gained general acceptance,[165] in reality the passage dictates only one, much more limited, chronological inference: Pasiōn's bank was under lease to Phormiōn in 371. Demosthenes' statement is generic, and should be understood generically: banking is a dangerous business; many *trapezitai* have failed even without the burden of lease payments. Gratitude is therefore owed to Phormiōn by the beneficiaries of his banking skills. Far from establishing mass trapezitic insolvencies in 371, there is absolutely no indication here, or elsewhere, that even a single banker failed in or around 371. Indeed, the text does not even suggest a simultaneous occurrence or interconnection of the bank insolvencies to which it alludes. Since the orator actually made his court presentation at least twenty years after 371 (see n. 155 above), the bankruptcies mentioned might have occurred at any time during the two decades following Pasiōn's death—or even prior to the initial leasing of the bank. Since Bogaert has also posited a second "banking crisis" only a few years earlier, why should one or more of the banking failures alluded to in Demosthenes 36 not have occurred during this earlier, purportedly cataclysmic period?[166] But in reality, the banking crisis of 377/6 is no less chimerical than that of 371.

A number of bankers encountered financial difficulties following their illicit

[165]Thus, for example, Pearson (1972: 241) alludes to "a financial panic in Athens not recorded in the historians, but [which] can be dated with reasonable certainty in 371–70." Cf. Isager and Hansen 1975: 55, 96.

[166]Humphreys (1970b: 253) has already noted the anomaly of *two* crises within so short a period and has suggested that in any case surviving evidence is compatible with a single crisis.

receipt of public funds from the Treasurers of the sacred funds of Athena, the officials who controlled the monies and valuables held in the Goddess's name (see above, pp. 114–15).[167] Yet from the mere fact that several banks reportedly failed in connection with this episode, a "banking crisis" has been constructed—and on the basis of a contorted, highly speculative, chronological argument, this "crisis" has even been dated with seeming exactitude to the year 377/6.[168] Inferences have even been made purporting to connect this otherwise unknown "banking collapse" with events known to have actually occurred in that year.[169] Yet virtually every aspect of this scandal is unclear. In fact, arguments have been advanced for dating this episode as early as 406.[170] Even if one prefers a later date (as I do),[171] the event can be attributed, with equally reasonable justification, to any year in the three decades between 385 and 354. In any case, the incident offers no basis for inferring widespread financial difficulty at any time.

The scandal is described in two separate ancient manuscript notes ("scholia") explaining Demosthenes' allusion, in his speech *Against Timokratēs*, to the imprisonment of the Treasurers of Athena and the Treasurers of the Other Gods after the Opisthodomos, the location of the divinities' funds, was burned.[172] One scholion explains:

[167]On these officials, see Aristot., *Ath. pol.* 47.1; Ferguson 1932 (pp. 129ff. there for this episode). They controlled the richest treasury in Athens: at the outbreak of the Peloponnesian War it contained about 6,000 talents (Thuc. 2.13.3), and despite its depletion during the war (toward the end, nonmonetary dedications had been melted down to meet the state's requirements, schol. Aristoph., *Ran.* 720 = Phil. 328 F 141a), this treasury was again rebuilt in the fourth century (see, for example, I.G. II² 1414.51, as revised by Woodward 1940: 391–92), partly from state surpluses, which at least on occasion were transferred to this fund. See I.G. II² 1443.12–13; Hansen 1986: 263.

[168]Bogaert 1974: 523: "Da verschiedene Banken zu derselben Zeit zusammengebrochen sind, kann von einer richtigen Bankkrise in Athen in dem Jahre, in dem der *Opisthódomos* durch Brand verwüstet wurde, gesprochen werden . . . ins Jahr 377/6."

[169]Bogaert cites as a possible cause of the "crisis" the Spartan fleet's effort in 376 to block grain shipments to Athens (1974: 525–26). But this initiative could not have caused bank losses on trade loans, or any other business difficulty. The interdiction was entirely ineffective and immediately eliminated; the Athenian navy escorted the grain ships safely to the Piraeus, and Chabrias followed with a decisive naval victory at Naxos, coming close to destroying the entire Lakedaimonian fleet. Diod. 15.34.3–4: ἃ δὴ πυθόμενος ὁ δῆμος τῶν Ἀθηναίων ἐξέπεμψε στόλον παραφυλάξοντα τὴν σιτοπομπίαν ὃς καὶ διέπεμψεν εἰς τὸν Πειραιέα τὴν κομιζομένην ἀγοράν. μετὰ δὲ ταῦτα Χαβρίας μὲν ὁ τῶν Ἀθηναίων ναύαρχος μετὰ τοῦ στόλου παντὸς πλεύσας ἐπὶ τὴν Νάξον συνεστήσατο πολιορκίαν. Cf. Xen., *Hell.* 5.4.60–61.

[170]Dörpfeld 1887: 44–45, 203; 1919: 20; Judeich 1929: 411–12; 1931: 263 n. 4.

[171]Although Xenophon (*Hell.* 1.6.1) reports a fire at "the old temple of Athena at Athens" in 406, this cannot be the blaze mentioned by Demosthenes in the context of the Treasurers' trial: the orator explicitly states that he is omitting examples of officials who had been imprisoned in cases prior to 403/2 (24.133: τοὺς μὲν οὖν πρὸ Εὐκλείδου ἄρχοντος ἐάσω).

[172]Treasurers, probably of Athena, are attested at Athens as early as the middle of the sixth

Some people say that the treasurers themselves stole from the funds; others, that they lent to some bankers the State's funds that had been placed in the Opisthodomos. Then, when the bankers were unable [to repay the funds], the treasurers, falling into an inability [to repay the funds], burned the place, so that they might attribute the loss to the fire. And these men were thus imprisoned, until the time when they were judged, as were the Treasurers of the Other Gods. For the latter also were implicated, even though they themselves had not burned [the place]. The Opisthodomos was in back of the Goddess, where the funds also were.[173]

The other note says:

It must be recognized that funds both from the Other Sanctuaries of the Gods and from Athena were placed in a certain building in back of the Akropolis, the so-called Opisthodomos, and certain treasurers had been assigned to the guarding of these. Once then, when considerable funds had been accumulated there, it was determined by the treasurers that, unknown to the State, they should lend these [funds] to the bankers, so that [the treasurers] themselves might profit thereby. After they had done this, the banks later happened to become insolvent. Then it was determined by them to burn the Opisthodomos, so that the funds should seem to have been consumed by the fire and not by themselves.[174]

The two notes are neither identical nor even entirely consistent. The first reports an alternate tradition, that the treasurers acted on their own, without any in-

---

century. See I.G. I³ 510; cf. Jeffery 1961: 72, 77, no. 21. The Treasurers of the Other Gods were created in the fifth century by decree of the Assembly (I.G. I³ 52), but (as with virtually every other aspect of the chronology for these two boards and their interaction) the date is highly disputed. (For a summary of the complex disputes that have raged about the fifth-century chronology, see Fornara and Samons 1990: app. 10, 182–87.) The two boards were amalgamated in the late fifth century (406/5?: see Ferguson 1932: 104ff.; Thompson 1970: 61ff.; Meritt 1978: 292ff.). They were separated again in about 385, but rejoined not later than 342/1 (346/5?: see Linders 1972: 74 n. 57). See generally Linders 1975.

[173]οἱ μὲν φασὶν ὅτι ἔκλεψαν ἀπὸ τῶν χρημάτων αὐτοί, οἱ δ' ὅτι τὰ χρήματα τῆς πόλεως κείμενα ἐν τῷ ὀπισθοδόμῳ, ‹ὥστε› τισὶ δανεῖσαι τραπεζίταις τοὺς ταμίας. ἀπορησάντων οὖν τῶν τραπεζιτῶν εἰς ἀπορίαν ἐλθόντες οἱ ταμίαι ἐνέπρησαν τὸν τόπον, ἵνα τῷ πυρὶ τὴν ἀπώλειαν λογίσωνται. καὶ οὗτοι οὖν ἐδεσμεύθησαν, ἕως ὅτε ἐκρίθησαν, καὶ οἱ τῶν ἄλλων θεῶν. καὶ οὗτοι γὰρ οἱ ταμίαι συνεσχέθησαν, μή ποτε αὐτοὶ ἐνέπρησαν. ἦν δὲ ὁ ὀπισθόδομος τὸ ὄπισθεν τῆς θεοῦ, ὅπου ἦν καὶ τὰ χρήματα (Dilts 1983–86: 272a).

[174]ἰστέον ὅτι χρήματα καὶ τῶν ἄλλων ἱερῶν τῶν θεῶν καὶ τῆς Ἀθηνᾶς ἔκειτο ἔν τινι οἰκήματι ὀπίσω τῆς ἀκροπόλεως τῷ καλουμένῳ ὀπισθοδόμῳ, καὶ ἦσάν τινες τεταγμένοι ταμίαι ἐπὶ τῇ φυλακῇ τούτου. ποτὲ οὖν πολλῶν χρημάτων ἀνενεχθέντων ἐκεῖσε ἔδοξε τοῖς ταμίαις, ὥστε λάθρα τῆς πόλεως δανεῖσαι ταῦτα τοῖς τραπεζίταις, ἵν' αὐτοὶ κερδάνωσιν ἐκ τούτου. ὡς δὲ τοῦτο ἐποίησαν, ἔτυχεν ὕστερον ἀνατραπῆναι τὰς τραπέζας. ἔδοξεν οὖν αὐτοῖς ἐμπρῆσαι τὸν ὀπισθόδομον, ἵνα δόξῃ τὰ χρήματα ὑπὸ τοῦ πυρὸς ἀναλωθῆναι καὶ μὴ ὑπ' αὐτῶν (Dilts 1983–86: 272b).

volvement with bankers ("the treasurers themselves stole the funds"). The location of the Opisthodomos is suggested variously ("in back of [the statue of] the Goddess"; "a certain building in back of the Akropolis").[175] The first note exonerates the Treasurers of the Other Gods for the burning of the Opisthodomos; the second specifies the motivation for the defalcation ("so that [the Treasurers] themselves might profit thereby"). But neither note in any way suggests that the insolvency of these specific bankers was part of an overall fiscal, financial, or trapezitic crisis. There is, of course, nothing inexplicable in the contemporaneous insolvency of several bankers who had been working together on an unlawful and corrupt plot. The routine financial interrelationships of various funding sources has been discussed above. As businesses producing risk-laden revenues from other people's money, Athenian banks were inherently subject to collapse. A specific example of an expected phenomenon does not justify the invention of an otherwise unattested but allegedly massively traumatic, state-wide, economy-wide dislocation.

The limited financial impact of the scandal may also explain the difficulty in dating its occurrence. Since Demosthenes and the two ancient notes all explicitly mention two separate boards of treasurers, those of Athena and those of the "Other Gods," the incident could not have occurred earlier than 386/5: in that year the two boards, which had been amalgamated in the late fifth century, were separated.[176] Dinsmoor in 1932 had sought, by long and tortuous argument, to establish from a multitude of topographical and epigraphical evidence (much of it subject to variant interpretation and highly disputed in scholarly polemic over many years[177]) that the specific year 377/6 was the necessary date of the fire that had been intended to obfuscate the Treasurers' defalcation, and therefore of the insolvency of the bankers to whom the Treasurers had advanced the sacred funds. Although Dinsmoor advanced a variety of tenuous contentions to support his conclusion,[178] the only objective evidence for the 377 date was a fragmentary inscription (I.G. II² 1654) dealing with Erechtheion accounts and making mention of the fire. By making questionable connections

---

[175]Scholars have been unable to determine even which of the buildings on the Akropolis contained or constituted the "Opisthodomos" referred to by the scholiasts. Candidates include the "ancient temple" of Athena, a term possibly applicable to either the "Erechtheion" or the remnants of the ancient Temple of "Athena Polias" (or of the so-called Hekatompedon); the western porch of the Parthenon itself; or an entirely separate, freestanding building otherwise unknown. For a summary of the possibilities and the debate, see Hopper 1971: 110–15.

[176]The last extant mention of a united board is in 389/8 (I.G. II² 1400), and the first subsequent reference to separate groups is in 385/4 (I.G. II² 1407). Since recordation of the treasurers of 385/4 atypically does not mention the board(s) of the preceding year, it has been inferred that this board was of a different nature and hence still unified: Ferguson 1932: 14–15, 142–43.

[177]See, for example, Lolling 1890: 653 n. 3; Körte 1898: 241 n. 1; Van Hille 1904: 431; Johnson 1914: 9; Paton 1927: 462–63, 473; Kolbe 1929: 264 n. 1, 1931: 82–83.

[178]D. M. Lewis (1954: 47–49) has demonstrated the equivocal nature, at best, of Dinsmoor's various arguments.

between the Erechtheion and the Opisthodomos mentioned by Demosthenes, and then between the fire mentioned in the Erechtheion accounts and the fire mentioned by the orator, Dinsmoor was able to insist that there was physical evidence confirming his 377/6 date: Erechtheion fragment 28 mentioning the fire could be dated only to 394–391 or 377–375; a fifth-century attribution was allegedly impossible because the nine individual workers mentioned in fragments 28 and 29 are persons different from those named in the fifth-century records ("the nine individuals mentioned . . . seem to belong to a new generation of workmen"; Dinsmoor 1932: 154). Of the two epigraphically possible fourth-century periods, the 390s were ruled out since the two boards of treasurers were not separated until 386/5. Therefore, Dinsmoor concluded, the only possible date for the crucial fragment was 377–375, refined by further argument to 377/6.

On this seemingly objective basis the "banking crisis" of 377/6 has rested, and Bogaert as recently as 1986 was still referring to his earlier studies based on Dinsmoor's work as justification for a "crisis" in that year (1986b: 29 n. 42). Epigraphical discoveries move on, however. Shortly after Dinsmoor's seminal publication, a new stone was added to Erechtheion fragments 27–28: refuting Dinsmoor's reliance on the "new generation of workmen," it carries the names of three workers who *are* mentioned in the fifth-century accounts (Schweigert 1938: 268–39). This new discovery eliminates all possibility that fragments 28 and 29, together with the fire they mention, can any longer be dated to the fourth century, as Dinsmoor himself acknowledged decades ago.[179] The only objective basis for a fiscal crisis in 377/6 has thus been removed. We know only that at some time between 386/5 (the date of the separation of the two boards of treasurers) and 354 (the date of Demosthenes' speech),[180] a fire occurred at the Opisthodomos that was attributed to defalcations by the sacred Treasurers and may have involved the financial insolvency of the particular bankers with whom these treasurers had dealt. No further inference is possible, except—once again—the methodological: sound economic history is impossible if the reality of business structure, and the social relationships affecting that reality, is ignored or distorted.

In fourth-century Athens, reality encompassed the complementary opposites of visible and invisible economies. Far from being mere pawnbrokers or money changers, the *trapezitai* functioned as true bankers through deposit and lending activities especially oriented toward the invisible sphere. They thus generated risk-laden revenues through other people's money, by the operation of a business organized through the *oikos*, with functions and procedures that reflected the polarities inherent in Athenian culture. In so doing, the *trapezitai* transformed themselves—and their society.

---

[179]Dinsmoor 1940: 175; 1947: 111 n. 14, 128 n. 93.

[180]The speech was probably delivered in the summer of 353. See Dionysios Hal., *First Letter to Ammaios* 4; Kahle 1909: 40, 42, 52.

WORKS CITED

Accame, S. 1941. *La lega ateniese del secolo IV a.c.* Rome.

Ackelsberg, M. A. 1983. " 'Sisters' or 'Comrades'? The Politics of Friends and Families." In *Families, Politics, and Public Policy: A Feminist Dialogue on Women and the State*, edited by I. Diamond, pp. 339–56. New York.

Adam, S. 1989. "Aspects de la sécurité de la navigation dans l'Antiquité grecque." In *Symposion 1985*, edited by A. Biscardi, J. Mélèze-Modrzejewski, and G. Thür, pp. 283–91. Cologne.

Adams, C. D., ed. 1905. *Lysias: Selected Speeches*. New York.

Alesia, D. 1949. *Lisia: Contro i rivenditori di grano*. Florence.

Allin, E. J., and W. P. Wallace. 1954. "Impurities in Euboean Monetary Silver." *The American Numismatic Society. Museum Notes* 6: 35–67.

Amit, M. 1965. *Athens and the Sea*. Collection Latomus, vol. 74. Brussels.

Anderson, B. 1983. *Imagined Communities: Reflections on the Origins and Spread of Nationalism*. London.

Andreades, A. 1929. "Antimène de Rhodes et Cléomène de Naucratis." *Bulletin de Correspondance hellénique* 53: 1–18.

———. [1933] 1979. *A History of Greek Public Finance*. Vol. 1. Translated by C. N. Brown. New York.

Andreau, J. 1977. "M. I. Finley, La banque antique et l'économie moderne." *Annali della Scuola Normale Superiore di Pisa*, 3d ser., 7: 1130–52.

———. 1987. *La Vie financière dans le monde Romain: Les Métiers de manieurs d'argent (IVᵉ siècle av. J.-C.–IIIᵉ siècle ap. J.-C.)*. Rome.

Andreyev, V. N. 1979. "Demosthenes on Pasion's Bank. An Interpretation." *Vestnik Drevnej Istorii* 1: 134–39. In Russian with English summary.

Ardant, H. 1966. *Technique de la banque*. 5th ed. Paris.

Aron, R. 1950. *La Philosophie critique de l'histoire, essai sur une théorie allemande de l'histoire*. Paris.

Ashburner, W. 1909. *The Rhodian Sea-Law*. Oxford.

Austin, M. M. 1988. "Greek Trade, Industry, and Labor." In *Civilization of the Ancient Mediteranean*, vol. 2, edited by M. Grant and R. Kitzinger, pp. 723–51. New York.

Austin, M. M., and P. Vidal-Naquet. 1977. *Economic and Social History of Ancient Greece*. London.

Bagnall, R. S., and R. Bogaert. 1975. "Orders for Payment from a Banker's Archive: Papyri in the Collection of Florida State University." *Ancient Society* 6: 79–108.

Bain, D. 1991. "Six Greek Verbs of Sexual Congress." *Classical Quarterly* 41: 51–77.

Balabanoff, A. 1905. *Untersuchungen zur Geschäftsfähigkeit der griechischen Frau*. Leipzig.

Balog, P. 1955. "Notes on Ancient and Medieval Minting Techniques." *Royal Numismatic Chronicle and Journal of the Numismatic Society*, 6th ser., 15: 195–202.

Barker, E. 1952. *The Politics of Aristotle*. Oxford.

Barthes, R. 1972. "The Structuralist Activity." In *Critical Essays*, edited by P. Sollers, translated by R. Howard, pp. 213–20. Evanston, Ill.

Beauchet, L. [1897] 1969. *Histoire du droit privé de la république athénienne.* 4 Vols. Amsterdam.

Becker, W. A. 1877–88. *Charikles.* Revised by H. Göll. Berlin. (Non vidi.)

Behrend, D. 1970. *Attische Pachturkunden.* Vestigia: Beiträge zur Alten Geschichte, vol. 12. Munich.

———. 1975. "Die ἀνάδιϰος δίϰη und das Scholion zu Plato Nomoi 937d." In *Symposion 1971,* edited by H. J. Wolff, J. Modrzejewski, and Dieter Nörr, pp. 131–56. Cologne.

Bellinger, A. R. 1956. "Greek Mints under the Roman Empire." In *Essays in Roman Coinage Presented to Harold Mattingly,* edited by R.A.G. Carson and C.H.V. Sutherland, pp. 137–48. Oxford.

Beloch, K. J. 1912–27. *Griechische Geschichte.* 4 vols. 2d ed. Strassburg, Berlin, and Leipzig.

Bergonzini, L. 1973. "Professionalità femminile e lavoro a domicilio. Questioni generali ed esti di un'indagine statistica in alcuni communi dell'Emilia Romagna." *Statistica* 33: 323–39.

Berkowitz, L., and K. A. Squitier. 1986. *Thesaurus Linguae Graecae: Canon of Greek Authors and Works.* 2d ed. Oxford.

Bernal, M. 1987. *Black Athena.* New Brunswick, N.J.

Besta, E. 1936. *Le obbligazioni nella storia del diritto italiano.* Padua.

Bianchini, M. 1979. "La συγγραφή ed il problema della forme contrattuali." In *Symposion 1974,* edited by A. Biscardi, P. Dimakis, J. Modrzejewski, and H. J. Wolff, pp. 245–62. Cologne.

Bibliographie zur Antiken Sklaverei. 1983. Edited by E. Herrmann. Bochum.

Bidez, J. 1943. "Hermias d'Atarnée." *Bulletin de la classe des lettres et des sciences morales et politiques de l'Académie royale de Belgique* 29: 133–46.

Biezunska-Malowist, I. 1966a. "The χωρὶς οἰϰοῦντες in Demosthenes' First Philippic." *Eos* 56: 66–72. In Polish with Latin summary.

———. 1966b. "Les Esclaves payant l'*apophora* dans l'Egypt gréco-romaine." *Journal of Juristic Papyrology* 15: 65–72.

Bikerman, E. J. [*sic*]. 1939–44. "Héliodore au temple de Jérusalem." *Annuaire de l'Institut de Philologie et d'Histoire* 7: 5–40.

Billeter, G. 1898. *Geschichte des Zinsfusses im griechisch-römischen Alterthum bis auf Justinian.* Leipzig. Reprint, 1970.

Bingen, J. [1972–76] 1984. "Inscriptions (III)." *Thorikos* 8: 175–87.

Biscardi, A. 1974. *Actio pecuniae traiecticiae. Contributo alla dottrina delle clausole penali.* 2d ed. Turin.

———. 1978. "Pecunia traiecticia e stipulatio poenae." *Labeo* 24: 276–300.

———. 1982. "Introduction à l'étude des pratiques commerciales dans l'histoire des droits de l'Antiquité." *Revue internationale des droits de l'antiquité,* 3d ser., 29: 21–44.

Biscardi, A., and E. Cantarella. 1974. *Profilo di diritto greco antico.* 2d ed. Milan.

Blass, F. 1887–98. *Die attische Beredsamkeit.* 2d ed. 3 vols. in 4. Leipzig. Reprint Hildesheim, 1962.

Bleicken, J. 1985. *Die athenische Demokratie.* Paderborn.

Bloedow, E. F. 1975. "Corn Supply and Athenian Imperialism." *L'Antiquité classique* 44: 20–29.

Boeckh, A. [1842] 1976. *The Public Economy of Athens*. 2d ed. rev. Translated by G. C. Lewis. New York. (Originally published as *Die Staatshaushaltung der Athener*. Berlin 1817.)

Bogaert, R. 1963. "Le Cours du statère de Cyzique aux Ve et IVe siècles avant J.-C." *L'Antiquité classique* 32: 85–119.

———. 1964a. "De Bankzaken van de Griekse Tempels." *Handelingen van de Koninklijke Zuidnederlandse Maatschappij voor Taal- en Letterkunde en Geschiedenis* 18: 107–20.

———. 1964b. "Encore le cours du statère de Cyzique aux Ve et IVe siècles avant J.-C." *L'Antiquité classique* 33: 121–28.

———. 1965a. "Banquiers, courtiers et prêts maritimes à Athènes et à Alexandrie." *Chronique d' Égypte* 40: 140–56.

———. 1965b. "Méthodes d'analyse et numismatique. Le Problème du cyzicène III." *L'Antiquité classique* 34: 204–13.

———. 1966. *Les Origines antiques de la banque de dépôt. Une mise au point accompagnée d'une esquisse des opérations de banque en Mésopotamie*. Leyden.

———. 1968. *Banques et banquiers dans les cités grecques*. Leyden.

———. 1974. "Die Krise der Banken in Athen im 4. Jahrhundert v. u. Z." In *Hellenische Poleis*, edited by E. C. Welskopf, 1: 521–30. Berlin.

———. 1976. "L'Essai des monnaies dans l'Antiquité." *Revue Belge de numismatique* 122: 5–34.

———. 1977. "Le Cours du statère de Cyzique à Athènes aux Ve et IVe siècles avant J.-C. État de la question." *Revue Belge de numismatique* 123: 29–33.

———. 1983. "Note sur l'emploi du chèque dans l'Égypte ptolémaïque." *Chronique d'Égypte* 58: 214–18.

———. 1986a. "La Banque à Athènes au IVe siècle avant J.-C. État de la question." *Museum Helveticum* 43: 19–49.

———. 1986b. *Grundzüge des Bankwesens im alten Griechenland*. Konstanzer Althistorische Vorträge und Forschungen, Heft 18. Konstanz.

Bolin, S. 1958. *State and Currency in the Roman Empire to 300 A.D.* Stockholm.

Bolkestein, H. 1939. *Wohltätigkeit und Armenpflege im vorchristlichen Altertum*. Utrecht. Reprint, 1969.

———. 1958. *Economic Life in Greece's Golden Age*. 2d ed. Leyden.

Bongenaar, J.C.A.M. 1933. *Isocrates' trapeziticus vertaald en toegelicht*. Utrecht.

Bonner, R. J. 1905. *Evidence in Athenian Courts*. Chicago.

———. 1920. "The Legal Setting of Isocrates' *Antidosis*." *Classical Philology* 15: 193–97.

Bourdieu, P. 1977. *Outline of a Theory of Practice*. Translated by R. Nice. Cambridge.

Brants, V. 1882. "Les Papiers de banque existaient-ils sur le marché financier d'Athènes?" *Le Muséon* 1: 196–203.

Breccia, E. 1903. "Storia delle banche e dei banchieri nell' età classica." *Rivista di storia antica* 7: 107–32, 283–309.

Breglia, L. 1964. *Numismatica antica. Storia e metodologia*. Milan.

Bremmer, J. 1981. "Plutarch and the Naming of Greek Women." *American Journal of Philology* 102: 425–26.

Brockmeyer, N. 1979. *Antike Sklaverei*. Darmstadt.

Browning, R. 1969. *Medieval and Modern Greek*. London.

Brucker, G. A. 1983. *Renaissance Florence*. Berkeley.

Brun, P. 1983. *Eisphora, syntaxis, stratiotika*. Paris.

Brunner, K., and A. H. Meltzer. 1971. "The Uses of Money." *American Economic Review* 61: 784–805.

Büchsenschütz, A. B. 1869. *Besitz und Erwerb im griechischen Altertum*. Halle. Reprint, 1962.

Buckland, W. W., and A. D. McNair. 1952. *Roman Law and Common Law*. 2d ed., rev. by F. H. Lawson. Cambridge.

Burford, A. 1963. "The Builders of the Parthenon." *Parthenos and Parthenon, Greece & Rome*, suppl. vol. 10: 23–35.

Burger, A. E. 1972. *The Money Supply Process*. Belmont, Calif.

Burke, E. M. 1990. "Athens after the Peloponnesian War: Restoration Efforts and the Role of Maritime Commerce." *Classical Antiquity* 9: 1–13.

Burnett, A. P. 1971. *Catastrophe Survived: Euripides' Plays of Mixed Reversal*. Oxford.

Burns, A. R. 1927. *Money and Monetary Policy in Early Times*. London.

Burstein, S. M. 1978. "I.G. II² 653. Demosthenes and Athenian Relations with Bosporus in the Fourth Century B.C." *Historia* 27: 428–36.

Busolt, G., and H. Swoboda. 1920–26. *Griechische Staatskunde*. 2 vols. Munich.

Buttrey, T. V. 1979. "The Athenian Currency Law of 375/4 B.C." In *Greek Numismatics and Archaeology. Essays in Honor of Margaret Thompson*, edited by O. Møorkholm and N. M. Waggoner, pp. 33–45. Wetteren.

———. 1981. "More on the Athenian Coinage Law of 375/4 B.C." *Quaderni ticinesi. Numismatica e antichità classiche* 10: 71–94.

Cagan, P. 1958. "The Demand for Currency Relative to the Total Money Supply." *Journal of Political Economy* 66: 303–28.

Cahn, H. 1977. Review of M. J. Price and N. M. Waggoner, *Archaic Greek Coins. The Asyut Hoard*. *Schweizerische Numismatische Rundschau* 56: 279–87.

Caillemer, E. 1876. "Le Contrat de dépôt, le mandat et la commission, le cautionnement sistendi causa." In *Mèmoires de l'Acadèmie de Caen*: 508–42.

———. [1877–1919] 1962–63. "Anaskeuazein." In Daremberg, Saglio, Pottier, and Lafaye [1877–1919] 1962–63, 1: 265. Paris.

Calhoun, G. M. 1914. "Documentary Frauds in Litigation in Athens." *Classical Philology* 9: 134–44.

———. [1926] 1968. *The Business Life of Ancient Athens*. New York.

———. 1930. "Risk in Sea Loans in Ancient Athens." *Journal of Economic and Business History* 2: 561–84.

Camp, J. M. 1986. *The Athenian Agora*. London.

Campbell, W. 1933. *Greek and Roman Plated Coins*. Numismatic Notes and Monographs 57. New York.

Cantarella, E. 1987. *Pandora's Daughters*. Translated, with revisions, by M. B. Fant. Baltimore. (Originally published as *L'ambiguo malanno* [1981].)

Carandini, A. 1979. *L'anatomia della scimmia*. Turin.

Carey, C. 1989. *Lysias: Selected Speeches*. Cambridge.

———. 1991. "Apollodoros' Mother: The Wives of Enfranchised Aliens in Athens." *Classical Quarterly* 41: 84–89.

Carey, C., and R. A. Reid. 1985. *Demosthenes: Selected Private Speeches*. Cambridge.

Cargill, J. 1981. *The Second Athenian League. Empire or Free Alliance?* Berkeley.

Cartledge, P. A., and F. D. Harvey, eds. 1985. *Crux: Essays in Greek History presented to G.E.M. de Ste. Croix*. London.

Cary, M. 1963. *A History of the Greek World from 323 to 146 B.C.* 2d ed. London.

Cassimatis, G. 1931. *Les Intérêts dans la législation de Justinien et dans le droit byzantin*. Paris.

Casson, L. 1957. "New Light on Maritime Loans." *Eos* 48, 2 (= *Symbolae Raphaeli Taubenschlag Dedicatae* 2 [Bratislava and Warsaw]: 89–93).

———. 1971. *Ships and Seamanship in the Ancient World*. Princeton.

———. 1976. "The Athenian Upper Class and New Comedy." *Transactions of the American Philological Association* 106: 29–59. (Reprinted in Casson 1984: 35–69.)

———. 1984. *Ancient Trade and Society*. Detroit.

———. 1986. "New Light on Maritime Loans: P. Vindob. G19792 (= S.B. VI 9571)." In *Studies in Roman Law in Memory of A. Arthur Schiller*, edited by R. S. Bagnall and W. V. Harris, pp. 11–17. New York.

———. 1990. "New Light on Maritime Loans: P. Vindob G 40822." *Zeitschrift für Papyrologie und Epigraphik* 84: 195–206.

Cataldi, S. 1983. *Symbolai e relazioni tra le città greche nel V secolo a.C.* Pisa.

Cataudella, M. R. 1986. "Aspetti e strumenti della politica monetaria ateniese fra V e IV secolo." *Sileno* 12: 111–35.

Cavaignac, E. 1951. *L'Économie grecque*. Paris.

Cawkwell, G. L. 1962. "Notes on the Social War." *Classica et Mediaevalia* 23: 34–49.

Christ, M. R. 1990. "Liturgical Avoidance and *Antidosis* in Classical Athens." *Transactions of the American Philological Association* 120: 147–69.

Civiletti, P. 1934. "Origini dell' assicurazione." *Atti Associazione Italiana di Diritto Marittimo* 1, 13: 115–37.

Clairmont, C. W. 1970. *Gravestone and Epigram*. Mainz-on-Rhine.

Clark, G. 1989. *Women in the Ancient World*. Oxford.

Clerc, M. 1893. *Les Métèques athéniens*. Paris.

Cloché, P. 1941. "La Démocratie athénienne et les possédants." *Revue historique* 192: 1–45.

Cohen, D. 1983. *Theft in Athenian Law*. Münchener Beiträge zur Papyrusforschung und antiken Rechtsgeschichte, Heft 74. Munich.

———. 1989. "Seclusion, Separation, and the Status of Women." *Greece & Rome*, 2d ser., 36: 1–15.

———. 1990a. "Late Sources and the 'Reconstruction' of Greek Legal Institutions." In *Symposion 1988*, edited by A. Biscardi, J. Mélèze-Modrzejewski, and G. Thür, pp. 283–93. Cologne.

———. 1990b. "The Social Context of Adultery at Athens." In *Nomos: Essays in Athenian Law, Politics and Society*, edited by P. Cartledge, P. Millett, and S. Todd, pp. 147–65. Cambridge.

Cohen, E. E. 1973. *Ancient Athenian Maritime Courts*. Princeton.

———. 1990. "A Study in Contrast: 'Maritime Loans' and 'Landed Loans' at Athens." In *Symposion 1988*, edited by A. Biscardi, J. Mélèze-Modrzejewski, and G. Thür, pp. 57–79. Cologne.

Collingwood, R. G. 1946. *The Idea of History*. Oxford.

Colmant, H. 1990. "The Evolution of Institutional Structures and Regulations." In *Banking in France*, edited by C. de Boissieu, pp. 51–79. London.

Colombos, C. J. 1959. *International Law of the Sea*. London.

Connolly, W. 1981. *Appearance and Reality in Politics*. Cambridge.

Connor, W. R. 1971. *The New Politicians of Fifth-Century Athens*. Princeton.

———. 1989. "After Smashing the Wedgwood." *American Scholar* 58: 533–41.

Cook, R. M. 1946. "Ionia and Greece in the Eighth and Seventh Centuries B.C." *Journal of Hellenic Studies* 66: 90–91.

Costanzi, V. 1927. *Le costituzioni di Atene e di Sparta*. Bari.

Costouros, G. J. 1979. "Early Greek Accounting on Estates." Working Paper no. 21 (1976). In *Working Paper Series*, vol. 2, edited by E. N. Coffman, pp. 1–6. Richmond, Va.

Crawcour, E. 1961. "The Development of the Credit System in Seventeenth-Century Japan." *Journal of Economic History* 21: 342–60.

Crawford, M. H. 1982. *La moneta in Grecia e a Roma*. Rome.

Crockett, A. 1979. *Money: Theory, Policy and Institutions*. 2d ed. London.

Crosby, M. 1950. "The Leases of the Laurion Mines." *Hesperia* 19: 189–312.

Da Cunha, M. C. 1985. "Silences of the Law: Customary Law and Positive Law on the Manumission of Slaves in Nineteenth-Century Brazil." *History and Anthropology* 1: 427–43.

Daremberg, C., E. Saglio, E. Pottier, and G. Lafaye, eds. [1877–1919] 1962–63. *Dictionnaire des antiquités grecques et romaines*. 5 vols. Graz.

Dareste, R., B. Haussoullier, and T. Reinach, eds. 1891–95, 1898–1904. *Recueil des inscriptions juridiques grecques*. 1st ser., 1891–95; 2d ser., 1898–1904. Paris.

D'Arms, J. H. 1981. *Commerce and Social Standing in Ancient Rome*. Cambridge, Mass.

David, E. 1984. *Aristophanes and Athenian Society of the Early Fourth Century B.C.* Leiden.

Davies, J. K. 1971. *Athenian Propertied Families, 600–300 B.C.* Oxford.

———. 1977–78. "Athenian Citizenship: The Descent Group and the Alternatives." *Classical Journal* 73: 105–21.

———. 1978. *Democracy and Classical Greece*. Stanford.

———. 1981. *Wealth and the Power of Wealth in Classical Athens*. Salem, N.H.

Davis, L. J. 1986. *Onassis: Aristotle and Christina*. New York.

Day, A.C.L. 1957. *Outline of Monetary Economics*. London.

Day, J. 1942. *An Economic History of Athens under Roman Domination*. New York.

Deaglio, M. 1974. "L'occupazione invisibile: Il caso di un comune piemontese." *Biblioteca della libertà*: 52–53, 69–108.

Degler, C. N. 1959. "Starr on Slavery." *Journal of Economic History* 19: 271–77.

De Martino, F. 1982. *Diritto privato e società romana*. Rome.

Diamond, I., and L. Quinby, eds. 1988. *Feminism and Foucault: Reflections on Resistance*. Boston.

Dilts, M. R. 1983–86. *Scholia Demosthenica*. 2 vols. Leipzig.

Dimakis, P. 1988. "Orateurs et hetaïres dans l'Athènes classique." In *Éros et droit en Grèce classique*, edited by P. Dimakis, pp. 43–54. Paris.

———. N.d. Ὁ θεσμὸς τῆς προικὸς κατὰ τὸ ἀρχαῖον ἑλληνικὸν δίκαιον. Athens.

Dinsmoor, W. B. 1932. "The Burning of the Opisthodomos at Athens." *American Journal of Archaeology* 36: 143–72.

———. 1940. "The Tribal Cycles of the Treasurers of Athena." *Harvard Studies in*

Classical Philology, supp. 1 (*Athenian Studies Presented to W. S. Ferguson*): 157–82.

———. 1947. "The Hekatompedon on the Athenian Acropolis." *American Journal of Archaeology* 51: 109–51.

Dittenberger, W., ed. 1915–24. *Sylloge inscriptionum graecarum*. 3d ed. Edited by F. Hiller von Gaertringen. 4 vols. Leipzig.

Di Tucci, R. 1935. *Studi sul economia genovese del secolo decimo secondo; la nave e i contratti marittimi, la banca privata*. Torino.

Doherty, F. C. 1927. *Three Private Speeches of Demosthenes*. Oxford.

Dopsch, A. 1930. *Naturalwirtschaft und Geldwirtschaft in der Weltgeschichte*. Vienna.

Dörpfeld, W. 1887. "Der alte Athenstempel auf der Akropolis II, III." *Mitteilungen des deutschen archäologischen Instituts, Athenische Abteilung* 12: 25–61.

———. 1919. "Das Hekatompedon in Athen." *Jahrbuch des deutschen archäologischen Instituts* 34: 1–40.

Dover, K. J. 1974. *Greek Popular Morality in the Time of Plato and Aristotle*. Berkeley.

———. 1978. *Greek Homosexuality*. London.

Dray, W. 1971. "On the Nature and Role of Narrative in Historiography." *History and Theory* 10: 153–71.

———. 1978. "Point of View in History." *Clio* 14: 265–83.

Drerup, E. 1898. "Über die bei den attischen Rednern eingelegten Urkunden." *Neue Jahrbücher für Klassische Philologie*, supp. 24.

Dreyfus, H., and P. Rabinow. 1983. *Michel Foucault: Beyond Structuralism and Hermeneutics*. Chicago.

Du Boulay, J. 1974. *Portrait of a Greek Mountain Village*. Oxford.

Eddy, S. K. 1970. "The Value of the Cyzicene Stater at Athens in the Fifth Century." *The American Numismatic Society Museum Notes* 16: 13–22.

Ehrenberg, V. 1962. *The People of Aristophanes: A Sociology of Old Attica Comedy*. New York.

Ek, Sven. 1950. "Nochmals φιλίον τράπεζα." *Eranos* 48: 127–28.

Endenburg, P.J.T. 1937. *Koinoonia en Gemeenschap van Zaken bij de Grieken in den Klassieken Tijd*. Amsterdam.

Engelmann, H. 1985. "Wege griechischen Geldpolitik." *Zeitschrift für Papyrologie und Epigraphik* 60: 165–76.

Epstein, S. 1969. *Capitalism, Primitive and Modern*. Manchester.

Erb, O. 1939. *Wirtschaft und Gesellschaft im Denken der hellenischen Antike*. Berlin. (Also found in *Schmollers Jahrbuch* 61 [1937]: 663–96, and 62 [1938]: 273–305.)

Erxleben, E. 1973. "Das Kapital der Bank des Pasion und das Privatvermögen des Trapeziten." *Klio* 55: 117–34.

———. 1974. "Die Rolle der Bevölkerungsklassen im Aussenhandel Athens im 4. Jahrhundert v.u.Z." In *Hellenische Poleis*, edited by E. C. Welskopf, 1: 460–520. Berlin.

Feige, E. L., ed. 1989. *The Underground Economies: Tax Evasion and Information Distortion*. Cambridge.

Fenves, P. 1986. "Marx's Doctoral Thesis on Two Greek Atomists and the Post-Kantian Interpretations." *Journal of the History of Ideas* 47: 433–52.

Ferguson, W. S. 1932. *The Treasurers of Athena*. Cambridge, Mass.

Figueira, T. J. 1984. "Karl Polanyi and Ancient Greek Trade." *Ancient World* 10: 15–30.

———. 1986. "*Sitopolai* and *Sitophylakes* in Lysias' 'Against the Graindealers': Governmental Intervention in the Athenian Economy." *Phoenix* 40: 149–71.

Fine, J.V.A. 1951. *Horoi. Studies in Mortgage, Real Security, and Land Tenure in Ancient Athens. Hesperia*, supp. 9.

Finley, J. H. 1938. "Euripides and Thucydides." *Harvard Studies in Classical Philology* 49: 64–67.

Finley, M. I. [Finkelstein]. 1935. "Ἔμπορος, ναύκληρος and κάπηλος." *Classical Philology* 30: 320–36.

———. [1951] 1985. *Studies in Land and Credit in Ancient Athens*. With new introduction by P. Millett. New Brunswick, N.J.

———. 1953a. "Land, Debt and the Man of Property in Classical Athens." *Political Science Quarterly* 68: 249–68. (Reprinted in Finley 1981: ch. 4.)

———. 1953b. "Multiple Charges on Real Property in Athenian Law." *Studi in onore di Vincenzo Arangio-Ruiz*, 3 (Naples): 473–91.

———. 1966. "The Problem of the Unity of Greek Law." *Atti del primo Congresso internazionale della Società italiana di Storia del diritto* (Florence): 129–42. (Reprinted in Finley 1975: ch. 8.)

———. 1970. "Aristotle and Economic Analysis." *Past and Present* 47: 3–25. (Reprinted in *Studies in Ancient Society*, edited by M. I. Finley, ch. 2 [London, 1974].)

———. 1973. *Democracy Ancient and Modern*. New Brunswick, N.J.

———. 1975. *The Use and Abuse of History*. London.

———. 1981. *Economy and Society in Ancient Greece*. Edited by B. D. Shaw and R. P. Saller. London.

———. 1983. *Politics in the Ancient World*. Cambridge.

———. 1985. *The Ancient Economy*. 2d ed. London and Berkeley.

———. 1986. *Ancient History: Evidence and Models*. New York.

Fisher, N.R.E. 1976. *Social Values in Classical Athens*. London.

Fogel, B. J., and S. L. Engerman, eds. 1971. *The Reinterpretation of American Economic History*. New York.

Forberg, F.-K. [1824] 1966. *Antonii Panormitae Hermaphroditus*, with *Apophoreta*. New York (original ed., Koburg). *Apophoreta*, translated by J. Smithson as *Manual of Classical Erotology*, 2 vols. (Manchester, 1884).

Forbes, C. A. 1933. *"Neoi": A Contribution to the Study of Greek Associations. Philological Monograph* 2 of the American Philological Association.

———. 1955. "The Education and Training of Slaves in Antiquity." *Transactions of the American Philological Association* 86: 321–60.

Fornara, C. W., and L. J. Samons. 1990. *Athens from Cleisthenes to Pericles*. Berkeley.

Forrest, W. G. 1970. "The Date of the Pseudo-Xenophontic Athenaion Politeia." *Klio* 52: 107–16.

Foucault, M. 1984. *The Foucault Reader*. Edited by P. Rabinow. New York.

Foxhall, L. 1989. "Household, Gender and Property in Classical Athens." *Classical Quarterly*, n.s. 39: 22–44.

Francotte, H. 1900. *L'Industrie dans la Grèce ancienne*. Brussels. Reprint, 1979.

Fraser, P. M. 1972. *Ptolemaic Alexandria*. 3 vols. Oxford.

French, A. 1991. "Economic Conditions in Fourth-Century Athens." *Greece & Rome*, 2d ser., 38: 24–40.

Frey, L. 1975. *Lavoro a Domicilio, Decentramento e Attività Produttiva*. Milan.

———. 1989. "How Large (or Small) Should the Underground Economy Be?" In *Underground Economies*, edited by E. L. Feige, pp. 111–26. Cambridge.

Frisk, H. 1960–72. *Griechisches etymologisches Wörterbuch*. 3 vols. Heidelberg.

Fuks, A. 1951. "*Kolonos misthios*: Labour Exchange in Classical Athens." *Eranos* 49: 171–73.

Gabrielsen, V. 1986. "φανερά and ἀφανὴς οὐσία in Classical Athens." *Classica et Mediaevalia* 37: 99–114.

———. 1987. "The *Antidosis* Procedure in Classical Athens." *Classica et Mediaevalia* 38: 7–38.

———. 1989. "The Number of Athenian Trierarchs after ca. 340 B.C." *Classica et Mediaevalia* 40: 145–59.

Gagarin, M. 1986. *Early Greek Law*. Berkeley.

Gajdukevič, V. J. 1971. *Das Bosphoranische Reich*. Berlin.

Gallo, L. 1984. "La donna greca e la marginalità." *Quaderni urbanati di cultura classica* 18: 7–51.

———. 1987. "Salari e inflazione: Atene tra V ed IV sec. a. C." *Annali della Scuola Normale Superiore di Pisa*, 3d ser., 17.1: 19–63.

Gara A. 1976. *Prosdiagraphomena e circolazione monetaria*. Milan.

Garlan, Y. 1982. *Les Esclaves en grèce ancienne*. Paris. (Translated as "Slavery in Ancient Greece" [Ithaca, N.Y., 1988].)

Garland, R. 1987. *The Piraeus*. Ithaca, N.Y.

———. 1990. *The Greek Way of Life*. Ithaca, N.Y.

Garner, R. 1987. *Law and Society in Classical Athens*. London.

Garnsey, P., ed. 1980. *Non-Slave Labour in the Greco-Roman World*. Cambridge.

———. 1985. "Grain for Athens." In Cartledge and Harvey 1985: 62–75.

———. 1988. *Famine and Food Supply in the Graeco-Roman World: Responses to Risk and Crisis*. Cambridge.

Gatti, C. 1967. "Aspetti della εὐεργεσία nel mondo ellenistico (a proposito di prestiti di privati a città)." *La parola del passato* 22: 192–213.

Gauthier, P. 1972. *Symbola. Les Étrangers et la justice dans les cités grecques*. Nancy.

———. 1976. *Un Commentaire historique des Poroi de Xénophon*. Genève and Paris.

———. 1980. "Études sur des inscriptions d'Amorgos (I. Biens 'terrestres' et biens 'maritimes')." *Bulletin de Correspondance Hellénique* 104: 197–205.

———. 1981. "De Lysias à Aristote (*Ath. Pol.* 51.4): Le Commerce du grain à Athènes et les fonctions des sitophylaques." *Revue historique de droit français et étranger* 59: 5–28.

Gera, G. 1975. *L'imposizione progressiva nell'antica Atene*. Rome.

Gernet, L. 1907. Review of "Salvioli, *Capitalisme*." *Notes critiques*, n.s. 7: 203–5. (Reprinted in *Les Grecs sans miracle* [Paris, 1983], pp. 87–88.)

———. 1909. "L'Approvisionement d'Athènes en blé au Ve et au IVe siècle." *Mélanges d'histoire ancienne* 25, no. 3 (Paris): 171–385. Reprint 1979.

———. [1938] 1955. "Sur les actions commerciales en droit athénien." In Gernet 1955b: 173–200. (Originally published in *Revue des études grecques* 51: 1–44.)

————, ed. 1954–60. *Démosthène, Plaidoyers Civils*. 4 vols. Collection des Universités de France. Paris

————. 1955a. "Aspects du droit athénien de l'esclavage." In Gernet 1955b: 151–72. (Originally published in *Archives d'histoire du droit oriental* [1950]: 159–87.)

————. 1955b. *Droit et société dans la Grèce ancienne*. Paris.

————. 1981. "Choses visibles et invisibles." Translated by J. D. B. Hamilton and B. Nagy. In *The Anthropology of Ancient Greece*, pp. 343–51. Baltimore. (Originally published in *Revue Philosophique* 146 [1956]: 79–86.)

Gernet, L., and M. Bizos, eds. 1924–26. *Lysias: Discours*. 2 vols. Collection des Universités de France. Paris.

Gianfrotta, P., and P. Pomey. 1981. *Archaeologia subacquea*. Milan.

Giglioni, G. Bodei. 1970. *Xenophontis de Vectigalibus*. Florence.

Giovanni, A. 1978. *Rome et la circulation monétaire en Grèce au IIe siècle avant Jésus-Christ*. Basel.

Glotz, G. 1910. *Le Travail dans la Grèce ancienne*. Paris.

Gluskina, L. M. 1970. "Some Aspects of Money and Credit Relations in Fourth Century Attica." *Vestnik Drevnej Istorii* 3: 17–43. In Russian with English summary.

————. 1974. "Studien zu den sozial-ökonomischen Verhältnissen in Attika im 4. Jh. v. u. Z." *Eirene* 12: 111–38.

Gofas, D. C. 1970. Δεῖγμα· ἱστορικὴ ἔρευνα ἐπὶ τοῦ Ἑλληνικοῦ Δικαίου τῶν συναλλαγῶν. Athens.

————. 1989. "Epiplous: Une Institution du droit maritime grec." In *Symposion 1985*, edited by A. Biscardi, J. Mélèze-Modrzejewski, and G. Thür, pp. 425–44. Cologne.

Goldin, C. D. 1976. *Urban Slavery in the American South 1820–1860*. Chicago.

Goldschmidt, L. 1889. "Inhaber-, Order- und Executorische Urkunden im klassischen Altertum." *Zeitschrift der Savigny-Stiftung für Rechtsgeschichte. Romanistische Abteilung* 10: 352–96.

Goldsmith, R. W. 1987. *Premodern Financial Systems: A Historical Comparative Study*. Cambridge.

Goldthwaite, R. 1980. *I Medici e la banca nel Quattrocento fiorentino*. Milan.

Goligher, W. A. 1907. "Studies in Attic Law. II. The Antidosis." *Hermathena* 14: 481–515.

Gomme, A. W. 1933. *The Population of Athens in the Fifth and Fourth Centuries B.C.* Oxford.

————. 1940. "The Old Oligarch." In *Harvard Studies in Classical Philology*, supp. vol. 1: 211–45. (Reprinted in *More Essays in Greek Literature and History*, edited by D. A. Campbell [Oxford, 1962], 38–69.)

Gomme, A. W., A. Andrewes, and K. J. Dover. 1956–1981. *A Historical Commentary on Thucydides*. 5 vols. Oxford.

Goody, J. 1986. *The Logic of Writing and the Organization of Society*. Cambridge.

Gordon, M. 1989. *Slavery in the Arab World*. New York.

Gould, J. P. 1980. "Law, Custom and Myth: Aspects of the Social Position of Women in Classical Athens." *Journal of Hellenic Studies* 100: 38–59.

Gouldner, A. 1965. *Enter Plato: Classical Greece and the Origins of Social Theory*. New York.

Grace, E. L. 1968. "Concubines in Classical Athens." *Vestnik Drevnej Istorii* 103: 28–52. In Russian with English summary.

————. 1974. "The Legal Position of Slaves in Homicide Proceedings." *Vestnik Drevnej Istorii* 128: 34–56. In Russian with English summary.

Graf, J. 1903. "Münzverfalschungen im Altertum." *Numismatische Zeitschrift* 35: 1–130.

Grundy, G. B. 1948. *Thucydides and the History of His Age*. Oxford.

Guépin, J. G. 1965. "Le Cours du cyzicène." *L'Antiquité classique* 34: 199–203.

Guillard, E. 1875. *Les Banquiers athéniens et romains, trapézites et argentarii*. Paris and Lyon.

Guiraud, P. 1893. *La Propriété foncière en Grèce jusqu'à la conquête romaine*. Paris.

Gurley, J. G., and E. S. Shaw. 1960. *Money in a Theory of Finance*. Washington, D.C.

Gutmann, P. M. 1977. "The Subterranean Economy." *Financial Analysts Journal* 33: 24–27, 34.

Hahn, F. H. 1982. *Money and Inflation*. Oxford.

Hallett, J. 1984. *Fathers and Daughters in Roman Society: Women and the Elite Family*. Princeton.

Halperin, D. M. 1990. *One Hundred Years of Homosexuality and Other Essays on Greek Love*. New York.

Halperin, D. M., J. J. Winkler, and F. I. Zeitlin, eds. 1990. *Before Sexuality: The Construction of Erotic Experience in the Ancient Greek World*. Princeton.

Hammer, J. 1908. "Der Feingehalt der griechischen und römischen Münzen." *Zeitschrift für Numismatik* 26: 1–144.

Hangard, J. 1963. *Monetaire en daarmee verwante Metaforen*. Groningen.

Hansen, M. H. 1982. "Demographic Reflections on the Number of Athenian Citizens, 451–309 B.C." *American Journal of Ancient History* 7: 172–89.

————. 1986. *Demography and Democracy*. Cophenhagen.

————. 1987. *The Athenian Assembly*. Oxford.

————. 1991. *The Athenian Democracy in the Age of Demosthenes*. Oxford.

Hansen, M. V. 1984. "Athenian Maritime Trade in the Fourth Century B.C.: Operation and Finance." *Classica et Mediaevalia* 35: 71–92.

Harrauer, H., and P. J. Sijpesteijn. 1985. "Ein neues Dokument zu Roms Indienhandel." *Anzeiger der phil.-hist. Kl. Österreichischen Akademie der Wissenschaften in Wien* 122: 124–55.

Harris, E. M. 1988. "When Is a Sale Not a Sale? The Riddle of Athenian Terminology for Real Security Revisited." *Classical Quarterly*, n.s. 38: 351–81.

————. 1989. "The Liability of Business Partners in Athenian Law: The Dispute between Lycon and Megacleides ([Dem.] 52.20–1)." *Classical Quarterly*, n.s. 39: 339–43.

Harris, W. V. 1980. "Roman Terracotta Lamps: The Organization of an Industry." *Journal of Roman Studies* 70: 126–45.

Harrison, A.R.W. 1968–71. *The Law of Athens*. 2 vols. Oxford.

Harrod, R. F. 1969. *Money*. London.

Harvey, F. D. 1966. "Literacy in the Athenian Democracy. *Revue des études grecques* 79: 585–635.

————. 1985. "Some Aspects of Bribery in Greek Politics." In Cartledge and Harvey 1985: 76–113.

Hasebroek, J. 1920. "Zum griechischen Bankwesen der klassischen Zeit." *Hermes* 55: 113–73.

———. 1923a. "Die betriebsformen der griechischen Handels im IV. Jahrhundert." *Hermes* 58: 393–425.

———. 1923b. "Zum Giroverkehr im 4. Jahr." *Klio* 18: 375–78.

———. 1931. *Griechische Wirtschafts- und gesellschaftsgeschichte.* Tübingen.

———. [1933] 1978. *Trade and Politics in Ancient Greece.* Translated by L. M. Fraser and D. C. MacGregor. Reprint. London. (Originally published as *Staat und Handel im alten Griechenland* [Tübingen, 1928].)

Havrilesky, T. M., and J. T. Boorman. 1982. *Money Supply, Money Demand and Macroeconomic Models.* 2d ed. Arlington Heights, Ill.

Head, B. V. 1911. *Historia Numorum.* 2d ed. Oxford.

Heichelheim, F. M. 1963. "Geld- und Münzgeschichte: (I) Anfänge und Antike." In *Handwörterbuch der Sozialwissenschaften,* edited by E. V. Beckerath, H. Bente, C. Brinkmann, E. Gutenberg, et al., vol. 4, pp. 273–82. Göttingen.

———. 1964. *An Ancient Economic History from the Paleolithic Age to the Migrations of the Germanic, Slavic and Arabic Nations.* 3 vols. Leyden. (Translation of *Wirtschaftsgeschichte des Altertums vom Paläolithikum bis zur Völkerwanderung der Germanen, Slaven und Araber.*)

Hemelrijk, J. 1925. "Πενία en Πλοῦτος." Diss., Utrecht.

Herfst, P. 1922. *Le Travail de la femme dans la Grèce ancienne.* Utrecht.

Herman, G. 1987. *Ritualized Friendship and the Greek City.* Cambridge.

Hermann, K. F., and H. Blümner. 1882. *Lehrbuch der griechischen antiquitaten.* Vol. 4, *Die griechischen Privataltertümer.* Freiburg.

Hertzfeld, M. 1985. *The Poetics of Manhood: Contest and Identity in a Cretan Mountain Village.* Princeton.

———. 1986. "Within and Without: The Category of 'Female' in the Ethnography of Modern Greece." In *Gender and Power in Rural Greece,* edited by J. Dubisch, pp. 215–33. Princeton.

Hicks, J. R. 1967. *Critical Essays in Monetary Theory.* Oxford.

Higginbotham, A. L., Jr. 1978. *In the Matter of Color: Race and the American Legal Process.* New York.

Hignett, C. 1952. *A History of the Athenian Constitution.* Oxford.

Hirschmeier, J., and T. Yui. 1975. *The Development of Japanese Business 1600–1973.* Cambridge.

Hock, R. F. 1976. "Simon the Shoemaker as an Ideal Cynic." *Greek, Roman, and Byzantine Studies* 17: 41–53.

Hopkins, K. 1978. *Conquerors and Slaves.* Cambridge.

———. 1983. "Introduction." In *Trade in the Ancient Economy,* edited by P. Garnsey, K. Hopkins, and C. R. Whittaker, pp. viii–xxv. Berkeley.

Hopper, R. J. 1953. "The Attic Silver Mines in the Fourth Century B.C." *Annual of the British School at Athens* 48: 200–254.

———. 1968. "The Laurion Mines: A Reconsideration." *Annual of the British School at Athens* 63: 293–326.

———. 1971. *The Acropolis.* London.

———. 1979. *Trade and Industry in Classical Greece.* London.

Huber, O. 1939. "Die wirtschaftlichen Verhältnisse Athens." Diss., Munich.

Humphreys, S. C. 1970a. "Economy and Society in Classical Athens." *Annali della Scuola Normale Superiore di Pisa,* 2d ser., 39: 1–26.

———. 1970b. Review of R. Bogaert, *Banques et banquiers dans les cités grecques*. *Journal of Hellenic Studies* 90: 252–54.

———. 1978. *Anthropology and the Greeks*. London.

———. 1983a. "The Date of Hagnias' Death." *Classical Philology* 78: 219–25.

———. 1983b. "The Evolution of Legal Process in Ancient Attica." In *Tria Corda: Scritti in onore di Arnaldo Momigliano*, edited by E. Gabba, pp. 227–56. Como.

———. 1983c. *The Family, Women and Death*. London.

———. 1985a. "Law as Discourse." *History and Anthropology* 1: 241–64.

———. 1985b. "Social Relations on Stage: Witnesses in Classical Athens." *History and Anthropology*, 1: 313–73.

Hunt, A. S., and C. C. Edgar. 1952. *Select Papyri I*. Cambridge.

Hunter, V. 1981. "Classics and Anthropology." *Phoenix* 35: 144–55.

Imbert, J. 1965. *Histoire économique des origines à 1789*. Paris.

Incarnati, L. 1953. *Moneta e scambio nell'antichita e nell' alto medioevo*. Rome.

Isager, S., and M. H. Hansen. 1975. *Aspects of Athenian Society in the Fourth Century B.C.* Odense.

Jacob, O. 1926. "Les Esclaves publics à Athènes." *Musée Belge* 30: 57–106.

———. [1928] 1979. *Les Esclaves publics à Athènes*. New York.

Jaeger, W. [1938] 1963. *Demosthenes*. Translated by E. S. Robinson. New York.

———. 1939. *Paideia*. Vol. 1. New York.

Jameson, M. H. 1977–78. "Agriculture and Slavery in Classical Athens." *Classical Journal* 73: 122–45.

———. 1983. "Famine in the Greek World." In *Trade and Famine in Classical Antiquity*, edited by P. Garnsey and C. R. Whittaker, pp. 6–16. Cambridge.

———. 1990a. "Domestic Space in the Greek City-State." In *Domestic Architecture and the Use of Space: An Interdisciplinary Cross-Cultural Study*, edited by S. Kent, pp. 92–113. Cambridge.

———. 1990b. "Private Space and the Greek City." In *The Greek City from Homer to Alexander*, edited by O. Murray and S. Price, pp. 171–95. Oxford.

Jardé, A. 1925. *Les Céréales dans l'antiquité*. Paris. Reprint, 1979.

Jeffery, L. H. 1961. *The Local Scripts of Archaic Greece*. Oxford.

Johnson, A. C. 1914. "An Athenian Treasure List." *American Journal of Archaeology* 18: 1–17.

Johnson, V. 1939. "Aristotle's Theory of Value." *American Journal of Philology* 60: 445–51.

Jones, A.H.M. 1948. *Inaugural Lecture: Ancient Economic History*. London.

———. [1957] 1977a. *Athenian Democracy*. Oxford.

———. [1957] 1977b. "The Social Structure of Athens in the Fourth Century B.C." In Jones [1957] 1977a: 75–96. (Originally published in *Economic History Review*, 2d ser., 8 [1955]: 141–55.)

Jones, J. E. 1975. "Town and Country Houses of Attica in Classical Times." In *Miscellanea Graeca*, fasc. 1, edited by H. Mussche and P. Spitaels, pp. 63–136. Gent.

Jones, J. W. 1956. *The Law and Legal Theory of the Greeks*. Oxford.

Jones, R. W. 1978. *International Trade: Essays in Theory*. Amsterdam.

Jordan, B. 1975. *The Athenian Navy in the Classical Period*. Berkeley.

Judeich, W. 1929. "Hekatompedon und alter Tempel." *Hermes. Zeitschrift für classische Philogie* 64: 391–415.

————. 1931. *Topographie von Athen*. 2d ed. Munich.

Juglar, L. 1902. *Quomodo per servos libertosque negotiarentur Romani*. Paris.

Just, R. 1985. "Freedom, Slavery and the Female Psyche." In Cartledge and Harvey 1985: 169–88.

————. 1989. *Women in Athenian Law and Life*. London.

Kagan, D. 1982. "The Dates of the Earliest Coins." *American Journal of Archaeology* 86: 343–60.

Kahle, F. 1909. *De Demosthenis orationum Androtioneae Timocrateae Aristocrateae temporibus*. Göttingen.

Kallet, L. 1983. "Iphikrates, Timotheos, and Athens, 371–360 B.C." *Greek, Roman and Byzantine Studies* 24: 239–52.

Karabēlias, E. 1984. "Le Contenu de l'oikos en droit grec ancien." In *Μνήμη Γεωργίου Α. Πετροπούλου*, edited by P. Dimakis, 1: 441–54. Athens.

Katayama, Y. 1970. "The Social Significance of Liturgies from the Viewpoint of the Participation of Metics." *Journal of Classical Studies* 18: 40–51. In Japanese with English summary.

Katzouros, P. P. 1989. "Origine et effets de la παραγραφή attique." In *Symposion 1985*, edited by A. Biscardi, J. Mélèze-Modrzejewski, and G. Thür, pp. 119–51. Cologne.

Kennedy, G. 1963. *The Art of Persuasion in Greece*. Princeton.

Kenyon, F. G. 1907. *Hyperidis orationes et fragmenta*. Oxford Classical Text. Oxford.

Keuls, E. C. 1985. *The Reign of the Phallus: Sexual Politics in Ancient Athens*. New York.

Kieso, D. E., and J. J. Weygarndt. 1980. *Intermediate Accounting*. 3d ed. New York.

Kirchner, J. 1901–3. *Prosopographia Attica*. Vols. 1–2. Berlin.

Kleber, P. 1890. *Die Rhetorik bei Herodot*. Vol. 1. Löwenberg.

Kliacko, N. B. 1966. "The *Hermokopidai stelai* as a Source for Slavery in the Fifth Century *B.C.*" *Vestnik Drevnej Istorii* 97: 114–27. In Russian. Summarized in *Biblioteca Classica Orientalis* 13 (1968): 281–82.

Knorringa, H. [1926] 1961. *Emporos: Data on Trade and Trader in Greek Literature from Homer to Aristotle*. Amsterdam.

Knox, B. 1989. *Essays Ancient and Modern*. Baltimore.

Kocevalov, A. 1932. "Die Einfuhr von Getreide nach Athen." *Rheinisches Museum für Philologie* 81: 321–23.

Kohn, D. L. 1976. "Interdependence, Exchange Rate Flexibility, and National Economics." In *Current Issues in Monetary Theory and Policy*, edited by T. M. Havrilesky and J. T. Boorman, pp. 485–94. Arlington Heights, Ill.

Kohns, H. P. 1964. "Die staatliche Lenkung des Getreidehandels in Athen (zur Lysias or. 22)." In *Studien zur Papyrologie und antiken Wirtschaftsgeschichte (Festschrift F. Oertel)*, edited by H. Braunert, pp. 146–66. Bonn.

Kolbe, W. 1929. "Zur athenischen Schatzverwaltung im IV Jahrhundert." *Philologus* 84 (n.f. 38): 261–67.

————. 1931. Review of *Athen, Akropolis* (Vienna, 1929) by O. Walter. *Berliner philologische Wochenschrift* 51, no. 3: 71–83.

Körte, G. 1898. "Der "alte Tempel' und das Hekatompedon auf der Akropolis zu Athen." *Rheinisches Museum für Philologie* 53: 239–69.

Korver, J. 1934. *De Terminologie van het Crediet-Wezen in het Grieksch*. Amsterdam.

————. 1942. "Demosthenes gegen Aphobos." *Mnemosyne*, 3d ser., 10: 8–22.

Koutorga, M. de. 1859. *Essai sur les trapezites ou banquiers d'Athènes*. Paris.

Kraay, C. M. 1964. "Hoards, Small Change and the Origins of Coinage." *Journal of Hellenic Studies* 84: 76–91.

————. 1976. *Archaic and Classical Greek Coins*. London.

Kränzlein, A. 1963. *Eigentum und Besitz im griechischen Recht des fünften und vierten Jahrhunderts v. Chr*. Berlin.

Kraut, W. 1826. *De argentariis et nummulariis commentatio*. Göttingen.

Krugman, P. R. 1978. "Purchasing Power Parity and Exchange Rates: Another Look at the Evidence." *Journal of International Economics* 8: 169–91.

Kuenen-Janssens, L. J. 1941. "Some Notes on the Competence of the Athenian Woman to Conduct a Transaction." *Mnemosyne*, 3d ser., 9: 199–214.

Kupiszewski, H. 1972. "Sul prestito marittimo nel diritto romano classico: Profili sostanziali e processuali." *Index* 3: 368–81.

Kussmaul, P. 1969. *Synthekai: Beiträge zur Geschichte des attischen Obligationemrechts*. Basel.

————. 1985. "Zur Bedeutung von συμβόλαιον bei den attischen Rednern." In *Catalepton. Festschrift für Bernhard Wyss*, edited by C. Schäublin, pp. 31–44. Basel.

Lacey, W. K. 1968. *The Family in Classical Greece*. London.

Lamb, W.R.M. 1930. *Lysias*. Cambridge, Mass.

Lang, M. 1957. "Herodotus and the Abacus." *Hesperia* 26: 271–87.

————. 1964. "The Abacus and the Calendar." *Hesperia* 33: 146–67.

Langdon, M. K. 1987. "An Attic Decree Concerning Oropos." *Hesperia* 56: 47–58.

Langfeldt, E. 1989. "The Underground Economy in the Federal Republic of Germany: A Preliminary Assessment." In *The Underground Economies: Tax Evasion and Information Distortion*, edited by E. Feige, pp. 197–217. Cambridge.

Langfeldt, E., and H. Lehment. 1980. "Welche Bedeutung haben Soderfaktoren für die Erklärung der Geldnachfrage in der Bundesrepublik Deutschland?" *Weltwirtschaftliches Archiv*. 116, 4: 669–84.

Lauffer, S. 1961. "Die Sklaverei in der griechisch-römischen Welt." *Gymnasium* 68: 370–95. (Also in *Rapports*, 11th International Congress of Historical Sciences [Uppsala, 1960], 2: 71–97.)

————. 1974. "Die Liturgien in der Krisenperiode Athens." In *Hellenische Poleis*, edited by E. C. Welskopf, 1: 147–59. Berlin.

Laum, B. 1922. "Kein Giroverkehr bei athenischen Banken." *Philologische Wochenschrift* 42: 427–32.

Launey, M. 1949. *Recherches sur les armées hellénistiques*. 2 vols. Paris.

Lepore, E. 1970. "Economia antica e storiografia moderna (Appunti per un bilancio di generazioni)." In *Ricerche storiche ed economiche in memoria di Corrado Barbagallo*, edited by L. de Rosa, 1: 3–33. Naples.

Lévi-Strauss, C. 1967. "The Structural Study of Myth." In *Structural Anthropology*, translated by C. Jacobson and B. Grundfest Schoepf, pp. 202–28. Garden City, N.Y.

Lévi-Strauss, C., and D. Eribon. 1991. *Conversations with Claude Lévi-Strauss*. Translated by P. Wissing. Chicago. (Translation of "De près et de loin." Paris, 1988.)

Levy, E. 1987. "Métèques et droit de résidence." In *L'Etranger dans le monde grec*, edited by R. Lonis, pp. 47–67. Etudes anciennes 4. Nancy.

Lévy, J. P. 1964. *L'Economie antique*. Paris.

Lewald, H. 1946. "Conflits de lois dans le monde grec et romain." Ἀρχεῖον ἰδιωτικοῦ δικαίου. *Archives de droit privé* 13: 30–77. (Reprinted in *Labeo* 5 [1959]: 334–69; German translation in *Zur griechischen Rechtsgeschichte*, edited by E. Berneker [Darmstadt 1968], pp. 666–90.

Lewis, B. 1990. *Race and Slavery in the Middle East*. Oxford.

Lewis, D. M. 1952. "Towards a Historian's Text of Thucydides." Diss., Princeton.

———. 1954. "Notes on Attic Inscriptions XIII." *Annual of the British School at Athens* 49: 39–49.

———. 1959. "Law on the Lesser Panatheneia." *Hesperia* 28: 239–47.

———. 1973. "The Athenian Rationes Centesimarum." In *Problèmes de la terre en Grèce ancienne*, edited by M. I. Finley, pp. 188–91. Paris.

Lewis, J. T. 1978. "Acquisition and Anxiety: Aristotle's Case against the Market." *The Canadian Journal of Economics* 11: 69–90.

Lewis, N. 1934. *L'Industrie du papyrus dans l'Égypte gréco-romaine*. Paris.

Lewis, N. 1960. "Leitourgia and Related Terms." *Greek, Roman and Byzantine Studies* 3: 175–84.

———. 1965. "Leitourgia and Related Terms II." *Greek, Roman and Byzantine Studies* 6: 226–30.

Lewy, H. 1885. *De civili condicione mulierum graecarum*. Breslau.

Licht, H. [P. Brandt.] [1932] 1952. *Sexual Life in Ancient Greece*. Edited by L. H. Dawson, translated by J. H. Freese. New York.

Limperopoulos, D. 1983. Ὠνάσης. Athens.

Linders, T. 1972. *Studies in the Treasure Records of Artemis Brauronia Found in Athens*. Acta Instituti Atheniensis Regni Sueciae, vol. 19. Stockholm.

———. 1975. *The Treasurers of the Other Gods in Athens and Their Functions*. Meisenheim am Glan.

Lipsius, J. H. [1905–15] 1966. *Das attische Recht und Rechtsverfahren*. 3 vols. Hildesheim.

———. 1916. "Die attische Steuerverfassung und das attische Volksvermögen." *Rheinisches Museum für Philologie* 71: 161–86.

Litewski, W. 1974. "Le Dépôt irrégulier." *Revue internationale des droits de l'antiquité*, 3d ser., 21: 215–62.

Littman, R. J. 1988. "Greek Taxation." In *Civilization of the Ancient Mediteranean*, edited by M. Grant and R. Kitzinger, 2: 795–808. New York.

Lloyd, G.E.R. [1966] 1987. *Polarity and Analogy: Two Types of Argumentation in Early Greek Thought*. Bristol.

———. 1990. *Demystifying Mentalities*. Cambridge.

Lo Cascio, E. 1981. "State and Coinage in the Late Republic and Early Empire." *Journal of Roman Studies* 71: 76–86.

Lofberg, J. O. 1917. *Sycophancy in Athens*. Chicago.

Lolling, H. G. 1890. "Περὶ τοῦ Ἑκατομπέδου· συμβολαὶ εἰς τὴν ἱστορίαν τῶν ἐπὶ τῆς Ἀκροπόλεως ναῶν τῆς Ἀθηνᾶς." Ἀθηνᾶ 2: 627–62.

Longo, O. 1983. "Eranos." In *Mélanges Edouard Delebecque*, edited by C. Froidefond, pp. 245–58. Aix-en-Provence.

Lotze, D. 1981. "Zwischen Politen und Metöken: Pasivbürger im klassischen Athen?" *Klio* 63: 159–78.

Lowry, S. T. 1969. "Aristotle's Mathematical Analysis of Exchange." *History of Political Economy* 1: 44–66.

———. 1974. "Aristotle's 'Natural Limit' and the Economics of Price Regulation." *Greek, Roman and Byzantine Studies* 15: 57–63.

———. 1987. *The Archaeology of Economic Ideas: The Classical Greek Tradition.* Durham, N.C.

McCulloch, R. 1979. "Trade and Direct Investment: Recent Policy Trends." In *International Economic Policy: Theory and Evidence*, edited by R. Dornbusch and J. A. Frenkel, pp. 76–105. Baltimore.

MacDowell, D. M. 1962. *Andokides "On the Mysteries."* Oxford.

———. 1976. Review of E. Cohen 1973. *Classical Review*, n.s. 26: 84–85.

———. 1978. *The Law in Classical Athens.* London.

———. 1986. "The Law of Periandros about Symmories." *Classical Quarterly* 36: 438–49.

———. 1989a. "The Authenticity of Demosthenes 29 as a Source of Information about Athenian Law." In *Symposion 1985*, edited by A. Biscardi, J. Mélèze-Modrzejewski, and G. Thür, pp. 253–62. Cologne.

———. 1989b. "The *Oikos* in Athenian Law." *Classical Quarterly* 39: 10–21.

———. 1990. *Demosthenes against Meidias.* Oxford.

McFee, W. 1951. *Law of the Sea.* London.

Machlup, F. 1952. *The Political Economy of Monopoly.* Princeton.

McKechnie, P. 1989. *Outsiders in the Greek Cities in the Fourth Century B.C.* London.

MacMullen, R. 1974. *Roman Social Relations, 50 B.C.–A.D. 284.* New Haven.

Macve, R. H. 1985. "Some Glosses on 'Greek and Roman Accounting'." In Cartledge and Harvey 1985: 233–64.

Maffi, A. 1972. "La capacità di diritto privato dei meteci nel mondo greco classico." In *Studi in onore di Gaetano Scherillo*, edited by A. Biscardi, 1: 177–200. Milan.

Makinen, G. E. 1977. *Money, the Price Level, and Interest Rates.* Englewood, N.J.

Manville, P. B. 1990. *The Origins of Citizenship in Ancient Athens.* Princeton.

Markle, M. M. 1985. "Jury Pay and Assembly Pay at Athens." In Cartledge and Harvey 1985: 265–97.

Marshall, F. H. 1905. *The Second Athenian Confederacy.* Cambridge.

Martin, T. R. 1985. *Sovereignty and Coinage in Classical Greece.* Princeton.

Martino, A. 1980. "Another Italian Economic Miracle." Mont Pelerin Society, Stanford conference. Mimeographed.

Marx, K. 1967–70. *Capital.* Translated by S. Moore and E. Aveling from the 3d German ed. of *Das Kapital.* 3 vols. New York.

Maschke, R. 1926. *Die Willenslehre im griechischen Recht.* Berlin.

Masi, V. 1963. *La Ragioneria nella preistoria e nell' antichita.* Bologna.

Mathieu, G., and E. Brémond, eds. [1928–42] 1963. *Isocrate.* Collection des Universités de France. 4 vols. Paris.

Mauss, M. 1923–24. "Essai sur le don. Forme et raison de l'échange dans les sociétés archaïques." *L'Année sociologique*, n.s. 1: 30–186.

Meiggs, R. 1972. *The Athenian Empire.* Oxford. (Reprinted with corrections, Oxford, 1975.)

———. 1973. *Roman Ostia.* 2d ed. Oxford.

Meikle, S. 1979. "Aristotle and the Political Economy of the Polis." *Journal of Hellenic Studies* 99: 57–73.

———. 1985. *Essentialism in the Thought of Karl Marx*. LaSalle, Ill.

———. 1989. "Et in Arcadia Chicago." *Polis* 8: 25–34.

Melvin, M. 1985. *International Money and Finance*. New York.

Meritt, B. D. 1945. "Attic Inscriptions of the Fifth Century." *Hesperia* 14: 61–133.

———. 1978. "The Chronology of the Peloponnesian War, II." *Proceedings of the American Philosophical Society* 122: 287–93.

———. 1982. "Thucydides and the Decrees of Kallias." *Hesperia*, supp. 19: 112–21.

Meyer, P. M. 1920. *Juristische Papyri*. Berlin.

Meyer-Laurin, H. 1965. *Gesetz und Billigkeit im attischen Prozess*. Gräzistische Abhandlungen, vol. 1. Weimar.

———. 1979. " 'Noxa caput sequitur' und Haftung des Verkäufers beim Sklavenkauf nach griechischen Recht." *Symposion 1974*, edited by A. Biscardi, pp. 263–79. Cologne.

Meyer-Termeer, A.J.M. 1978. *Die Haftung der Schiffer im griechischen und römischen Recht*. Zutphen.

Michell, H. 1957. *Economics of Ancient Greece*. 2d ed. Cambridge.

Migeotte, L. 1984. *L'Emprunt public dans les cités grecques*. Quebec.

Millett, P. 1983. "Maritime Loans and the Structure of Credit in Fourth-Century Athens." In *Trade in the Ancient Economy*, edited by P. Garnsey, K. Hopkins, and C. R. Whittaker, pp. 36–52, 186–89. Berkeley.

———. 1989. "Patronage and Its Avoidance in Classical Athens." In *Patronage in Ancient Society*, edited by A. Wallace-Hadrill, pp. 1–33. London.

———. 1990. "Sale, Credit and Exchange in Athenian Law and Society." In *Nomos: Essays in Athenian Law, Politics and Society*, edited by P. Cartledge, P. Millett, and S. Todd, pp. 167–94. Cambridge.

Mitteis, L., and U. Wilcken. [1912] 1963. *Grundzüge und Chrestomathie der Papyruskunde*. Vol. 2. Juristischer Teil. Hildesheim.

Modrzejewski, J. 1970. *Loi et coutume dans l'Égypte grecque et romaine*. Paris.

Momigliano, A. 1931. "La eisphora e la sostanza di Demostene." *Athenaeum*, n.s. 9: 477–96.

———. 1934. "La κοινὴ εἰρήνη dal 386 al 388 a.C." *Rivista di Filologia e di Istruzione Classica* 12: 482–514.

———. 1950. "Ancient History and the Antiquarian." *Journal of the Warburg and Courtauld Institutes* 13: 285–315.

———. 1952. *George Grote and the Study of Greek History*. London.

———. 1974. "Historicism Revisited." *Mededelingen der Koninklijke Nederlandse Akademie van Wetenschappen*, Afd. Letterkunde, n.s. 37.3: 63–70. (Reprinted in *Essays in Ancient and Modern Historiography* [Oxford, 1977].)

Mondaini, G. 1942. *Moneta, credito, banche attraverso i tempi*. 2d ed. Rome.

Montgomery, H. 1986. " 'Merchants Fond of Corn.' Citizens and Foreigners in the Athenian Grain Trade." *Symbolae Osloenses* 61: 43–61.

Moore, J. M. 1986. *Aristotle and Xenophon on Democracy and Oligarchy*. Berkeley.

Morgan, M. H., ed. 1895. *Eight Orations of Lysias*. Boston.

Morrison, J. S., and J. F. Coates. 1986. *The Athenian Trireme*. Cambridge.

Morrow, G. R. 1960. *Plato's Cretan City. A Historical Interpretation of the Laws.* Princeton.

Mossé, C. [1962] 1979. *La Fin de la Démocratie Athénienne.* New York.

———. 1972. "La Vie économique d'Athènes au IVème siècle. Crise ou renouveau?" In *Praelectiones Patavinae*, edited by F. Sartori, pp. 135–44. Rome.

———. 1973. *Athens in Decline 404–86.* London.

———. 1979a. "Citoyens actifs et citoyens 'passifs' dans les cités grecques: Une Approche théorique du problème." *Revue des études anciennes* 81: 241–49.

———. 1979b. "Les Symmories athéniennes." In *Points de vue sur la fiscalité antique*, edited by H. van Effenterre, pp. 31–42. Publications de la Sorbonne, Études 14. Paris.

———. 1983. "The 'World of the Emporium'." In *Trade in the Ancient Economy*, edited by P. Garnsey, K. Hopkins, and C. R. Whittaker, pp. 53–63. Berkeley.

Murray, A. T. 1936–39. *Demosthenes: Private Orations.* Vols. 4–6. Loeb edition. Cambridge.

Musti, D. 1981. *L'economia in Grecia.* Bari.

———. 1990. *Storia Greca: Linee di sviluppo dall'età micenea all' età romana.* 2d ed. Rome.

Nasse, E. 1891. "Banken." In *Handwörterbuch der Staatswissenschaften*, edited by J. Conrad, L. Elster, W. Lexis, and E. Lopning, 3d ed., 2: 12–40, 47–63, 66–68.

Neale, W. C. 1957. "The Market in Theory and History." In Polanyi, Arensberg, and Pearson 1957: 357–72.

Nenci, G. 1978. "Il problema della concorrenza fra manodopera libera e servile nella Grecia classica." *Annali della Scuola Normale Superiore de Pisa*, 3d ser., 8: 1287–1300.

Netting, R., R. R. Wilk, and E. J. Arnould. 1984. *Households: Comparative and Historical Studies of the Domestic Group.* Berkeley.

Nicholas, B. 1962. *An Introduction to Roman Law.* Oxford.

Niemeyer, T. 1889. *Depositum irregulare.* Halle.

Noonan, T. S. 1973. "The Grain Trade of the Northern Black Sea in Antiquity." *American Journal of Philology* 94: 231–42.

Norden, E. 1923. *Die antike Kunstprosa.* 2 vols. Leipzig and Berlin.

Ober, J. 1985. *Fortress Attica: Defense of the Athenian Land Frontier 404–322 B.C.* Leiden.

———. 1989. *Mass and Elite in Democratic Athens.* Princeton.

Oertel, F. 1928. Review of J. Hasebroek, *Staat und Handel im alten Griechenland. Deutsche Literaturzeitung* 49: 1618–29.

Officer, L. H. 1982. *Purchasing Power and Exchange Rates: Theory, Evidence and Relevance.* Greenwich, Conn.

Oliva, P. 1960. "Die Bedeutung der antiken Sklaverei. Kritische Bemerkungen." *Acta Antiqua Academiae Scientiarum Hungaricae* 8: 309–19.

Oliver, J. H. 1935. "Greek Inscriptions." *Hesperia* 4: 5–70.

Ormerod, H. A. [1924] 1987. *Piracy in the Ancient World.* Liverpool.

Osborne, M. J. 1972. "Attic Citizenship Decrees: A Note." *Annual of the British School at Athens* 67: 128–58.

———. 1981–83. *Naturalization in Athens.* 4 vols. Brussels.

Osborne, R. G. 1985. *Demos: The Discovery of Classical Attika*. Cambridge.

———. 1988. "Social and Economic Implications of the Leasing of Land and Property in Classical and Hellenistic Greece." *Chiron* 18: 279–323.

Paley, F. A., and J. E. Sandys. [1896–98] 1979. *Select Private Orations of Demosthenes*. 3d ed. 2 vols. Cambridge.

Panagos, C. T. 1968. *Le Pirée*. Athens.

Pantazopoulos, N. 1946. *Αἱ Ἑλληνικαί "Κοινωνίαι."* Athens.

Paoli, U. E. 1924. "Grossi e piccoli commercianti nelle liriche di Orazio." *Rivista di Filologia* 52: 45–63.

———. [1930] 1974. *Studi di diritto attico*. Milan.

———. 1976. *Altri studi di diritto greco e romano*. Milan.

Parsons, T. 1951. *The Social System*. Chicago.

Partsch, J. 1909. *Griechisches Bürgschaftsrecht*. Leipzig.

Passamaneck, S. M. 1974. *Insurance in Rabbinic Law*. Edinburgh.

Paton, J. M., ed. 1927. *The Erechtheum*. Cambridge, Mass.

Patterson, C. 1981. *Pericles' Citizenship Law of 451–50 B.C.* New York.

———. 1986. "*Hai Attikai*: The Other Athenians." *Helios* 13, 2: 49–67.

Pearson, L. 1966. "Apollodorus, the Eleventh Attic Orator." In *The Classical Tradition: Literary and Historical Studies in Honor of H. Caplan*, edited by L. Wallach, pp. 347–59. Ithaca, N.Y. (Reprinted in Pearson 1983: 211–23.)

———. 1969. "Demosthenes, or Pseudo-Demosthenes, xlv." *Antichthon* 3: 18–26 (Reprinted in Pearson 1983: 224–32.)

———. 1972. *Demosthenes: Six Private Speeches*. Norman, Okla.

———. 1983. *Selected Papers*. Edited by D. Lateiner and S. A. Stephens. Chico, Calif.

Pečirka, J. 1966. *The Formula for the Grant of Enktesis in Attic Inscriptions*. Prague.

———. 1967. "A Note on Aristotle's Conception of Citizenship and the Role of Foreigners in Fourth Century Athens." *Eirene* 6: 23–26.

———. 1973. "Homestead Farms in Classical and Hellenistic Hellas." In *Problèmes de la terre en Grèce ancienne*, edited by M. I. Finley, pp. 113–47. Paris.

———. 1976. "The Crisis of the Athenian Polis in the Fourth Century B.C." *Eirene* 14: 5–29.

Peradotto, J., and J. P. Sullivan, eds. 1984. *Women in the Ancient World: The Arethusa Papers*. Albany.

Perotti, E. 1972. "Una categoria particolare di schiavi attici, i χωρὶς οἰκοῦντες." *Rendiconti Istituto Lombardo di Scienze e Lettere* 106: 375–88.

———. 1976. "Contribution à l'étude d'une autre catégorie d'esclaves attiques: les ἀνδράποδα μισθοφοῦνται." *Actes du colloque 1973 sur l'esclavage. Annales Littéraires de l'Université de Besançon* 182: 179–94.

Pesando, F. 1987. *Oikos e ktesis: La casa greca in età classica*. Perugia.

Phōtiadēs, P. S. 1923. "Juridical Commentary on the Paragraphē against Zēnothemis." *Ἀθηνά* 36: 109–32. (In Greek.)

Pickard-Cambridge, A. W. [1914] 1979. *Demosthenes and the Last Days of Greek Freedom*. New York.

Plant, R. 1979. *Greek Coin Types and Their Identification*. London.

Pleket, H. W. 1971. Review of R. Bogaert, *Banques et banquiers dans les cités grecques*. *Mnemosyne* 24: 433–37.

Pöhlmann, R. 1925. *Geschichte der sozialen Frage und des Sozialismus in der antiken Welt.* 2 vols. 3d ed. Edited by F. Oertel. Munich.

Polanyi, K. 1944. *Origins of Our Time: The Great Transformation.* New York.

Polanyi, K., C. M. Arensberg, and H. W. Pearson, eds. 1957. *Trade and Markets in the Early Empires.* New York.

Pomeroy, S. 1975. *Goddesses, Whores, Wives and Slaves: Women in Classical Antiquity.* New York.

Pope, H. 1935. *Non-Athenians in Attic Inscriptions.* New York.

Postan, M. M. 1944. "The Rise of a Money Economy." *Economic History Review* 14: 123–34.

Powell, A. 1988. *Athens and Sparta. Constructing Greek Political and Social History from 478 B.C.* London.

Prachner, G. 1980. *Die Sklaven und Freigelassene im arretinischen Sigillatagewerbe.* Wiesbaden.

Préaux, C. 1958. "De la Grèce classique à l'époque hellénistique. La banque-témoin." *Chronique d'Égypte* 33: 243–55.

Preisigke, F. 1910. *Girowesen im griechischen Aegypten.* Strassburg.

———. 1915. *Fachwörter der öffentlichen Verwaltungsdienstes Aegyptens in den griechischen Papyrusurkunden der ptolemäisch-römischen Zeit.* Göttingen.

———. 1925–66. *Wörterbuch der griechischen Papyrusurkunden.* Edited by E. Kiessling. Vols. 1–3: Berlin, 1925–31; vol. 4: Marburg, 1944–66.

Price, M. J. 1976. Review of L. Weidauer, *Probleme der Frühen Elektronprägung. Numismatic Chronicle,* 7th ser., 273–74.

Pringsheim, F. 1916. *Kauf mit fremden Geld.* Leipzig.

———. 1950. *The Greek Law of Sale.* Weimar.

———. 1955. "The Transition from Witnessed to Written Transactions in Athens." In *Aequitas und Bona Fides: Festgabe für A. Simonius,* pp. 287–97. Basel.

Pritchett, W. K. 1956. "The Attic Stelai, Part II." *Hesperia* 25: 178–317.

Purpura, G. 1987. "Ricerche in tema di prestito marittimo." *Annali del Seminario Giuridico dell' Università di Palermo* 39: 189–337.

Ragazzi, G. 1973. "Theories of the Determinants of Direct Foreign Investment." *International Monetary Fund Staff Papers* 20 (July): 471–98.

Rahe, P. A. 1984. "The Primacy of Politics in Classical Greece." *American Historical Review* 89: 265–93.

Randall, R. H., Jr. 1953. "The Erechtheum Workmen." *American Journal of Archaeology* 57: 199–210.

Rehdantz, C. 1845. *Vitae Iphicratis Chabriae Timothei.* Berlin.

Reiske, I. I., ed. 1770–71. *Oratorum Graecorum quorum princeps est Demosthenes.* Leipzig.

Rhodes, P. J. 1972. *The Athenian Boule.* Oxford.

———. 1981. *A Commentary on the Aristotelian Athenaion Politeia.* Oxford.

———. 1982. "Problems in Athenian Eisphora and Liturgies." *American Journal of Ancient History* 7: 1–19.

———. 1986. "Political Activity in Classical Athens." *Journal of Hellenic Studies* 106: 132–44.

Riezler, K. 1907. *Über Finanzen und Monopole im alten Griechenland.* Berlin.

Robert, J., and L. Robert. 1980. Review of T. V. Buttrey, "The Athenian Currency Law of 375/4 B.C." *Bulletin épigraphique* 93, no. 195: 391.

Roberts, J. T. 1986. "Aristocratic Democracy: The Perseverance of Timocratic Principles in Athenian Government." *Athenaeum*, n.s. 74: 355–69.

Robinson, E.S.G. 1951. "The Coins from the Ephesian Artemision Reconsidered." *Journal of Hellenic Studies* 71: 156–67.

———. 1960. "Some Problems in Later Fifth Century Coinage of Athens." *The American Numismatic Society. Museum Notes* 9: 1–15.

Rodbertus, J. K. 1867. "Zur Geschichte der römischen Tributsteuern seit Augustus." *Jahrbücher für Nationalökonomie und Statistik* 8: 453–58.

Rodinson, M. 1973. Preface (in French) to P. Chalmeta Gendron, *El 'señor del zoco' en España*. Madrid.

Rogers, C. 1989. *Money, Interest and Capital: A Study in the Foundations of Monetary Theory*. Cambridge.

Roll, R. 1973. *A History of Economic Thought*. 4th ed. London.

———. 1979. "Violations of Purchasing Power Parity and Their Implications for Efficient International Commodity Markets." In *International Finance and Trade*, edited by M. Sarnat and G. Szego, 1: 133–76. Cambridge, Mass.

Roover, F. Edler de. 1945. "Early Examples of Marine Insurance." *Journal of Economic History* 5: 172–200.

Rosenvallon, P. 1980. "Le Développement de l'économie souterraine et l'avenir des sociétés industrielles." *Le Débat* 2: 15–27.

Rostovtzeff, M. 1930. "Rhodes, Delos, Hellenistic Commerce." In *The Cambridge Ancient History*, vol. 8, edited by S. A. Cooke, F. E. Adcock, and M. P. Charlesworth. Cambridge.

Rougé, J. 1966. *Recherches sur l'organisation du commerce maritime en Mediterranée sous l'Empire Romain*. Paris.

———. 1981. *Ships and Fleets of the Ancient Mediterranean*. Translated by Susan Frazer. Middleton, Ct. (Originally published as *La Marine dans l'antiquité* [Paris, 1975].)

Rousselle, A. 1983. *Porneia*. Translated by Felicia Pheasant. Paris. (Translated as *Porneia: On Desire and the Body in Antiquity* [Oxford, 1988].)

Ruschenbusch, E. 1966. *Solōnos Nomoi*. Wiesbaden.

———. 1978. "Die athenischen Symmorien des 4. Jh. v. Chr." *Zeitschrift für Papyrologie und Epigraphik* 31: 275–84.

———. 1985. "Ein Beitrag zur Leiturgie und zur Eisphora," and "Die trierarchischen Syntelien und das Vermögen der Synteliemitglieder." *Zeitschrift für Papyrologie und Epigraphik* 59: 237–49.

———. 1987. "Symmorienprobleme." *Zeitschrift für Papyrologie und Epigraphik* 69: 75–81.

Ste. Croix, G.E.M. de. 1953. "Demosthenes' Timema and the Athenian Eisphora in the Fourth Century." *Classica et Mediaevalia* 14: 30–70.

———. 1956. "Greek and Roman Accounting." In *Studies in the History of Accounting*, edited by A. C. Littleton and B. S. Yamey, pp. 14–74. London.

———. 1970. "Some Observations on the Property Rights of Athenian Women." *Classical Review*, n.s. 20: 273–78.

———. 1972. *Origins of the Peloponnesian War*. London.

————. 1974. "Ancient Greek and Roman Maritime Loans." In *Debits, Credits, Finance and Profits* (Essays in Honour of W. T. Baxter), edited by H. Edey and B. S. Yamey, pp. 41–59. London.

————. 1981. *The Class Struggle in the Ancient Greek World.* London.

Salin, E. 1921. "Zu Methode und Aufgabe der Wirtschaftsgeschichte." *Schmollers Jahrbuch* 45: 483–505.

Salvioli, G. 1907. *Le Capitalisme dans le monde antique.* Paris.

Sanborn, F. R. 1930. *Origins of the Early English Maritime and Commercial Law.* New York.

Santillana, D. 1926. *Istituzioni di diritto musulmano malichita, con riguardo anche al sistema sciafita.* Vol. 1. Rome.

Sbordone F., and C. Giordano. 1968. "Dittico greco-latino dell'Agro Murecine." *Rendiconti della accademia di Napoli* 43: 195–202.

Schäfer, A. 1858. *Beilagen* [Supplement] to First Edition of Schäfer 1885–87. Leipzig.

————. 1885–87. *Demosthenes und seine Zeit.* 3 vols. 2d ed. Leipzig.

Schaps, D. M. 1971. "The Woman Least Mentioned: Etiquette and Women's Names." *Classical Quarterly* 71: 323–60.

————. 1979. *Economic Rights of Women in Ancient Greece.* Edinburgh.

Schiller, A. A. 1971. "The Business Relations of Patron and Freedman in Classical Roman Law." In *An American Experience in Roman Law*, edited by R. S. Bagnall and W. V. Harris, pp. 24–40. Gottingen.

Schläpfer, P. L. 1939. *Untersuchungen zu den attischen Staatsurkunden und den Amphiktyonienbeschlüssen der demosthenischen Kranzrede.* Paderborn.

Schmalzriedt, E. 1960. "Systematisches zum Problem der Falschen Münzen antiker Zeit." *Studium Generale* 13: 299–312.

Schodorf, K. 1905. *Beiträge zur genaueren Kentnis der attischen Gerichtssprache aus den Zehn Redners, Beiträge zur historischen Syntax der griechischen Sprache.* Vol. 17. Würzburg.

Schönbauer, E. 1964. "Παραγραφή, διαμαρτυρία, exceptio, praescriptio. Zur antiken Einrede der Unzulässigkeit des Streitverfahrens." *Anzeiger der phil.-hist. Kl. Österreichischen Akademie der Wissenschaften in Wien* 10: 203–31.

Schucht, H. 1892. "De documentis orationibus Atticis insertis et de litis instrumentis prioris adversus Stephanum orationis Demosthenicae." Diss., Königsberg.

————. 1919. "Ueber die Echtheit attischer Rednerurkunden." *Philologische Wochenschrift* 39: 1120–28, 1143–51.

Schuhl, P. 1953. "Adēla." *Annales publiées par la Faculté des Lettres de Toulouse, Homo: Études philosophiques*, I (May): 86–93.

Schuller, W. 1985. *Frauen in der griechischen Geschichte.* Konstanz.

Schumpeter, J. A. 1954. *History of Economic Analysis.* New York.

Schwahn, W. 1933. "Die attische eisphora." *Rheinisches Museum für Philologie* 82: 247–84.

Schwarze, K. 1956. "Geld und Geldverkehr im Alterum." *Das Alterum* 2: 90–102.

Schweigert, E. 1938. "Inscriptions from the North Slope of the Acropolis." *Hesperia* 7: 264–310.

Seager, R. 1966. "Lysias and the Corn-dealers." *Historia* 15: 172–84.

————. 1974. "The King's Peace and the Balance of Power in Greece, 386–362 B.C." *Athenaeum* 52: 36–63.

Sealey, R. 1990. *Women and Law in Classical Greece*. Chapel Hill, N.C.

Segal, C. 1986. "Greek Tragedy and Society: A Structuralist Perspective." In *Greek Tragedy and Political Theory*, edited by J. Peter Euben, pp. 43–75. Berkeley.

Segal, E. 1983. "Euripides: Poet of Paradox." In *Greek Tragedy: Modern Essays in Criticism*, edited by E. Segal, pp. 244–53. New York.

Segrè, A. 1947. "Note sull' economia di Atene nel IV secolo av. Cr." *Studi Italiani di Filologia Classica* 22: 133–63.

Seibert, J. 1979. *Die politischen Flüchtlinge und Verbannten in der griechischen Geschichte*. Darmstadt.

Seidl, E. 1957. Review of *Symbolae Raphaeli Taubenschlag Dedicatae. Studia et documenta historiae et iuris* 23: 358–62.

Shear, T. L., Jr. 1987. "Tax Tangle, Ancient Style." *Newsletter of the American School of Classical Studies at Athens* (Spring): 8.

Simônetos, G. S. 1939. "Das Verhältnis von Kauf und Übereignung im altgriechischen Recht." In *Festschrift Paul Koschaker*, edited by M. Kaser, H. Kreller, and W. Kunkel, 3: 172–98. Weimar.

Sinclair, R. K. 1988. *Democracy and Participation in Athens*. Cambridge.

Soubie, A. 1973–74. "Les Preuves dans les plaidoyers des orateurs attiques." *Revue internationale des droits de l'antiquité* 3d ser., 20: 171–253; 21: 77–134.

Soudek, C. J. 1952. "Aristotle's Theory of Exchange." *Proceedings of American Philosophical Society* 96: 45–75.

Stalin, G. 1946. *Questioni del leninismo*. Moscow.

Stanley, P. V. 1979. "*Agoranomoi* and *Metronomoi*: Athenian Market Officials and Regulations." *Ancient World* 11: 13–19.

Starr, C. G. 1958. "An Overdose of Slavery." *Journal of Economic History* 18: 17–32. (Reprinted in *Essays on Ancient History*, edited by A. Ferrill and T. Kelly [Leiden, 1979], pp. 43–58.)

——. 1987. *Past and Future in Ancient History*. Lanham, Md.

——. 1989. *The Influence of Sea Power on Ancient History*. New York.

Staveley, E. S. 1972. *Greek and Roman Voting and Elections*. London.

Steinwenter, A. 1925. *Die Streitbeendigung durch Urteil, Schiedsspruch und Vergleich nach griechischem Rechte*. Munich.

Steltzer, E. 1971. "Untersuchungen zur Enktesis im attischen Recht." Munich, diss.

Stigum, M. 1978. *The Money Market: Myth, Reality, and Practice*. Homewood, Ill.

Stockton, D. 1990. *The Classical Athenian Democracy*. Oxford.

Strauss, B. S. 1986. *Athens after the Peloponnesian War*. Ithaca, N.Y.

Stroud, R. S. 1974. "An Athenian Law on Silver Coinage." *Hesperia* 43: 157–88.

Stumpf, G. 1986. "Ein athenisches Münzgesetz des 4. Jh. v. Chr." *Jahrbuch für Numismatik und Geldgeschichte* 36: 23–40.

Suhle, A. 1930. "Wertbezeichung." In *Wörterbuch der Münzkunde*, edited by F. von Schroetter. Berlin and Leipzig.

Talamanca, M. "Contributi allo studio delle vendite all'asta nel mondo antico." In *Atti della R. Accademia dei Lincei*, ser. 8, vol. 6, fasc. 2, pp. 34–251. Rome.

——. 1975. "Giudizio paragrafico ed ammissibilità dell'azione nel sistema processuale attico." In *Symposion 1971*, edited by H. J. Wolff, J. Modrzejewski, and D. Nörr, pp. 125–29. Cologne.

Tapio, H. 1975. *Organization of Roman Brick Production*. Helsinki.

Tarn, W. W. 1948. *Alexander the Great*. 2 vols. Cambridge, Mass.

Taubenschlag, R. 1936. "Die Geschichte der Rezeption des Griechischen Privatrechts in Aegypten." *Atti del IV Congresso internazionale di papirologi, Firenze 1935*. Milan. (Reprinted in *Opera Minora* [Warsaw, 1959], 1: 573–600.)

Thalheim, T. 1913. *Lysiae orationes*. Leipzig.

Theil, H. 1968. *Optimal Decision Rules for Government and Industry*. Amsterdam.

Thiel, J. H. 1922. *ΞΕΝΟΦΩΝΤΟΣ ΠΟΡΟΙ*. Amsterdam.

Thielmann, G. 1963. *Die römische Privatauktion*. Berlin.

Thomas, R. 1989. *Oral Tradition and Written Record in Classical Athens*. Cambridge Studies in Oral and Literate Culture, 18. Cambridge.

Thompson, D. B. 1960. "The House of Simon the Shoemaker." *Archaeology* 13: 234–40.

Thompson, H. A., and R. E. Wycherley. 1972. *The Athenian Agora*. Vol. 14. Princeton.

Thompson, W. E. 1970. "Notes on the Treasurers of Athena." *Hesperia* 39: 54–63.

———. 1974. "Tot Atheniensibus idem nomen erat." In *ΦΟΡΟΣ: Tribute to B. D. Meritt*, edited by D. W. Bradeen and M. F. McGregor, pp. 144–49. Locust Valley, N.Y.

———. 1976. *De Hagniae Hereditate: An Athenian Inheritance Case. Mnemosyne*, supp. 44. Leyden.

———. 1978. "The Athenian Investor." *Rivista di studi classici* 26: 403–23.

———. 1979. "A View of Athenian Banking." *Museum Helveticum* 36: 224–41.

———. 1980. "An Athenian Commercial Case: Demosthenes 34." *Tidjschrift voor Rechtsgeschiedenis* 48: 137–49.

———. 1981. "Apollodoros v. Phormion: The Computation of Damages." *Revue internationale des droits de l'antiquité*, 3d ser. 28: 83–94.

———. 1983. "The Athenian Entrepreneur." *L'Antiquité classique* 51: 53–85.

———. 1987. "The Commercial Dispute at D. 52.20." *American Journal of Philology* 108: 600–602.

———. 1988. "Insurance and Banking." In *Civilization of the Ancient Mediteranean*, edited by M. Grant and R. Kitzinger, 2: 829–36. New York.

Thomsen, R. 1964. *Eisphora*. Copenhagen.

Thomson, G. 1966. *Aeschylus and Athens*. 3d ed. London.

Threpsiades, J., and E. Vanderpool. 1963. "Πρὸς τοῖς Ἑρμαῖς." *Ἀρχαιολογικὸν Δελτίον* 18A: 99–114.

Thür, G. 1972. "Der Streit über den Status des Werkstättenleiters Milyas (Dem. or. 29)." *Revue internationale des droits de l'antiquité*, 3d ser. 19: 151–77. (Reprinted in *Demosthenes* [Wege der Forschung, 1978], pp. 403–30.)

———. 1977. *Beweisführung von den Schwurgerichtshöfen: Die Proklesis zur Basanos*. Vienna.

———. 1987. "Hypotheken-Urkunde eines Seedarlehens für eine Reise nach Muziris und Apographe für die Tetarte in Alexandreia." *Tyche* 2: 229–46.

———. 1989. "Wo wohnen die Metöken?" In *Demokratie und Architektur*, edited by W. Schuller, W. Hoepfner, and E. L. Schwandner, pp. 117–21. Konstanzer.

Tilli, G. 1984. ". . . Postremo vetita versura." *Bullettino dell'Istituto di diritto romano* 86/87: 147–63.

Tinberger, J. 1952. *On the Theory of Economic Policy*. Amsterdam.

Tod, M. N. 1948. *A Selection of Greek Historical Inscriptions*. Vol. 2. Oxford.

Todd, S. 1990a. "The Purpose of Evidence in Athenian Courts." In *Nomos: Essays in Athenian Law, Politics and Society*, edited by P. Cartledge, P. Millett, and S. Todd, pp. 19–39. Cambridge.

———. 1990b. "The Use and Abuse of the Attic Orators." *Greece and Rome*, 2d ser. 37: 159–78.

Toutain, J. F. 1929. *L'Economie antique*. Paris. (Translated by M. R. Dobie, *The Economic Life of the Ancient World* [New York, 1930]; reprint New York, 1979.)

Travlos, J. 1971. *Pictorial Dictionary of Ancient Athens*. New York.

Treggiari, S. 1969. *Roman Freedmen during the Late Republic*. Oxford.

Trenerry, C. F. 1926. *The Origin and Early History of Insurance*. London.

Triantaphyllopoulos, I. 1968. Ἀρχαῖα Ἑλληνικά δίκαια. Athens.

Tuplin, C. 1984. "Timotheos and Corcyra. Problems in Greek History, 375–373 B.C." *Athenaeum*, n.s. 72: 537–68.

Turner, E. G. 1968. *Greek Papyri*. Oxford.

Valensi, L. 1974. "Anthropologie économique et histoire: L'Oeuvre de Karl Polanyi." *Annales* 29: 1311–19.

Van Effenterre, H. 1979. "Réflexions sur la fiscalité dans la Grèce des cités archaïques." In *Points de vue sur la fiscalité antique*, edited by H. van Effenterre, pp. 19–30. Publications de la Sorbonne, Études 14. Paris.

Van Groningen, B. A. 1963. "ΕΚΔΟΣΙΣ." *Mnemosyne*, 4th ser., 16: 1–14.

Van Hille, E. 1904. "De lapide nuper Athenis in arce invento." *Mnemosyne* 32: 325–48, 420–34.

Van Hook, L. 1945. *Isocrates*. Vol. 3. Loeb ed. Cambridge, Mass.

Vannier, F. 1988. *Finances publiques et richesses privées dans le discours Athénien aux Ve et IVe siècles*. Centre de Recherches d'Histoire Ancienne, vol. 75. Paris.

Vatin, C. 1970. *Recherches sur le mariage et la condition de la femme mariée à l'époque hellenistique*. Paris.

Vélissaropoulos, J. 1977. "Le Monde de l'*emporion*." *Dialogues d'histoire ancienne* 3: 61–85.

———. 1980. *Les Nauclères grecs*. Geneva.

Vermeule, C. C. 1954. *Some Notes on Ancient Dies and Coining Methods*. London.

———. 1956–57. "Minting Greek and Roman Coins." *Archaeology* 9: 100–107.

Vernant, J.-P. 1983. "Hestia-Hermes: The Religious Expression of Space and Movement in Ancient Greece." In *Myth and Thought among the Greeks*. London. (Translation of *Mythe et pensèe chez les grecs*, 2d ed. [Paris, 1969].)

Vernant, J.-P., and P. Vidal-Naquet. 1969. *Mythe et tragédie*. Paris. (Translated as *Tragedy and Myth in Ancient Greece*, translated by Janet Lloyd [Brighton, 1981].)

Veyne, P. 1971. *Comment on écrit l'histoire, essai d'épistémologie*. Paris.

Vidal-Naquet, P. 1986. *The Black Hunter: Forms of Thought and Forms of Society in the Greek World*. Translated by A. Szegedy-Maszak. Baltimore. (Translation of *Le Chasseur noir: Formes de pensées et formes de société dans le monde grec* [Paris, 1981].)

Vince, J. H. 1935. *Demosthenes*. Vol. 3. Loeb ed. Cambridge, Mass.

Vinogradoff, P. 1922. "The Legal Background of Demosthenes' Speech in Zenothemis v. Demon." *Revue d'histoire du droit* 3: 163–74.

Voemel, J. T. 1843. *Demosthenes: Opera*. Paris.

Vondeling, J. 1961. *Eranos*. Groningen.

Von der Lieck, K. 1933. *Die xenophontische Schrift von den Einkünften*. Cologne.

Von Herrmann, J. 1958. *Studien zur Bodenpacht im Rechte der gräco-ägyptischen Papyri.* Münchener Beiträge 41. Munich.

Walbank, M. B. 1983. "Leases of Sacred Properties in Attica, Parts I–IV." *Hesperia* 52: 100–135.

———. 1984. "Leases of Sacred Properties in Attica, Part V." *Hesperia* 53: 361–68.

Wallace, R. W. 1989. "The Athenian *Proeispherontes.*" *Hesperia* 58: 473–85.

Wallich, H. C. 1982. "The Evolution of the International Monetary System." In *The International Monetary System: Choices for the Future*, edited by M. B. Connolly, pp. 280–92. New York.

Wankel, H. 1983. "Bemerkungen zu dem athenischen Münzgesetz von 375/4." *Zeitschrift für Papyrologie und Epigraphik* 52: 69–74.

Watson, A. 1987. *Roman Slave Law.* Baltimore.

Weber, M. [1909] 1924. *Agrarverhältnisse im Altertum.* Tübingen.

———. 1921. "Die Stadt." *Archiv für Sozialwissenschaft und Sozialpolitik* 47: 621–772. (Reprinted in *Wirtschaft und Gesellschaft* [Tübingen, 1925]; English translation, *The City*, translated and edited by D. Martindale and G. Neuwirth [Glencoe, Ill., 1958].)

———. 1961. *General Economic History.* Translated by F. H. Knight. New York. (Translation of *Wirtschaftsgeschichte*, 3d ed. [Berlin, 1958].)

———. [1958] 1976. *The Protestant Ethic and the Spirit of Capitalism.* Translated by T. Parsons. New York. (Translation from *Gesammelte Aufsätze zur Religionssoziologie*, 3 vols. [Tübingen, 1920–21].)

Webster, T.B.L. 1969. *Life in Classical Athens.* London.

———. 1973. *Potter and Patron in Classical Athens.* London.

Weidauer, L. 1975. *Probleme der frühen Elektronprägung.* Freiburg.

Weiss, E. 1923. *Griechisches Privatrecht auf rechtsvergleichender Grundlage.* Leipzig.

Welles, C. B. 1970. Review of R. Bogaert, *Banques et banquiers dans les cités grecques. Gnomon*: 804–10.

Welskopf, E. C. 1980. "Free Labour in the City of Athens." In Garnsey 1980: 23–25.

Wenger, L. 1906. *Stellvertretung im Rechte der Papyri.* Leipzig.

Westermann, W. L. 1931. "Warehousing and Trapezite Banking in Antiquity." *Journal of Economic and Business History* 3: 30–54.

Whitcombe, E. 1985. "The Benevolent Proprietor and the Property Law: A British-Indian Dilemma." *History and Anthropology* 1: 373–79.

Whitehead, D. 1977. *The Ideology of the Athenian Metic.* Cambridge.

———. 1983. "Competitive Outlay and Community Profit: φιλοτιμία in Democratic Athens." *Classica et Mediaevalia* 34: 55–74.

———. 1986a. "The Ideology of the Athenian Metic: Some Pendants and a Reappraisal." *Proceedings of the Cambridge Philological Society* 212, n.s. 32: 145–58.

———. 1986b. "Women and Naturalisation in Fourth-Century Athens: The Case of Archippe." *Classical Quarterly* 36: 109–14.

———. 1986c. "Festival Liturgies in Thorikos." *Zeitschrift für Papyrologie und Epigraphik* 62: 213–20.

Wiedemann, T.E.J. 1987. *Slavery.* Oxford.

Wilcken, U. 1925. "Punt-Fahrten in der Ptolemäerzeit." *Zeitschrift für ägyptische Sprache und Altertumskunde* 60: 86–102.

Will, E. 1954. "Trois quarts de siècle de recherches sur l'économie grecque antique." *Annales (E.S.C.)* 9: 7–22.

———. 1975. "Les Sources des métaux monnayés dans le monde grec." In *Numismatique antique. Problèmes et méthodes*, edited by J. M. Dentzer, P. Gauthier, and T. Hackens, pp. 97–102. Nancy.

Wille, K. 1984. *Die Versur. Eine rechtshistorische Abhandlung über die Zinskapitalisierung im alten Rom. Schriften zur Rechtsgeschichte.* Vol. 33. Berlin.

Willetts, R. F. 1967. *The Law Code of Gortyn. Kadmos*, supp. 1. Berlin.

Wilson, F. W. 1935. "Studies in the Social and Economic History of Ostia: Part I." *Papers of the British School at Rome* 13: 41–68.

Winkler, J. J. 1990. "Laying Down the Law: The Oversight of Men's Sexual Behavior in Classical Athens." In Halperin, Winkler, and Zeitlin 1990: 171–209.

Wolff, H. J. 1944. "Marriage Law and Family Organization in Ancient Athens." *Traditio* 2: 43–95. (Reprinted in *Beiträge zur Rechtsgeschichte Altgriechenlands und des hellenistisch-römischen Ägypten* [Weimar, 1961], pp. 155–242.

———. 1952. "Die Grundlagen des griechischen Eherechts." *Tijdschrift voor Rechtsgeschiedenis* 20: 1–29, 157–81. (Reprinted in *Atti del 3º Congresso di diritto comparato* [Rome, 1953], 1: 213–57.)

———. 1961. *Beiträge zur Rechtsgeschichte Altgriechenlands und des hellenistisch-römischen Ägyptens.* Weimar.

———. 1966. *Die Attische Paragraphe.* Weimar.

———. 1968. "Die Grundlagen des griechischen Vertragsrechts." In *Zur Griechischen Rechtsgeschichte*, pp. 483–533. Darmstadt. (Originally published in *Zeitschrift der Savigny-Stiftung für Rechtsgeschichte. Romanistische Abteilung* 74 [1957]: 26–72.)

———. 1969. "Methodische Grundsatzfragen der rechtsgeschichtlichen Verwendung attischer Gerichtsreden." In *Atti del II Congresso Internazionale della Società Italiana di Storia del Diritto*, pp. 1–13. Firenze. (Reprinted in *Opuscula dispersa*, edited by J. G. Wolff and F. Wieacker [Amsterdam, 1974], pp. 27–39).

———. 1975. "Juristische Graezistik—Aufgaben, Probleme, Möglichkeiten." In *Symposion 1971*, edited by H. J. Wolff, J. Modrzejewski, and D. Nörr, pp. 1–22. Cologne.

———. 1978. *Das Recht der griechischen Papyri Aegyptens in der Zeit der Ptolemaeer und des Prinzipats.* Vol. 2: *Organisation und Kontrolle des privaten Rechtsverkehrs.* Handbuch der Altertumswissenschaft Abt 10, T. 5. Munich.

Wood, E. M. 1988. *Peasant-Citizen and Slave.* London.

Woodward, A. M. 1940. "Two Attic Treasure-Records." *Harvard Studies in Classical Philology*, supp. 1 (*Athenian Studies Presented to W. S. Ferguson*): 377–407.

Wormell, D.E.W. 1935. "The Literary Tradition concerning Hermias of Atarneus." *Yale Classical Studies* 5: 55–92.

Wright, F. A. [1923] 1969. *Feminism in Greek Literature: From Homer to Aristotle.* Port Washington, N.Y.

Wycherley, R. E. 1957. *The Athenian Agora.* Vol. 3, *Literary and Epigraphical Testimonia.* Princeton.

———. 1978. *The Stones of Athens.* Princeton.

Wyse, W. [1904] 1967. *The Speeches of Isaeus.* Hildesheim.

Young, J. H. 1956. "Studies in South Attica. Country Estates at Sounion." *Hesperia* 25: 122–46.

Youtie, H. 1960. "Notes on Papyri." *Transactions of the American Philological Association* 91: 239–71.

Ziebarth, E. 1896. *Das griechische Vereinswesen.* Leipzig.

———. 1929. *Beiträge zur Geschichte des Seeraubs und Seehandels im alten Griechenland.* Hamburg.

Ziebell, W. 1937. *Olbia. Eine griechische Stadt in Süd-Russland.* Hamburg.

INDEX OF PASSAGES CITED

2.8.1–5: 71n.48
3.11.4: 6n.14
Oik.: 84n.112
1.1: 62n.3
1.5: 101n.200
2.6–7: 195
3.10–15: 87n.128
7.3: 106n.221
7.32: 87n.128
7.33: 78n.85
7.36–42: 87n.128
9.15: 87n.128
9.19: 87n.128
20.22–28: 31n.15
20.29: 31n.15
Por.
2.3: 163–64n.219
3.9: 47, 53, 162n.214
3.10: 47, 53
3.13: 48n.35
3.14: 164n.225
5.3: 20n.84, 32n.18, 41n.1, 61n.1,
141n.128
Symp.
4.30–32: 195n.21
4.31: 49–50
8.25: 6n.14

INSCRIPTIONS AND PAPYRI

Arch. Delt.
17 (1961–62). Khronika 35, no. 4: 15,
24n.107, 35

Bagnall and Bogaert 1975: 17n.66
Berliner Griechischen Urkunden
14.2401–16 (1980): 17n.66
Bingen [1972–76] 1984
no. 75: 198n.44

Corpus inscriptionum graecarum
2056: 131n.90
Corpus inscriptionum latinarum
16.1.10–13: 103n.209

Dareste, Haussoullier, Reinach
1.457: 108n.234
Dilts 1983–86
272a, b: 222

Dittenberger 1915–24
364.42.46: 201n.70
955: 50n.43
1194: 35n.29

Erechtheion Fragments
27, 28, 29: 224

Fine 1951
no. 28: 79
Finley [1951] 1985: 34–35
no. 3: 15, 24n.107, 35
nos. 11–101 and App. 3: 167
no. 12A (App. 2): 35
nos. 30–32, 42, 70, 110: 208n.111
no. 39: 32n.18
no. 114A (App. 3): 79n.86
no. 135: 32n.18

Hesperia
5 (1936)
397, ll. 175ff.: 63n.6
14 (1945)
119–22, no. 11: 20n.83
19 (1950)
210, no. 5: 82n.104, 82n.105
219, no. 6: 82n.104
236, no. 14: 82n.104
240, no. 15: 82–83n.105
277, no. 29: 82n.104
22 (1953)
240ff.: 6n.15
26 (1957)
2, no. S2: 82n.105
30 (1961)
23ff.: 6n.15
56 (1987)
47–58: 6n.14
Hunt and Edgar 1952
no. 1: 51n.52

Inscriptiones Graecae
I³ 18/30: 150n.165
I³ 52: 222n.172
I³ 236: 195n.26
I³ 369: 143n.135
I³ 370: 150n.165
I³ 378: 150n.165
I³ 475–76: 22n.92
I³ 510: 222n.172
II² 34: 102n.205

public sphere: and gender, 92–93, 101; and
  private life, x, 61, 86, 224. See also *oikos*
purchasing power: of drachma, xiv, 22n.92,
  205
Pyladēs (*trapezitēs*): and Demosthenes' inheritance, 121–22, 126, 171–72
Pyrilampēs: *oikos* of, 82–83n.105
Pythias (niece of Hermias and wife of Aristotle), 80n.93
Pythodōros the Acharnian: and Apollodōros,
  16n.64, 99n.183
Pythodōros the Phoenician: and Pasiōn, 89,
  99n.183, 147
Pythodōros the shopkeeper: and Pasiōn:
  16n.64, 89, 98–99; as well known citizen,
  25, 99

race: and slavery, 91–92
racing: victories of Dēmadēs and Dēmētrios,
  89n.141
ransoming: loans for, 15, 26–27, 33–34, 92,
  211–13
real estate: as alternative to maritime investment, 51; bankers' handling of assets and
  loans, 133; and bank loans, 15; as collateral, 24, 132–36; commingling of personal and banking assets, 65; and
  concealment of wealth, 193n.4, 194; and
  eggeios ousia, 131–33; and *eisphora* on,
  196–97; Finley on market for, 31–32; in
  inheritances, 131, 191n.4; and noncitizens,
  58–59, 83n.105, 89n.141, 99–100, 104,
  108, 120–21, 133–34, 145–46; owned by
  Lysitheidēs, 82; and public disclosure of financing, 145–46; and sale with right of redemption, 167; as source of cash for
  investments, 153; speculation in, 31n.15,
  143, 215, 217; as visible asset, 8, 194,
  201; woman as lender, 79. See also agriculture; farms; *horoi*-stones
receipts: not used, 119. See also contracts;
  grammata; recordkeeping; witnesses; written agreements
recordkeeping: assets and liabilities of bank,
  185, 187; and bankers' loans from personal
  funds, 136; and bankers' wives, 77–80; of
  Demosthenes (father), 120–21, 124–25;
  depiction of, on gravestone, 145; and
  destruction at time of repayment, 207;
  equipment for, 69; *hypomnēmata*, 17; importance of bankers' books, 72; legal recognition of, 205–6; maritime loan

agreement (sole surviving), 42, 51–52, 54–
  57, 135, 146–47; and omitted transactions,
  206; routine for banks, 124; and third-party
  transfers, 119. *See also* accounting
reeds: as building materials, 78
regulation: absence of, in banking, 9, 41–44,
  183–84; and bank insolvencies, 217; of
  grain imports, 42–43, 151, 166n.235, 173;
  and invisible economy, 192
reinvestment: of cash flow, 184; opportunities
  for marine, 57
relationships: bank employee and client, 72;
  banker and agent, 98–101; banker and
  client, 33–34, 116–19; business and social, 65–66, 210–11; clandestine business,
  139; network of bankers', 67; role in economy, 5–6. *See also* disembedded economy;
  embedded economy; kinship; *koinōnoi;
  oikos*; partnerships; syndication
rent: paid while leasing bank, 219–20; payable in cash, 6n.14, 186; as source of cash
  for investments, 153
rentiers: as money-lending class, 151–53
repayment: guarantee of, 181; obligation of,
  111–12, 164–65, 185
representation. *See* agents; intermediation
retail businesses: bank financing of, 15; and
  currency exchange, 19; perfume, 94, 210,
  214–15; and slaves, 93; women in, 78
Rhodes: and maritime trade, 55, 59n.95,
  165–66, 168
risk: and bankers' records, 206; and bank failures, 217–18; of banking, 220; credit, 144,
  146, 169; and maritime contracts, 53–57;
  relation of, to yield, 53–54, 142–43; of
  transfer of funds outside bank, 119
risk-laden revenues: characteristic of banks,
  10, 140–41; nonmaritime, 143–44
Roman banking: definition of, 10; and maritime lending practices, 53n.69
Roman law: and concept of deposits, 112; on
  women's property rights, x
Roman slaves: commercial pursuits and manumission of, 73

sacrifices: and *epidoseis*, 197
safekeeping: of documents 22–23, 144n.140;
  of precious goods, 10, 22–23, 113, 120
Ste. Croix, G.E.M. de: on maritime loans,
  153n.179, 163, 166, 167; on Marx, ixn.3
sale: Athenian law of, 14; with option of redemption, 166–67